William Wheeler

Letters of William Wheeler of the Class of 1855, Y.C.

William Wheeler

Letters of William Wheeler of the Class of 1855, Y.C.

ISBN/EAN: 9783337137748

Printed in Europe, USA, Canada, Australia, Japan

Cover: Foto ©ninafisch / pixelio.de

More available books at **www.hansebooks.com**

In Memoriam

LETTERS

OF

WILLIAM WHEELER

OF THE CLASS OF 1855, Y. C.

> My heart leaps up when I behold
> A rainbow in the sky;
> So was it when my life began;
> So is it now I am a man;
> So be it when I shall grow old,
>   Or let me die.
>   WORDSWORTH.
>
> The childhood shows the man
> As morning shows the day.
>   MILTON, *Paradise Regained.*

PRINTED FOR PRIVATE DISTRIBUTION
1875

RIVERSIDE, CAMBRIDGE:
PRINTED BY H. O. HOUGHTON AND COMPANY.

TO THOSE IN THE CLASS OF '55

WHO LOVED MY SON,

AND WHO CHERISH HIS MEMORY,

THIS VOLUME

IS RESPECTFULLY DEDICATED,

BY HIS MOTHER.

PREFACE.

THOSE for whom these letters are especially compiled will not need an apology if some brief sketch of the early life of the writer is prefixed to them.

William Wheeler was born in the city of New York, August 14, 1836. He was very attractive as a little child, and early manifested those qualities which made him a great favorite with his friends and companions.

His love of knowledge, exhibited at a very early age, led him to learn to read, and then he gratified this love without restraint. He was very happy, when four years old, to sit by his mother's side, with the Family Bible, and entertain himself by the hour, with the stories which it contained. He became a diligent student of the Bible, and attendance at the Sabbath-school was to him a pleasure, as well as a duty.

He did not go to school till he was eight years of age, when he was ready to take his place with those considerably older than himself. His teacher had a remarkable faculty of inspiring his pupils with a love of study, and William was not slow in responding to the influence. He loved play as well as study, and when released from school, he and his friend, Robert Edwards, who was a near neighbor, found, in a lot which had been inclosed next his home, as a play-ground, unfailing means of amusement, where invention could be allowed full play without interfering with the rights and pleasures of others.

When between eight and nine years of age, he would collect his boy playmates on some door-step in his neighborhood, and entertain them with stories of his own imagining, which would be continued from evening to evening, — a youthful Improvisatore.

His father being unable to use his eyes except for the necessary duties of his profession, William spent his winter evenings in reading to him such books as Prescott's "Mexico," Shakespeare, Alison's "History of Europe," etc.

The next day he would entertain himself in arranging his toy soldiers in the order of the battles of the Great Captain, which impressed them very forcibly upon his mind. He was also instructed by his father in the game of chess, for which he had ever a great fondness, and in which he was much skilled. When ten years of age he was sent to boarding-school at Stamford, where he made much progress in some branches of study.

In the spring of 1847 his parents removed to Brooklyn, and in the fall of that year, after the death of his father, in August, William was placed at the school of Rev. B. W. Dwight, where he continued until he entered college in September, 1851. At this school he advanced in his various studies with great rapidity and delight, varying them with sports favorable both to physical and mental development. He here formed friendships which were a source of happiness during his life. His friend, Robert Edwards, having removed to Brooklyn shortly before him, the childish friendship was here continued (R. being also at Mr. D.'s school), and formed one element of his future enjoyment, sadly ended for this life by Robert's death at the taking of Fort Wagner.

Those who knew William at College do not need to be informed of his character or acquirements, as they had better opportunities of judging of him, in both respects, than those whose relationship might lead them to look upon him with partial eyes.

He was not without faults, being of an excitable temperament, and was led sometimes to exhibitions of passion; but he was generous in acknowledging when he had wronged any one; he was unselfish, giving up his own pleasure for the gratification of others, a loving son, a devoted and tender brother and friend.

His course in College was pursued, not so much to take the first honors of his Class, as to acquire such stores of knowledge, on various subjects, as would fit him to enjoy and appreciate learning. Of science he was not very fond, nor was the character of his mind such as to make high attainment in it practicable.

His letters will show what his course was after leaving College, and their perusal is submitted to the kindly regard of those who have urged their preparation for the press.

I.

LETTERS OF THE WOODS, AND COLLEGE DAYS.

1850–56.

I.

LETTERS OF THE WOODS, AND COLLEGE DAYS.

HUNTER, *August* 14, 1850.
In the Catskill Mountains.

DEAR MOTHER, — . . . . I am now fourteen years old, and yet I seem the same person that I was six years ago. Time ; how it flies ! . . . . I would like to give you a little account of an expedition which we made a week ago. Last Wednesday, Ogden, Robby, a young man named Jonas Mann, and myself, started off early in the morning for the Stony Cove, in an old wagon, with fishing-lines and a basketful of provender. We went on as far as it was possible for a wagon to go, and then Ogden unharnessed the horse and went over to Olive, while we three commenced the ascent of a high mountain, on the other side of which was the brook in which we were to fish. After a tiresome journey over the mountain on foot we came to the brook down which, that is towards the mouth of which, we were going to fish till we should come to the shanty where we were to pass the night and meet Ogden, at the mouth of the brook. We fished and fished, sat down and ate our dinner, and then fished on, but no shanty appeared. At length a most terrific thunder storm came on. Situated in a deep valley between two mountains, the thunder was echoed from cliff to cliff most awfully, the ground seemed to shake under us, the sky was one blaze of lightning, while torrents of rain poured down on our unprotected heads. Not a single fish could we catch during this shower, which lasted several hours. We toiled on through rain, and fallen logs, and brushwood, expecting every moment to see the shanty where we were to get our supper and spend the night. But seeing nothing but the brook with its thick woods on each side, we were almost ready to give up in despair; when we saw a path leading up to the woods we followed it, got lost in the woods (all this time the rain pouring down in torrents), wandered about for a long time, and at length we got out of the woods into a clearing where we saw a house. We got our supper and stayed all night; went off the next morning without breakfast expecting to get it at the place where we were going to meet Ogden. We travelled on, but no house appeared till in the evening, about 7 P. M., we came to a house where we got some supper and spent the night. The next day we hired a wagon to go home, being completely wearied out with the exertions of the preceding day, in which we had walked fifteen or twenty miles. We reached home well tired with our two days' expedition, and with two hundred trout. Of these my share was seventy-two, being the number that I had caught. Blackberries are becoming very plenteous. I went out this evening before supper time and picked four quarts in a very short time. Somebody rides on horseback every day at the Colonel's, and I have become quite a horseman.

NEW HAVEN, *February* 23, 1852.

While reckoning up the time this morning, I found that it was three weeks since I had written to you. I was very much surprised to discover that time had passed so rapidly. Indeed this whole term has seemed like a short dream of a day, so incessantly have I been occupied. My love for college life is continually increasing, and I think that Ike Marvel has done well in setting it down as the most pleasant part of the life of man . . . . Here is the place to form friendships for life, which shall be unending till death. Our class is a remarkably still, quiet, well behaved one, and has performed so far but very little mischief. I have seen here at college but very little of that spreeing which is laid so heavily to the charge of institutions of this kind. It is chiefly confined to the upper classes, Freshmen having better things to do than to carry on.

So you have rented the house! It really makes me feel very bad to think of leaving it so long. You give up a great deal for me, dear mother, and I will strive to repay you by my heart's affection, and by becoming worthy of such a sacrifice. But I doubt not that before long you will become as much attached to New Haven as to Brooklyn, if not more. For my part nothing can diminish my affection for the Empire State. The prizes for Greek translation were not read off this evening after all; if I take a first prize I will send you a telegraphic dispatch. But it is growing late, and I must get up early to-morrow morning to study. Wishing you all good that an affectionate son can, I am yours, lovingly,   WILLIE.

P. S. Please gently hint to Aunt E. that for some more of those snaps she will receive most hearty thanks.

NEW HAVEN, *March* 13, 1852.

DEAR MOTHER, — On going to the Post Office Tuesday evening I found your long-expected letter. I also, at the same time, received a long and very interesting letter from B. W. D. It was from beginning to end full of his go-ahead spirit. I think he is the most consistent man in carrying out his professed principles that I know of . . . . Tutor D. told W. that our class was a very moral one, and that it exerted a very good influence. Some are surprised to see so many "blue fellows," as they call them here, but I must say that I have always had a very high opinion of those "blue fellows," ever since I have been in college. But the bell rang some time ago, and I must go to dinner, so good-by.

Monday, March 15. I would have completed my letter on Saturday, but I was interrupted. We have just completed five books of Euclid, which is more than any class before us has ever done. The fifth book was in my humble opinion very tough. I had to study on it pretty hard, as we had no diagrams to assist us. In Homer's Odyssey we have nearly completed the tenth book, and in Livy are laboring away towards the end of the twenty-second. There was quite a time here yesterday on account of four students, two Sophs and two Juniors, who were caught in the interesting occupation of cementing up the bell. Five tutors besieged them in the belfry, and caught these four, while several more escaped. The delinquents will be either suspended or rusticated; that is, they will have the benefit of country air for a term or two. You need not fear that I will embroil myself in any of these scrapes. I am improving in speaking and reciting in my Secret Society, which I would uphold did the Faculty condemn them never so much. They bring one into connection and intercourse with some of the best scholars and finest fellows in the class. · It cherishes that social feeling which is so necessary to the student, and makes him feel as if his society fellows were his brothers. I look forward with much pleasure to the time when I shall be gobbling poor Freshmen for the Brothers'. I shall have a very fine opportunity for so doing, as I shall have all vacation as well as at Commencement . . . I should like to have a little time during vacation to solve the prize mathematical problems, which will at that time be given out.

From a letter written when alone at —

NEW HAVEN, *January* 24, 1854.

I am very lonely here all by myself. I give a German lesson three times a week, which affords me an opportunity of seeing other specimens of humanity, besides our two domestics and the old gray cat. I seriously contemplate getting a housekeeper who won't charge wages, and presenting mother when she returns with a second edition of " Mrs. Wheeler." It is most stupendously cold here. The fire itself froze the other morning. I would send you a piece, but for fear it would melt and burn a hole in the paper. The thermometer stood last night at *one below zero in the shade !* Ah ! you can't comprehend how peculiarly adapted is this season of the year for going out to prayers at 6½ A. M. The delightful sensation of finding the water frozen in the bowl, and the morning so dark that it would take a Drummond light to brighten it up. Then the pleasure of tumbling down a half dozen times or more in running up to chapel, the unmitigated hardness of the seats, the sudden change to an over-heated recitation-room, all render "sleeping over morning prayers," "a consummation devoutly to be wished."

NEW HAVEN, *May* 24, 1854.

.... I do not dare to write "as funny as I can," for I should then be obliged to send you several grosses of buttons, and hooks and eyes, to repair the damages which my irresistible humor had caused. ... I feel dreadfully sentimental this morning. Primo, because it is one of the fairest days that ever shook the dew from her "saffron· robe;" secundo, because I passed close by Miss ——'s house this morning; tertio, because we are going to have a whaling big eclipse, and the Junior class are dismissed from recitation to look at it. We don't have it annular here; it is going to look like a moderate-sized cheese-paring!

YALE COLLEGE, *September* 18, 1854.

The long vacation is over, and we students have got back again to our books, universally recruited in health and spirits. You are most probably aware of the important and interesting fact that I have arrived at the dignity of Senior! And what dignity! Could· you behold the ineffable majesty with which I pace the streets, ogle the ladies, and cut my friends in the lower classes, you would be impressed with a vast idea of mental and moral grandeur. It is indeed hard work for me to maintain my Senior dignity, and in fact during the vacation, I thought of summoning to my aid a *pair of whiskers!* With this in view I began assiduously to cultivate said whiskers; but finding that their powers of increasing were exactly the opposite of Jack's bean-stalk, and that in all human probability I should be obliged to wait many months before they would become distinctly visible, I seized a razor and with one fell swoop detached them from my countenance. Alas! humanity weeps over such wholesale destruction, and I draw the veil over the heart-rending recital.

NEW HAVEN, *February* 20, 1855.

.... Speaking of Commencement reminds me that my course here is almost completed; already we have begun to make preparation for Presentation Day, the day on which we are "presented" for graduation. In the morning of this day, after the ceremony of presentation is completed, we have the Class Valedictory Oration, and Poem; these are not appointments for scholarship, but elected by the class. On the afternoon of this day we have a grand pow-wow on the college green. We have a circle of seats constructed on which the class sit, and in the hollow space within is the orchestra, which is composed entirely of members of the class.

We are going to have a very good orchestra. The air is to be supported by about four flutes, and by two flageolets; the second, by four flutes; the tenor, by five violins and two guitars; the bass by the violoncello and sax-horn. Besides this, we are to have a piano, a triangle, the bones, and drum.

We practice every Wednesday afternoon, and are coming along very finely. Perhaps you have been surprised at hearing me say "we" all along here, and perchance are already inquiring, "Pray, what instrument does my tuneful cousin play?" Be it known unto you then, oh most scornful and satirical of females, that actuated by a desire to help the class along in their laudable endeavors after good music, I have taken hold of Jack's sax-horn and am learning with the most astounding rapidity.

Occasionally I amuse myself by throwing North College into an uproar by a few well-timed blasts, which bring Professor Hadley to my door with the injunction of "a little less noise in study-hours." We do our practicing in the new hall of the Brothers' Society, and after we get through, we have dancing of all sorts, wishing, moreover, that ladies of our acquaintance were present. I wish you could be here at

THE WOODS, AND COLLEGE DAYS. 9

Presentation Day, for the exercises are much more interesting than those of commencement. It is the last time we all meet together as a class, before breaking up, never to meet again, as in all human probability some will die before our meeting in 1858. It is a very strange circumstance that not one of all our class has died during the college course, and we are so nearly through. . . . .

NEW HAVEN, *March* 23, 1855.

DEAR M., — . . . . This term hath flown away literally on eagle wings; it seems scarcely yesterday that I came from New York, where I had such a delightful vacation, and prepared to " bone down " to study again. And it makes me feel sad enough to see the end of this term approaching, and now so near, and to think that in a few short weeks our class, who have stood together for four long but pleasant years, must now separate, and go away to the four winds of heaven, never, perhaps, to meet again, and never, surely, to meet again with their young thoughts, and hopes, and aspirations. Perhaps, when a lessening band of time-worn and world-battered old men, we, the class of Fifty-five, may once more gather in sadness around the hearth-stone of our Alma Mater, and relight the torches of our hearts at the ceaseless flame which ever burns there, from the sources of science and of truth, — But stop, I appear to be falling into a sermon, or rather a funeral discourse; but in good truth, dear coz, the thoughts of parting make me so sad that it is hard to be still, for you know that " out of the abundance of the heart the mouth speaketh."

NEW HAVEN, *April* 7, 1855.

. . . . The principal circumstance which has made me so busy lately, is the fact that I am entering into competition for the Berkeley Scholarship, as perhaps I told you in my last letter. The examination is upon Homer's Iliad, Greek Testament, Xenophon's Cyropædia, Tacitus, Horace, and Cicero's Tusculan Disputations. I have read eight books of

Homer's Iliad, and felt very glad that we did not have it in Freshman year, when we could not appreciate it one half so well, and when we would have studied it upon compulsion. It is a vast field of beauty and power, where a student may roam for hours and days, and yet be perpetually culling fresh flowers of noble thought — it is a perennial stream where he can for a lifetime satisfy his thirst for the sublime and the beautiful. .... I do indeed, agree with you, in loving best "the happy summer time ;" and through all pleasures of gayety in winter, and the capricious fancies of spring, I am ever looking forward to the time when —

"From brightening fields of ether fair disclosed,
Child of the Sun, — refulgent Summer comes."

I am keeping my "Isaak Walton," which your dear father gave me, to read *then*, lying under a shady tree, or perhaps with a fishing-rod in my hand, upon the bank of some good trout-stream. I have only dipped into it (the book, not the trout-stream), but I came across one exquisite passage which I must give you : —

"The lark when she means to rejoice, to cheer herself and those that hear her, she then quits the earth and sings as she ascends higher into the air ; and having ended her heavenly employment, grows then mute and sad to think she must descend to the dull earth which she would not touch but for necessity."

Is it not a sweet thing?

NEW HAVEN, *September* 26, 1855.

I spent a quiet, but very pleasant week at Tarrytown, and then left for Pennsylvania. After a two days' journey, in the evening glow of a charming day, I saw from the top of a lofty hill —

"On Susquehanna's banks fair Wyoming."

The vast champaign, falling in gentle declivities down to the banks of the river on the one hand, and cultivated to the very summits of the hills on the other, the rich fertility of the soil, the beautiful river, which at seasons overflows, and fertilizes all around, causes it to seem not strange to us that the Indians should regard with the eye of hatred, and massacre, with the hand of midnight murder, the pale faces who would deprive them of this beautiful spot, which their own poetic nation cherished by the name of Wyoming, or the Lovely Valley.

.... I went down a coal-shaft and entered a coal-mine, which was a scene as new to me as very well could be. The sooty miners looked like fiends, were it not for the star-like lamps in their caps, which made one think of the Irish fairy tales of the fairies who had stars in their foreheads. The walls were black, the roof was black; it looked like some vast funeral vault draped for a burial. The polyglot swearing of the miners, who assaulted us on all sides, for "backsheesh," soon removed the delusion. I was glad enough to see the light again, yet the miners who spend their lives here assert that it is both pleasant and healthy. "*Chacun à son goût.*" And that is n't my "goût."

NEW HAVEN, *February* 2, 1856.

.... Imagine that it is now the beginning of December, instead of the beginning of February; that it is now two weeks and not two months, since I received your good, long letter; and also imagine that you received a note from me on New Year's Day, and not I one from you; in fact, imagine such a train of circumstances as shall make me a decent young man, and not such a good-for-nothing, dilatory procrastinator as I really am ; for, I am sure, I need all the assistance which I can so obtain to avert from my guilty head your most righteous execrations. Still, I must have a hearing. We will have the case, in our imaginary court, Davenport against Wheeler; and your justice and good sense shall be the jury, your resentment and terrible ferocity shall be the counsel for the plaintiff, and a sort of lingering kindness, which I hope you still have for me, shall be the counsel for the defendant. And shall not the verdict be "Guilty, but recommended to mercy." Be so good as to recollect that I am the secretary of the class, and consequently have no less than ninety correspondents, or thereabouts, and after I have finished a batch of letters, I feel so disgusted with letter-writing that I do not pen another epistle for months. With regard to yourself it is different; I enjoy writing to you immensely, but then, you know, there must be a beginning, and that is hard to make.

You don't seem to me to be enjoying boarding-school as much as you might. Ah, how I did groan, when I heard you were not coming to spend the winter in New Haven. What pleasant times we would have had; I am sure that both you and I would not have neglected our studies, and when playtime came, would we not have improved it jollily? The rides in October and November, with air pleasantly warm yet bracing, with skies as clear and pure as if not a single mist intervened between us and the heavenly blue of the divine dome above; the sleigh-rides, in January and February, over the crisping snow, through our amphitheatre of hills, with East and West Rocks, like ermine-clad giants looking down upon us; and, oh, the walks in the pleasant, lovely days of Indian Summer, through woods painted in all their tree leaves by unearthly artists, in earth-surpassing colors,— hills, whose every rock was covered with most delicate shades of green and purple mosses; penetrating to spots before unknown, save to the squirrel and partridge, often repeating these pleasant strolls, until our feet knew,—

> "Each lane and every alley green
> Dingle or bushy dell of the wild-wood
> And every bosky bourn from side to side."

NEW HAVEN, *July* 18, 1856.

DEAR M.,— .... I have been for nearly three weeks absent from New Haven on a trip to the Northern Adirondacks, in New York State, in Franklin and Essex counties, and on the Saranac Lakes and the Racquette River. We slept eight nights in the woods, partly in a tent, and partly with no covering but the blue heaven, around the cheerful camp-fire. There are wondrous charms about such a life; the freedom from all restraint, the consciousness of perfect independence, the invigorating effects of the labors of the hunt, the evening trophies, whether a deer, a string of noble trout, a score of pigeons or ducks, or occasionally a brace of partridges; and then, last of all, sweet sleep, which is only the companion of health and hard labor. And in the depth of the woods my thoughts often reverted to you, and it was an amusing idea to think in what widely different scenes our daily life was laid; yours in the centre of life, in the midst of breathing millions, and surrounded by the art-works of ages; mine, in the depths of the pathless forest, many miles from human habitation, with no signs of life around me save my companions, and the mute denizens of wood and wave. . . . . American politics form a theme of great interest to almost every one in this country, especially to the young men, who are peculiarly enthusiastic either on one side or the other, but especially on the side of Fremont, — and I assure you that *I* do not fail to partake of the general rage. Whatever a young and feeble voice and a weak influence can do shall be given to the cause of the Republican party. Hurrah for Freedom and Fremont! Do you hear anything said in England about American internal politics; anything about the Presidential election, or the Brooks outrage? I am too sensitive and passionate and nervous ever to become a politician or a *wire-puller*, but so long as I have a voice to raise and a vote to cast, the one shall be raised and the other cast in behalf of intelligence and Freedom.

From a letter written —

NEW HAVEN, *March* 17, 1857.

. . . . Very neglectful have I been of you for a good while past, but this time it has not been on account of sickness as it was last Fall, but of real good, honest, downright work. I have at last learned what it is to study in earnest; that is, not merely con over one book or one set of books, but dash out into a wide sea of general reading and learning. Would to heaven that the day was forty-eight hours long instead of twenty-four! I divide my time now somewhat as follows: Law school Studies and recitations, eight hours; exercise and meals, three hours; general studies, eight hours; arms of Murphy, five hours. This last I consider time thrown away, and do frequently lament that mankind was not so constituted as to do without it.

II.

LETTERS OF FOREIGN TRAVEL AND ART.

1857–58.

II.

LETTERS OF FOREIGN TRAVEL AND ART.

SHIP AUSTRALIA, Off Sandy Hook,
Saturday, 1 P. M., *May* 9, 1857.

DEAR MOTHER, — We 're off! Hauled off from the dock at about 10 A. M., and were towed down the bay by the tug *S. A. Stevens*. This note I shall send back by her.

My grief after I left you was checked in its violence by the carriage stopping at the jail and taking in two men, — one, the sheriff, very drunk; the other, an insane man, very foolish. This latter poor man's miseries somewhat diverted my mind from my own, and I did all I could to make him comfortable. On board the boat he was badly deserted by the sheriff. The poor man was doubly unfortunate; he was crazy, and could speak no English, so I had an opportunity of conveying consolation to him in German. The crew of the ship amount to fourteen, and are, most of them, Yankees from Salem. About an hour ago they hoisted the anchor to the —

"Yeo heave yeo, and the heave away,
And the sighing seaman's cheer."

Monotonous it was, and a deep grunt at every "long pull, and strong pull, and pull all together," served as basso profundo. There is a delightful long swell, and pitch of the ship, which in good time will doubtless produce upon me a stomach-stirring, if not a spirit-stirring effect. The Ericsson steamer is coming after us, and I must go on deck and see her. Love to J.; hope he did not come down, as it would have been too late to see me. Love to all. Yours on the deep.

SHIP AUSTRALIA, *May* 17, 1857.
Lat. 40° N., 52° 39' W. Long.

DEAREST MOTHER, — My feelings, and a sufficient amount of steadiness in the vessel, at length permit me to use pen and ink without danger of involving myself in any very dread or dirty catastrophe; this letter may be sent by ship, but probably will be obliged to wait until we arrive at Marseilles. I suppose I must not tell you how often I have longed to be at home and regretted that I had ever left it, nor how often Harry and I have talked about it together; and, having made all due allowance for difference of time, have wondered what you were all doing at home just then, and if you were thinking of us as intently as we were of you — at both homes. No, mother, I never was made for a traveller; the thought of "Home, sweet Home," as the end and crown of all travel, will ever be to me an incitement to press hastily on, and rejoin that home circle which is incomplete without me, and without which I feel myself *so* incomplete — such a fraction. Even on this beautiful Sabbath afternoon, with the gorgeous sea foaming in majesty around, and the fresh breeze urging on our ship at eight knots an hour, even now, I would give all this beauty and grandeur, all these dark waves, with their sapphire crests and tracks of foam, to be transported to our pew in church where you are now sitting, and to walk home with you under the budding elms on this sweet May Sabbath afternoon. Not that we have not had a sermon; at five bells (2½ P. M.) the crew was mustered on the main deck, and H. went through the motions of a regular Orthodox service. The hymns were rather a fizzle; as H. and I were not disposed to exhibit ourselves in a grand duet, he was compelled merely to read them. The sermon also was a poor affair, being one which he read from a volume of Sermons, or rather Moral Essays, which the captain had on board. The prayers, however, were delivered with much unction, and the whole service was as interesting as it was novel, having never been performed on the vessel before. H. intends to prepare himself to speak extempore next Sunday, so that he will not be obliged to resort to any such miserable stuff again. You probably feel an interest in knowing how seasick I was. The moment dreaded by all landlubbers arrived on Saturday evening, soon after the departure of the pilot-boat. For about two hours I steadfastly held my head over the bulwark and contemplated the dark rolling wave, *et voilà le tout !*

The next day I was out of bed, brisk enough, and I have not been sick since; and as far as I am concerned, I don't think seasickness is what it is bragged up to be. I rather entertain a decided contempt for it. My two fellow sufferers, however, would tell a different tale. H. and Mr. D. have been more or less sick ever since we started, and their disappearances from the festive board have frequently been both sudden and amusing. The seats nearest the door were voted to them by acclamation. Captain K. is a right nice fellow, maintains his dignity like a gentleman, and seldom or never swears at the men. He is, I imagine, a very favorable specimen of the captains of merchant vessels. "The monotony of sea life," dryly remarked the Captain, " is varied by two incidents, — sometimes you see a ship, and sometimes you ship a sea." So the other morning, at four bells (6 A. M.), we all tumbled out of bed and up on deck, to see a large ship which was passing near us; we hailed her, and there came back from her deck the following delicate and poetical query: "How's freights?" They were requested to report the ship *Australia*, so perhaps you will soon hear of us through the newspapers. On Friday we had a regular storm; every particle of sail was taken in, and for a day and a half we plunged around amid driving rain and roaring winds and mountain waves, not seeing sun, moon, or stars, and having a most indistinct idea of where we were. Victor Cousin, I think it is, who says that however grand a scene may be, if the sensation of fear intrude, the latter destroys all idea of grandeur, and usurps its place. Had he said, the sensation of seasickness, I think he would have been nearer right; but I cannot believe that the sensation of fear, in relation to what is grand, can fail to give it a more sublime and lofty bearing of power; and surely the fear I felt, lest our ship should never emerge from the mountain billows into which she plunged, did but serve to make me more conscious of my own littleness in comparison with this greatest of God's works, this —

> "Mighty mirror, where the Almighty's form
> Glasses itself in tempests."

May 31, Lat. 37° 48' N., Long. 15° 42' W.

We spend the day on board ship somewhat as follows: at 7 A. M., the captain begins his rousing exertions upon the three passengers; by 7½ his exertions are crowned with success and we get up. At 8 A. M., we breakfast and then generally walk the deck for half an hour or more, if promenading be practicable, then we are to be seen stretched out at full length on the quarter-deck. Here we read or sleep as taste of the individual inclines, and also amuse ourselves with watching the captain at his observations, and the making and taking in of sail. The throwing of the log occurs every two hours, but our vessel though advertised as "The fast sailing clipper *Australia*," does not give a very good account of herself at the log, her speed being seldom over eight and never over nine miles an hour. Punctually at 1 o'clock our sable Ganymede announces dinner, at which we sit for nearly an hour. In the afternoon we copy the pursuits of the morning and again assemble at table at 6 P. M. The evening, if pleasant, is spent on deck in climbing, jumping, playing chess, checkers, or dominoes, and in talking under the moonlight which so sweetly spreads over this vast expanse of ocean. Nothing could be more lovely than the last two or three nights; the ocean, calm and quiet, scarcely moved by any wave save the long swell and heave which ever lives in its bosom; the moon, turning into gold and diamonds the silent sea on which it sleeps, a flood of glory as far as the eye can reach; the ship herself with every sail of snowy canvas set, looking like some great and beautiful bird asleep upon this fairy lake, poised on white wings and gently swaying with the "swell of the long waves." Nor when the moon has gone down, does this scene of beauty cease; in the white foam of the ship's wake are seen thousands of marine animals, which emit a phosphorescent light, and as they shine from the foam look like stars rolled out of the folds of an angel's snowy mantle. Beautiful, beautiful exceedingly, is a night at sea ; and thanks to the holy eyes of the watch stars which transport us to the dear ones at home, who are perhaps even then gazing on them and praying them to be propitious to the wanderers at sea. Bright and electric sparks of love are they whose sphere of influence extends o'er sea and shore, and sheds the light of memory and home upon ocean-track and mountain path alike.

You will see from this division of the day, that the circumstances of most importance are the three meals, oases in the desert of daily life ; cities of refuge to us pursued by the murderous hand of ennui ; epochs up to which to date the events of the day. "Up to which," I say, not from which ; in other words, we are influenced by hope rather than by memory, and we count forward to the prospective meal as did the Romans to their Kalends, Ides, and Nones. As for our fare, it is good enough, and thanks to sundry goodies brought by each of us from home, shows home comforts and nice things more than you would expect in a rough merchant vessel. The gingersnaps are yet a few of them in existence; although unanimously applauded by both captain and passengers, and eaten when brought out with a remarkable relish, I have thought fit to keep them in a very miserly way, and dole them out as a great favor, for I look upon them as the last link that binds me to home. Many, many thanks to my dear aunt for her kindness ; little though the act of love, it was the seed of much pleasant thought and thankfulness.

We are in the midst of a calm just now, and although the weather is perfect, we do not get on at all, and shall be a long time in accomplishing the four hundred and eighty miles between us and Gibraltar. Up to this time we have had a very good run, and unless this calm continues, we shall reach Gibraltar in three days. Calm weather is very good for writing letters, but not for much else.

Good-by for to-day.

OFF THE BALEARIC ISLES,
Lat. 39° 16', Long. 1° 2' E., *June* 16.

I laid down my pen two weeks ago on the Atlantic, expecting soon to resume it, but the soft enervating climate in which we were enveloped after passing the Azores threw its balmy fetters even on the powers of thought and converted the quarter deck into a real "Castle of Indolence."

The ship, too, seemed affected by these drowsy influences, and for a week we lay within one hundred and fifty miles of Gibraltar, but making little progress through the becalmed ocean. But at length on the 8th, as I was sitting in the cabin, land was announced! Up I started, throwing maps, grammars, and hand-books in wild confusion, and in a moment stood on the deck. There was the land, the land which for a month I had longed for, hoped for, looked for, more than all save home and friends; there it lay, a mere blue line to be sure, but still the land; — not Europe, the object of my pilgrimage, but dark, wild, mysterious Africa, the home of fetichism, the mystic parent of the more mystic sources of Nile and Niger, the fountain head of dark debasing slavery.

The next day we passed the Strait of Gibraltar, and there, between the pillars of Hercules, I thought of the solemn "Ne Plus Ultra," which for so many years kept back the timid ancients on their voyages, and of which motto we ourselves were so convincing a contradiction; and then I thought of Don Roderick and Cava, and how, to revenge his private wrong, Count Julian brought ruin on his country, and infamy on himself, when the Moors at his instigation crossed the narrow strait and quenched the Christian altar fires with the blood of the "Last of the Goths." And in more modern times the gallant defense of Elliott, when human valor and skill seemed unavailing against an overwhelming force, has made his name a part of that fortress, whose title is a synonym for strength. And still later how these regions must have echoed to the cannonades of Trafalgar, on that day when the last maritime force of France and Spain vanished before Nelson's mighty genius and impetuous valor, like mists before the sunbeam. And so we sail into the Mediterranean Sea, most classic of all ages, washing the shores of all lands of ancient story, furrowed by the keels of the ships of Ulysses, Æneas, and Hercules, and strewed with the wrecks of Persian, Grecian, Carthaginian, and Roman fleets. So then it is rather a fall from the heights of romantic history, when I think that on this sea, the scene of knightly valor and Turkish desperation, swept now by Corsair Sultans, and now by Emperors, I should now be sailing not to rescue the Holy Sepulchre from the Infidels, not to succor the glorious Knights of St. John in their rockbound Malta, not to strike a blow for Grecian or Italian independence, but bound for Marseilles, in the merchant ship *Australia* consigned to Rabaud Brothers & Co., and, oh! horror, laden with alcohol (I smell it now), stores, wheat, and bacon. But all the alcohol and bacon in the world would not suffice to quench the enthusiasm that I felt, when as beating along the shore of Africa, we came in sight of the coast of Granada, and saw the snow-covered mountain tops,

"Where bleak Nevada's summits tower
Above the beauty at their feet."

Granada! it was like a trumpet note, in whose echoes throng the histories of the olden times, resounding with tecbir and gong, and kettle-drum, and clarion note, and cries of God and our Lady, St. Iago for Spain, defiantly answered by the Allah il Allah, of the fanatic Mohammedan.

There among yonder mountains the heavy armed, uneducated Goth contended with the polished, brave, and learned Saracen for the Alhambra, that delight and glory of the earth. Alas for Spain! the soldier has passed away, but the mark remains.

"Fair, fair but fallen Spain, 't is with a swelling heart
I think on all thou might'st have been, and look at what thou art.
But the strife is over now, and all the good and brave
That would have raised thee up, are gone to exile or the grave.
Thy fleeces are for monks, thy grapes for the convent feast,
And the wealth of all thy harvest fields for the pampered lord and priest."

Yet, perhaps, in the progress of the ages, a better future is in store even for Spain. Surely such energy as they displayed in past times is not entirely dead, and could the right impulse be given and the dread spell of priest-craft be exorcised, Spain might yet send forth new Cids, new Cervantes, new Lope de Vegas, men worthy of a land so fair.

We have just come in sight of the Balearic and Pityusæ Islands, Majorca and Iviça, uncelebrated in ancient story that I can recall, save that their inhabitants were distinguished archers, having been trained bowmen and slingers from childhood, and when young, dependent for their breakfast on their skill, since it was fastened to the tops of tall trees, and they were obliged to bring it down with their bows or slings, before they could eat it. Imagine the dilapidated condition of the breakfast upon reaching the ground! A most peculiar way of teaching the young idea how to shoot.

MARSEILLES, *June* 24.

Here we are at last, on shore in Europe. After a tedious voyage of just forty-five days from Sandy Hook, we find ourselves once more on terra firma, and that too the land of my hopes, thoughts, expectations. I was the first to leap ashore, and such was my state of excitement that I could scarcely refrain from kissing the ground and crying " France, I salute thee." From what seemed a long and troubled dream of sea life, I have awaked to find myself in another dream in which the actors are most new, strange, and fantastic. Everything we see does but go to remind us that we are far, far away from home, and it is a great relief to glance from the swarthy faces and dark, suspicious-looking eyes to the frank, manly countenance of Captain K. On reaching shore, we got a cab and made a bee-line for Rabaud & Brothers, and were there just in time before the shutting up. Letters were handed to the captain, H., and D., but none to me. I felt as though my heart would burst, and had it not been for the by-standers, I should have given way to all the bitterness of disappointment; but a moment's further search brought to light my letters. Can you imagine how eagerly I tore them open, and with what avidity the contents were devoured.

To L. R. P.

SHIP AUSTRALIA, *June* 21, 1857.
Mediterranean, Lat. 40° 52', Lon. 2° 42' E.

. . . . This is our forty-third day at sea ; think of it, my dear friend, and commiserate me. We are distant from Marseilles less than two hundred miles, and yet have been for the last week so pestered with calms and head winds, that our arriving at the end of our voyage seems to be rather a subject for conjecture than for hope. Had not the weather been perfectly charming, this protracted imprisonment would have been perfectly unendurable, but such air and such a sky! For the past four weeks we have had but one unpleasant day; and even that cleared off, and ended with a most gorgeous sunset ; lovely troops of gold and silver-robed clouds attended

"The bridal of the sea and sky,"

which lay "like lovers after a quarrel, embraced in one another's smile."

For thirty days we saw nothing around except the sea, and occasionally the white sail of a vessel ; but on the afternoon of the thirtieth, signs of approaching land began to be perceived. Small tropic birds of weak wing flew around the ship, and two turtle-doves settled upon the mast. Our first mate, probably having never read Coleridge, shot one of them with his pistol ; I have been expecting ever since to see him visited with some condign punishment by the spirit

"That loved the bird that loved the man
That shot him with his" revolver.

Surely our first mate went to greater lengths than the "Ancient Mariner," for I do not think that we read that that unfortunate person fricasseed the albatross. While yet a hundred miles from shore the land breeze brought to us a sweet scent of the shore, and of trees and flowers, of the bursting buds of the balsam-tree, and the rich perfume of orange groves. The topgallant cross-trees were often sought, to get a glimpse of the shore, and at length a blue misty line lay faint in the dim distance, but still no mist, no cloud, no, the land, the land! I think that I can safely say that the vexed question whether two men can give three cheers was finally settled by the howl which C. and I set up on the occasion. As evening advanced, a levanter sprang up, and the sea was fairly whitened with the sails of a fleet of vessels of all sizes issuing from the Straits. Towards night the wind changed, and by day-dawn we were sailing bravely along past Tangiers, Tarifa, Centa, and Gibraltar, past the sunny vine-clad slopes of Andalusia, and the rugged hill-sides of Morocco, into the classic Mediterranean, dear to the artist, to the adventurer, to the scholar. Truly it is no great hardship to sail upon the sea where Bacchus, Theseus, and Ulysses sailed; to cross the track of Hercules and of those intrepid voyagers who scorned the mandate "*ne plus ultra*," and found the Orkneys; to gaze upon the water from which Venus rose and into which Sappho sprang; and, underneath a kindred sky, and breathing a kindred air, to muse upon those stars, " Gods, or the home of Gods," and upon those mystic transformations of antiquity, Ariadne with her crown, the sword of Orion, and the hair of Berenice. And when not long ago we had a storm, and *Eurusque Notusque* were rushing around in the giddy mazes of a rotary storm (see Olmsted's Nat. Phil., Redfield's theory), I almost expected to see the venerable head of old Nep. rising from the waves and stilling the vagabond winds with his fragmentary but highly suggestive ' *Quos ego.*' (There is a large and very unclassical-looking shark playing around the vessel; I think of Jonah, and shudder at the idea of being nipped off at the knees.) Our great want on board ship is space to exercise in; climbing ropes and pacing the deck become quite stale after the first month. I would like to try a little boxiana, but my two fellow-passengers, C. and a young Massachusetts man, are so pusillanimous that I cannot arouse them even by offering to take them both together. Ah, boy, if I only had you here, I would at the same time amuse myself and improve my digestion by giving you one of those scientific dressings down of the olden time, which used to conduce so highly both to your physical and moral condition. For thus runs the argument; if when I was sick, and thin, and weak, I used occasionally to sit on you and hold a pugilistic inquest, much more so now when I am improved in weight, health, and toughness. .... Our captain is to be married as soon as he returns from this voyage, and consequently is in rather a Benedictine state of mind; so every Saturday night out comes the bottle and Bayard Taylor's poems, and he invites us, in the words of that poet, —

> "To drink to sweethearts and to wives,
> On Saturday night at sea."

I, though destitute of both these precious articles, especially the sweetheart "*in esse*," do gravely top off my whiskey with my mental optic fixed on my lady-love "*in posse*," my spouse *in futuro*, my bride prospective, my wife in the "dim shadowy." (See Crosby.)

"*Tuesday, June 23d. Gulf of Lyons.* Since writing the above, we have experienced a youthful tempest, and the "stormy Gulf of Lyons" has preserved its reputation. Unable to sleep on Sunday night, I dressed myself at 3½ A. M., and went on deck, where I witnessed a scene both outré and magnificent. A heavy gale was blowing, and our vessel was plunging wildly around with an occasional sea dashing over the bulwarks, but the sky was cloudless, and in the east a few faint pencils of light heralded the coming day. The sunrise which followed I am unable to describe; but can scarcely imagine a more remarkable union of the Beautiful and the Sublime than a clear sunrise during a storm at sea. The best conception one can have, without actually seeing it, would be to combine in one picture Everett's description of the Mayflower's passage in 1620 with his most poetical account of a sunrise in his speech at the Dudley Observatory Inauguration. Every rose, however, has its thorn. As I was sitting out on the bowsprit-bitts, enjoying this scene, my eyes were suddenly blinded by a shower of spray; I clung fast to the nearest ropes, and found myself enjoying a sea-bath; when I opened my eyes again, I saw a perfect flood washing across the bows, and carrying away sundry unlashed articles into the sea. The captain was soon advertised of my slightly adventurous position, and I was ordered down. The uneasy motion of the vessel brought on my fellow-passengers a return of seasickness, and I barely escaped. But to-day the weather is glorious, the coast of La Belle France in full sight, and by to-night or to-morrow morning we hope to be in the city of the ancient Phocæans, and of the brawny wretches who led the massacres of the French Revolution with the thrilling Marseillaise. . . . Hoping to meet you before long in the "old country," I am yours in bonds never to be broken.

PARIS, HOTEL MEURICE, *June* 28, 1857.

Marseilles conveyed to my mind a most vivid conception of that slightly warm place which no gentleman will allow himself to mention; but still we spent one pleasant evening when it was comparatively cool, in visiting the Chapelle of Notre Dame de la Garde. This is perched upon the very tiptop of a high and steep hill, commanding an admirable view of both the harbor and the city. Here is a most enormous bell, weighing more than 22,000 pounds, and requiring eight men to ring it. A large church is to be built here, and lotteries are held to assist in the erection. The notices of these lotteries are attached to the very doors of the Chapelle. The interior of the building is most interesting; the walls are literally covered with small "ex votos" pictures representing persons in every style of danger and disease, both by land and sea; especially sick beds and apparently inevitable shipwrecks; everywhere the Virgin with the Child in her arms appears, and the disease is arrested, or the storm calmed. One very remarkable ex voto is a piece of stone which was taken from the bottom of a ship. She had run upon a rock and dashed a hole in her bottom, but a piece of the rock broke off, and, remaining in the hole, had preserved the ship from sinking. This seemingly apocryphal fact is not impossible, since a similar accident and preservation happened to the celebrated clipper ship *Flying Cloud* in one of her voyages to New York. The next day we left for Avignon, where we made arrangements to go to Vaucluse, and then strolled out to see the Cathedral and Palace of the Popes. This latter was very interesting; we saw the very oubliette in which Nicholas di Rienzi was confined; rightly called *oubliettes*, for shut up thus, one must have seemed forgotten by both God and man. The torture-rooms of the Holy Office of the Inquisition were then showed to us. The furnace in which persons suffered the dreadful torture by burning sulphur; the rooms of the Strappado and the Rack, and the large stone bath into which a man was put, and then it was heated red-hot! This was called the first torture; I should think that it would have been likely to be also the last. The next morning we got up very early, and started by half past five for Vaucluse, with a nice carriage and driver. A very pleasant ride of three or four hours brought us to that lovely place which Nature has clothed in her fairest garments, and around which Romance and Poetry have woven their most bewitching spells. The Fountain of Vaucluse and the Home of Petrarch! The first, is an altar at which the lover of the strange and wild in Nature delights to bow; the last, a shrine of love and poetry well worth a scholar's pilgrimage. Dark blue, like the sea, is the fountain; of immeasurable profundity, and has been supposed to have a communication with the Lake of Geneva. After its first appearance in perfect quietude at the foot of the tremendous precipice, it disappears under ground for a few rods, and then bursts forth again in three bright, sparkling springs, whose united volume forms at once a river, whose clear, sky-blue course can be traced far off through the fertile fields of the broad champaign of Provence. In this calm, quiet place of repose, rightly called Vaucluse, or the Close Valley, so completely is it shut in by the high hills, it is pleasant to imagine Petrarch as living, engaged in the culture of his garden and his orchard, and in writing those lovely pastoral letters which shew the stamp of the poet, more than those sickly groanings and repinings at the virtuous cruelty of one who was the wife of another man. No, let the thought of Laura and of worldly passions be absent from this secluded place, which should only be the home of pure and holy thoughts. We stood in Petrarch's house, sat under his laurel tree, and drank from the little stream which murmured through his garden just as it does now, and on whose brink he used to sit and feed his fishes and meditate. But the Yankee spirit never satisfies itself with thinking and musing — it must have work, so we set out to climb the precipice above the fountain. After an arduous climb, through narrow clefts and up abrupt ascents, where our only hold was on the precarious support of an old tree, we reached the top, from which we had a glorious view of the whole level country of Provence, the land of chivalry and song, of the troubadour's lute and the herald's coat. Here reigned good King Renè, the father of the imperious Margaret of England, and around him were gathered the poets, the painters, and the *beaux esprits* of the day, at a time when the gentle and beautiful arts were, in other lands, neglected for civil and foreign war, and the heavy sword and ponderous lance crushed out of sight the brush, the chisel, and the lute. The land is now degraded and inferior; even the soil has lost much of its exuberance and fertility, but yet a ray of light is left upon it, and one still hears the sweet Provençal tongue, and still seès the tasteful caps and kirtles covering graceful forms and raven hair; and everywhere the dark-brown cheeks and flashing eyes, which he had seen in imagination long before. The Durance and Vaucluse rivers are plainly seen, but how different! The former, dingy and muddy, the latter, clear and blue, and accompanied in all its course by a fresher and greener verdure than can be seen elsewhere in the Champaign.

HOTEL MEURICE, PARIS, *July* 12, 1857.

DEAREST MOTHER, — . . . . I cannot tell you a tithe of all I have seen in Paris; in fact, I have been so nearly bewildered, ever since I have been here, that the attempt at recounting sights seen, sounds heard, and smells endured, would prove a failure. It is but just to say, that from the last mentioned attraction, that of bad smells, Paris is remarkably free; but in some of our rambles in the Faubourgs, in passes and cul-de-sacs, I have had that delicate organ, the nose, grievously offended. It is said that Paris is the most beautiful city in Europe, and I can easily believe this to be the case; wherever you turn, something new to the eyes and grand or beautiful meets the sight; here an obelisk, there a palace, and a little farther off a magnificent arch. The Place de la Concorde strikes me as the most surpassingly beautiful out-of-doors object in Paris. On account of the light-colored asphalt pavement, and many marble statues, it looks too glaring in the daytime, but at night, when the moon shines through the ever-falling fountains, and the glittering lights of the Champs Elysées and the Rue de Rivoli stretch away endlessly in brilliant avenues, and across the Seine the beautiful dome of the Invalides looks solemnly on; when we remember what has been done and what suffered upon this spot; that here rose the awful guillotine, and here fell the unhappy Marie Antoinette and the heroic Charlotte Corday; that here the glorious Girondists sang the birth-song of freedom for their own death song, and here that song died gradually away until the thrilling tones of Vergniaud were left alone to sing —

"Amour sacré de la patrie," —

these combined attractions of sad memory of the past and of beautiful nature and art in the present, have given me more pleasure than almost anything here. In fact, I am very susceptible of what is historically interesting, and I am truly thankful that my life has been spent so much among books, and that I have thus stored up information of the olden time which comes out with most pleasant distinctness, when I am in the presence of the places and relics of that same olden time.

We take great tramps all over the city and outside of it; and are practicing the pedestrian art, so that when we go to Switzerland we may have muscles well prepared and toughened, to take journeys of twenty, thirty, or forty miles per day. We walked out on the Fourth of July to Vincennes, since there was no celebration of the day among the Americans here. No! the eagle drooped his beak and lowered his majestic tail, and nobody took interest enough to gather together the scattered tribes, and to sing his praises in the Declaration of Independence, or in Hail Columbia. So we went out to Vincennes, a good stout tramp of five or six miles each way, but it was a delight to escape from the bewildering tumult of this ever active and noisy city. We walked down the Rue de Rivoli, past the Louvre and the Hotel de Ville, stopped for a few minutes to examine the Column of July, which stands upon the very spot formerly occupied by the gloomy Bastile, which was captured in 1789, and destroyed in 1790. It was constructed, says the inscription, "To the Glory of the French Citizens who armed themselves and fought in defense of the public liberties in the memorable days of 27th, 28th, and 29th of July." The sides of the column are filled with the names of five hundred and four patriots, who were killed in 1830, and many also of those who were slain at the barricade of 1848, are buried here, with the heroes of eighteen years previous. Here also the throne of the Orleans Dynasty was burned, in February, 1848. Thence down through the Rue du Faubourg St. Antoine, that fruitful nest of Republicanism and rebellion in all times, to the Barriere du Trône, which is one of the limits of the city. Passing between the pillars, with their colossal statues of St. Louis and Philip the Fair, we are in the country, and soon at Vincennes. Most of the fortifications and barracks are recent, but the Donjon has remained intact since 1333, and bids fair to rear in defiance its massive walls for five hundred years more. It is a chubby, chunky-looking affair, and until one attempts to climb to the top, he cannot have a realizing sense of its height. How inseparable is Walter Scott from a donjon tower or keep; I also thought of Mrs. Browning's rhyme, and considered the Duchess May as decidedly a strong-minded woman, if she had such a taste for riding the castle wall. In the little chapel of the Barracks, not in plain sight, but in a side chapel, is the monument of the unhappy, murdered Duc D'Enghein. He is represented as being supported by Religion, and wept over by France, while Vengeance, or, as the guide politely said, Discord, holds a blazing torch. This is one of the very few Bourbon reminiscences still remaining in Paris which are capable of being removed to gratify the present dynasty. I asked the guide to show me the spot where the Duc was shot, but he peremptorily refused, and not even the magic sheen of a piece of silver could soften his obduracy; he seemed to have had decisive orders to the contrary. It is thus that the nephew strives to cover over the crimes and blunders of his uncle, but Napoleon the First is as great, with all his faults unexcused, as he could be even if Napoleon the Third should spend his life in his vindication. He has always been my idol from my boyish days; his genius, his wondrous destiny, his dreadful fall and sad death, have ever had a charm for me, which nothing could lessen or destroy, and my youthful sympathies were so strongly enlisted for him, that his enemies were my enemies. I hated Wellington; and were it possible to hate a sailor, I should have hated Nelson, and I must confess that never have I been filled with emotions of such deep and heartfelt worship, as when I stood before that little coffin, surmounted by the cocked hat and gray coat, in the Hotel des Invalides, while, from the gloomy panelings of the chapel, the mighty names of Marengo, Jena, Austerlitz, and Wagram look down like guardian giants of the fame of him who now sleeps there so peacefully. Below the flooring of the church, but open above, so that it can be seen from the pavement, is the pavilion which contains the grand sarcophagus; this is surmounted and covered by a gigantic slab of porphyry, weighing 135,000 pounds. Every Monday this is removed, and the coffin is placed in the chapel, which I have abovementioned, and where it can be easily seen by all. The pavement of this lower crypt, containing the sarcophagus, is splendidly inlaid in mosaic, and inwrought with the names of several of Napoleon's most brilliant and important victories. Around the sarcophagus stand twelve colossal figures, caryatides in white marble, representing War, Legislation, the Arts and Sciences. In fine, the entire furniture of this subterranean crypt is most imposing and magnificent, and its cost can be reckoned only by millions; but never can it be as touching as that little cocked hat and sword, nor can any epitaph be written, which will more endear him to the French, than those last words of his which are his fitting epitaph: " Je désire que mes cendres reposent sur les bords de la Seine, au milieu de ce peuple Français que j'ai tant aimé." Everywhere here, in galleries and in offices, is seen his noble head, with that brow of almost superhuman thought, and those eyes which seem more divine than those of any sculptured hero or demigod of antiquity.

The nephew's head shows a most decided contrast; I should scarcely think that he would like to place his bust beside that of his uncle, when he must know that his subjects, however loyal, cannot fail to draw comparisons unfavorable to him.

Last night we walked out to the Bois de Boulogne, and on our way stopped at the Chapel of St. Ferdinand, which was erected on the very spot where the Duc d'Orleans, the oldest son of Louis Phillippe, was thrown from his carriage and killed, on July 13th, 1842. The picture of his death is most touching, his noble and manly face being without expression either of feeling or pain, as he was unconscious during the four hours which intervened. At his feet bends the unhappy king in the deepest grief, the Prince utterly forgotten in the Father. On his tomb, his drooping figure is supported by a beautiful angelic being, which his own sister Marie of Orleans had executed, little thinking that it would be for her own brother's tomb. One clock points ever to the hour when he fell from the carriage, ten minutes before twelve, another to the moment when he died, ten minutes past four. There also are some of the instruments of exercise and amusement which once were his; and what interested me more than all, his little boat, an Indian canoe, with its flag and rudder, in which he used to row himself on the Seine. As I looked at these, I forgot that he was the heir of a vast kingdom, and thought of him only as a dear young man, who was the truest of friends, and the kindest of brothers. We walked some distance from the chapel before our sadness was sufficiently dispelled to speak to each other; it cast a shade of melancholy over the whole evening. This Bois de Boulogne is as beautiful as anything so completely artificial can be; woods, dark groves, rural lanes, lakes, streams, water-falls, grottos, and rustic bridges, all constructed by the hand of man, strive to rival the beauties of God's own forests; but in my opinion they "can't come it." A herd of red and fallow deer went bounding along near the road, and for a moment my blood thrilled with recollections of Adirondack; but the next instant I rejected any comparison between these puny creatures and the swift-footed wild deer of America. The last amusement of the evening was a row, which we took on one of the artificial rivers, in a nice little boat about the length of the *Una*, but much broader, the crack boat in fact of the stream. I first astonished the boatman by a description of the proportions of the *Una*, and endeavored to convey to his mind some faint conception of the way in which she could be sent through the water, and I then excited his loud approbation by the manner in which I handled my oars. My arms were rather weak from inactivity on board ship, but I put in all the "fancy touches," and rowed rather with regard to elegance than to strength. I suppose I should have told this to J. rather than you; just make this part of the letter over to him, and pardon me for troubling you with so much of my boating slang.

We have been very agreeably disappointed in the preaching here; on Sunday morning we go to a Wesleyan Chapel near the Madelaine, where a Mr. G. reads the Episcopal service, but preaches sermons which in practicality and fervor are almost equal to those of Dr. C. himself. At 3 P. M. we go to the American, or rather the French Chapel, which is at present occupied by the Americans during part of the day, until their own, now being erected in Rue de Berri, shall be completed. We had an excellent sermon there last Sunday from Dr. Kirk on the Life of Paul.

The Americans, and more especially the English, keep the Sabbath at Paris, but the city otherwise is "wholly given to idolatry." On Sunday evening the streets are filled with carriages and pedestrians, all the shows are open, and the open air concerts, which are bad enough on work-days, are embellished on Sundays with additional attractions (?). We have seen the most absurd and indecent dancing and buffoonery on Sunday evening. I am sorry to say that the Americans on the continent have not nearly so good a reputation for church going as the English, who have a chapel in almost every place which is much frequented by strangers. So H. and I have provided ourselves with an English-prayer book, that we may do all things decently and in order.

GHENT, *July* 20, 1857.

MY DEAR JACK, — We have just arrived in this queer old place, and have been refreshing ourselves, after the dusty railroad ride from Brussels, with a cup of excellent tea. I take this opportunity of being in Belgium, and in Ghent, which are familiar to you from the pages of Prescott, and in themselves intensely interesting, to write you a long letter. We have taken this detour into Belgium and Holland, at the advice of T. D., who has been with us in Paris for a couple of weeks, and who had recently taken it himself. I expect we shall enjoy it very much, judging from what we have seen of Belgium thus far.

Our three weeks' stay in Paris was quiet, and, but for the heat, would have been extremely pleasant. We spent one delightful day in the pleasant walks and excellent museums of the Garden of Plants. This is a most admirably collected and conducted institution, affording to the common people, who are all admitted free to the Gardens and lectures, a grand opportunity to become completely familiar with the most interesting and valuable parts of Natural History and the other sciences. I cannot imagine a better place for studying the sciences than Paris; I met a young Swede at Waterloo, with whom I had a grand talk in German. He had been studying Mathematics and Astronomy in Paris for some time, and was very loud in his praises of the Observatory, in which Lalande, La Place, and Bailly wrought: of the Garden of Plants, and of the Botanical Gardens of the Luxembourg; in this last we ourselves saw many students busily employed, with their large books, in gathering and classifying flowers and plants. It seems difficult to reconcile these three qualities which seem so prominent in the French character, namely, their fondness for the exact sciences, their romantic love of glory, and their total want of all true poetry. Their taste seems to be for the showy and tawdry; their greatest ambition is to get a medal or a cross. I went to the Opera twice in Paris, and heard William Tell and Trovatore. The scenery and all the accessories were splendid enough, but the singing was pretty poor, as all the best singers have gone into the country. I was greatly disgusted with the claque, and had a great mind to pitch into some dough-faced fellows near me, who, without a spark of enthusiasm or capacity to enjoy good music, clapped away whenever their leader gave the signal. I doubt not that any demonstrations which I might have chosen to make would have been supported by the gentlemen around me, for they looked as disgusted as I felt. What a glorious enterprise, the crusade against the Claque! From one of the salesmen at Galignani's I obtained a complete list of nice and cheap hotels on our whole route, many of them of a class which are not mentioned in the otherwise invaluable Murray.

We have a very nice room fronting on the Kauter or Place d'Armes; and as it is the eve of a fête, namely the Anniversary of the Accession of Leopold I., King of the Belgians, we have been having grand doings out in front, and this letter has been several times interrupted, for me to run to the window to listen to most exquisite music, both vocal and instrumental.

July 22, — Since the first part of this letter was written we have been to Bruges and returned. It would be difficult to say which of the two cities, Bruges or Ghent, possesses the most historic interest. Bruges being the residence of the Counts of Flanders, has more souvenirs of the nobles, but Ghent is renowned for its grand republican burgher spirit, which found such a noble exponent in Jacques and Phillip Van Artevelde. We had not intended at first to go to Bruges, but finding that it had for ages been celebrated for its pretty girls, of course it would not do for two such connoisseurs as H. and myself to neglect it. There is a sad, deserted air about this city of Bruges, which was in 1250 one of the most splendid cities in Europe. The town seems asleep; no vehicles in the streets, no vessels in the canals, no faces at the windows of the principal houses. In the suburbs, on the contrary, swarms a filthy population, and they, too, seem totally devoid of all energy and enterprise.

We saw a great number of paintings by artists of the early Flemish school, some of them of very great delicacy and beauty. Minuteness of detail also seemed much striven after. I have been especially pleased with the works of the brothers Van Oost and John Van Eyck. I think that Rembrandt's reputation has been vastly overrated.

In the church of Notre Dame, I saw the monuments of Charles the Bold and his daughter Mary of Burgundy. The interest I take in this part of the country is greatly increased by my remembrance of the vivid descriptions in Quentin Durward, which are remarkable, seeing that Scott drew upon his imagination for his facts. We also climbed the "Belfry of Bruges," and having surmounted its 402 steps, had a fine view of the flat country round, even as far as Ostend and the sea. They have here a chime which is played by very costly and intricate machinery, and is said to be the finest in Europe, but I do not like it nearly so well as the one at Ghent, which is continually playing the jolliest tunes. We see everywhere here in Belgium memorials of Alva, Charles V., Philip II., and the Counts of Egmont and Horn. At Brussels, in front of the Hotel de Ville, is a venerable building called the Bradhuis, in which the two counts spent the night previous to their execution, and from the windows of which Alva is said to have looked while the execution was going on. The prison is now standing on the site of the Hotel de Luxembourg, in which the confederates held their meetings, and from the balcony of which the leaders presented themselves with the beggar's staff and wallet, and gave to the movement the name of the Insurrection of the Gueux. Alva out of revenge had the unoffending building leveled with the ground. One of the oddest and most remarkable things I have seen is what is called the Beguinage. It is a convent in this city, which is a little city itself, comprising streets, rows of houses and canals, all the buildings being occupied solely by the nuns. They number about seven hundred; they do not bind themselves to a perpetual seclusion by taking the vows, but are allowed to return to the world again if they don't like it. Those whom we saw about the streets, dressed in the faillè, or large black cloak with a hood, did not have the appearance of having spent their valuable time in fasting and macerating, or, if they had, it certainly agreed with them most remarkably. I could easily imagine all the younger sisters up some night on a spree of somewhat the same nature with those that are described as taking place at B.

THE HAGUE, *July* 25, 1857.

DEAREST MOTHER,—We have just arrived here from Rotterdam after a delightful ride in the treck-schuyt or canal-boat, and are now comfortably settled in the best room of that very respectable hotel, the Bull's Eye, and have just washed down an excellent beefsteak with some excellent tea. My mind is now at rest for a couple of days, and freed from cares touching hotel bills and francs, centimes, guilders, and stivers, so I can write to you who are never out of my mind.

I think of you day and night, and long most truly for the time which will bring me back to the house roof and to you. We arrived at Antwerp having crossed the Scheldt from the Tête de Flandre, which is noted as being the place where the people of Antwerp cut through the dyke and inundated the country that the provision ships from Zealand might sail across the land and relieve the city from the strict blockade which the Duke of Parma had been carrying on. Had this measure been taken sooner, the city would have been saved.

The next day we employed in studying Rubens at the Museum and in the Cathedral. The pictures in the Museum greatly disappointed me. The two principal ones are the "Crucifixion," and the "Adoration of the Magi." In the former of these, the moment is selected when the soldier pierces the Saviour's side, while others are breaking the legs of the two thieves: it is certainly a picture of wonderful power, and would appear to the most advantage if viewed at a distance of something under an eighth of a mile; the figure of the thief who railed, and who in his agony has forced one of his legs loose from the cross, is a miracle of expressive force and correctness of drawing; but upon a near examination the faces have a blotched and unfinished look like that of Murillo's pictures, but without that grand spirituality which makes one forget all faults in Murillo. The "Adoration of the Magi" struck me as rather comic than grand; the principal figure, one of the Magian Kings, has an expression on his face in which I could not read any holy awe, but rather a feeling of disappointment that he had come so far to see so little. But a pleasing disappointment was reserved for me at the Cathedral: here I saw Rubens' great master-piece, called "The Descent from the Cross," and am now ready to acknowledge him as a truly great master, but not one to my heart. I should think, however, that the drawings, the position of the figures, and most especially the drooped form of Christ, are wonders of art. In the opposite transept of this Cathedral is a very good painting, the "Elevation of the Cross," also by Rubens. In this he has introduced a most admirable dog and horse, to exhibit his power of representing animals. But however fine may be the coloring of Rubens, and however powerful his groupings, I can now say with certainty that he is not the painter for my worship, since form is his object rather than expression.

I have been much pleased with the pictures of the Flemish

school, which are so devoted to minuteness of detail and delicacy of finish, especially of Hans Hemling and the two brothers Van Eyck, the inventors of oil painting. Their pictures, 425 years old, are as bright and clear as the first day they were painted, and preserve wonderfully their original beauties. I will speak only of the master-piece of this school, which is in the Cathedral of St. Bavon at Ghent. It is called the "Adoration of the Spotless Lamb," and is by the two Van Eycks. Not more than three feet wide and four feet high, it still contains more than three hundred faces, some of them portraits, and all of the highest excellence. Above is the Father, with St. John the Baptist on the one hand, and the Virgin on the other. The face of the latter combines with the beauty and softness almost of a miniature, an expression of spirituality unsurpassed by any of Raphael's Madonnas that I have yet seen. Below is the Lamb upon the Altar. He is approached by four groups of worshipers, from four opposite directions ; first the prophets, next the apostles and New Testament saints, thirdly the virgins and female saints, and fourthly the bishops and founders of monasteries. In this last group the painters have introduced their own portraits. Yet with all this delicacy and completeness of finish, the pictures of this school say nothing to the heart and soul ; they are rather to be carefully examined with the microscope than to be gazed at with full eyes and a swelling heart.

AMSTERDAM, *July 25.*

Since I began this letter I have changed my place of abode, and three days have intervened. We left the Hague yesterday afternoon, and were very sorry to leave it, for, besides the fact that we had most comfortable quarters, the city is a lovely one, and everywhere reigns that sense of order and cleanliness and freedom from show, which reminded me most powerfully of my New England home. And here let me put in a word for the Dutch. I had a long-standing prejudice that they were a coarse, stupid people, as broad as they were long, drinking and smoking all the time, and totally devoid of those qualities that interest and endear. But I was most agreeably disappointed when I came to see them. The men are in general a fine and intelligent looking class; one meets with many a manly figure and sensible face to remind him that he is among the descendants and fellow-countrymen of the De Witts and Van Tromps, of the Prince of Orange and the Counts of Egmont. Their faces are generally free from the stupidity of the Belgians, and the mean frivolousness of the French. Among the women I have, within the last four days, seen more beauty than in the four weeks previous. True it has been of rather a solid, substantial kind, and wanting that face lighted by the fires of the soul which we have at home, but yet a good, honest look, which makes one think of a quiet home, and well swept house, and a crowd of chubby children around the neat hearthstone.

Our ride from Delft to the Hague, in the treck-schuyt or canal-boat, was one of great pleasure and beauty. The ordinarily unpoetic canal was completely embosomed in verdure, and its sides were lined with charming little country-seats, upon whose gates the owner had inscribed some sentiment indicative of his intense satisfaction and contentment, such as "Lust en Rust," *i. e.* Pleasure and Ease; "Bosch Lust," Wood Pleasure; "Pax Intrantibus," Peace to the comers in; "Meer Lust," Sea Delights, etc.

Along the sides of the grand canal were stately rows of fine trees, which gave an exclusive and aristocratic air to our humble highway, and gave to it the dignity of an avenue. Everywhere there was the richest green; everywhere the most flourishing prosperity. I doubt if there be a country on the face of the earth where the people are so well off and so universally prosperous, or where property is so equally distributed among all classes. One sees here no beggars, of whom there are a plenty in Belgium: in fact, they form there a large part of the population. In Bruges alone there are over 15,000. But in this country, conquered from the sea, and in which there is a continual contest going on between land and water, with a dingy sky and rainy climate, it would seem as if the very exertion to support existence, and preserve life from the angry waves, had also kept alive in the natives a spirit of freedom and independence which is unknown to the other Continental nations. The habit of demanding a fee for every trifling device is not practiced here. For example, this afternoon H. dropped his cane into the canal and had given it up for lost, when it was picked up by a canal-boatman and returned. I threw him a piece of money, which he took only after many remonstrances. I like the Dutch extremely, and were I not an American, and were it not for the Dutch language, I would be willing to be a Dutchman. This Dutch language is odd enough, but has certain strong resemblances both to the English and German, and by a judicious shingling of these I manage to get along capitally with the lower order of persons, who speak neither French, English, nor German. But if I should ever come abroad again, I should previously prepare myself in every language which there was any probability of my using. Lord Bacon most truly says, "He that travelleth into a country before he hath some entrance into the language goeth to school and not to travel."

We have visited, to-day, Broek, which is celebrated as being the cleanest village in the world. All visitors are obliged to take off their shoes upon entering a house, or at least to wipe them extremely clean. A weekly scrubbing of the most radical character takes place. The houses are very often painted to keep them looking handsome, and even the cows' tails are held up by a rope running over a pulley, with a weight at the further end, that they may not dangle in the muck and get dirty. The bricks are laid out in figures similar to those which form mosaics, and the gardens are clipped into forms both regular and fantastic.

One room of the house is sacred, and is not shown to visitors. This the housewife enters once a week, dusts it and returns, locking the door and leaving it to solitude until the next week shall come round. Good manners also seem to receive much attention. Every child we met greeted us with an uncouth salutation, and some of them even made abortive attempts at saying, "Monsieur, guten Tag?" This was very pleasant, and I wish I could see more of this true courtesy, which is really from the heart. This expedition we did on foot, and on our way back we were sprinkled with sundry and various showers. One of them was so heavy that we were forced to take refuge under a hay-stack, where we lay for some time moralizing on the oddness of our condition. We have an extremely independent way of getting along. We speak to no English, unless they speak to us first, and even then we make them no advances; but we converse as much as possible with the natives wherever we go, take things as they come, grumble at nothing, and consequently enjoy ourselves as much as it is possible for two such home bodies to do away from home.

HEIDELBERG, *August* 7, 1857.

DEAR J.,— At last the long looked for, wished for, sickened for letters are in my possession, and I am in a state more nearly approaching to happiness than I have been since I got ashore and obtained my letters at Marseilles. After reading them, my heart was so full of joy that I seemed ready to suffocate, and I was obliged to spend a couple of hours in the open air, and around the old castle, before I could sufficiently command myself to sit down and answer yours. Your news, all so good and pleasant, and mindful of everything that would please me most, every item, however apparently trivial to one at home, was most eagerly devoured, and every well-remembered and dearly cherished name of a friend went right to my heart, giving full assurance that absence from home does but endear it more completely to one ; or, to speak mathematically, the home feeling increases directly as the square of the absence.

What a glorious time you must have had this summer; picnics, parties, and, above all, boat rides ; you aggravate me terribly by painting such a picture of New Haven life, and cause me to wish myself at home more heartily than I am in the habit of doing about three times a day. However, you have not enjoyed these pleasures alone. I have been very frequently present, both in sleeping visions and in wakeful daydreams I have walked up Hillhouse Avenue, and laid down on the oars of the *Una.* You give me a lively idea of the gayety of N. H., and an idea that could only be given by an actor in the gay scene. Alas ! and has thy young nature been drawn into the fatal maelstrom of society?

I suppose you would like to hear where I have been for the last week or two, since I wrote from Ghent and Amsterdam. Cologne disappointed my high-strung expectations in the smell line. I sniffed everywhere, without discovering the —

"four and twenty stenches
All well defined and separate stinks;"

nor did I regret them, especially as the city was disagreeable enough, with heat and dust, to satisfy any one, without the least argument addressed to the nose. On Friday afternoon we were off "up the Rhine." For quite a long time the scenery was of the most uninteresting nature; but as we approached Bonn, the beautiful blue range of the Siebengebirge loomed up one after another, looking much like the Catskills to one viewing them from down the river, although not equaling the Catskills in height and grandeur, yet making a most agreeable change from the flat lands of Holland and Belgium.

We spent the night at Bonn, and heard the students yelling and singing around the streets, which sounded very natural and home-like, and my heart warmed towards the noisy fellows. Students are students all the world over, and there is a sort of freemasonry about them all which gives them a kindly feeling for one another, and draws a line between them and the outer world. The next morning we began our foot tramping, and ended it also the same day. We made what we supposed the necessary arrangements for having our luggage sent to Coblentz, where we were intending to pass the Sabbath, and each with a good stout stick in his hand, jogged sturdily along the post road.

Passing the old ruined castle of Godesberg, built by the warlike Archbishops of Cologne, we held on through the village to the ferry, which takes one across the river to Königswinter and Drachenfels. When we reached the water's edge, the ferry-boat was some little distance from the shore, and still receding; but as I did not wish to wait an hour for the next boat, I waded out into the shallow water and got on board, an example which H. was obliged to follow. At the village of Königswinter we began the ascent of the far-famed Drachenfels, and if ever the sun fell hot on my back and head, it was then. "Feen wedder for de grubs" (fine weather for the crops), as an English-speaking German said to me; but not fine weather for attempting the ascent of such a perpendicular heart-breaking hill as Drachenfels. Several times did we sit down, almost in despair, and wish that we had not so scornfully rejected the offers of the boys who stood at the foot of the hill with such tempting looking donkeys. Finally we gained the summit of this most picturesque of crags, and sat down among the crumbling ruins of that ancient castle, where Siegfried of the Niebelungen Lied slew the dragon, and gained himself an immortal name, and where his successors lived and so oppressed the peasants and unwarlike vassals, that they soon wished the Dragon back again instead.

The view is not equal to that at Rolandseck, across the river, which is also the scene of one of the most romantic and truly touching of all the Rhine legends. There, upon the beautiful island of Nonnenwerth at our feet, once stood the convent into which the fair Hildegard, the betrothed of Roland, entered when she was falsely persuaded that he had fallen at Roncesvalles; and here, at this gateway, the true knight sat, day after day, for two years, ever gazing upon the convent windows, if perchance he might see her face appearing there, or might hear her voice mingling in the vesper hymn. And here he was one day found sitting, dead, with his face still turned towards the convent window.

This little story Schiller has embodied, with some changes of name and place, in one of his most exquisite ballads. Read Ritter Toggenberg, and think of me as on the spot where —

"Gazing upward to the convent
Hour on hour he passed,
Watching still his lady's lattice
Till it oped at last.

"Till that face looked forth so lovely,
Till the sweet face smiled
Down into the lonely valley,
Peaceful, angel-mild."

But to return to our walk; we tramped along by the side of the river, examining the fine specimens of prismatic basalt which lie around everywhere, and which is used for fences, steps, and posts.

In the church of Apollinaris, a beautiful Gothic gem just above the town, we made an odd acquaintance, nothing more nor less than a young German artist from Dusseldorf, who was copying frescoes and paintings. We agreed to go to Coblentz together, and on the boat had a very jolly time talking about student and artist life, German and American universities and dwellings. We joined in singing Gaudeamus, Lauriger Horatius, and Edite Bibete.

BADEN BADEN, *August* 10, 1857.

DEAR MOTHER, — It is now nearly two weeks since I wrote to you, and they have been filled with interest and variety, so that it seems impossible that it can be so short a time. We have seen Cologne, and the long windings of the Rhine, as far as Mayence, including Bonn, Coblentz, and Bingen, with transient views of many a rock-girt ruin, which time would fail me to enumerate. Indeed, my dear mother, I do not wish to fill my letters with descriptions of pictures, cities, and views; far rather would I talk simply and quietly, as when I was at home; but I find that my experiences and surroundings give a peculiar tinge to my mind, just as the red wine-cup, in which I drank some Niersteiner at Cologne, gave to the wine within it the ruby brightness of the sparkling Asmannshaüser, king of the red Rhine wines. So you must expect to know something of what I have seen; and first of all the Cathedral of Cologne. As we rode in the cars towards the city, while yet a long distance off, I saw a strange unfinished pile, which my heart at once told me was the world renowned cathedral. You know there is an old tradition that it was built by the Devil. Now I can easily imagine the presence of the Devil's handiwork in the heavy pillars of the Madeleine, which looks more like a heathen temple than a church of the Christian's God, or in the gaudy marbles of St. James at Antwerp. But he never could have touched those graceful, airy reeds, which shoot up ever heavenward, leaving behind in upward flight all ideas of the gross and material. Here one does not feel crushed and confined, as in many Gothic and most Grecian churches. In that wondrous choir, one hundred and sixty-one feet in height, one seems to see a direct avenue to the sky, and the vault is so far remote that one may easily be pardoned for supposing that he sees the blue dome of heaven itself. I can easily pardon the rustic ignorance which is enthralled by such architecture; its effect must be dangerous upon the sensitive minds even of the highly cultivated order; and when you add to all these glorious pillars and sculptured saints, and relics well-nigh vying with the church itself in antiquity, the golden light streaming through painted windows, and the answering voices of the choristers, while above all peals the solemn organ, I am not the person to blame the weak mind that sinks down by my side and exclaims, "Sancta Maria, ora pro nobis." For myself, these rites and ceremonies, which I would not call mummeries, and cannot call worship, have only the effect to make me long more sincerely than ever for the simple service of our church at home, which I have not heard since I came away, and which I shall learn to appreciate more thoroughly when I return. Cologne well deserves to be called the "town of Monks and Bones." Two churches are entirely devoted to the reception of the osseous remains of two separate sets of martyrs; one, of those of St. Ursula and her eleven thousand Virgins, and the other of the Theban Legion of St. Gereon, who were slain in one of the persecutions under Diocletian, though how they got up here from Thebes I am unable to relate. I was not well at Cologne, and did not go around much. On the second day we took the boat for Bonn and embarked on Father Rhine, who is extremely uninteresting until the Seven Mountains heave in sight, and his real beauties do not begin until you leave Coblentz. I shall long remember that most delightful sail. The banks were high and richly cultivated, and upon their summits perched many a crumbling and ancient castle, with whose names were identified legends of the olden time, breathing of love and defiance, of rapine and war, of knightly generosity and undying love. I was much pleased with that which is connected with the Castles of Liebenstein and Sternberg, which stand side by side upon two crags, and were inhabited by two brothers, who were both deeply in love with a fair young girl, a ward of their father. The elder, perceiving that she preferred his brother, nobly retired and gave the young lady up to him. The younger one, instead of profiting by his brother's generosity, went off to the crusades, and left his affianced bride in the charge of his elder brother; he was still faithful to his noble character, and treated her like a sister. After a time the younger brother returned, bringing with him a Grecian wife from the East; whereat the elder sent him a fierce defiance, and a bloody conflict would have taken place, had it not been for the entreaties of the ill-used lady, who had entered into a convent. The false younger brother was punished by the perfidy of his Grecian bride, who ran away from him. Ever after the two brothers lived happily together, and never saw again the unhappy fair one for whom they had striven. As if for an emblem of their legend, a white convent lies at the foot of the two rival castle crags. Also the rock of the water-nixie Loreley or Lurley, and the seven sisters who were turned into stone by her, for their coldness and capriciousness. The magnificent ruin of Rheinfels is redolent with stirring war tales, both of the Middle Ages and of modern times.

In the Castle of the Cat or Katzeneln bogen lived the noble family whom Irving has made famous to Americans by his tale of the "Spectre Bridegroom." Just above Boppart is a sharp turn in the river, and before reaching it one seems sailing upon a beautiful lake, so completely closed up do both entrance and exit appear. At this point the echoes from the rock of Lurley can be heard repeated fifteen times, but I am inclined to think this an exaggeration ; at least, such was not our experience. And so we go gliding on between the vine-clad banks, beholding —

> "The negligently grand, the fruitful bloom
> Of coming ripeness, the while city's sheen,
> The rolling stream, the precipice's gloom,
> The forest's growth, and gothic walls between
> The wild rocks shaped as they had forests been,
> In mockery of man's art" —

until we reach Bingen, famed by song as "calm Bingen on the Rhine." And indeed, not only did we find it calm, but also very slow. However, we were very nicely settled, with a fine room overlooking the Rhine, and commanding a good view of the Niederwald, upon which we gazed with a longing eye, impatient to get at it. The next day we were satisfied. Early in the morning we got a boat and rowed out into the river. From this point we surveyed three independent States, — the Dukedom of Nassau, the Electorate of Hesse in which Bingen stands, and the Kingdom of Prussia. We passed through the Bingen loch, a place obstructed by rocks, which caused a whirling similar to that at Hell Gate.

We had a good look at the Mouse Tower, celebrated as being the residence of Bishop Hatto, about whom a legend is told ; how, when the grain was scarce and the people clamorous for bread, he invited them to come to his barns and get corn ; and when a goodly number were gathered there, he shut the doors and burned them all to death. Soon after this he was attacked in his palace by the rats, and obliged to flee to this tower, in the centre of the river ; but even there the rats found him out, and completely devoured him, picking his bones uncommonly clean. We then landed and climbed up to the Castle of Rheinstein, one of the oldest castles on the river, which is inhabited by the Prince of Prussia, who has restored it to the condition of a castle of the Middle Ages, and has filled its walls with old furniture, odd suits of armor, and the windows are provided with stained glass of great antiquity. The walls are covered with antique weapons, and many interesting relics ; among them, the iron hand of Goetz of Berlichingen, autographs, and an ale mug of Luther's, which latter showed the great Reformer to have been a decided opponent of the Maine Law. This castle is a place to live and die in ; and I had a strong desire to request the head servant who showed us around, and who bears the antique title of Schlossvogt, to propose to the Prince Frederick, who was in the room above us, to take me in for a few weeks to board. How the venerable fragment would have opened his eyes. The rock upon which the castle stands is falling to pieces, and it is found necessary to bind it together with iron chains.

We returned to our boat and crossed the river to Assmannshausen, where we commenced our ascent to the Niederwald ; the top being gained, we refreshed ourselves at the hunting castle of the Duke of Nassau, and went into the wood. Here we found ourselves once more in the presence of nature, not Dutch or French nature, clipped into straight or curved lines, but wild and willful nature, unrestrained, and indulging in a thousand fantastic forms, with gnarled roots and uncouth branches. We came first to the Magic Cave, a strange bower, completely surrounded by trees, through which three vistas of great length have been cut, and there, at the end of them, some three or four miles off, we see the opposite side of the Rhine, set, as it were, in a beautiful framework of leaves, and producing an effect both magical and beautiful. A little further on is an artificial ruin, upon the very pitch of the rock. From this we can see the three rivers which here unite, and can easily distinguish them from each other by their color, the Nahe being brown, the Main, reddish, and the Rhine clear green. They do not mix, it is said, until they meet in the deep pool of Lurley, several miles below. Still further on, is the Temple, a small building erected upon the most suitable spot for enjoying the finest view on the Rhine, which Bulwer calls, "one of the noblest landscapes upon earth," and it would be difficult to imagine a more beautiful panorama than this, which takes in all that lovely district known as the Rheingau or Bacchanalian Paradise, and extends far off towards the fair Heidelberg Bergstrasse, and the dark masses of the Odenwald. But I cannot give you any idea of the scene in words; it would be as easy to convey in language a smell or a sound; enough for me to say, that upon this spot alone, was I willing to justify the extravagant encomiums that have been bestowed upon the Rhine, or to give it a place among rivers, beside that majestic stream near whose banks I was brought up, and which wants nothing but historic names to make it superior in every respect, in beauty, majesty, and fertility, to any river in the world. We continued, on that day, the ascent of the river to Mayence; but we had seen already the beauties of the Rhine, and nothing more of interest was to be seen, except the hills which produce the Johannisberger, the Marcobrunner, and the Steinberger; the three most delicious and expensive wines in the world.

The cathedral tower of Mayence at length announced to us the end of our journey for that day. This very ancient building we viewed with much interest. The oldest part dates from 978. In it are the tombs of the powerful archbishops of Mayence; also that of Henry Frauenlob, or Praise the Ladies. He was a canon of Mayence, and did so exalt the female sex in his songs, that when he died he was borne to the grave by eight ladies, who poured into his grave libations both of tears and wine, and has ever since borne the title of the Ladies' Minstrel.

Frankfort pleased me much; and, as soon as I got there, I walked out to see the house in which the great author of "Faust" and "Wilhelm Meister" was born. It is a house of ordinary exterior, but now forever marked out from those which stand around it. A very fine colossal statue of Goethe also stands in the square, before the theatre, the pedestal of which is covered with bas-reliefs taken from the subjects of his works. On one side Mephistopheles leans sneering over the shoulder of Faust, and Iphigenia is led to the altar of sacrifice. Behind we have scenes from "Egmont" and "Tasso," while the third side is occupied with "Wilhelm Meister," and in the corner the grave of Werther.

The environs of Frankfort are quite beautiful. The former ramparts have been laid out in gardens, with walks and fountains. But the great art beauty of Frankfort is Dannecker's lovely statue of Ariadne and the Panther. This is surrounded by curtains so arranged as to throw a rosy light upon the marble, and give it a flesh-like appearance. .

This does not show the Ariadne as deserted by Theseus, and gazing ever after the lessening sails of his vessel, but rather the Ariadne consoled by Bacchus, and therefore she is crowned with the vine leaf and the ivy, and seated upon one of the wine god's chariot-drawing panthers. The position is remarkably easy, — a reclining one, — with one foot drawn up under her with one hand. The face is pleasantly, but not severely, Grecian, and indicates a sort of dreamy repose; the panther, on the contrary, is all life and action.

In one day more we were in Heidelberg, the most charming spot in which I ever set my foot, and rendered doubly dear by being the place where I found my letters from home. I felt as though I could stay there a month, but was obliged to be satisfied with three days, a large part of which time was delightfully spent in roaming through the woods and over the old castle, which we visited about three times a day. This is the noblest of all ruined German castles, and gives one some idea of what must have been the power and magnificence of the Elector Palatine, by whom it was built and occupied. In 1764 a dreadful conflagration destroyed all the interior of the palace which war and pillage had hitherto spared, and its noble courts and halls, which once echoed to the laughter of high-born ladies and the rattle of knightly spurs, now lies silent and deserted.

One of the interior façades is very beautiful; its graceful Italian architecture and slim pilasters are the work of Michael Angelo, and are in strong contrast to the heavier and more Romanesque style of the front adjoining.

To the garden one passes through a fine gate, resting upon

pillars richly carved, and entwined with ivy leaves. It was erected in one night, by the Elector Frederick V., as a surprise to his bride Elizabeth, the daughter of James the First. To this day it is called the Elizabethan Gate. The handiwork of the ferocious Count Tilly, the perpetrator of the massacre of Magdeburg, is here to be seen. The massive tower at the right extremity was blown up by him, while the rest of the tower looms up like a grand torso. He, too, it was who littered his horses in the elector's splendid library, and, when straw was scarce, tore up valuable old manuscripts for the animals to rest upon. Along the front runs the enormous balcony, large enough for a hundred people to dance upon. It is grand to lean over the parapet and see the town below, and the silver Neckar and the vineyards on the other side. Upon this balcony is shown a large and deep foot-mark, said to have been made by the foot of a lady, who was pursued by a ruffian, and sprang from the highest window of the castle. In the vaults of the castle is shown the enormous cask called the Heidelberg Tun, which holds eight hundred hogsheads. Very naturally by the side of it is placed a statue of the court jester, who never used to go to bed without drinking fifteen to eighteen bottles of the wine. Homer lamented that the arms of men were not as strong as they were wont to be. I think we have degenerated in strength of stomach, and we might search far and near without finding the man who could drink fifteen bottles of wine nowadays.

We met a number of friends here, four Yale men and six or seven from theological seminaries. They were all very kind to us, and we had a right jolly walk with them.

Tuesday, August 11. — We are just in the very den of that great giant whom Bunyan does not mention, but who carries off victims bodily, as well as either Pope or Pagan. It does seem hard that every healing spring must have a poison fountain by its side, and that the sick cannot come to cure their bodies without putting soul and substance in peril by the contagious influence of the gaming table. It had been my intention to risk a few francs at rouge et noir, just to try the experiment; but, when I saw the poor people seated round the green board, some with ill-affected looks of unconcern, others with their very eyes protruding with excitement, but all fascinated there, as it were, by a snake's eye, I felt all the blood tingling in my veins to play high, and ride upon the highest wave of passion and fever-heat; and I tore myself away almost by main force, knowing well that I should never stop while I had a sou left. I breathed freer when I found myself in safety in the open air. But truly these gaming houses are a disgrace to the sovereigns by whom they are licensed, and who derive from them the greater part of their revenues. Their argument is that gambling will go on, and it is better that they should license and regulate it; but I think that this merely shows their weakness and cupidity, in that they are not able to cut them up root and branch. The water in the springs is intensely warm, varying from 212° to 144°. It is much more abundant than is needed for medicinal purposes, and some of the springs are used by the country people for scalding pigs and poultry. In taste the water resembles chicken broth.

The Black Forest begins here behind the town, and stretches its gloomy length over eighty miles to Schaffhausen. We should have liked to walk through it, but our intended trip to Strasburg will make it out of the question.

FRIEBURG IN BADEN, *August* 12.

We had a most delightful journey yesterday. On the French border we came near being sent back because we had not the *visé* of the Baden police to enter France, but, by dint of very considerable soft sawder and politeness to the head gens-d'arme, he finally consented to keep our passports at the guard-house until we should return. So we jogged into France in a way quite jolly, but very irregular. Our gaze was of course immediately directed towards the splendid minster, which looms up grandly, and can be seen from a long distance, and naturally, since it is the highest building in the world, — four hundred and eight feet in height, or twenty-four feet higher than the great pyramid. Like Cologne cathedral, this glorious pile is unfinished, the other lofty tower being necessary to complete it and to fill it out symmetrically. The exterior is very light and chaste, and the spire is wholly made of beautiful open-work, so fine and delicate that it rather seems like iron than stone. But within how different! The pillars are perfectly enormous, and the roof, which is not very high, is vaulted in a style rather Romanesque than Gothic. The change from the round to the pointed style can here be read, the choir being a fine specimen of the heavy round style, while the rest is a sort of cross between round and pointed. Nowhere is seen that airy and spiritual-pointed arch which so captivates the senses and touches the heart at Cologne. You might imagine that it was an underground palace built by the gnomes for their king, or the court where the stern Minos and Rhadamanthus give their eternal decrees, rather than a glorious temple of the living and beneficent Deity. The south transept is supported by a single beautiful pillar, surrounded by three rows of figures, the lowest of saints, the next of the angels of praise, and the highest, the angels of love. The statue of the architect, Erwin von Steinbach, is seen leaning from a small Gothic gallery, with his eye constantly fixed upon this pillar, which was one of his favorite pieces. When he died the building of the cathedral was carried on by his daughter Sabina.

We walked back to Kehl, and had a very pleasant ride to this place in the third-class cars, a place which we had not as yet explored. There are decided advantages about the third-class cars; in the first place, one is sure to avoid the English; then it is more open and airy, thus giving a better view of the country; and, finally, it is much the best place to see the people of the country. Here all are at their ease, and talk together as if they had known each other for years. The Germans whom I have seen much of, and with whom I have taken occasion to converse, strike one soon as being very full of a spirit of humanity and kindness, although at first their slow and phlegmatic temperament may lead one to consider them indifferent and regardless of the comforts of others; but this is not so. Their politeness is always aroused by the wants of any person, and this is based upon true courtesy and goodness of heart. One thing has troubled me ever since I came to Europe, and that is the immense amount of labor performed by the female sex. Cows and women work in the fields with oxen and men. This is sorely prejudicial to female beauty, and thus blowsed and burnt by wind and sun, the fairest face soon becomes moderately frightful; consequently a pretty face is almost a wonder in the agricultural districts. Our ride was a very pleasant one, lying as it did all along the edge of the Black Forest Mountains, which gave a continual variety of surface, with an occasional castle or old tower.

SCHAFFHAUSEN, *August* 12.

At last I am in Switzerland, and from this first Swiss town this letter shall be mailed, I am determined. Our ride through the Black Forest has been perfectly splendid. Soon after leaving Frieburg, the wildness of the scenery began. We ascended a hill called Heaven, and thence descended into a dark and narrow dell which goes by the name of the Valley of Hell. At the Gate are two very picturesque and frowning rock pillars. This is called the Stag's Leap, from an old tradition, that a stag, hard pressed, sprang across the chasm from one rock to the other. He must have taken a very long run to it. The scenery is much like that of the Catskills, only hardly so wild and new, but these magnificent forests of pine, fir, and hemlock, are unequaled by any woods that I have ever seen. In walking through them the foot sinks into the soil as into a cushioned carpet, and everywhere is that delightful woody smell that I love so much.

When about half way to Schaffhausen I saw what looked like clouds, and yet did not move like clouds; they were the sky-piercing snow-clad summits of the Alps, but so overwhelming was their height that I could scarcely believe my eyes. What must they be near at hand! We crossed the frontier by passing over a little brook; and I threw my hat in the air to think that I was in a free land, and no more subject to police or custom-house. Day after to-morrow we shall probably shoulder our knapsacks to walk. It strikes me as a strange coincidence; and perhaps also as an omen, that on the same day I begin my independent travel, I also take my first steps upon the road of life as a man. Perhaps the toilsome walk will be only emblematic of a life of toil and suffering. Be it so! I have a strong faith in what Carlyle says in "Sartor Resartus," about the worship of Sorrow. But I hope at least that walking will do us both good. You must forgive everything in these fragmentary letters; were my body settled, my ideas would be more so.

ZURICH, *August* 20, 1857.

We arrived in this place last night after a week's tramping, and found our letters from home. I mailed my last letter to you at Schaffhausen. We put our carpet-bags into the Post restante, directed to ourselves at Zurich, and having all cares of luggage off our minds, we left our knapsacks at the hotel, and tramped off to see the celebrated Falls of the Rhine, which have the reputation of being the finest water-fall in Europe. This claim has been contested, however. I have never seen Niagara, you know, and consequently was the better able to appreciate this very beautiful cascade, for it scarcely deserves the name of a great water-fall. Its characteristics are rather fairy-like beauty, than grand sublimity. It excites delight rather than awe. For myself I was charmed with it, so far did it surpass any fall which I had ever seen. With such violence does the water dash down upon the rocks, that it is separated into millions of diamond spray drops, from which arises a column of white mist which is visible in the night-time at a long distance. A castle has been built by an artist on the rock, beside the fall, and permission is given to travellers to go out on a platform at the foot of the castle, which is directly under the fall. This is the finest spot to see the shoot, which passes directly over one's head, and seems continually about to rush in and overwhelm the spectator. Occasionally a larger burst than common invades the platform, and gives every one on it a right good soaking. We put on some India-rubber coats, and presented ourselves in the very teeth of the cataract. Breath, sight, and hearing were quickly taken away, but it was a grand sensation to feel the cataract all around me, and to imagine myself one with the roaring and rushing flood. The rainbow on the spray is lovely, and with a gentle wave-like motion it rises and falls with the undulations of the mist, now mounting to the very summit of the spray crest, now resting below on the seething bosom of the basin. Nothing can be more beautiful than the snow-white foam garment in which the Rhine Undine has arrayed her favorite cascade. It makes me think of a snow-drift blown at once onwards and yet in rolling columns.

We returned to the hotel, girded up our loins, fastened on our knapsacks, with our good canes in hand, and tramped on the road to Constance, intending to walk seventeen miles to Steckborn, as we had already walked four miles to and from the Rhine fall, and at Steckborn to take the evening boat for Constance, since thirty-three miles was rather too long a walk for the first day. Of our first exercise in walking what shall I say? How we walked seven miles, and stopped to dine at a small inn, where we were astonished at the cheapness of our fare. How beautifully looked the clear green Rhine, how pleasantly the wind blew down from the hills and through the valley, cooling us when heated, and removing the fatigue we deserved for not starting off earlier; and how, when about a mile from the town of Steckborn, after we had just arisen from a pleasant rest by a brook, we saw the steamboat for Constance, which we had been told would not come till an hour later, rushing along past us, and how for a little while we tried youthful spunk against steam in a race, but finally were obliged to give in dead beat, and reconcile our minds to spending the night at Steckborn. Here we had a grand bath, and with limbs all fresh and reinvigorated made our entry into Steckborn, and were soon devouring a tremendous supper of bread and milk and honey, at the Lion. And here let me tell you what care we are obliged to take of our feet. Every night, before going to bed, they are carefully rubbed with tallow and brandy, mixed in the palm of the hand, to strengthen and keep them soft. In the morning the stockings (thick, woolen ones), are soaped on the inside, then all sores or blisters, especially on the shoulders where the knapsack straps come, have to be treated with arnica and brandy, and all lameness removed with good rubbings and bathings. Our hours of rising and lying down are very primitive; instead of going to bed at four and getting up at eight, as I sometimes did at home, I now go to bed at eight and rise at four, that is to say, when pedestrianizing. These early hours are beginning to lose their horrors for me, and I think that upon the whole my constitution will survive the shock. To return to Steckborn, I passed the last night of my minority in a furious battle with numerous fleas past and present, the former having already left their itching mementoes upon me, and the latter being desirous to imitate their example. Although dreadfully tired, I could not sleep. It struck me as being perhaps a kind of initiation into manhood. As the aspirants to the honor of knighthood in the good days of chivalry were bound to wake the night before and protect their armor, so I, who have been for many years an anxious aspirant for manly honors, was obliged to lie awake and protect my armor. Finally I devised a plan for treeing the insects, a plan which I flattered myself was ingenious, original, and poetical. It was this. The moonlight was streaming in at the window, and lay on the bed in a broad band of silver light, cutting off the pillow and a little more from the rest of the bed. Upon the pillow I curled myself up and watched intently to see if any unlucky insect would dare to set foot on the sacred stream; had any done so he would have "died a flea's death"; but no one made his appearance, and behind this Diana's shield, I was safe. Sleep at length overcame the sentinel, but it was undisturbed, and I awoke in the morning slightly cramped, but jubilantly victorious, and twenty-one years old. This levity may seem out of place in one who has a right to style himself a *man*, but I feel so jolly at receiving letters that my spirits find an outlet in every direction.

We left early for Constance, and at the entrance saw the meadow in which John Huss and Jerome of Prague were burned. The hole is still shown in which the fatal stake was set. This is one of the spots of holy ground, where the Protestant breathes a blessing on the noble martyrs whose ashes have whitened the soil, and whose blood has soaked the sod. In this decayed old city we also saw the large Guild Hall, where the grand council was held which condemned Huss to death, and in the minster is shown the stone upon which he stood when his sentence was pronounced. They say that this stone always remains dry when the stones around are wet. The city, in fact, is redolent of Huss; they show the house where he was captured, and the castle where he was confined. In fact, the martyrdom of John Huss is the stock in trade of Constance, now that most travellers are Protestants, and all pilgrims passing through must see the places associated with the history of the "Bohemian Goose," from whose wing Luther plucked the quill with which he wrote his thesis.

The Lake of Constance, or Bodensee, as it is called, is one of the largest, but not the most picturesque, of the Swiss lakes. On it we took boat and sailed for Rorschach, which is an extensive corn market, on the southern shore, and at the end of the road leading to St. Gall. The scenery on the lake was quite flat and tame at first, but as we approached the southeastern side, the rugged and lofty mountains of Appenzell made their appearance, and towering above them all, the snow-covered Sentis, of which more anon. We were too tired and sleepy to enjoy anything very much, and dropped into a quiet nap, which lasted until we found ourselves near Rorschach, when we rubbed our eyes and prepared to go ashore. As we approached the pretty and flourishing city of St. Gall, we met the younger portion of the population out for an evening walk. We saluted them all, high and low, with the regular German address "Guten Abend."

The inn in which we slept was of an humble exterior, but very good; the room was hung round with cards filled with extremely practical and straightforward Scripture texts, showing that our hosts were reformed to the backbone. Rising very early the next morning, we proceeded towards the canton of Appenzell, celebrated as being the land of the great original "Ranz des Vaches," and also for its wild and picturesque scenery. It has also the advantage of being rather out of the ordinary course of travel, and is not overrun in every direction by the English.

It is divided into two sections, Outer and Inner Rhoden, which are most singularly opposed to each other in religious matters, for two parts of one canton. Outer Rhoden contains 42,746 Protestants to 875 Catholics, while Inner Rhoden has 11,230 Catholics to 42 Protestants. The difference is soon perceived on passing from one to the other. Outer Rhoden has all the signs of life and prosperity. It is principally engaged in farming and manufactures. Inner Rhoden, on the contrary, a people of shepherds and graziers, is characterized by that happy moral and physical soil, compounded of dirt, vice, and laziness, in which Catholicism seems so readily to take root.

The capital, Appenzell, is branded by the guide books as a dirty and decayed place; so we satisfied ourselves with regarding it from the top of the highest hill, and then went on to a small place two or three miles further on the mountainside, called Weissbad. The nucleus of the place is a large hotel, called Molken Kûr, or milk cure. Many Swiss and Germans come here to restore their health by drinking goats' milk, and breathing the mountain air, and many come for no particular reason at all. This was Saturday. We engaged a guide to take us over the great Mt. Sentis on Monday morning, and resigned ourselves to passing Sunday in a place where not a soul spoke English but ourselves, and in a canton where, as I have said, there were only forty-two Protestants. We of course made forty-four. The houses and barns of Weissbad are very prettily scattered over the gentle slopes which lead up to the frowning rocky range beyond, and several foaming brooks flow through the little valleys.

From the tops of the surrounding hills we heard in the

evening the "Ranz des Vaches." It is not, as I had supposed, any regular air or set of airs, but is, as Sam Weller remarks, according to the taste and fancy of the singer. The airs are very rude and simple, and derive pretty much all their charm from the echoes of the hills, and the peculiarly romantic nature of the accompanying scenery. On the Meglis Alp I heard a singer, or yodler as they call them, whose voice and song were remarkably sweet. This, I am inclined to believe, is an exception to the general rule.

On Sunday it rained, and I was dreadfully homesick, — a complaint which I had thought completely cured. My want of occupation threw me back upon memories of the past, and there of course the home-light was most conspicuous.

This Zurich is a very pretty place, although there is no wild scenery about it. The Lake of Zurich empties itself here by the river Limmat, whose water is so clear that one can see the bottom all the way across. We are delightfully situated at the Stork Hotel, on the Limmat. Just in front is the great minster, in which the dauntless and gallant Zwingle preached the real Reformation. His name is peculiarly honored here, and the house is shown in which he passed the last six years of his life.

I send you a sweet little sprig of "Vergiss mein nicht," from the foot of old Sentis, not because I am afraid that you will forget me, but the sweet little flowers blooming close by the snow were just like those we have at home.

I shall always be your own boy.

RIGHI KULM, *August* 25, 1857.

MY DEAR AUNT, — The "rabies scribendi" has attacked me in full force here, 5,550 German feet above the sea, and as I cannot in decency attack mother or John again, having dispatched a rather lengthy letter from Zurich, you see you are the victim. It has seemed to me that it would perhaps be a pleasure to you to recall to your mind some of the delightful scenes through which you passed six years ago, and which are undoubtedly sweeter in the recollection than in the actual enjoyment. For my part I can easily imagine that when I shall once more be seated by the family fireside, I can enjoy these scenes in memory without that eternal longing for the home-roof which now mingles with all I see or do. Then, too, the point of view from which I regard matters and things must be so different from that in which they appeared to you, that they will have a certain aspect of novelty. We left Zurich last Friday afternoon, and began our tramp over the Albis range towards Zug; the ascent of the Albis is not at all difficult, especially for youths who had just overcome the difficulties of the Sentis Pass in the canton of Appenzell, which is one of the hardest and wildest in Switzerland. Over our shoulders we saw as we ascended, "the margin of fair Zurich's waters" peeping out in separate spots, which looked like a long line of isolated little lakes, and when we reached the top, the lake of Zug looked up with its figure 8 of a bed; this, however, we could not trace till later.

There was one object of interest by the roadside near Cappel, which had the effect of exciting my enthusiasm powerfully; it was the monumental stone of Ulric Zwingle. He always was a hero of mine. His noble boldness, and true enthusiasm for the great cause in which he was engaged, ever stood, to my mind, in strong contrast with the comparative timidity and scholastic quiet of Luther. Then, as a reformer, he was so much more thorough and decided than Luther; in him was no clinging to old forms, no adherence to Mother Church, no undue reverence for *old* corruptions simply because they were *old*. The results of the labors of these two reformers, are not equal at the present day; while the weak Lutheranism of modern Germany is yielding on all sides to the attacks made upon it, to Roman Catholicism on the one side, and to skepticism and indifference on the other, the Protestantism of the reformed cantons is still nourished in life and strength; and not uselessly, for it brings with it prosperity and self-respect, — witness the activity and power of Berne and Zurich, the first cantons in Switzerland. Then to the end of all things — *Death* — how different; one scarcely knows how Luther died, but we all have heard of Zwingle's martyr death — how on the battlefield of Cappel, when the "sword of the Lord and of Gideon" had fallen from his nerveless hand, an enemy found him lying, and ran him through with his lance, how he gasped out, "You can kill the body but not the soul," and died. I was much pleased with the simplicity of the memorial which was raised just upon the place where he fell. It is a huge, shapeless mass of stone, into the middle of which is let a plate with the inscription. At Zug we crossed the Lake of Immensee, and continued our tramp towards Luzerne. Near Küssnacht we came suddenly upon Tell's Chapel, amid the wooded height from which he winged the fatal arrow, and followed it with the bitter taunt, "Thou knowest the shorter, look not for another?' There are several things about the story of Tell which are so confused and contradictory, that I scarcely know what to believe. There is the best reason to suppose that he was not entirely a myth, for, besides the old and numerous country traditions, we have an account of the dedication of Tell's Platte, on the spot where he sprang ashore from the boat of Gessler, at which, thirty-one years after the death of Tell, one hundred and thirteen persons were present who knew him personally, and assisted in the ceremonies. I dislike, extremely, the ordinary portrait that is drawn of him, viz.: that of a spouting patriot, into whose mouth are put all sorts of flat sentiments about Liberty and Fatherland. Now it is certain that Tell was not one of the conspirators at Rutli, from which place he would never have absented himself had he been such a character as he is described to be. How much more satisfactory is the man whom Schiller shows us; a character said to have been originally suggested by Goethe; the swift mountaineer with an intense love for his family and his home, and an intense enjoyment of the free blue sky, but happily untainted by those modern ideas of abstract liberty in which it is the fashion to clothe every hero of the past. His nature is made up of sweet domestic traits, that noble simplicity which is the foundation of all that touches and interests, even when finally he draws the fatal bow-string, with such words as these: —

> "Till now the father never went from home,
> But joy, sweet joy awaited his return —
> He always brought back something for the children,
> Some Alpine flower, rare bird, or precious fossil,
> Such as the wanderer finds by stream or mountain.
> Alas! how different his employment now!
> He sits by the wild way with thoughts of death,
> 'T is his foe's life for which he lies in wait,
> And yet, dear children, he but thinks of you,
> Even now 't is to preserve your lives, 't is to
> Save your sweet innocence from wrong and danger
> He now sends forth his bolt at the destroyer."

So pure and beautiful are the traits of his nature that we revolt from his shooting Gessler from behind a bank, assassin-like, even to protect his children from the evil to come. Still his whole life, as drawn by Schiller, makes to the mind's eye a charming home picture, fit to be cherished in the heart.

Leaving the chapel and the ruined castle of Gessler behind us, we soon came in sight of the beautiful Lake of the Four Cantons, had a delightful stroll along its pleasant banks, till, from a little eminence, we saw Lucerne. What a lovely place it is; everything in the background so wild and rugged, Pilatus frowning above all, and in the foreground all so peaceful and picturesque — the old city walls with its towers, the crystal stream of the Reuss, and the fair lake sleeping so quietly in the sunlight. I was perfectly charmed with Luzerne, and had time suffered would have stayed there several days and attempted the ascent of Mount Pilatus, which would have been right spicy and interesting from the danger which attends it. How were you pleased with the Lion of Luzerne, erected as a memorial of the Swiss Guards who were massacred at the Tuilleries in 1792? For myself, I could only regard it as a work of art; as such it has a power and simplicity which are remarkable, and serve as an additional proof of the vast genius of Thorwaldsen, who could thus desert the beaten track, and hew from the very bosom of the rock an image which is wonderful, both from its colossal proportions and life-like attitude and expression. But I cannot blend with this any glow of admiration or enthusiasm for the men whose fidelity it was erected to commemorate; their motives were mercenary and mean; had they beaten off the mob, probably they expected that their pay would have been doubled, — as it was, their blood was bought for gold, and at the service of the master who could pour it out where and when he would. How much more honorable the trophies of Swiss bravery to be seen in the Arsenal there, and which were won by deeds of antique bravery, upon fields whose names are now like a trumpet call — Sempach, Morgarten, Morat. The signet-ring of Charles le Temeraire, taken from his finger as he lay stretched on the field of Morat; the ducal robe of Austria worn at Sempach, when Arnold von Winkelried offered up his heroic life and "Death made way for Liberty;" the heavy iron collars in which the Austrian noble intended to confine the free necks of the Swiss — these are trophies well worth fighting for, and proudly pointing to when won. . . .

These glorious Alps, how they satisfy my longings after wild free nature!

In Belgium, Holland, and France, I wandered among palaces which dazzled and picture galleries which bewildered my mind, ignorant of art, and through scenery where the hand of man had robbed Nature of her glorious forest crown, and had placed upon her brow, instead, the tinsel ornaments of parks and vineyards. I stood in churches and cathedrals where religious architects had done their best, but I could not comprehend, in a full degree, the language spoken by slender pillars and pointed arches, purpled pinnacles and painted windows; but here nature's vast book is wide open, and a child like myself, who has always loved her, can easily read the pages upon which the gigantic characters are snow capped mountains and rushing streams and deep blue lakes. I wish for no other cathedral than the great forest dome, and for no fairer pictures than the sun paints at noon in the waveless lake, and at evening in the rosy clouds. Of course, as time passes

I hope that I may come to have a more complete and intelligent appreciation of art, but for some time yet I desire to be Nature's alone. The glaciers I am looking forward to with great anticipations of delight, and am afraid I shall be half crazy when I get into the Bernese Oberland, and the region of Mont Blanc.

GRINDELWALD, *September* 1, 1857.

MY DEAR J., — During the past week I have had my fill of mountain climbing: we have been over the Pass of the St. Gothard, crossed the mountain range which separates this canton of Tessin from Italy, crossed back over the Gries Glacier to Switzerland, over the Grimsel to Meiringen, and to-day have climbed the great Scheideck to this place. To-morrow we cross the Wengern Alp, which has the reputation of being one of the hardest mountains in Switzerland to ascend. All the natural laziness in me trembles at the idea of the scramble which we shall probably enjoy.

I wrote a letter to Aunt E. from the Righi, but as I finished it in the evening I had no chance to describe the magnificent sunrise which we had the next morning. At a very early hour the whole population of the Culm were aroused by a stunning racket in the entries, which reminded me more of college than anything else, and in about three quarters of an hour, some hundred or more shivering persons were assembled on the summit, many of them scantily clad, and some wearing around them for shawls, the bed blankets which they had carried off in spite of the prohibitory notice stuck up in all the rooms. I, arrayed in my heavy overcoat, could afford to laugh compassionately at my miserable fellow beings. Long before the sun rose, faint streaks of light came streaming up, heralds of the glory to come. As the light grew bright, the few clouds in the heavens were illuminated and the distant glaciers of the Bernese Oberland were overspread with a most beautiful rosy light. Beneath our feet all was cloud and mist, through which not a glimpse of the habitable world was to be obtained, while around and above the glorious day had already begun; it was as if we were separated from the world by a thick veil and the sun was rising for us alone. As the sun rose to plain sight, over the mountain top, a shepherd blew on his horn the welcome to the sun, and there was very speedily a scattering to the breakfast-table. We were soon through breakfast and off with our new *compagnons de voyage* E. N. W. and B. L.

I have been installed paymaster, linguist, and commander-in-chief of the party, a post which my previous experience in money and hotel slang, together with total disregard of the wrath of landlords and waiters, render me peculiarly fitted for. We came down from the Righi to Gersau, and crossed the Lake of the four-wood cantons to Fluelen, and thence to Altorf, where we took dinner, with the scenes of Tell's great exploit on every side of us. We stopped at the Hotel de William Tell; just above us was a fountain where the father stood, with his cross bow; just below, another fountain occupying the spot where was once the linden tree, under which the boy stood, with the apple on his head. On the hills just beside the town, stands the little village in which Tell was born. I hope by this time you will see what a tell-tale place it must have been. We reached Amstäg that night, and left right early in the morning, since H. C., who is an early bird, started us all up by 4 A. M.

With the frowning mass of the Bristenstock above us, we left the extremely picturesque village of Amstäg, and came ever, as we ascended higher and higher, into wilder and wilder regions, the scraggy mountains above, and the roaring, foaming Reuss below. Beauty was abundantly added by the many fountains which were seen on every side, pouring from a great height, in one pure, foamy stream, or else, in an almost endless succession of little laughing and jumping cataracts.

The road was an admirable one; built of heavy masonry, in places where the streams would be liable to wash it, spanning the gulf of the Reuss with numerous bridges, which in any other place would be thought most picturesque, and protected in some spots by long stone galleries, from the destructive effects of the winter avalanches. One of the bridges crosses a cleft of very great depth, though not more than eighteen or twenty feet wide ; tradition says, that once a monk leaped across this chasm, with a damsel in his arms, and thus preserved her from some ruffians, who were pursuing her ; he must have been a more clean-limbed and springy fellow than most of the monks I have seen, to have got across the cleft alone, to say nothing of the slightly cumbersome additional weight which he carried. The story is rather a stretch both for the monk's legs and my imagination.

Further on, the scenery grows still wilder, and the name of the Teufel is frequently used in describing prominent objects. The Teufel's Stone is an immense block of rough rock, which Mr. Teufel was said to have been seen by a peasant, carrying on his shoulder, and upon the peasant's making a pious ejaculation, Old Clooty dropped his burden and put for the Styx instead of the Reuss. Might it not have been that the peasant was deceived by some spectral illusion, like that of the Brocken Spectre, caused by the reflection of his own shadow, upon a bank of mist, greatly magnified? But the most tremendously wild and weird thing in the valley, is the Teufel's-brücke, or Devil's Bridge. There are two, both spanning the immense and roaring gorge with a single leap. The older one was built by the Devil's permission, as described in the Golden Legend, and the other, finer, but less picturesque, built in 1830, by the canton ; taken together, they produce a very strange effect, especially as the lower one is all overgrown with moss and grass. The rock rises immediately behind the bridge, in a most strikingly savage manner, and on every side are seen precipices so steep, cliffs so jagged, streams so headlong, vegetation so scanty and desolate, with the mocking wind sweeping in great blasts through the narrow defile, that to me, it surpassed all that I ever had imagined of savage grandeur.

But even the horrors of this tremendous valley must have been increased, when, in 1799, the French and Austrians fought here a most bloody battle, partly upon the very bridge itself, and when they, being obliged to retreat, blew up the bridge, or rather a part of it, and plunged friend and foe together into the abyss below. The fall of the Reuss is here very considerable, and peculiarly noticeable for its tremendous fury; a beautiful rainbow stood on it when we saw it. But I must bid you good-by, for the present, as we are going out to look at the glacier which seems almost to come in at my window.

Sept. 2. — We did not go to the Wengern Alp to-day, after all. At 3½ A. M. we were waked according to order, but it was raining hard, and all ideas of climbing the arduous mountain are out of the question? We accordingly may on to Interlaken to-day, and from that place I will finish this letter.

Sept. 2, Afternoon, Interlaken. — What a glorious batch of letters I have just received here, and how perfectly happy I am! . . . . The news of which you spoke was news indeed to me, as for some time past we have been roaming in a wild and desolate country, which has no papers of its own, let alone "Galignani," the "London Times," or the "New York Herald;" and I am as totally ignorant of anything which has been going on in the civilized world, as if I had been living in the planet Jupiter. Last Saturday, my dear Jack, was your birthday, and I remembered you most affectionately, as I rose to see the sunlight of the 29th of August, in the Val Formazza and to hear the roar of the magnificent fall of the Tosa, which leaps over the precipices in an immediate fall of four hundred feet, and falls a thousand feet in a short distance. To my taste, it was superior to the fall of Schaffhausen, although I think many would prefer the vast volume and graceful beauty of the latter, to the wild grandeur and terrific height of the Tosa Fall. I shouted to the echoes here, "Many happy returns to you, dear Jack!" and the echoes most faithfully repeated, "You, dear Jack!" I would have written you a letter here on that day, but the first two thirds were occupied in a most tremendous climb, over the steep and precipitous mountain range which separates Sardinia from Switzerland, a walk across the Gries Glacier, and a very long descending walk to the town Obergestelen, which we reached by about 2 P. M. This trip is described in the guide books as a very tough day's work, but we did it in less than seven hours, and could, if necessary, have done fifteen miles more before bedtime. As it was, we were all fatigued enough to eat a good dinner and go to bed very early, and so I was obliged to give up my cherished plan of wishing you many happy returns upon the day itself.

I am now a man, my dear brother, as well as yourself. We stand together now, shoulder to shoulder, in the battle-field of life; and from this reconnoitering post of August, 1857, would it not be well to look down and survey the field of the future, and think of some general plan for the campaign of the world. For myself, it does not seem as if I should ever be married, and should prefer to live with you and mother in the old style, until something inexorable shall occur to drive our barks into separate seas. . . . . I now feel anxious for difficulties to appear, in order that I may meet and vanquish them; it is hard to persuade a man who has surmounted the steepness of the Alps, that there is any difficulty which can detain, or danger which can daunt him.

I was prepared to be disappointed in the glaciers. I think it requires a sort of preliminary education before one gets to really appreciate what wondrous things they are, and how vast the phenomena must have been from which they had their origin. I have now come to consider them as they should be considered, the miracles of the mountains.

The first specimen of which we had a view was not a very favorable one; it was the Gries Glacier, lying between two lofty peaks of the Nufenen range, and though of considerable extent, yet it wants that wonderful depth and beautiful azure tinge which make so many of the other glaciers so attractive. We crossed it completely, and that after the time (10½ A. M.) when it is safe to cross. By 11 or 12 M. the snow melts the ice, which is formed during the night, over the clefts and cracks. The whole surface was quite soft and slushy, and it seemed as if we were in danger of falling in every minute, but when we came to a crack the deep, thick ice walls assured us that we were walking on a floor nearly as solid as the earth itself. In fact our less practiced companions often thought that we were walking on the ground, from the heaps of stones and heavy dirt through which not a particle of ice could be seen, but every now and then a deep cleft or the sound of gurgling water underneath assured them of their mistake.

The great Glacier of the Rhone we passed, and, although we did not go very near it, we had a fine opportunity to observe its remarkable shape, and the purity and clearness of its ice. Its shape is much that of a heavy glove, and from this similarity Longfellow has drawn one of his most admirable comparisons. He calls it a gauntlet which the old Winter King has thrown down to Summer, and which every year the Sun, the champion of Summer, strives in vain to raise upon the point of his glittering sunbeam-spear. From a deep cavern within the glacier rises the noble river Rhone, which is certainly more interesting in its youth, among the mountains of Switzerland, than in its turbid and turbulent old age on the plains of southern France.

But the most beautiful glacier that I have yet seen has been the Glacier of Rosenlaui, which we visited last Tuesday. It is small in size, and lies imbedded between the craggy peaks of the Wellhorn and the Engelhorn. On account of the freedom of the surrounding rocks from marl and the softer beds, the virgin whiteness of the ice is not deformed by masses of dirt and impurity, as is the case with many glaciers, but its hills and bergs shine in crystal purity, and in all the clefts the separated sides of the ice are of the most beautiful blue imaginable, as lovely as a summer sky. By a series of rather slippery and dangerous steps we climbed up on to the glacier, and examined these blue ice-holes, which go stretching downward like the clear ocean on a calm day, but with a purer and more heavenly azure than even the ocean depths. The rough rocks, and the whole gap above the glacier, have in their outline a resemblance to a human face, and they say that it is the Mountain Spirit who thus watches over the beautiful treasure which lies so cold and icy on his rocky breast, and have given it the name of the "Watcher of the Glacier."

To L. R. P.

INTERLAKEN, *September* 2, 1857.

. . . . Can't you meet me at or near Geneva, on or before the 1st of October, and travel with me for about a month and a half in Italy? C. expects to go home at the end of our Swiss tour, which will probably terminate in about three and a half weeks, bringing us to Geneva by the 25th of September. Near that time you can come on; and right glad shall I be to shake you by the hand on the shore of this Old World. We could have a classical tour of the most delightful description; you shall do the classical allusions, and I will do the art, since I have studied it somewhat in the last two months. . . . I should be delighted if you would join us at Martigny, which we shall reach in about ten days. These Alps are perfectly glorious, and I know you would enjoy them immensely. They freshen a man up, and give him new soul-life to go back to society and art, and to enjoy them with a new zest. . . . What do you want to spend a month in Heidelberg for? Certainly not to learn German; that is the greatest farce in the world, to say nothing of the fact that pretty poor German is spoken in Baden. The students of German there don't seem to learn enough in a year to ask decently for their daily bread and butter. You could gain far more profit by drinking at the grand old Italian fount of learning and inspiration, and treading those fields which have been so often trodden by the lords of the world. Greece, too, is not impossible to men once in Italy. . . . By the way, there was no name at the bottom of your letter, but, from sundry touches, I suspected the writer; safer to sign the name, however, unless you have got married and taken your wife's name, as is the custom in some nation I have read about.

INTERLAKEN, *September* 3, 1857.

I have been for a week past in regions wild and desolate, else I should have written to you sooner. I am enjoying intensely my trip through Switzerland, which is now about one half completed; and I am looking forward with great eagerness to the solemn glories of Chamounix and Mont Blanc. Oh, how beautiful is this Bernese Oberland! The grand chain, of which the Jungfrau, the Monk, and the Finster Aarhorn are such prominent members, stand like a band of sentinels around these lovely valleys, their summits clad in eternal snow, and on their shoulders resting the mighty glaciers, those monstrous rivers "upon which Winter has breathed, and they are still." But perhaps you would like to know how I got here. I bade farewell to Aunt E. on Mont Righi, and, with J., I have gone along the road in the valley of the Reuss as far as the Devil's Bridge, and now I will travel the rest of the way with you. We passed through the broad, green, silent meadow of Andermatt, which is very remarkable as being perfectly flat and even, while all around it tower lofty mountains of the most rugged and precipitous nature. Just above the village church is a very remarkable wood, which is shaped like a wedge, with the point up the hill, and is of great service in protecting the village from avalanches, which split in two upon the sharp point of the wood, and rush off to the two sides, thus passing beyond the village and doing no injury. Of course no one is allowed to cut down any trees in this wood, but they are guarded with the most jealous care. From Andermatt our course lay up the magnificent road of the St. Gothard, which is obliged to be carried across and back, in numerous zigzags, in order to avoid a too abrupt ascent, which would be very hard on the draught-horses used in the Italian trade. So very winding is the road that sometimes one sees it just forty or fifty feet above his head, but distant half a mile if he follow all its windings. Fortunately for foot-travellers there are a great many cross-cuts which are easily accomplished by those willing to put forth a little exertion, and strike the road most wonderfully, so that we could easily beat a horse and wagon, although going at a good speed. As evening approached we had ascended high above the sea, and the cool air began to blow down from the glaciers, so that we were glad to button up our coats and walk at a rapid rate, keeping a sharp look-out for the Hospice on the summit, where we were to pass the night. At length a building loomed up on the very top ridge of the pass, and a large St. Bernard dog came bounding down towards us, reminding me most forcibly of the dog stories I used to read and how these noble animals rescued travellers from the snow, imparting to them their own warmth. In the interior of the Hospice I saw some rude pictures representing scenes of this description, and in all the dog of St. Bernard figured as a conspicuous character. One of these dogs, who had died after greatly distinguishing himself, I observed standing in a niche on one of the staircases, nicely stuffed and preserved. The accommodations were plain but good. Travellers are charged nothing for what they have, but are expected to put into the box a sum equivalent to what they would pay for the same at an inn; poor persons pay nothing.

The next morning we started to descend this pass in the grand old range of the St. Gothard which gives rise within a small distance to four large and celebrated rivers, which flow to all four points of the compass; the Reuss to the North, the Rhine to the East, the Ticino to the South, and the Rhone to the West. It has justly been called the cradle of mighty streams. The road descends by a most remarkable series of zigzags, similar to those upon the northern side; but previously to its construction a most bloody battle was fought here in 1799, between the French Republicans and the Russians under Suwarrow, upon paths which had hitherto been known only to hunters and shepherds. Upon one of the rocks is inscribed in large letters, "SUWARROW VICTOR," in honor of his driving the French from the pass, which he did by a very curious piece of clap-trap; his soldiers being thrown into disorder by the fire of the French rifle-men, and beginning to flee, he ordered a grave to be dug, and then lay down in it, saying that he would die on the spot where "his children" had disgraced themselves; the effect of this demonstration was wonderful, and upon Suwarrow's getting out and putting himself at their head, they charged most impetuously, and drove the French from their position.

The valley into which we descended is known by the name of the Val Tremola, on account of the great danger of the avalanches, which fall here continually in winter, and one has reason to tremble indeed when he reads of the numerous sad life-destroying accidents which occur here from year to year, a single one of which destroyed three hundred persons. However, as it was summer we went through it with great equanimity, and arrived at Airolo, when I had to put in practice my very small amount of Italian, but to my great surprise found myself able to make myself understood, which I could scarcely have expected, not having studied Italian at all since I left home. And best of all, I met an old man on the road who had a brother at St. Louis, and with him I had quite an animated conversation on the subject of America, to which my companions listened with respectful admiration. Indeed I am beginning to believe that I have quite a taste for language-learning, and do reap the full benefit of my old fondness for philology by my ability now to talk with the people of a country in their own language, which is the only way to really study their character.

We passed though the Val Bedretto, which is as miserable a country as you could easily imagine. Bedretto, the valley capital, is a petty and filthy little place, not so large as one of our Irish suburbs, and equally respectable. But our great adventure was getting lost among the mountains while trying to cross them to the Val Formazza. Through some carelessness, we lost the path, and wandered about the whole afternoon, seeking it again, but without success until we were half tired to death, and the shades of evening were beginning to draw on; and we were making up our minds to pass the night in the nearest wood, striving to keep up a fire that we might not get frozen, when we made one last desperate attempt, and by crossing right over the top of a high mountain, succeeded in reaching a path which led into the neighboring valley. It was quite dark when we arrived at the village where we had proposed to spend the night. When arrived there, imagine our vexation at finding it almost totally uninhabited, the shepherds who usually dwell in it being all otherwise engaged with their flocks upon the mountain pasture. They spend the winter months at this wretched place, which is called Kehrbachi and is the highest winter residence any where around. After hunting around for a long time, I found an Italian who could not understand me, nor I him; but he scared up a German, whom I persuaded to admit us into an empty house and let us have a place to sleep. I never in my life saw anything eatable like the black bread which he got for us; it was as hard as the nether millstone and evidently had been lying in the house ever since the inhabitants left it on the departure of winter. Eating it was out of the question, so nibbling became the order of the day. This German also managed to concoct for us a large bowl of rice soup, which he placed smoking upon the table, with four large ladles, one for each man, and all were requested to go in miscellaneously. More execrable stuff I have scarcely tasted since we embraced Homœopathy. An attic with most suspicious beds, where sleep was difficult, not to say impossible, and another meal of rice soup, were poor preparations for the hard day's work which we were about to undertake,— the passage over the Gries Glacier, and so through the Eginen Thal to Obergestelen, where we were obliged to pass the Sabbath. The ascent of the mountain to the glacier was extremely arduous, but a good part of the descent was a lovely woodland walk, and, at one turn, we suddenly came in full sight of the grand mountains of the Bernese Oberland, at which we all gave one shout of joy. At Obergestelen we passed the Sabbath very pleasantly; we had a little service together, which E. W. conducted, and in the evening we walked out by the banks of the Rhone, and sang hymns, which were probably rather new to the inhabitants of this extreme Catholic place.

INTERLAKEN, *September* 5.

. . . . Well, I suppose you would like to know something more about my wanderings. I think you left me at Obergestelen, where we passed the Sabbath, and had a service in our rooms. In the afternoon we visited the churchyard, and in a small chapel, which was perfectly open, we saw a large pile of human bones, heads and arms, being the sad remains of eighty-four persons who perished here at one time in an avalanche. This seems still more melancholy when one reflects that one half of all the population of the place must have been swept away by this tremendous calamity, and not a family left unscathed. The next morning we rose blithe as larks, after our day of rest, and set off very early, without any breakfast, to try the pass over the Grimsel, on an empty stomach, and without a guide, which is our regular plan. A guide is a great nuisance, to say nothing of the expense and disgrace. By a careful observation of the pass, and continually using the compass, in connection with our excellent Swiss map, we succeeded in reaching the top, where we came out in the midst of the wildest scenery, and were now at length really within the Bernese Oberland. The beautiful Rhone glacier was on our right hand, and in front, what was far more beautiful to hungry men, the Hospice. I improved the occasion to inform the crowd that the next time they took a fancy to walk on an empty stomach it should n't be on mine, which was never fitted either by nature or education for such a performance. Close by the Hospice is a lake which bears the agreeable title of the Dead Sea, so called, some say, because no fish will live in it, but really for a much more interesting and tragical reason. In 1799 the Grimsel was held by the Austrians, and the position was considered both by themselves and their enemies, the French, as inexpugnable; and General Gudin, the French commander, might have wasted his forces in vain attempts, notwithstanding he had positive orders from Massena to capture the pass. In this dilemma a native offered, for a high reward, to lead some troops round by the peaks above and behind the Austrians, and thus surround them on every side. A body of troops was intrusted to him; but when they were within an hour of the summit, the horrors of the way so terrified them, that they believed the guide to intend treachery, and threatened him with instant death if he did not lead them back to their camp. It required all the exertions of the officers to make them advance. At length by paths known only to chamois hunters, they reached the Austrian rear, and, while General Gudin made an impetuous attack in front, they assailed the Austrians from behind. These latter looked upon them as dropped from the clouds, and, becoming panic-stricken, fled in all directions. Those who remained, in sullen despair dashed their muskets and sabres to pieces on the rocks, and perished almost to a man. The far larger number of the slain perished by falling from the precipices than by the hands of the French. The dead were buried in the lake, and thence its name. Even to the present day swords and muskets are found, and occasionally a skeleton in a mouldering white uniform. How horrible the position of the Austrians must have been, so surrounded by deadly foes, and that in the midst of such a savage country!

A stout walk of two hours brought us to the falls of the Aar at Handeck; this is a most magnificent fall, ranked never lower than the third in Switzerland, and considered by some as the finest of all. It comes thundering down from its source in the glacier of the Aar, and here falls in an undivided body of water for two hundred feet; such is the fury with which it dashes upon the rocks below that a vast volume of spray rises up, and by hiding the actual depths of the abyss, suggests to the imagination the idea that it is almost bottomless. The water of the Aar is not very pure, as it flows over marly rocks; but as if in an intentional contrast, the river Aerlinbach pours its lovely crystal stream over the same precipice with equal fury, and mingles its snowy spray with the dingy foam-cloud of the Aar, heightening the effect by this strange contrast, as well as greatly increasing the volume of water. We spent an hour very pleasantly here, mostly on a platform built right over the abyss, amidst the spray-mist, and should have enjoyed a longer stay, but an English party were coming down the hill, so we considered discretion the better part of valor, and hastily took our flight, not wishing to hear the beautiful fall characterized by the young ladies as "very nice," nor by the young men as "beastly." We had agreed to spend the night at Meiringen, thus making a day's march of about twenty-eight miles, and when we supposed ourselves within a few miles of the place, L. and I walked ahead to reach it before the others, and secure good rooms at the "Bear" Inn. Now the valley of Meiringen is celebrated for its beauty, and when, therefore, we emerged from the narrow gorge into a lovely vale, we supposed of course that this was our destination, and inquired of some men where the den of "The Bear" was situated? they pointed us up the road, having misunderstood the question, and off we tramped, looking in every direction for the inn, and, in fact, for the town, which seemed to us very small for such a large place as Meiringen. However, as Meiringen is spoken of in "Hyperion" as "embowered in cherry-trees," we supposed that the trees hid the town from sight, and so tramped on. But as we went further and further, the country grew wilder, and we thought it prudent to turn back; when we got to the point from which we started, we found there our friends C. and W., quietly drinking beer under a piazza, and laughing at our mistake, for to our horror we were told that this was not Meyringen, but Imhof, a place three miles before it. We acknowledged the error, and started fiercely off, determined to find Meiringen or perish in the attempt. The first damper to our enthusiasm was the lofty dam, six hundred and fifty feet high, through a narrow cleft in which the Aar bursts its way. It would seem as if the whole valley had at one time been a lake, until it had been able to empty itself through this wall of rock. The road over the dam runs in a very winding zigzag, which was peculiarly annoying to us who were in such a hurry to get over it, and this annoyance was by no means decreased by the troops of little boys and girls who assailed us, some with Alpine songs and flowers, and some with out-and-out begging. It was rather amusing, though, to see a little imp perched on a rock on the watch for travellers; as soon as we appeared, he uttered a shrill cry, and, like

Roderick Dhu's soldiers, a band of little imps started out from unseen crevices, and, arranging themselves along the road-side, began to perform a doleful imitation of the "Ranz des Vaches;" but in vain, for to such appeals I am always obdurate and stony-hearted. At the summit of the dam, Meiringen appeared to our eyes, and L. and I thought that all our mistakes and troubles were over, but we were most grievously deceived. On entering the town, a beautiful village embowered in trees, in the heart of a really Alpine valley, we inquired for the "Bear," and were most maliciously and abominably directed wrong again, and, arriving at the inn door to which we were sent, we asked if that was the "Bear." "Oh, yes," was the reply — so we engaged two double-bedded rooms, and supper for four, and then sat quietly down to await the arrival of W. and C., who were only about a half a mile behind us. Long and anxiously we waited, but they came not, while the desire for supper grew ever stronger; at length it occurred to me that this might perhaps not be the "Bear" after all, and this indeed I found to be the case. Of course I was quite furious, but it did n't do any good, and after supper, I was obliged to drag my weary body, guided by a boy, to the real "Bear," where I found our friends hard at work feeding, and after arranging a plan for meeting and going away the next morning, I dragged myself back, having thus added to my long day's tramp an additional walk of at least a mile and a half. Indeed, it was a day full of mistakes, and yet all unavoidable ones, since they all arose from the stupidity and mendacity of these Bernese peasants. My first impressions of this great Protestant canton were not very favorable.

We had agreed the next morning to rendezvous on a certain bridge at $5\frac{1}{2}$ A. M. I was the first one there, and while waiting, had an ample opportunity to observe and admire the beauties of the Hasli-Thal, of which Meiringen is the capital. A great addition to the attractiveness of the scenery is the number of magnificent water-falls, which plunge down from the mountains on both sides; on the south the celebrated Reichenbach Falls, and on the north the three fountains which form the Alpbach. This latter stream is governed by a most mischievous mud-nymph, who often rushes forth from the Hasliberg, and covers whole fields with a thick flood of clay and water, which completely spoils the soil for agriculture; in 1762 a mud-stream of this description destroyed half the village.

The others soon came up, and we began the ascent of the pass which leads over the Greater Scheideck to Grindelwald. It was on this march that we had an opportunity to visit the beautiful Glacier of Rosenlaui, of which I think I spoke in my last.

Of our march to Grindelwald I will say nothing, except that it was dreadfully fatiguing, and more especially so for us who had worked so hard the day before. The view from the Scheideck of the great Eiger 12,800 feet high, and of other snow-covered giants, was astonishingly fine. There is one thing on this route of which I must speak, and which I had nearly forgotten. On the descent to Grindelwald is a most magnificent echo, which repeats several times from the towering crags of the Wetterhorn, and the sound of the Alpine horn blown here produces a most remarkable effect; in itself it is an instrument of the most disagreeable tone, — the sack-horn is nothing to it for ear-splitting; but just as in the kaleidoscope, a few rough pieces of glass become beautiful by reflections and combinations, so these harsh tones, when reflected and multiplied from the rocks around, lose their original character, and are changed to chords of wonderful sweetness. At first the notes are heard sharp, clear, and distinct from the mountain, a faithful repetition, only more chorded, but before this ceases, the sound is heard again farther off, but now with a soft solemnity which breathes of some vast wood-chapel with chanting Druid priests and an organ from some "fountain-lighted" cave; and even this chant is interrupted by a wild, far-off strain, from the recesses where the mountain-spirits still remain, and sing sad laments for the happy hillsides from which the foot of man has driven them. Nor is this all. From the highest peaks music still mounts aloft, and now in that sweet murmur from mid-sky, one hears no Druid priests, no organ tones, no Dryad wailings, but an angel band with Æolian harps, who receive the aspiring sound, and take it to its heavenly home. This is by no means an exaggeration; I have often heard an Alpine horn in connection with an echo, but never anything like this wonderful music and variety of sound which one enjoys at the foot of the frowning Wetterhorn.

We took our supper at Grindelwald, and then walked out to examine the glaciers. The upper glacier is much purer and freer from mud than the lower one, but the latter was much more accessible, coming in, as it seemed, at our bed-room window, although in reality it was three quarters of a mile distant. In the side of the ice a long, circular hole had been cut, large enough to admit us standing, and extending quite a distance back into the glacier; here we sang "Home, Sweet Home," and the notes, especially the rich key-note of the bass, were finely lengthened out by the reverberations of the cave. By means of some ladders we then ascended into the ice, and walked for some distance on the glacier, until we came to an enormous crack large enough to take in a coach and six, when we thought it prudent to return, especially as it was growing dark. On our return we again entered the ice-cavern, which was now illuminated with torches, which an old man and two boys waved at intervals under the ice-dome. The effect of the bright light reflected from the glassy walls was very beautiful, and reminded me of the "most magnificent and mighty freak" of the "imperial mistress of the fur-clad Russ," which Cowper so elegantly describes: —

> "A watery light
> Gleamed through the clear transparency, that seem'd
> Another moon new risen, or meteor fallen,
> From Heaven to Earth — of lambent flame serene."

We were greatly delighted, and caused the illumination to be repeated several times with fresh lights.

The next day we marched to Interlaken, the sick and

wounded, viz., L. and C., by carriage, and the main body, W. and myself, on foot. I am rather disappointed in Interlaken ; my expectations had been raised to too high a pitch, and I was astonished not to find a little village consisting almost entirely of hotels, an earthly paradise. Still it is a very lovely place, and the view obtained of the Jungfrau through a series of gaps in the valleys, is superb, considering the distance, and affords a fine opportunity to persons who cannot climb passes, to see this most beautiful mountain from a comfortable situation. The lakes, too, are charming; that is to say, the Lake of Brientz is, and that of Thun also, judging from a glimpse that I have had of it.

BATHS OF LEUK, CANTON VALAIS, *September* 11, 1857.

MY DEAR COUSIN, ... You know yourself, no one better, the affectionate interest with which you all at Albany are regarded by all the family circle, and most especially by our little circle at New Haven. Even now I look in hope and fancy forward, through many months of time, and across many leagues of space, to some future Christmas week, which I shall spend by your fireside as in the happy days gone by, and join in everything with that same boyish pleasure which was my wont, and which I hope may never leave me, although I am now nominally a man. I feel with Wordsworth, —

> "My heart leaps up when I behold
> A rainbow in the sky ;
> So was it when I was a boy,
> So is it now I am a man,
> So shall it be when I am old,
> Or let me die."

It strikes me that there is among young men, a tendency to drop into an aged state when they begin to enter upon the duties of life, and the sweet and fragrant flowers of boyish enthusiasm and frankness are withered by the chilling breath of that strange, stern formality called Dignity. If it be possible, such shall never be the case with me, and if it ever is, from that moment the sight of sky and stars, and the enjoyment of life will not be what it was before. But stop; I am prosing when I should be praising and setting before your mental optics in exalted terms the beauties of these glorious Alps; don't blame me if in a heedless moment I should splurge somewhat, for when a mind accustomed to ordinary life, and ordinary terms, comes among scenes of inspiring sublimity and beauty, the natural tendency is to use a language which is more elevated, and expressions more extravagant. A dinner may be *good*, but a snow-capped mountain is *grand;* a book may be interesting, but an avalanche is awful; so I shall not entirely repress this natural tendency, for I have been encouraged in it by a remark of Rev. Dr. Skinner's which I recently heard: "If a young man is flowery in his youth, there is hope that he may get over it in manhood, and bear fruit; but if he is dry when young, what will he be when he is old?" And first you shall have a daguerreotype of the animal known as W. W., somewhat different from that taken during the second week of May, 1857, and also sketches of his three companions; he representing the genus Pedestrian, and they the different individuals known as C., L., and W. A strong flannel shirt much like that worn by the boating clubs, with a small collar of the same material, which decreases the undress and barbarous appearance, and renders a linen collar unnecessary, except on great occasions, a pair of extremely heavy pantaloons, a vest buttoning up to the throat like a minister's, and serving as an over-coat except in very severe weather, a stout coat with numerous pockets within and without, a broad-brimmed hat of a most peculiar drab color, but admirably adapted for keeping off the rain, and last but not least, an enormous pair of boots whose mammoth soles would shock all my lady acquaintance, complete my costume when *en grande tenue* for a long tramp. Add to these, the heavy knapsack on my back, weighing some fifteen pounds, and my trusty alpenstock in my hand, and I stand before you fully prepared to walk thirty miles and enjoy it grandly, and to eat a tremendous supper when evening comes on. Somewhat similarly appareled are the rest; C., six feet high, black beard, and tremendous stride; W., the shortest man in the party, yellow mustache and goatee, of the class before me in college, and just graduated from the Union Theological Seminary; L., a fine, handsome fellow, twenty-four years old, son of the Bishop of ——, and just beginning the medical practice; such is our party, a most harmonious and pleasant one, which has travelled now for two weeks together, with the greatest satisfaction. But these three humbugs are insisting that I stop writing and prepare to accompany them down the Valley of the Rhone, so good-by."

SIERRE, VALLEY OF THE RHONE, *September* 11, 1857.

.... I cannot tell you a tithe of all I have seen and enjoyed. So I will take up my wondrous tale (like the moon), from the point of my leaving Interlaken. If you have ever seen a picture of Interlaken, you must have noticed a long row of poplar trees introduced as prominent characters, and occupying the foreground; in fact my idea of the place was a strong sensation of windows peeping out from among " the tall popular-trees " (" Villikins and his Dinah "); but although I was at Interlaken nearly a week and actively engaged for a large part of the time in searching for said trees, it was never my fortune to find more than one, or two at the most; the windows I saw, as the town is principally made up of staring boarding-houses, but the trees were most decidedly not. Imagine then my triumph and satisfaction, when getting well out into the Lake of Thun, and going in the opposite direction, to see upon looking back, the poplar-trees there sure enough, and looking just like the picture; where they started from, or whether they are not actual, but merely an imaginary part of the landscape, it " passed my persimmon " to say.

A pleasant sail of an hour brought us in sight of Thun, where we landed and spent the rest of the day. A more enchantingly lovely place, it was never my fortune to behold; in fact no town I have ever seen has come into the most remote comparison with it in those qualities of calm repose, exquisite mingling of land and water, hill, mountain, and level champaign, and above all that gentle lustre of sunlight which streams over all, and in which inanimate nature seems to bask and be perfectly happy. Other spots are eminent in loveliness, but Thun excelleth them all. Heidelberg is charming, with its long, straight Bergstrasse, its glorious old castle — that wonder of the Middle Ages, — and its shining Neckar; Lucerne is wonderfully picturesque from its situation on the Lake of the Four Cantons, at the foot of Mount Pilatus, and from its ancient city wall embellished with frequent towers; but Thun with neither forest lake, grand feudal tower, nor city wall, possesses beauties of its own that are unsurpassed. Through the middle of the city flows the bright blue Aar, embracing in his arms, most lovingly, many an island, while the city on the hill-side looks down with a perpetual smile, as if to thank the river for the zone of heavenly blue which he had bound around her waist. To the east lies the broad Lake of Thun, surrounded by craggy and lofty mountains, while to the west and north no high mountains are seen, but a pleasant rolling land of hills, so that Thun seemed to me a lovely herald, placed upon the borders of that rugged mountain land, to silently proclaim, by its peaceful beauty, an entry into a land no longer bleak and desolate, but a sunlit fruitful land, where no avalanche ever comes to astonish or destroy. In a place of so much beauty I felt an interest in visiting that quiet dwelling-place, so appropriately called by the Germans "God's Field," or the "Court of Peace," and I found much in it to delay me there. I always like to walk in a Sleeping Place, for so means the word cemetery; and be very silent and reverent, for fear of disturbing those spirits who may be revisiting the scenes which they loved so well. It was so sad to think that the enchanting view from the church-yard wall was nothing to those that slumbered there; perhaps their eyes had opened on scenes of calm repose of which this was but a faint type. Very sad too, it was to see the English graves, so remote from their island-home, and to think that they had died here in a strange land; although perhaps there were kind hands to fold the arms across the breast and to plant the bright red roses thickly on the stranger's grave. And saddest of all is the tomb of a bridal party, thirteen in number, who were drowned in crossing the Aar and were buried here side by side. Their weather-worn tombstone tells that it was more than an hundred years ago, but still, thanks to those never-failing fountains of sympathy in the human heart, their sad fate is mournfully mentioned, and strangers kneel to trace on the crumbling stone the names of the unhappy party.

. . . . But now I must be off immediately on the top of a diligence, or to speak classically, *summâ diligentiâ*, to Berne, that fine old city of the bears, who from time immemorial, ever since one of them had the good luck to be killed on the side of the city by Duke Berchtold of Zähringen, have been, in a Protestant way, the patron saints of the city and canton. A very respectable family of bruin's race are still maintained at the public expense in a large trench outside the city, and crowds of enthusiastic citizens are at all times to be seen attending at the den of the favorites. I could not help reflecting that the bear is a caricature of the more slow and heavy, but very reliable, portions of the Swiss, just as the monkey is a slight exaggeration of the volatile character of the mob that every day surrounds his cage at the Jardin des Plantes at Paris. I have quite a fondness for seeing thus resemblances between a people and the animal to which they are most attracted. The English are like their own bull-dogs, the Germans, like their quiet and peaceful poodles; while I think that the American can be compared to no actual creature, but rather to that strange chimera known as being made up of " half man, half alligator, and half steam-boat." But to return to our bears and to Berne, which, by the way means a bear itself, and is what the French call an " Armoire Parlante," or name corresponding in significance with the coat of arms. The favorite animal looms out on every side. Here he stands in full armor on a fountain, supporting in one paw the old city banner, and in the other a sword. On another fountain he acts as squire of the body to some ancient Bernese hero; and when the clock over one of the city gates indicates the hour, a long procession of bears march out of the towers, and pass solemnly along before a seated figure in oriental dress, bowing as they pass, while a bear on his left hand strikes the number of the hour on a bell. The view of the Bernese Alps from the Palace Terrace here is perfectly superb. A long stretch of the grandest snow-capped mountains — the Virgin "veiled to all eternity," as the Germans call her, the Monk by her side, the sharp peak of the Finster Aarhorn, and near by, the Schreckhorn or Peak of Terror, whose precipitous sides have never been trodden by the foot of human being. This was the grand old chain under whose shadow we had been wandering for the two weeks previous, and whose craggy ridges and bold outlines looked to us like the face of a friend inviting us back again, and we all felt an answering sentiment of longing to be among them; so the next day we were on our way back to Thun, and the next day up the valley of the Kander to Kandersteg, where we took a rest of half a day in reposing our wearied limbs, bathing our sore feet, and exploring the region round about for water-falls, in which last point we were eminently successful. We discovered no less than five very beautiful ones, none of them less than eighty to a hundred feet in height, and one so high that its small body of water was resolved into a fine cloud of dust-spray, like the celebrated Staubbach in the valley of Lauterbrunnen. From Kandersteg we started very early in the morning to go through the Pass of the Gemmi to the Baths of Leuk before the sun had become too hot. Five o'clock saw us well off and toiling up an ascent which was rather steeper than anything we had yet attempted; although the morning was very cool, the perspiration poured down from every available inch, and we were not sorry when we stood upon the summit of the pass, more than eight thousand feet above the sea, and looked far down the rugged rocks to the distant valley, where lay the place of our destination. The descent here is extremely remarkable, as it is down the side of a precipice, which, when viewed from below, seems perfectly insurmountable, and it is difficult to believe it possible that a good broad path winds up its side. This path is a miracle of daring engineering; in frequent zigzags it proceeds along a narrow ledge, and thus accomplishes by gradual steps what could never be done by a straight road; in many places a plumb line dropped from the edge of the path would fall upon that immediately below, and in some cases one can look sheer down the rock and see nothing of the path, which pursues its way in a gallery directly under his feet: thus, for example, we heard a party of ladies talking and laughing very near under us, but we could see nobody at all by looking over, and it was not until we had turned a point in the road that we met the fair donkeyestrians toiling up the rock-side; a task which I would not be hired to undertake, as it is far steeper here than on the side to the north. In one place the precipice falls off in a perpendicular line for over sixteen hundred feet, and, as if to add to the horror of the cliff, its top projects some twenty feet, so that anything falling from the brink would take nearly ten seconds to reach the bottom, without taking into consideration the resistance of the atmosphere, which would probably about double the time. The idea made me sick and dizzy, and I was careful to withdraw myself quickly from the edge, to avoid the bad consequences of both an accidental fall and a morbid impulse; this latter I always feel very powerfully, and am obliged to guard against whenever I look over a very lofty precipice. This Pass of the Gemmi is not a splendid carriage road, like those of the St. Gothard, the Simplon, and the Splügen, but on account of its wonderful descent down the precipitous rock, is more grand and picturesque than them all, unless it be a part of the Splügen called the "Via mala," which I have not yet seen. We reached the Baths of Leuk in four and a half hours from Kandersteg, a remarkably rapid walk, as the guide-books allow seven and three-quarters hours for it, but we take a great deal of satisfaction in abbreviating the times in the guide-books: in fact we have discovered that we walk a German hour in about forty-five minutes. The Baths at Leuk are both hot and medicinal, and the time spent in the water is the longest I ever heard of, being about five hours in the morning and three in the afternoon; and in order to dispel the ennui which must necessarily arise, the bathers, mostly French, bathe together in large baths which hold from fifteen to thirty persons of all sexes, sizes, ages, and ranks, and many have floating before them on the water little tables on which are books, newspapers, flowers, and contrivances of all descriptions, to while away the weary hours which the invalids must spend in the water in order to make a cure effective. These baths are open to the public view at all times, and any one can amuse himself by looking at the bathers, provided he will take off his hat and shut the door after him. Some of the rules for the behavior of the bathers are very amusing; as all excitement is injurious to that placid frame of mind and body so requisite for recovery, it is stated that all manner of discussion on the subject of religion is absolutely forbidden; a very wise regulation, since probably nearly every creed in Europe is at times represented here. Near these odd baths is something still more strange; it is a village standing on the edge of the precipice which overhangs the baths, and the approach to which can only be made by a series of eight ladders fastened against the perpendicular rocks. Up and down these ladders the inhabitants pass at all hours of the day and night, but it is rather dangerous for persons to go up who are not accustomed to ladder-climbing, and extremely perilous to come down. We did not succeed in visiting these, although we kept a sharp lookout for them. What an odd idea, going down a straight face of rock to go to a party, and then going up again to go to bed! Still, I imagine that to them their airy home is very dear, and that they love their rocky nests as well as the birds do theirs.

MARTIGNY, *Sept.* 12. — This letter, you see, is destined to be finished at odds and ends of time, for I find it very difficult to command any number of solid hours. I can't say, my dear coz, that I dreamed of you last night after writing the above to you, since I slept scarcely at all, and was right glad this morning to take things easily, and be contented with a saunter of nine miles before dinner, and a ride of twenty miles in the omnibus after dinner, which brought us to this place; we did not ride because we were lazy, but because the road was flat and uninteresting. Our morning's walk lay through vineyards which were laden with magnificent bunches of white and purple grapes, which fairly made our mouths water; so, having reached a village which was pretty well embowered in vines, we repaired to a house and sent the woman for a quantity. She soon returned with a basketful, coyly peeping out from among leaves, and such immense bunches! There was a dead silence for some minutes in the party, interrupted only by an occasional murmur of satisfaction. You may form some idea of the size of the bunches when I tell you that I devoured one large one and two small ones, and then was obliged sadly to desist, for I could do no more; W. got through about two thirds of a very large bunch, and was obliged to raise the siege and lay down the remainder. We got here by 6 P. M., and I was much disappointed not to find letters from home as I had expected. Now, my dear coz, I suppose I have bored you with talking guide-book so much, and interfering so with the province of those who write "Tours in Europe;" and it would be far more pleasant to me to chat with you about old times, were it not that public opinion expects that a traveller should give some account of what he has seen.

CHALETS DU MOTTET, FOOT OF MT. BLANC,
September 16, 1857.

DEAR J., — Having written a letter to A., describing my course from Interlaken down into the Valley of the Rhone, and as I have a great dislike of rehashes, I will simply trace out our daily course until we arrived at Martigny. On September 1st, L. and W. having letters at Berne, took the earliest boat, while H. and I followed at the more dignified hour of noon. . . . .

We took the diligence to Berne; found our companions at the Stork. The inn was very crowded, and we had four beds put up in one room, and slept like boarding-school boys in a dormitory.

The next day was of course devoted to doing Berne. There is not a great deal in it worth seeing, except, of course, the bears, animate and inanimate; unearthly representations of the latter kind surmount innumerable fountains, gates, and doorways, and do their best to maintain the long supremacy which Bruin has exercised over the town.

The Bundespalast, or Palace of the Union, in which the National Assembly of Switzerland meets once in three times, its rivals being Luzerne and Zurich, is a very splendid new building, of a light stone, with a terrace in front, from which is commanded a most unequaled view of the distant Bernese Alps.

The next morning we returned to Thun. In the evening we resumed our knapsacks, which had now been neglected for four days, and walked about thirteen miles up the Kienthal to Mühlinen; passing on our way the Niesen, which is remarkable for being, from top to bottom, on the north side, of a regular pyramidal shape. We rose early in the morning to put in execution a plan of mine for crossing the Dündengrat, a very difficult and dangerous pass, and then through the Oeschinen Thal to Kandersteg, a path abounding in most magnificent scenery, and running just at the foot of the grand snow mountain called the Frau (not the Jungfrau). But most unfortunately there was no guide at Kienthal, and as we could not go without one, we were reduced to the disgusting expedient of retracing our steps to Mühlinen, and of there taking the public road. By this detour we walked some nine miles out of our way, and as the sun was high, we suffered greatly before arriving at Kandersteg. Here we spent the night, and the next morning passed the Gemmi, which was the highest and most striking pass which we had as yet seen. Sloping up quite gradually on the northern side, it falls off to the south in steep precipices down which the road winds in zigzags, some of which are directly over others, and are astonishing pieces of engineering.

We dined at the Baths of Leuk, of which I have no room to speak at present, and pushed on down into the valley of the Rhone to Sierre, on the Simplon road, where we dried up, having done a very good day's work, thirty-one miles, and more than half of it over a very steep and difficult pass. The next day we walked about ten miles on the great road to Sion, and having stopped on the way at St. Leonard, a place perfectly embowered in vineyards, and eaten grapes enough to make an army feel uncomfortable, we took the diligence at Sion, very glad to get so rapidly over a road so uninteresting.

We spent a very pleasant Sunday at Martigny, and met some nice English people, among them the minister, who officiated twice in a small room to a congregation of about twenty. We left early in the morning for the Great St. Bernard, and had a cool walk for several hours up into the mountains. At a place called St. Pierre we stopped to dinner. Soon after we left it we had quite a little adventure. L. and I were abstracting some half-ripe currants from a bush, and two char-a-bancs were coming up the road, when suddenly we heard a crash followed by the howls of the two drivers, and upon looking round saw one of the char-a-bancs upset and broken. I dropped my Alpstock and ran like a deer, thinking of course of Doctor Antonio and Lucy. I got there just in time to see a very pleasant English gentleman whom we had seen at Martigny emerge looking very much worried, and then hand out his daughter. Fortunately no bones were broken, and the char having been mended we repeated our condolings and offers of service and plodded along. As we mounted higher, all became bleaker and wilder, and finally we passed into a cloud of mist, and arrived at the Hospice cold and tired. Nothing could exceed the politeness and true courtesy with which we were received by the Brethren. Our wet clothes were dried, and we took the opportunity, before it was yet dark, to go and see the Morgue, where the bodies of those lost in the snow are kept until recognized and claimed. The coldness of the air preserves them to a great degree from putrefaction, but still a more shocking sight I never saw. Some were still standing erect, some leaning over, and some had slid down so as to be all in a heap. As I looked through the grating, and my eyes became accustomed to the darkness, I could even distinguish the expressions of the features. In one corner was leaning a mother who had perished with a child in her arms, and even at this time they are not separated. I thought, perhaps, she had once been beautiful, but the features are now fearfully distorted, and, from the dark recesses, those dead eyes stand out in a horrible stare, that haunted me all night. The ladies, and the gentlemen with them, took their supper in the salle-a-manger, where they were entertained by the Superior. But all of us single gentlemen took supper with the monks in the refectory, an arrangement which pleased me very much, as I wished to see as much as possible of these noble-hearted and devoted men.

We sat along a great table with a Brother opposite to each guest, and what with the monks' good dinner, their sober and pleasant conversation, and their wine which they helped out liberally, the evening meal passed most pleasantly, after which we were right glad to get to bed and escape the cold. This, at nearly 8,400 feet above the sea, the highest dwelling in Europe, is always very severe. At 5 A. M., all were aroused by the ringing of the bell, and at 6 we attended service in the chapel. It was a remarkable scene; the chapel was splendidly decorated, in this respect contrasting with the extreme plainness of the Hospice. The cold was so intense as quickly to condense every particle of breath; upon the floor were kneeling in extreme devotion some twenty peasants; all wore an aspect of great dreariness, when suddenly the monks began the service, and the fine organ rolled out a resounding chant, which seemed a song of victory and triumph over the horrors of the weather and the trials of the frost. To me there was something most sublime in the chanting of men who were so near to heaven — in their piety as well as their habitation, and whose self-sacrificing devotion is so unparalleled, in these selfish days; the rigor of the climate soon kills them, and even those who outlive the term of their vow, seven years, seek a warmer climate with broken constitutions.

A thick mist hung around the Hospice, and it seemed as if there was about to be a heavy rain. Notwithstanding, we set out, with our guide, to descend to warmer and clearer regions — with our guide, I said, and such a guide! We got him at Martigny to take us through what is called the tour of Mont Blanc; that is, from Martigny to St. Bernard, thence to Courmayer, and from there over several passes to Chamouni. Having a thorough contempt for guides, we went up to St. Bernard without him, trusting he would make his appearance before morning, which indeed he did. As we discovered that he had a penchant for going slow, we adopted the rather novel expedient of keeping half a mile ahead of him and then blundering upon the right path with a precision which was to be acquired only by extensive Alpine scrambling. At St. Remy we entered Sardinia, and underwent a polite overhauling at the custom-house, our guide taking the opportunity to engage a guide there to guide him over the Col de Serena, the pass which interposed between us and Courmayer. I feared it would be something like the blind leading the blind; but as there was a well-defined path and we led the way, the two unhappy guides succeeded in getting along safely. At a shepherd's chalet near the summit of the Col, which we entered, the shepherd brought us a pailfull of clear cream, and another of milk to dilute it with. We discovered a large cake of corn bread. I took so much of this, with clear cream, as to make me decidedly sick. We finally reached the high-road and had a walk upon it which seemed interminable, but all our toils and troubles were fully recompensed by our first view of Mont Blanc.

Without doubt this is the grandest feature in all Switzerland, and should always be reserved for the last, since thus the emotions can be, as it were, educated, and rise in a gradual scale of intensity, until finally the climax is reached on seeing this most sublime work of God's hands.

They say that just the point from which we saw it, when approaching from Courmayer, is just the place par excellence; from behind a peak itself lofty, suddenly a solemn, snow-clad mass came looming forth, very distinct, but still overtopping all the nearer peaks, and seeming to hang right over us; the first emotion was that of half-terrified awe; the rest of most unmingled joy and admiration.

The sun was approaching its setting, and clad the whole mountain with a flood of light; around his waist was the glorious cincture of golden and silver clouds, while his head stood proudly forth in the undiminished splendor of stainless snow. It must have been from this point, and at a moment like this, that the poet describes him, —

> "Mont Blanc is the monarch of mountains,
> They crowned him long ago
> On a throne of rocks, in a robe of cloud,
> With a diadem of snow."

Would that I had time and space to tell you of our three days' march around his base, and among his frozen rivers; but we are now at Chamouni, and the next two days must be devoted to the wonders which lie so thickly around this strange and beautiful valley. I have written this letter in sundry times and in divers places; wherever we rested I have taken a book upon my lap and scribbled as much as possible.

CHAMOUNI, *September* 20, 1857.

DEAREST MOTHER, — After a week of hard work, sweetened by wondrous pleasure, the day of rest has arrived, been well and pleasantly spent, and now on this lovely Sabbath evening I sit by the window in the twilight, just bright enough to see to write, and talk with you before the candles are brought, just as we used to talk on Sunday evenings at home.

The setting sun has tinged all the mountains with a rosy light, and at the foot of Mont Blanc the glaciers shine with a subdued and softened color far more beautiful than the sun-glare, forming a scene which one might suppose reserved for dreams and the imaginings of fancy. But, gloriously fair as it is, there is something about that little word "home" which throws a shade of sadness over it all; and it is peculiarly at such moments that I wish J. and yourself at my side to make complete my enjoyment. If I think of you and all the dear ones at home on one day more than another, it is on Sunday — that day so sacred to me from both habit and education. But whom do you think I saw this morning upon entering church? Close by the door loomed up the majestic figure of Hon. I. A. R., and upon proceeding a little further I saw the long wavy locks of our old friend A. P. I touched him on the shoulder, and we had a good handshake and a few whispered words between the pauses of the service. After church was over we had quite a jubilant time together; and he informed us that they had been following us everywhere, till at Thun they had seen our names for the last time.

He saw L. P. at Heidelberg, and cheered him somewhat, as P. had just arrived. He had already written me two letters, which showed very evidently that he had begun to appreciate the sadness and desolation of being a stranger in a foreign land. For myself I am happy to be able to say that while still retaining my love of home, I have lost the cat-in-a-strange-garret feeling to a sufficient degree to be able to enjoy myself immensely in these wild mountains whose endless variety satisfies without satiating. I tried in my letter to J. to say something about our tour around the base of Mont Blanc, but there was so much previous, that my letter filled up before I was aware of it; and, as it was one of our most difficult as well as most pleasant trips, I must e'en trouble you with a melange of snow-capped mountains, lofty passes, Alpstocks, glaciers, and hungry young men. We left Courmayer bright and early, our guide having aroused himself from the semi-dormant state in which he had been the day before, and which he attributed to the hard bed at the Hospice of St. Bernard; but now his foot was on his native heather, and he knew the way, every foot of it. Our confidence in his acquaintance with the country was greatly restored by seeing him shake hands with numerous friends on the road, to say nothing of the compliments which he bestowed very lavishly upon many a sun-burned representative of the fair sex. Our course lay for a long distance through a narrow valley known as the Allée Blanche, which runs along in a deep gorge at the very foot of Mont Blanc. The peak of the great mountain itself was here not so prominent as some others which were nearer and more imminent. The Col du Geânt is a most magnificent snow mountain, the path over which is extremely difficult; still it was passed by some ladies some years ago, but only with great labor and the assistance of eight or ten guides. Our course proceeded by the side of an immense moraine, brought down by the Glacier de Miage. The piled-up rocks, stones, and dirt gave the appearance of a small mountain, and suggested the vast length of time, and violence of natural causes, which must have been in operation in order to transport such enormous masses. In some places the glacier was so concealed by the debris that it was almost impossible to believe that it was anything but a mud plain. The morning was exceedingly pleasant, and we walked six hours steadily without noticing how time passed, and climbed a very high pass called the Col de la Seigne, upon whose top we found new-fallen snow, and had quite a jolly snow-ball fight. When arrived at the summit, we saw in the valley far below the Chalet du Mottet, where we expected to dine. Upon sight of this, our guide set up an unearthly howling and yelling, in which we could recognize no articulate words; but still it seemed to have a meaning, since when we reached the chalet we found the dinner ready and waiting for us. Our guide's yodling evidently had the effect of a spell, and conjured up some good cutlets, etc., which suddenly disappeared, with two bottles of wine, and left us almost as hungry as before. After the usual halt for a couple of hours after dinner, we left the hospitable chalet, and stretched our legs towards pass number two, which was decidedly the hardest one we had been over. On reaching the top of a lofty hill we supposed it to be the summit of the Col des Fours, but to our dismay the guide informed us that it was still three-quarters of an hour to the top. And such a three quarters of an hour! Right up perpendicularly almost, over beds of slate. We were soon above all traces of vegetable life, even of the coniferous trees and hardy mountain grasses, rock on every side being all that could be seen, and even this rendered more dreary by dark patches of dirty snow, which lay on the rifted crags. Upon a tall peak sat, in solitary state, the vulture of the Alps, while near him were perched two crows, probably his satellites, the only living things that could be seen anywhere. The steep ascent was almost too much for all of us. When arrived at the top we were at a height of more than nine thousand feet above the sea, by far the highest point which we had yet attained. The other slope, where we were to go down, was covered with snow, and we had a little coasting party, using the seat of our pantaloons instead of sleds. Here we descended, and crossed a great plain called the Plaine des Dames, because, a long time ago, a lady of high rank perished there, with her whole train, in one of those dreadful snow whirlwinds called "tour mentes," for which this spot has rather an unpleasant reputation. A cairn of stones has been piled upon the fatal spot, to which the guides request travellers to add a stone in remembrance of the tragedy.

After a walk of eleven hours, the hardest day's work which we had ever done, we saw, beaming before us, a small light, which the guide informed us was in the hamlet where we were to pass the night, and before long the whole party were peacefully snoring, with the exception of myself, who was not so much knocked up as the rest, so I sat up to write a letter to J., which will account for the stupidity with which it is redolent. Sleep was a wonderful restorative, and the entire used-up crowd made their appearance in the morning quite fresh and blooming, and walked over the Col de Voza to the Valley of Chamouni, where we are now snugly ensconced in the Hotel de l'Universe, with a magnificent view of Mont Blanc and the Glacier des Bossons, from our bedroom window.

R. has come in, and, as the fellows wish to sing, I must give up all attempts at writing on this to-night, so goodnight. To morrow we intend to go over the Tête Noire, back to Martigny. I expect to revel in the letters which I hope to find there. R. accompanies us on foot; his father and mother go on mules.

To L. R. P.

GENEVA, *September* 26, 1857.

MY DEAR BOY, — I have just now got time and breath enough to answer your very reasonable, but not at all friendly or enthusiastic letter, which I received at Martigny, just before commencing the tour of Mont Blanc, and, although I could not deny any of your well-stated premises, was much disgusted with the inevitable conclusion. I shall probably be obliged to visit Italy alone this autumn, as C. expects to leave me in a day or two, and I am not the man to go with anybody, Tom, Dick, or Harry, to that wonderfully rich old land. To one who had as yet done no travelling, the plan you lay out would afford very great attractions, but you must know that I "did" both Frankfort and the Rhine very thoroughly last summer, and am not inclined at present to go over the same ground again especially as I was much disappointed in the "exulting and abounding river," with the exception of the range of the Siebengebirge and the Rheingau, between Coblentz and Bingen. And, by the way, as I am an old hand along there, let me give you a word or two of advice which may save you some money and trouble. If you expect to stay in Frankfort a couple of days, as I suppose you will, and desire to go to a hotel where you will *have* to talk German, the Landsberger Hof is very comfortable, and during the two days that C. and I were there we did not see a single Anglo-Saxon. Then take a third-class ticket on the Rhine boats; you can get one at Mannheim or Mayence, which will last you all the way to Cologne, and allow you to get off and climb castles and steal grapes as often as you wish. There is no earthly difference between the second and third class except the price, and the bow of the boat is always more pleasant than the stern for looking out. You will of course stop at Bingen, "dear Bingen on the Rhine;" if either you or S. have a *penchant* for good Rhine wine, you can get, at the "White Horse," such Assmannshäusen as you never tasted before, and probably never will again; it grows on the hill behind the hotel, and can be relied upon as genuine.

I hope that while at Bingen you will make an excursion to the splendid castle of Rheinstein, and to the Niederwald; it will do your heart good to get into a fine, wild, untrimmed forest once more; besides, the view from the temple on the brow of the hill is called by Bulwer "one of the noblest landscapes upon earth," and at the Tauberhohle⁻ is a vista cut through the trees, which shows the opposite side of the river as in a frame, and with the effect of a diorama. We did not stop at St. Goar, but wish we had, as it lies in the very midst of the most beautiful scenery, and from it you can so easily get up to that immense old ruin of Rheinfels. Then from Coblentz you can visit the castle of Stolzenfels, and the splendid fortress of Ehrenbreitstein; the view from the top of the latter is very fine, and will repay your trouble, even if you don't care for the fortifications. Of course you will visit personally the ruins of Rolandseck and Drachenfels, which are so fairly teeming with old historic and traditional interest; and by the way, it would be a good idea for you to buy, at Jügel's, in Frankfort, a little book called "Lays and Legends of the Rhine;" most of the poetry is rather raspy, but the legends are well given, and you need something of the sort to really enjoy the Rhine. Schiller's ballad on the story of Rolandseck, the sweetest legend on all the Rhine, always pleased me extremely, and you will find a respectable translation of it in the book mentioned above. Near Remagen, which is a short distance above Rolandseck, stands the beautiful little modern church of St. Apollinaris; if you get any opportunity to visit it you will be repaid by the fine frescoes on the walls. I should like above all things to stand with you in the Frankfort Museum, before those fine pictures of Lessing's, and once more to gaze upon the lovely Ariadne of Dannecker; and to whisper to you in the Rossmarkt, before that grand statue of Goethe, the secret admiration which I have always entertained for him; to drink Rhine wine with you at Bingen, and to climb together the steep sides of Drachenfels, and then to stand by your side under the heaven-aspiring arches of Cologne Minster, that angelic architecture. But so it moughten't be; my lessening hours warn me to make the most of my time and see North Italy this fall; God willing, we will meet in Berlin in the month of November, and touch hands once more.

GENEVA, *September* 28, 1857.

. . . . Our most glorious stay at Chamouni was filled with scenes so grandly beautiful, that I have scarcely language to express what I felt and still feel in connection with that spot.

> "Where with God's own majesty
> Are touched the features of the earth." — BRYANT.

I think that I have already told you of how we made the tour of Mont Blanc, and of our day's walk across the Col de la Seigne and the Col des Fours. This last was really too much for any one, however practiced and hardened to mountain climbing, and pretty well used up all the party except myself. I believe that we all arrived at Chamouni with a sort of indistinct hope that here we were to be allowed to rest a little, and digest all that we had seen; but never was any one more grievously disappointed. It was no more like rest than going into a fierce battle after a long march can be called rest. Oh no, our time was too short and precious, and there was too much at Chamouni to be seen, to allow of any wasting of time in rest. The valley of Chamouni, considered by itself, is not entitled to any great reputation for beauty. It is devoid of those innumerable chalets, those leaping fountains, and that rich green of fertility, which give the Lauterbrünnen such a loveliness; and at the same time its position is not sufficiently elevated to destroy all verdure, or to give it that magnificently wild and scathed aspect, which is so very impressive in many high passes. But it has what is far better than all, and that is the glorious snow-mass of Mont Blanc, and the gorgeous immensity of the Dome du Gouté, to say nothing of the sky-piercing Aiguilles, which arise on every side. But really to know the wonders which belong to Chamouni, one must have the enterprise to visit and explore mountains, rocks, and glaciers, and nowhere more than here is seen the truth of that old proverb, that there is nothing good or beautiful to be obtained without hard work. So by half-past five, H. roused up the other two capable men of the party, and off we started to the Flégère. We had reëngaged our guide to conduct us around Chamouni, and then take us back to Martigny, and the night before he had been profuse in his promises to be on hand to go with us to Flégère ; but at starting time he was nowhere to be seen, and, as we did not want the trouble of waking him up and dressing him, we were e'en glad to get off without him, a guide being unnecessary, and rather a piece of borous ceremony than anything else. We had a very easy climb of what most people consider pretty tough, and the only trouble which I had was about half way up, and that of a rather amusing character than otherwise ; as we passed through a flock of goats, the two gentlemen of the flock, the Gulielmi Capricornici, or to speak vulgarly, Billy-goats, were having a fight together. One of them being quite small and the other a very patriarchal William, I thought it my duty to approach and back up the little one as much as possible, considering the fearful odds against which he was contending; but to my intense disgust, they both made common cause, and came up the rocks after me in a manner which I did not like, nor Dr. L. either, if one can judge by the alacrity with which he devolved the post of honor and danger upon me. I held my Alpstock in rest to defend my own rear as well as that of the party, and caused the animals to desist. At the Pavilion, upon what is called the Summit, the view is very fine, and almost everybody satisfies themselves with that ; but the innkeeper told us that from the Needles, about an hour and a half from the house, was a point of view to which scarcely anybody ever went, which was very much superior to that from the Pavilion. So H. and I left L. hard at work sketching, and stretched our legs toward the real summit. The landlord's "hour and a half" proved a fifty minutes' climb for us, all extremely steep, and, finally, right up the almost perpendicular, rocky ridge, until we found a place large enough to sit down on without being sure to tumble off, and we received a most royal reward for our pains. From this height one can really see and appreciate the immense height of Mont Blanc's summit, a thing which cannot be done from below, since the Dome du Gouté stands forth as the principal object, and on account of its comparative nearness, looks far higher and larger than that distant, rounded peak. But here the grand old mountain is seen rising above the rest, like Saul, by a head a king confessed, although his lofty attendant princes form a bright and brilliant throng. What a solemn court! For thousands of years they have stood thus, silent before that great white throne, and silently have they listened to the commands of their matchless mountain monarch, who speaks only in his avalanches, and who can see nowhere upon his portion of the earth's curve, anything equal or even second to himself. Indeed, this mass of whiteness was so awful in its immensity, that all individuality seemed gone, and the snow-mountain seemed the only object before me. But soon the spell began to be broken, and I saw that besides Mont Blanc there was a vast and varied field of vision; the noble glaciers which stream down from his feet — the Glacier des Bossons distinguished for beauty, and the Mer de Glace for vastness, the double moraines of the latter appearing with great distinctness to a great distance back into the heart of the mountains; those strange, sharp peaks, so well named the Aiguilles Rouges et Vertes, which in their angular acuteness bear such a striking contrast to the smooth, well-rounded tops of the adjoining snow mountains; and what was most unexpected of all, we could look right over the Col de Balme into the Valley of the Rhone, and distinguish there the precipitous pass of the Gemmi; and beyond this our dear old friends the Bernese Alps, with their well-known outlines, the Blümlis Alp, the Schreckhorn, and the Jungfrau; we recognized them all, called them all by name to bid a last farewell, and thought of the two jolly weeks which we had spent at their feet, or wandering among their romantic and picturesque passes. So delighted were we with this unexpected pleasure, that we could scarcely tear ourselves away, and when we did descend from our dangerous position, it was only to encounter another serious delay, as we found a splendid field of whortleberries, which it was impossible to neglect; so I found a good place, where the berries were thick, and sank down among them, with my face ever turned toward the mountain, that I might enjoy both Mont Blanc and whortleberries at the same time, and experience together the two sensations of lofty sublimity and lazy satisfaction. We had a grand run down the steep side of the mountain for nearly an hour, steady jumping and dodging all the time. We took dinner, and, as we intended to go in the afternoon to the Glacier des Bossons, we sent for our guide, who soon appeared, and that in a most jubilant and happy state. As he marched along in front of us, I observed that his colossus-like legs frequently crossed each other, and that his general course described a line much resembling that of a Virginia rail-fence. I questioned him, and discovered that he had been drinking two bottles of champagne with one of the hotel-keepers, and was consequently "a few points in the wind;" but as he solemnly remarked, "he was as good a guide when he was drunk as when he was sober, and a great deal happier into the bargain;" so I let him go on, thinking that a fall into a crevasse would sober him, if it did n't finish him entirely. But I soon saw how mistaken I was in the idea that any amount of water would sober him. As we came to one of the

"Five wild torrents fiercely glad,"

he was afraid to trust himself to the narrow bridge, but waded through instead, and declared that he must have some Cognac to keep out the cold. This was the climax, and now the angles of the zigzag became constantly more and more acute, so that I was almost afraid to let him go on the glaciers; but there was a kind of method in his madness, and I observed that in spite of little knocks and falls, he took very good care of his carcass; so when we reached the glacier, he sat comfortably down on a dry spot in the middle of it, while we cruised all over, partly to examine the glacier, and partly to accustom ourselves more to ice-walking, as we were to spend a good part of the coming day upon the Mer de Glace. This Glacier des Bossons is a perfect gem of an ice-field, both on account of its perfect purity, in which no other can remotely compare with it, and also for the fantastic but picturesque manner in which the ice is thrown up into waves, pinnacles, and bergs, principally at its lower extremity, which runs far down into the valley, and is consequently a very prominent and attractive object on first seeing the vale from the surrounding ridges. It is across the upper end of this glacier that the road lies by which a few fools every year ascend Mont Blanc. The two young Americans, of whom you have heard, went up on this road and spent the night at the Grands Mulets, a miserable chalet, and then employed the second day in going to the top and returning to Grands Mulets, the third in coming back to Chamouni ; so that it is altogether only one hard day and two easy ones for a hardened climber, and not by any means the dreadful thing that it is bragged up to be. Our guide informed us that it was no more dangerous than the road to the Jardin, to which we went the next day, as I shall tell you. The view is seldom fine on account of the clouds below, and even when it is, the rarefied air and the extreme cold do not allow one to remain on the summit more than ten or twenty minutes, so that the only earthly reason for going up is to be able to say that you have been. Even those who have been up themselves frankly acknowledge that it is not worth the expense, and is altogether a foolish business. The greatest danger, I am inclined to believe, arises to the health from breathing the rarefied air ; the firing of cannon, and all that, is merely a dodge to throw a halo of eclat around an expedition rather uninteresting. The morning we went to the Jardin, we were all up and dressed 4 A. M., breakfasted at $4\frac{1}{2}$, and shortly before 5 were well started on our way across the valley, and up the hills to Montanvert, our guide carrying on his back a huge knapsack stuffed with those three great standby's of human existence, bread, meat, and wine. A more glorious morning I never saw. All was still, save now and then the distant thunder of an avalanche; not a cloud was in the sky, and on the mountain's brow hung in silvery lustre the morning star, which did not seem to sink and disappear as we approached the mountain's base, but to be fixed there as a perpetual jewel, and I fully understood the opening lines of Coleridge's sublime hymn. Indeed, there is not a word in it all which I did not feel in my heart most fully " before sunrise in the vale of Chamouni." The pleasure, too, was of an unmixed nature; so perfect was the stillness, that there was nothing to interrupt the still small voice of praise, which is continually going up to the Creator everywhere in the fresh dawn; and here, where all is so magnificent, this voice is very loud, and audible by human hearts, if they listen aright. How grand were the mountains in their gray twilight robes; how beautifully calm the glaciers, untouched by the sun glare, while the angry air raged on as ever, regardless of the holy quiet. But we must hasten on, for Mont Blanc has caught the sunbeams on his crown of snow, and we must finish our climb to Montanvert before the "glorious orb" gets over into the valley and on to our backs, which will make us sweat like daylaborers; so up we go at our best speed in the usual order, I first, H. close after me, and Dr. L., whose legs are unfortunately not so long as ours, some little distance in the rear; the guide's position was very variable, sometimes half a mile ahead, and then a mile behind, but in every case equally useless. We reached the inn on the Montanvert in an hour and forty minutes, at least I did; it usually takes two hours and a half. This Montanvert is a steep mountain shoulder, about as high as the Flégère, thrust forward into the Mer de Glace, and consequently commanding a fine view of the pinnacles and icebergs of the lower end, which is called the Glacier des Bois, but a very confined and limited one of the vast plains and ocean-like waves of the real Mer de Glace, its immense crevasses, and its mountainous moraines.

People go up to Montanvert as a day's job, and when they have stared about them a little, and have gone down and walked on the ice a few steps, in a place provided with artificial stairs chopped out, perfectly nice and comfortable, they go back and say that they have seen it and walked over it. This reminds me of Chicken Little's declaration that the sky was falling, and that part of it fell on her tail, when it was only a rose-leaf. But this is quite absurd: for the view, although very fine, is rather of the Glacier des Bois than of the Mer de Glace, and I would not waste my time and breath to obtain a view of the Mer de Glace, which is inferior to that seen from the Flégère. No; really to see and understand this Sea of Glass which lies at the foot of the great White Throne, a visible type of the invisible, one should penetrate into the very heart of those snow-clad mountains, and stand at the junction of those three ice streams, whose confluence produces the Mer de Glace. We had to go through many places, difficult, and some dangerous, but at length we got down to the level of the glacier, and began climbing the moraines to get upon its surface. This moraine climbing is an extremely ticklish business, for so loosely does the mass hold together, that the foremost one is forced to be continually rolling down large piles of stone and dirt, which the lower ones have to be careful to dodge. How I escaped spraining my ankle a hundred times I don't know, but attribute it to an overruling Providence, and the stoutness of my boots, for I received many a blow, which would have cut an ordinary pair all to pieces. When once on the glacier, the walking was much easier, and from this cause, and also the novelty of the situation, the time passed away very rapidly. Besides its vast extent, the Mer de Glace presents phenomena which are either peculiar to itself, or at least are far more fully developed and striking than in any other glaciers. The most noticeable of these are its double line of moraines, and its immense stones on icy pedestals, the supporting stem of ice having been shaded from the sun by the flat stone above. Of these latter we saw many fine specimens, and many others which seemed very recently to have lost their centre of gravity, and to have toppled over. The ice of the Mer de Glace is purely white, and instead of showing a deep azure in its crevasses, as is the case with many other glaciers, there is little else besides perhaps a tinge of green. Crystals are found in great numbers among the rubbish of the moraines, and here one sees a superb mineralogical cabinet collected from all rocks and strata, and arranged together by the mere force of water. We had not time to stop and collect any specimens. On crossing to the other side, our rascally guide attempted to take us to the Jardin by a cross cut, over a very steep crag, for, as it afterward turned out, the glacier had changed so much that he did not know the way by the path, and consequently made tracks for the unchanging hills. So up we went after him, in momentary danger of breaking our necks, up a crag almost perpendicular, with nothing to take hold of except weak roots and tufts of grass, and all this with the uncomfortable feeling, that if our guide, who was not over active, should fall upon us with his weight of over two hundred pounds, he would inevitably sweep us away. We were all very indignant at being thus wantonly brought into danger, but as I happened to look up, I forgot my wrath, for from a hole in Jean Michel's breeches fluttered out what seemed and what undoubtedly was, the extremity of his chemise ; I could n't resist the temptation of pointing it out to the fellows, and comparing it to the white plume of Henry IV., at the battle of Ivry.

"Press, where ye see that white rag wave, all up the dangerous hill;
And be your oriflamme to-day, the shirt-tail of Michael."

So we all held on tight, and had a good laugh, which was grimly echoed by the guide up the cliff, who always considered it his duty to laugh when we did. After six hours of steady hard work, we crossed the Glacier de Taléfre, and arrived at the Jardin, a rather extravagant name for a field of short grass, upon which a few miserable goats pick up a living ; but perhaps deserved by the astonishing contrast, which its dingy green verdure bears to the dazzling white of the glaciers which surround it on every side. But how glorious to be right in the heart of all the snow and ice, and white-robed mountains,

"The palaces of Nature, whose vast walls
Have pinnacled in clouds their snowy scalps,
And through eternity, in icy halls,
In cold sublimity, where forms and falls
The avalanche, the thunderbolt of snow!"

From immense heights the three mighty glaciers of Talèfre, Lechaud, and the Giant, come sweeping down in glittering Mississippis of ice, and form the Mer de Glace, which is scarcely vaster or grander, than the three streams which are its feeders. Notwithstanding the vast quantities of ice and snow all around us, the sun was very hot, and we made a tent of shawls, under which we lay and feasted, and drank bumpers in sparkling Aste wine, which had been nicely cooled by leaving it in a crevice of the glacier. The unanimous opinion was, that as Mont Blanc was the crown of our Swiss tour, so the Jardin was the finest view around Mont Blanc, and we praised ourselves as smart fellows for having kept the best for the last. On going back, the sun was very glaring on the ice, and H. and I proved the good qualities of some colored spectacles which we had bought in Paris for the very purpose, and which relieved our eyes very pleasantly. We reached Chamouni, not very tired, and having done in one day, with ease, what takes most people two days' hard work. So ended our Alpine experience, if I except the passage over the Tête Noire; and now, farewell to Alpstock and knapsack, to fatiguing walk, rude appetite, and heavy sleep; I must now plunge into the sea of Art, and be a hard student during the coming month in Italy. I read the papers here and am very enthusiastic about the English troubles in India; would that an American legion might be formed to fight beside their English cousins, and that I might have the privilege of striking a blow for decency and civilization; all the dislike I have borne for the English is turned into pure sympathy, especially when the prayers are read on Sunday, "for the suffering countrymen in the East," and I see old ladies wiping sad tears from their eyes, for friends and relatives there.

MILAN, *October* 6, 1857.

.... There is one point in your letter which I wish to notice, and am sorry that I did not speak of before, as it might, perhaps, have saved you a great deal of anxiety; it is with regard to my going into danger, and running risks. Now let me assure you once for all, dear mother, that I am past that youthful folly which might once have prompted me to go into danger simply for the sake of saying so; and I hope you think more highly of my good sense than to suppose, for a moment, that I would uselessly risk a life which is happy and might be useful. But I believe that every young man has in him a consciousness of what he can do, and so far he is fully justified in going. Surely it would be the part of cowardice to turn back from a little danger, which good nerves are certain to overcome. Besides, I am getting over that tendency to giddiness with which I was wont to be troubled, and can now look down a precipice, if necessary, as well as any other man. Indeed, I often think of you at home, and of the sorrow which you would feel if anything should happen to me; and this thought has cleared my eye and steadied my nerves many a time, and I have whispered to myself, "It won't do to fall on any account." I must, however, recognize in some cases a Protecting Hand which saved me, not perhaps from killing myself, but from leg-breakings and ankle-sprainings innumerable; indeed, as I recall our expedition to the Jardin, I can scarcely see how I escaped some severe injury to my limbs, from the dangerous nature of the moraines, over which we walked so much. But I think I have bored you enough already with the Jardin, and I also recollect that my stories about Chamouni completely expelled all account of my impressions of the city of Geneva, where I remained no less than ten days, and got heartily sick of it. All the city of the lake is new, and its fine quays and stately hotels present a very imposing appearance to one coming down the lake. When I say "imposing" I mean to use the word in its bad sense; for although it looks, from the lake, like a splendid city, it is really very ordinary when one gets into it, and, with the exception of three or four, the streets are narrow and dirty. Calvin and J. J. Rousseau are the two guardian genii of the place, and each has left traces of his influence behind him, although this influence takes different ways of showing itself. Thus Rousseau's name is carefully preserved and honored; the street in which he was born is called after him, and a beautiful little island in the lake, close by the bridge which joins the old and new town, and on which is a public promenade, also bears his name, and is adorned with a fine bronze statue of him. Calvin's name, on the contrary, is extinct as far as physical signs would show; the house in which he lived no longer stands. I searched for it, but a new one occupies the spot; his very grave is deserted, for he was buried, at his own desire, without monumental stone, and now even the graveyard has been given up to other purposes. But his influence still survives among the descendants of those whom he kept in such strict order, and undoubtedly it would do his grim shade good to see the Calvinists of the nineteenth century, setting their faces as firmly against the opera and theatre, as did the Calvinists of the sixteenth. Some of the strict rules of his time, however, have been repealed or have fallen into disuse, and plush breeches are no longer hunted down with an unrelenting fury. I think that some of the laws which were enacted under Calvin's popedom are to be equaled in absurdity only by the most ridiculous of our Connecticut Blue Laws. Geneva bears in some respects a very strong resemblance to Paris, especially around the quays and on the banks of the river, and one sees the washerwomen plying their daily labor on rafts fastened to the shore, just as it is on the Seine. Far be it from me, however, to compare the Seine to the Rhone, the mud and dirt of the former with the crystal azure of the latter, as it darts from the lake in "arrowy rushings." It was quite nice to see the Rhone for once of a decent appearance, for in his babyhood among the Grimsel Mountains and his native glaciers, in his youth, flowing through the valley which bears his name, and in his old age as he rushes desperately to the sea through the level south of

France, he's as dirty as one could wish to see; it is only here, after a good washing in the indigo tub of Lake Geneva, and before he meets the muddy Arve, that he assumes an appearance of decency; thus he goes, muddy for some hundreds of miles, clean for some hundreds of feet. The environs of Geneva are said to be very beautiful, but I was seized with such a feeling of despair when H. went away that I walked about very little. I met J. C. the other day, and we had a very pleasant walk together to an eminence called Grand Jaconnex, outside the city; the air was very clear and the sky cloudless, so we had a most superb view of Mont Blanc and his companions; the whole range is perhaps better seen and appreciated in its entire extent from this point than from any other. I hung on at Geneva with the faint hope that B., of my class, who is travelling in these parts, might come along and bear me company into Italy; but he did n't appear. Mrs. C. wanted me to wait until her husband returned from Paris, and then travel to Milan with them; and this I should have been almost tempted to do, had not the day of his return been very uncertain. So I bade good-by to all the pleasant people at the Pension Boret, and took the boat across the lake again towards Villeneuve, thus exactly retracing my steps, a proceeding which is at any time distasteful to me, but was particularly so then, as I had no companion to assist me in whiling away the weary hours. Instead, however, of going directly to Villeneuve, I landed at Montreux, and walked to the Castle of Chillon, which I did most incontinently, not because I cared to go over it, but simply to tell people who might ask that I had been there. To any person who is not a very great admirer of Byron, this must always be the reason for going; people go there to see the place where Byron located his "Prisoner of Chillon," and not to view the spot made holy by the imprisonment of Bonnivard, for the sake of liberty and conscience; indeed, when Byron wrote his rather poor poem, he had never heard of Bonnivard, and consequently his thrilling picture sinks immediately to a fancy sketch. I rather admired the building, however, and the vault in which Bonnivard was imprisoned, and where he wore a hollow by his incessant pacing, is a fine old piece of architecture, with heavy pillars and rounding arches. I then walked on to Villeneuve, took the evening train to Bex, and joined a young fellow in getting a carriage to go on to Martigny, which we reached about 8 P. M. The diligence was full, and I was obliged to resort to the more expensive mode of posting, and joined interests with the young fellow mentioned above; he had travelled a great deal, and was then on his way to the East, having with him a Greek courier, who spoke all modern languages quite indifferently. We came up the valley of the Rhone to Brieg, a most tedious journey, and then crossed by the Simplon Pass to Lake Maggiore. This magnificent work was built by Napoleon for the purpose of transporting his cannon into Italy, his previous passage over the St. Bernard having given him enough of bad mountain roads. The Swiss side presents but little that is remarkably fine except one fine view of the Bernese Alps. I bade those good old friends a last adieu from this point. Almost at the very summit is the Hospice, a dreary great building inhabited by a detachment of monks from the Great St. Bernard. Here, as well as at the town of Simplon, a little further on, the winter lasts eight months; indeed, I saw much fresh snow lying on mountain tops not very high above the pass. The descent on the Italian side is magnificently picturesque; it surpassed in beauty, and equaled at least in wildness, all the passes we had been over. The Gemmi is perhaps more striking in its steepness, but that is a mere mule-path, and dangerous at that, while the Simplon is a splendid carriage road over which six horses can go finely at ten miles an hour. In many places it has been necessary to protect the road from avalanches by means of long galleries, some built over and some hewed out of the solid rock. Notwithstanding all their precautions, the road was destroyed twice between 1830 and 1840, and put the Swiss republic to a vast expense in mending their share. The Italian government has taken the less honorable but more convenient course of not mending their side at all. Perhaps the most striking of all these galleries is the one called the Gallery of Gondo, cut for six hundred and eighty-three feet through the solid rock. Immediately on emerging from the darkness of this gallery, a large body of water seems to rush right down upon you, forming a beautiful waterfall; the surrounding walls of rock here tower up two thousand feet above the road in shear, unbroken precipices, which in some spots even jut out and overhang, producing a most unpleasant sensation in the person passing underneath. Add to this a long vista up the valley, including waterfalls and numerous picturesquely-arching bridges, and you have a scene which is said to surpass even the celebrated Via Mala on the Splugen Pass.

MUNICH, *October* 25, 1857.

DEAR MOTHER, — It had been my intention to delay writing this until I reached Berlin, where I should find and be able to answer home letters that I should probably receive, but as I have been delayed on my journey, I dispatch a short letter to let you know that I have come thus far safely, and that you may be relieved from all anxiety. I have just attended divine service for the first time in four weeks; during three weeks I have been travelling in Austrian Italy, where it is quite difficult to get permission to establish a Protestant church; consequently in several large cities, which swarm with English and Americans, there is no chapel or service of the English Church, and as it has not entered into my calculation to go to the Romanist Church, I do not go at all. Far, far more pleasant was it when our party was travelling together in Switzerland, and when we were in a manner independent of English chapels, and could spend Sunday most delightfully by ourselves, in reading, singing, and strolling under the shadow of the mountains, engaged in conversations which were as profitable as they were pleasant.

I hope that hereafter I shall always manage to make any Sunday stoppages at civilized places, and have made a firm resolve never to travel alone again; for my recent experience has taught me that nothing can be more dreary. Oh, how frequently during the last month I have longed for the dear and quiet delights of home. I sigh for rest and the sound of home voices, the music of home songs, the light of loved eyes and faces, and instead, I am whirled along in the activity of sightseeing, and hear nothing but a harsh foreign tongue, see none but unpleasant foreign faces, until it seems to be all some horrid dream, and that if I could only thoroughly wake up, I should find myself in my own room at home, and should hear your voice calling me to get up. I have almost wished that the present state of money affairs might affect us to a sufficient extent to make it necessary for me to return home. I feel quite defiant sometimes when I feel the young life and health bounding in my veins, and I should be so proud if I could do something with my strong young arms for you, to repay all the love and kindness that you have lavished upon me for twenty-one years. It shall be the object of my future life, to repay you with love, at least, and a devotion which has always been latent in my heart, but of whose intensity I have never been aware until the cruelty of circumstances removed me a solitary exile, transplanted me to the unkindly soil of Europe, where I can never thrive, and from which I shall most joyfully remove to the much loved shadow of our home. . . . .

I saw at the table to-day a pretty fair development of the German system of morals, as regards the observance of Sunday. When dinner was about over, and most of the guests had left, four Germans and French sitting together began to throw dice to see who should pay for the champagne which they were to drink in the evening. Positively the rattle of the dice-box made me sick, and my indignation was not diminished when I was told that it was their regular practice. I seem to be on a little island in the boundless ocean; everywhere there is the same restless, unruled life, regardless of all that I have been taught to hold most sacred, and among these unholy waves it is most difficult to maintain a footing on the sure ground. English and Americans, as well as others, seem to have a travelling set of morals, and a conscience of a different texture from that which regulates their home conduct;

the guiding motto is no longer: "Do what you believe to be right," but, "When in Rome do as the Romans do." For myself, I can't understand it.

I hope that in Berlin Messrs. D., P., S., and I will be able to make a little society, in which all spare time may be pleasantly spent.

You will be glad to learn that here in Munich I have succeeded in finding some one to talk English to, a young man named F., from Hartford, who had seen that I was an American student, and offered kindly to assist me in any way. As he is an art student, he has been able to be of much service to me in this city, which fairly teems with art.

I am very anxious to reach Berlin, and settle down for the winter, as the weather is growing quite chilly and unpleasant for travelling.

Munich is a very unhealthy place, from its being so very flat; there are always numerous marshes which exhale fever miasmata; few foreigners live here long without catching what is called the slime fever. I will tell you where I have been, and what I have seen when I reach Berlin.

Tell J. that on this day, the 25th, I wished a certain fair friend of ours many happy returns of her birthday.

BERLIN, *November* 2, 1857.

Here I am at last, settled in my own winter home, having arrived here on Friday, the 30th October. Met P., D., S., and T. D., and most glorious of all, received a perfect flood of letters, upon which I have been feasting ever since. Just " phansy my pheelinx," as Chawles Yellowplush says! In fact, the accumulations of more than a month were gathered in that blessed poste restante, fully compensating me for my lonely Italian pilgrimage, when I was companionless, letterless, and generally miserable. If anything sweetens a journey, heightening its pleasures and alleviating its troubles, it is a packet of dear, warm-hearted letters, breathing of home and loved ones. The non-reception of letters when I was at Milan, Venice, and Munich, was perhaps even a greater drawback than the want of a companion. Notwithstanding, however, I enjoyed myself most fully in Italy, keeping my eyes pretty wide open for matters and things in general. I must tell you a little something about my return from Venice to Milan, which was very pleasant, and also of my last day or two at Venice. On Thursday, October 15th, I had everything ready packed for departure, when I discovered that in my hunting after pictures, palaces, and churches I had omitted to visit the Arsenal, and very willing was I to delay another day on any pretext whatever; for the quiet charm of the grand, old amphibious city was gradually stealing over me, and, with a friend, I should have been most happy to have spent a month there, among scenes which I believe to be unequaled of their kind, and like the poet, I can say,

> "I loved her from my boyhood; she, to me,
> Was like a fairy city of the heart."

But to the Arsenal: we sailed down the Grand Canal, past the Ducal Palace and the Bridge of Sighs, and turning up into a smaller canal, I soon stood before the two splendid ancient marble lions, which in years gone by stood on the Piræus of Athens. They could not easily have surveyed a fairer scene there than here, but yet their new masters have become as low and slavish as the Athenians, and the glorious name of Lepanto has, like that of Salamis, been veiled with a cloud of subsequent disgrace. Venice is no longer a queen, with an unequaled dower, but, alas! a crushed and cowering slave, her years of empire forgotten, her children corrupt and enervate, and a foreign master lords it over them; speaking, too, the same language with that proud Emperor Barbarossa, who in this very city humbled his haughty neck beneath the foot of the insulted pontiff. Within the Arsenal Museum are many objects of interest; prominent among them hangs the great Standard of the Turkish Admiral, taken at the battle of Lepanto, where the Christians struck a mighty blow for the Cross, and the Crescent went down for the first time in a sea of blood. But the most interesting thing of all was the sword of old blind Henry Dandolo, who, when ninety years old, stormed the walls of Constantinople at the head of the crusaders, and then refused the crown which he had so bravely won, preferring to remain Doge of Venice rather than become the Emperor of the East. Here also is kept the model of the famous Bucentaur, the galley from which the Doge every year, on Ascension Day, espoused the Adriatic. A right gorgeous vessel she must have been, with her banks of oars rising in ranks above each other, and the whole exterior richly gilded. The original vessel was burned in 1824, and this model is now the only memorial of her. In the afternoon I took my last row on the Grand Canal, and took my fill of gazing at the old decayed palaces, which tell of a splendor vanished, far beyond what is seen in modern times, and not only remarkable as the homes of merchant princes, but also for their intrinsic architectural beauty and richness, —

"Glowing with the richest hues of art,
As though the wealth within them had run o'er."

The next morning I took an early train for Padua, and you can easily imagine that it was with deep regret that I left this enchanting city, and for the last time

"Looked to the winged lions' marble piles,
Where Venice sits in state, throned on her hundred isles."

A ride of some two hours brought me to Padua ; this fine old city presents quite an imposing appearance, at a short distance, as it is built very compactly in a solid mass, from above which arise the domes of several very noble churches, and also the lofty roof of the Municipal Palace, about which is told quite a strange and interesting story. An Augustine friar, Fra Giovanni by name, had travelled very extensively, for the purpose of collecting architectural drawings and models. One of these was of a palace in India, which had an immense unsupported roof ; with this the Paduans were so much pleased that they ordered him to arrange the roof of their Town Hall in a similar manner ; it is said to be the largest roof in the world unsupported by pillars. The interior of the hall is decorated with strange great frescoes, mostly emblematical and founded upon the science of astrology, for which Padua was once greatly celebrated. Among other objects of interest in this hall, including the monument of my old Freshman friend Titus Livy, what interested me considerably was the bust of Belzoni, a native of the place, between two Egyptian statues which he presented to the city. It is pleasant thus to see genius and enterprise honored even after death, although the great man may have been shamefully neglected while living.

A large open square or parade ground has received the name of the Piazza of the Statues, from its being surrounded by a double row, seventy-eight in all, of statues of the distinguished men who have at any time been connected with the history of Padua; unfortunately their stock of great men ran out before their space was covered, and they were consequently obliged to appropriate quite a number of foreign names, whose connection with Padua was of the most dim and undefined nature, such as Petrarch, Tasso, and Gustavus Adolphus.

But by far the most interesting feature connected with Padua is the chapel of Maria dell' Arena, whose walls are covered with very old and fine frescoes by Giotto, which have at the same time doubled his reputation, and have also served to show the condition of the art of painting, when it had passed the earliest age of stiffness and angularity, and although with a certain sweetness and beauty of their own, are yet far behind the school of Raphael, which followed two centuries afterwards.

The subjects of the frescoes are entirely illustrations of sacred history, and it gives a deep additional interest to know that Dante lived in the same house with the painter, and doubtless by his deep spiritual advice did much to influence the character of the young artist. I have not space here to tell you what I thought of all these tender and pious works of mediæval art, but will mention two or three to give you an idea of the wonderful beauty and grace that was attained even by the pre-Raphaelites. The Raising of Lazarus was peculiarly powerful; the newly-raised body stands on end, but still motionless, being swathed with the burial garments, but in the face appears a remarkable struggle between life and death, the eyes being just faintly raised, as if the vital element had not yet spread fully over the body. The Marriage in Cana of Galilee, was full of graceful female forms, while in the Burial of Christ were united many qualities seeming quite remarkable in a painter of that period ; to the accuracy and minuteness which are so observable in the old painters was added a graceful pose of the figures, and a sweet expression of devotion in the faces, such as the old painters tried hard to attain, but produced only clumsy parodies of upturned eyes and distorted features. So that here we see a long stride in advance of the past, and towards that high ideal which was not realized until more than two centuries later, in the masterpieces of Leonardo da Vinci and Raphael. To me it is peculiarly pleasant to think of Dante as standing by Giotto's side, and explaining to him the deep and hidden meaning of Scripture allegory and metaphysical law, thus demonstrating that the rules which govern in the art of poesy are none the less valuable when that poesy is made tangible, and spread in colors on the canvas or the wall.

But I perceive that I am getting slightly borous. I am, moreover, growing very sleepy, so give me a kiss, and goodnight, dearest mother.

November 3. — I have just finished the first breakfast that I have taken alone, as P. left yesterday.

Our way of life is arranged in a very pleasant manner, and one calculated to allow abundant opportunities for study, and yet bringing us together in a social party two or three times during the day. It is after this fashion : we rise in the morning, and each one takes his coffee in his own room ; then generally come lectures, or studies, which are carried on according to the taste or fancy of the particular student; at 1 P. M. we meet and take a good sharp walk for one hour, after which we all, five in number, take dinner together at the Hotel Bellevue. After dinner come perhaps more walks, or we disperse, each to his own room, and work until 8 P. M., when we all meet again in Mr. D.'s room to take tea. On this occasion no English is allowed to be spoken, or even read. Last night, Mr. D. and I had pretty much all the conversation to ourselves. I, however, broke the rule by sundry sly and surreptitious glances at the " New York Weekly Times," for October 17th, in which were many items of interest, not only as touching the money crisis, but also concerning the recent election in Kansas. I shall look with much impatience for the next mail, to see whether the Free State men have nobly triumphed, or whether they have been jockeyed out of their victory by the frauds and ballot-stuffing of Leavenworth County border ruffians. To return, I think that these evening meetings of ours will be not only profitable but also pleasant.

I must tell you something more of Italy. Retracing my steps towards Milan, I spent the night at Verona, and went, early the next morning, to Brescia, where I spent a most delightful half day, in wandering among its fine churches and antique ruins. A Roman temple was dug up here, and many beautiful antiques discovered, among them a bronze winged statue of Victory, which struck me at once by its wonderful elegance, seeming to stand right out from everything else around it. It seems indeed strange that the old Greeks and Romans, with nothing but a Pagan religion and Pagan devotion to inspire them, should have succeeded in giving to their works of art a beauty and power which it is the highest ambition of the moderns faintly to approach. I speak of sculpture rather than painting, for the latter was undoubtedly a flower which blossomed much later, and received its highest nutriment from the gentle dew of Christian devotion.

In Brescia, too, I could dream over some of my old dreams of the time of Chivalry, inseparably connected as it is with the names of two of my favorite heroes, Gaston de Foix, and Bayard, the "chevalier sans peur et sans reproche." Gaston de Foix, I am sorry to say, acted like a rapscallion, as he stormed the city and then led his soldiers, the flower of chivalry, into pillage and slaughter, which lasted for seven days, and in which 46,000 of the inhabitants perished. In the midst of all these horrors the gentle Bayard shone like a bright, mist-dispelling star. I have not space to tell the whole story, how when grievously wounded and carried into a house, he forgot his own pain to care for the safety of his hostess and her daughters ; how for many weeks he lay there nigh unto death, but ever kind and courteous, thinking less of himself than of others; and how, when he went away, he refused all ransom, and with such sweet and gentle speeches (much, by the way, like those of dear old Don Quixote), that it really warms one's heart to read them. Oh, to see in those dark times a character like this, as brave, high-spirited, and able as any, but more gentle, devout, and generous than all, reminds me of Cogia Alhabdal's diamond, in the "Arabian Nights," which shone brightest when all the lights were extinguished, and everything else was dark.

In the afternoon I went to Bergamo, which is a most picturesque city, the most wealthy portions of the inhabitants living on a lofty hill with very steep sides, thus literally the "upper ten," while the larger portion of the town lies at the base of the rock. Most of the fine churches and public buildings are in the Citta, or upper part, and look splendidly, from their being at a great height, and consequently visible at a long distance. The view from the Castello of Bergamo I thought even superior to that from the top of the Cathedral of Milan. To the north are seen the Alps, to the west the cathedral spires of Milan and Monza, and the region watered by the Adda, while to the south the fertile plain of Lombardy, the valley of the Po, stretching far off to the Appenines, sprinkled thickly with noble towns and cities, and glowing, as I saw it, with the rich hues of a superb Italian sunset. I could scarcely refrain from crying aloud, —

"Where 's the coward would not dare
To fight for such a land."

But, alas! the times must produce a new race of men before Italy shall shake off the Austrian yoke, or even gain for herself her ancient feudal privileges, which were wont to be the substitute for freedom.

The day after I was at Milan, across the Lake of Como, and by night-fall, over the Splügen Pass to Chur, in the Canton of the Grisons. The Lake of Como, of which Bulwer gives such a rapturous description in his "Lady of Lyons," I had expected to be disappointed in, but was not at all. I had intended to tell you about my ride over the Splügen, but as I wish to answer grandpapa's by this mail, I must hand it over to J.

Your loving son.

BERLIN, *November* 3, 1857.

MY DEAR J., — One letter at a time from you has hitherto been sufficient to inspire me with the most joyful emotions, but my demonstrations slightly passed the bounds of decency, when in the bundle of letters handed to me with a benevolent smile by the postmaster, I discovered that there were two from you. I repaired to P.'s room, and having opened all my letters, twelve in number, upon the table, I performed a war dance over them, in total uncertainty as to which I should open first, and it is no exaggeration to say that it was two days before I had completed the perusal of them all. I have just read your two letters over for the third time. Your second letter was peculiarly interesting to me, from the many items it contained — it really seemed as if you were sitting in my study at home and telling it all to me face to face. . . . .

Wednesday, November 4. — It is very cold this morning, and all the exposed wood-work is covered with a coating of frost ; I shall have a fire this afternoon in my big porcelain stove, and shall rejoice that I am not now crossing the Splügen Pass, as I was doing two weeks ago last Monday, for it was cold enough there then to satisfy any one. We had at first some very bad weather, and I feared that the beauties of the celebrated Via Mala would be spoiled for me, as during our ascent there was a fierce and continual storm of mingled snow and rain. But at the village of Splügen, where we stopped to take dinner and warm up, the clouds cleared off, and down towards the Swiss side everthing looked bright, and sunlit, and beautiful. I got the conductor to let me sit with him in his seat on top, and so had almost as good a view of the scenery as if I had proceeded on foot. Indeed it was a shame to ride over this pass, but I had more baggage than I could carry on my back, and was besides pressed for time, and was therefore compelled to adopt that method of progression, which is most disagreeable to me. The scenery, in most parts of this pass not very remarkable, was, in one district about a mile and a half long, extremely wild and picturesque. Imagine walls of rock, rising above you on either hand to a height of some 1600 feet, in perfectly smooth precipices, while below a vast chasm stretches away to an immense depth, and at its bottom flows the stream of the here youthful Rhine, or rather his lower branch, the upper one coming from the St. Gothard range. You can form some idea of the extreme narrowness of these clefts, through which the road passes and the river flows, when I tell you that in one place a short bridge carries the road over the abyss which is not more than six or eight feet wide; a cleft through which, in long forgotten times of the Pass, the Rhine has broken his way from the mountain-glaciers to the plains below. The bridge itself was so narrow that the diligence had not more than two feet to spare on either side, and as the top projected considerably over the wheels, I could look straight down into the chasm, whose two sides seemed to have been split apart quite recently, so near were they to each other, and so well did the opposite sides fit. But, with the exception of this short pass, the Splügen road is rather ordinary than otherwise, and not such a remarkable exhibition of grandeur and wildness as I had been led to expect. The Simplon I think superior to it in every respect; besides being one of the finest roads I ever saw, it passes through nobler snow mountains, is overhung by more imposing glaciers, the walls of rock which close it are higher and grander, and above all the magnificent coup d'œil which one gets in looking backward, while going down the Italian slope, surpasses anything on the Splügen. Of all the mountain passes which I have been over, including (besides the four great ones, the St. Gothard, the St. Bernard, the Simplon, and the Splügen) some fifteen passes of lesser note, the Simplon is the one over which I should most enjoy going again.

At Reichenau, where we stopped to change horses, I had an opportunity of seeing the union of the upper and lower branches of the Rhine, who from this time becomes quite a respectable river, and in springtime I should imagine a rather dangerous one, as his banks are very low, and are lined on each side by "moraines," so to speak, of stones which he brought down when swelled by the spring floods. I think that by this time I ought to be acquainted with old Father Rhine, having seen him in all his phases: a glacier torrent roaring through the Splügen, a little river flowing muddy into Lake Constance, but flowing out "clear as diamond spark," and furrowed by the keels of steamboats as far as Schaffhausen; there plunging down in rapids and cataracts and on to Strasburg, where it is a fierce, unnavigable stream, and rushes through the bridge piers with great rapidity. At Mayence we saw him again, and from thence to Cologne, in the quiet and tranquillity of his manhood, with his robe and crown of orchards and vineyards: once more at Leyden, sinking away and losing himself in the sands of ocean. We spent the night at Chur, the capital of the Grisons. This is a very strange canton, the largest in Switzerland, and the least thickly settled. In its mountains there is said to be still capital sport of chamois shooting; in fact I dined for two days on chamois venison, which is rather poor stuff, and not comparable to the rich meat which we shot for ourselves last year in the Adirondacks. But the most remarkable thing about this canton is the language which they speak. It is called the Romaic dialect, and is a heterogeneous mixture of Latin, German, French, and Italian, the Latin and Italian predominating. But still the language as I heard it spoken has very little of Italian softness. The language spoken in several valleys is said to bear a very strong resemblance to the Latin of the Roman peasants, as described by Livy. I went the next day to Lake Constance, which I crossed to Lindau, where I was anxious to meet the train to Augsburg. When I arrived I found that I had only fifteen minutes to get to the depot, and, to add to my trouble, I was attacked by both the police and custom-house officers, as I was now passing from Switzerland into Bavaria. Discretion was the better part of valor, so I seized my traps and bolted for the depot, which fortunately was close at hand, shouting out to the astonished officials that it was all O. K., and managed to get to the cars just in time. My journey from Lindau to Augsburg, and from thence to Munich, was very uninteresting. However, I spent a very pleasant half day at Augsburg, which is a very fine old city. The inn at which I put up is one of the oldest in Europe, dating from the fourteenth century. It is called Die drei Mohren, and is now kept in the finest house in Augsburg, formerly the palace of the Fugger family, who were for so many generations so celebrated for their wealth. I saw the room in which Anthony Fugger burned the three million florins I. O. U. which he held against Charles V., on the occasion of that Emperor spending some time in the house. The cellar of the Drei Mohren contains the most celebrated collection of wines which is known anywhere in these parts, and it is said that one is sure of getting them pure and genuine here, though he pays a pretty good price for them. Among these are the Immortal Massic and the Falernian of the Romans, from Palestine the Dew of Carmel, and Hill of Bethlehem wine, and also one from Ithaca called Schloss-Ulysses. This last rather took me down.

I was much interested in several things in Augsburg, especially the water-works and the room where the "Augsburg Confession" was publicly read to Charles V. This room has been entirely modernized, as was to be expected from a Catholic sovereign, who would efface with pleasure all that could remind one of the Reformation; but still I determined to see it, that I might be able to tell mother that I had been upon the very spot where Melancthon's celebrated paper was published, which produced such great results both for good and evil. The room was very uninteresting in its appearance, and the places where the distinguished persons stood are not known, but it is very easy to see where the throne must have stood, and also to define the spot where Bayer, the Chancellor of Saxony, stood, who when requested by the Emperor to read the Confession in Latin, replied, "Your Majesty surely does not desire it to be read in a tongue which the people do not understand;" and then proceeded to read in such a loud tone of voice that it was not only heard in the apartment but even by the crowd without. Augsburg is now about two fifths Protestant to three fifths Catholic, and I was informed that they get along very peaceably together.

I perceive that I shall not have space enough to tell you what were my impressions of the Munich Gallery, and consequently will not touch upon it.

But I must give you an account of a glimpse of student-life, especially as here in Berlin there appears to be very little student life at all, the fellows being older, and not so much attached to beer and duels as at Bonn, Heidelberg, and Munich.

A young artist from Hartford named F. was very kind to me, and, after taking me to the Pinacothek and Glyptothek, and also to some galleries to which no unintroduced person can be admitted, offered to take me to the Student's Kneipe the night before I came away. I gladly accepted, as I was anxious to see how they did these things down here in Bavaria; I was also urged to go by a German member of the Chor or society, named Farmbecker, who had been F.'s teacher in German, and with whom I had had some very pleasant talks about our mutual friend. I do not wonder that T. liked him, for he had a very quiet, gentlemanly manner, and struck me as being a German translation of Doc. M. About 8 P. M. we dropped into the house in which the Chor of the "Isarians" holds its meetings, and entered a small room, very plain and decorated with little else than shields, upon which were painted the colors of the club — green, blue, and white; green being the color of the river Isar, from which they take their name, and blue and white the colors of Bavaria. Around a long table were seated some dozen or fifteen fellows, busily engaged in drinking and smoking, wearing caps decorated with the same colors as above, the body being green with a blue and white rim underneath. These colors are carried out very completely in watch ribbons and pipe decorations.

Some of them wore what is called the Festmütse or Feast cap, which is a very small smoking-cap without any tassel, which is placed upon the top of the head, and gives a highly rakish and jolly appearance.

I was received with true student cordiality, and placed opposite to a tall fellow, who, I was informed, was the best schlager, or fighter, in the university; and, although he had fought very often, had received scarcely a single scratch. This is the highest praise which they could possibly bestow upon a fellow student, and could not be increased if he had the learning of Erasmus and the eloquence of Abelard. A jolly student song then followed, not a compound of yells and howls such as go to make up the students' chorals at Yale, but a really sweet, well-executed song, which deserved the name of a lay. Some of the voices seemed very good, and all were harmonious. The song over, a vigorous beer-drinking set in; large mugs of beer, containing nearly a quart, were drunk on every side. I began a conversation with the huge swordsman opposite me, and, after a few words, he suddenly challenged me to "drink out," that is, to empty my mug at one pull, without breathing. A quart is a pretty good mouthful for a man whose drinking days had been over for two years, but it would n't do to hesitate, so we clinked our mugs together, there was a short pause, then not a drop fell from the inverted mugs which we brought down upon the table with a simultaneous clang. From that moment I was looked upon as a jolly fellow, and was overwhelmed with attentions. The fighting Junior, whose name was Schenk, drew me a picture of a duel, which I was assured was exactly correct, and which I enclose to you, only requesting that you will preserve it carefully, as it is quite nicely done, though dashed off in a moment. I should also like to keep it as a remembrance of my meeting with the Munich students.

Schenk was very anxious that I should stay and study in Munich, and take lessons from him in fighting. He offered to be my second in all my fights, and parry all the bad blows, "so that the cuts you get will be merely ornamental," said he. I was obliged to refuse his tempting offer. Students are the same the world over, and it was most delightful for me to get another glimpse of student life, at once similar to and so different from my old life at Yale.

BERLIN, *November* 8.

For really severe study the opportunities and inducements at this place are very numerous and valuable, and the distractions, especially for a stranger, are extremely few. The Library of the King contains the respectable number of five hundred thousand volumes, besides several thousand manuscripts; upon these a student ought to be able to browse to his heart's content, and have no need to complain that his acquaintance in the city is confined to three or four male friends. And as hereafter I shall have positively nothing to write about, save the dry and uninteresting details of a quiet, studious life, I take this opportunity to speak once more of the interesting objects which I have seen in coming to this place, for I would by no means have you suppose that my visits to Munich and Nuremberg were not filled with enjoyment and admiration of the ancient and the artistic. In Munich there were some things which pleased me, and others which decidedly did not. I did not like at all the uniform appearance of almost all the new buildings, which, with their spick and span aspect, made them look as if they had all been built in blocks by contract, or else turned out of some Yankee machine for manufacturing houses, some great public-building turning-lathe. This is especially noticeable in the magnificent Ludwigstrasse, where the uniformity is most dreary. The unfilled appearance of many of the finest streets is mentioned by some as a defect; but to me it seemed rather an ornament than otherwise, as the vacant spaces left between the houses were occupied with gardens or little clumps of shrubbery, which imparted a charm to the stiffness of the city, and reminded me very forcibly of some of the prettiest parts of New Haven or Norwich. In fact, the Briennerstrasse, through which I walked about every day, was very much like Temple Street, although, of course, it had no such glorious elms, whose equals I have as yet seen nowhere in Europe.

You can imagine that I reveled in the treasures of the

Pinacothek. This is said to be one of the very best arranged, lighted, and managed picture galleries in Europe, and although there is nothing in it which in any very peculiar degree excited my emotion, yet it was a place where I could have spent a good deal of time most pleasantly and profitably. The collection is peculiarly rich in the old German masters, from the very earliest times, when the Byzantine was dominant in Germany, and William of Cologne at the head of it, down to later times, when the German artists had begun to make pilgrimages to the Italian cities, and to sit at the feet of those great masters who so beautifully united the tender with the majestic. There are also many fine specimens of the early Flemish school, in which such rapid steps were made onward; among them the Jan Van Eyck was of course the finest, although there was nothing in the Pinacothek equal to his great picture of the "Adoration of the Spotless Lamb," which I enjoyed so much at Ghent, which is immeasurably the masterpiece of that early school.

The great room, however, is the hall of Rubens, in which are collected no less than ninety-five of the works of this jolly man, whose free rich life seemed to find an appropriate type and perpetuation in the gorgeous coloring and unfettered motion which he lavished on his paintings.

I cannot, however, in my own feelings, accord to Rubens that position which many give him, nor can I assent to all that Sir Joshua Reynolds, at once his critic and his panegyrist, chose to say. In some styles of painting, not generally the highest, he is perhaps the most able and successful painter that ever lived. But it appears to me, that when he takes up subjects of a more high and holy nature, he fails, or at least meets with inferior success. He was, however, unfortunate in his models, and as a man can produce only what is within and around him, it is scarcely to be expected that his characters should possess an elevated beauty such as he had never intimately studied, or be spiritualized by an expression of love and devotion such as he had never felt. He was a gloriously gifted man, and painted in the most gorgeous colors known in the art, the most beautiful women, the noblest men, and the wildest animals, which he knew, and grouped all together with the originality and power of a wonderful imagination. For all this we can give him the highest praise and admiration, but cannot go further and acknowledge his magic as strong enough to touch the heart or bow the knee.

What pleased me most of all in this gallery were those charming pictures of Murillo, representing scenes from the lowest classes of the Spanish. Nothing could be more natural and beautiful than those two boys eating fruit — one a bunch of grapes, and the other a melon, with a melon seed already sticking to his cheek. Spite of rags and poverty, they are in the full enjoyment of the "dolce far niente," and the humor which glitters and sparkles in their eyes is of that keen and racy kind which lights up so cheerfully the pages of Cervantes.

But enough of art, although I have still a great deal more to say of Albert Dürer, and Teniers, and Gerard Dow, and of the rich landscapes of Claude Lorraine, Both, and Ruysdael, to which my attention was particularly directed by my companion, a young artist from Hartford, who is studying landscape painting in Munich.

This is my dear mother's birthday, and I wish for her many returns of the day, all happy with that health and quiet pleasure which it shall be my aim to increase, — my warmest love to her from her absent son. Tell her I have thought much of her to-day, and most of all when we met in Mr. D.'s room this evening, and sung those old hymns and tunes, which never fail to bring back to my mind the place where, and the lips from which I first learned them.

To H. N. C.

BERLIN, *November* 13, 1857.

. . . . Were not your first few days after reaching home perfectly rich with happiness? days to be remembered through a lifetime, for the peculiar charm in which they were clothed? When you answer this, I want you to particularize about the little minutiæ of your own return home, at least as far as you think fit, and also to tell me every word spoken and every look given when you first met my mother and brother. I don't care if you don't say much else, or even if you omit a disquisition on the money crisis, with which I have been bored for two weeks past, if you will only, in addition to a full detail of your own voyage and experiences, tell me everything you noticed in my home-circle. A man more lonely and miserable than myself after you left would have been a difficult thing to find.... In Venice I spent a week, and had you been with me, we should doubtless have squandered there a fortnight of our valuable time. For her palaces and pictures, her canals and churches, her rich blue sky and oriental bearing, over all which blows the fresh sea breeze from the Adriatic, form a glorious combination of the gorgeous, the beautiful, and the strange, which not only delighted and astonished me, but gave me new ideas of beauty and excellence, and taught me that, however wonderful art may be, the power of the human mind in seizing and enjoying it is still more wonderful..... At Munich I also attended a German Kneipe, or society meeting, and had a very jolly time, being as it were transported back to the dear old days of whist and whiskey-punch in ———'s and ———'s rooms. I will tell you all about it when I see you, for it is probably the only sight of student social life which I shall get, as they have positively no student-life at this University of Berlin, which is a kind of extra-nice, advanced, finishing-off establishment, where the object is rather study and profit than fun ; the students are older, more earnest and sober, and consequently frown down, rather, all attempts at societies, beer-drinking, and duelling, which appear to be the chief end of man at Heidelberg, Bonn, and Munich. From Munich I went up to Nuremberg, which is the finest old Gothic city in Europe ; every house is just as it was three hundred years ago, and in the good old times when Albert Dürer painted, Peter Vischer and Adam Krafft carved, and the cobbler Hans Sachs poured forth his inspiriting war songs. The appearance of antiquity about the houses is much greater and more general than in Ghent or Bruges ; in fact, there is scarcely anything modern about the whole town to remind one that he is in the nineteenth century, and thus call off the dreamer's mind from the past. I was delighted with the city, and would have willingly given up Milan, cathedral and all, if necessary, in order to visit it."

TO THE SAME.

BERLIN, *January* 10, 1858.

An ulcer in my leg, in which I caught cold, gave me considerable pain, and reduced me to the humiliating necessity of calling in a German doctor; fortunately for me he understood English, and I did not have such a ludicrous time in relating my symptoms as " My Uncle " did in " Up the Rhine." The Herr Doctor however made one pretty bad bull, though it was rather in a professional line: I asked him if I might eat apples, whereupon he replied that he " had no *injections* to it." The Partingtonism was too much for the politeness of the crowd who had come in to hear whether I was in immediate danger or not, and we all collapsed in a most hearty laugh, in which the jolly doctor joined; and then my landlady's little girl was sent out for a fabulous quantity of apples, which, with the help of my sympathizing friends, disappeared with astonishing rapidity. . . . During my lonely days upon my sofa, I read again and again your letter, both alone and in connection with one I received from home nearly at the same time; it is *so* pleasant to view the home circle from different points, and the little sketch which you gave me was such a charming one, and seemed to bring those dear ones so clearly before my mental eye, that I cannot sufficiently thank you for it. No one can better appreciate my feelings than a devoted lover of home life like yourself, so you may fill out yourself the state of feeling in which I was by imagining how you would like it if you had remained in Europe, and I had written you from America a jolly little account of two evenings spent by me in the light of that Tarrytown fireside. . . . . I never was celebrated for my faith in doctors, nor for my obedience to their prescriptions. This doctor the other day, after looking very owlish, and writing out a long list of medicines to be swallowed inside and rubbed outside, informed me that I was to eat no meat! You cannot thoroughly appreciate the full horror of this command, for at the large hotels which you and I frequented, the bill of fare had been much influenced by English travel, and consequently we did not see German cookery rampant, nor have you any idea of the vile weeds which are brought on to the table under the name of vegetables. Cut off thus from meats, a vast desert of *Kraut*, an endless Sahara of *Kohl*, stretched out before my disgusted eye. I tried the no meat system for one day, and then made up my mind that if I ate meat, I *might* die of an ulcer, but that if I did not eat meat I should certainly die of starvation. So I adopted the rule of self-preservation and defied the doctor, whom I now believe to be the secret emissary of some seller of vegetables.

BERLIN, *November* 18, 1857.

. . . . I now sit down to answer the last letters from home, and hope that you will not wholly despise my letters, which will henceforth want the enthusiastic interest of the traveller, but which will rather be replete with the dull reflections and observations of the student. The ordinary events of commonplace life, in an unpicturesque city, will be henceforth the subject of my story, and they will want to you that charm which all your home matters have to me, namely, a previous interest in them, which becomes ever stronger the further and the longer I am removed from them. . . .

The Italian readings which I hold with Mr. D., the tea-drinkings in his room, and our walks together before dinner, are the pleasantest episodes in my daily life; but at other times he is fearfully busy with lectures and hard study, so that I do not feel myself justified in disturbing him. After a few trials of talking German at our evening tea-drinkings, in which Mr. D. and I were pretty much sole interlocutors, we gave it up and have since eaten our evening meal in peace. . . .

It is peculiarly disagreeable to have people turn round and stare at you in the street, simply because they hear you speaking English. I don't think I shall be thoroughly well settled till I have thrashed a couple of these broad-faced, stupid

Berliners for their impolite way of fixing their fishy eyes upon every one whom they take to be a foreigner; there are several who sit near me at the dinner-table, with whom I should like to begin. I am afraid that the German dishes are not good for me; at any rate they make me extremely choleric towards the unhappy specimens whom I see every day feeding on them.

But I feel quarrelsome and abusive this afternoon, so I will leave off writing until I can get into what you would call "a better frame of mind," that is to say, one less complaining and grouty, but I feel dreadfully blue and melancholy just now.

11 P. M. — I have been to supper, and after a quite pleasant talk in T. D.'s room, I have come back quite humanized and soothed down, although I feel just about as remorseful as ever.

When I get into one of these states of mind, after sighing in vain for that home which I was so foolish as to leave, I begin to look back with regret upon the pleasant passages of travel over which I have recently been, and during which the continual occupation drove away, in a great measure, melancholy thoughts. Among these passages, the last and most delightful was Nuremberg, which I visited just before coming on here, which I would by no means have you suppose that I passed over or neglected.

I left Munich on Tuesday, October 27, and spent the night at Augsburg, from which I took the early morning train, and so jogged along northward, through Bavaria, at the slow pace of a German train. At Donauworth I had the pleasure of gazing for a few moments upon the Danube, which I can truly believe to be a noble and glorious stream, far superior to the Rhine; for although here one does not hear its torrent's thunder shock, nor does it seem magnificently rude, as Campbell describes it, yet even at that distance from its mouth it is navigable by steamers, and a large bridge is necessary to span its rushing waters. I have a sort of hankering to sail down its yet unhackneyed stream, and to view its scenes of wild grandeur,

"Imperial Danube's rich domain,"
but one can't see everything, and I ought to be thankful for having even got a partial glimpse of the noble old River King. Near the place where we crossed the Danube lies the little village of Blenheim, celebrated in song by Dr. Southey, who informs us, through the medium of Wilhelmina, Peterkin, and their Grandfather, that *there* was a famous victory. So on to Nuremberg. On entering the gates of this grand old relic, one is immediately carried back three centuries, and sees around him the same streets, the same houses, the same city, which the noble and pious artists, Albert Dürer, Peter Vischer, and Adam Krafft saw at the end of the fifteenth century. Long rows of strangely-built, richly-ornamented houses, with high-peaked roofs, in which are several tiers of windows, looking like the cannon port-holes in the sides of a man-of-war; fountains of all kinds, from the grotesque old German style to the elegant tracery of Gothic open-work, noble mediæval churches of the truest and purest style of Gothic, with the pointed arch, the style of Cologne Cathedral, and the unvarying antiquity of the appearance of the streets, in which seldom can be seen anything in the least degree modern, produce the effect almost of a spell of glamour; like the enchanted castle in the "Sleeping Beauty," where everything had been laid to sleep by a charm, and so preserved for a hundred years, so the Genius of the Middle Ages has laid his spell, and has preserved to himself this city, whole and entire, saying to the wild waves of progressive modernism, "Thus far shall ye come and no farther, for here I have set up my last tower of strength; into this have I retired as into my last citadel, and here shall ye not place your profaning foot; but here let the student and the mystic come as from the glaring heat of a summer's day, into the soft coolness of a church aisle; and here I will show him old pictures in the chapel aisles, mellowed by the light of the past and ages long gone, from Frederic Barbarossa to Wallenstein, and will sing him old songs which were made in the infancy of mediæval poetry, and have since come echoing down

through the corridors of time; and he shall go forth with quiet pleasure from his communion with the spirit of the olden days."

This was what the spirit said to me at least, and I was right glad that I could understand it, and could enter with a feeling of intense enjoyment into the contemplation of the particular beauties of art with which the old city is replete. The churches, pictures, and images, which were set up and adored by the Catholics, still remain in great perfection, for notwithstanding the strong Protestant tendencies of the city for several hundred years, the change produced by the Reformation was a quiet and gentle one, and not disgraced by outbursts of iconoclastic fury; they have been rather inclined to divert to their own use the religious apparatus of the Romanists, though with a nobler faith and purer devotion.

The awakening of inventive thought, as well as of religious reform, also made its appearance near the beginning of the sixteenth century in Nuremberg; its citizens were the Yankees of their time, and among their inventions may be reckoned the watch, the air gun, the paper mill, and the first cast cannon, besides sundry musical instruments and ornamental arts, the latter mostly imported from Italy. But the most interesting view which can be taken of Nuremberg at that active and wide-awake period, is that which regards its artists, wood carvers, bronze casters, sculptors, and painters, of whom a large number of remarkable ability were engaged in various works in the city at just the same time. Preëminent in the bronze-casting and sculpture department stands old Peter Vischer, with whose great work, the shrine of St. Sebald, I was much charmed. It is the most elaborate piece of casting I ever saw; it consists of five hundred separate pieces, all worked up in the richest Gothic style, and employed the artist thirteen years of hard labor to finish it. But it is something more than a mere work of elaborate art; in the calm, sweet faces of the twelve apostles, which surround the shrine and are the most prominent figures, in their noble forms and gracefully-flowing garments, can be observed the influence of that beautiful spiritual Italian school which had recently been making rapid strides in Germany, and showed its effects even in such rough material as bronze. For this seems to be a step above most ordinary castings, whose highest aim seems to be to give a correct imitation, or at most a very rough or gross expression, but in this extraordinary piece of work everything is finished with the beauty and nicety of the chisel, not a fault nor sign of bad taste being visible throughout the whole. Very different in its general style is a lofty stone spire in the St. Lawrence Church, of Gothic open-work, called the Sacrament House, and intended to receive the consecrated wafer. Although the service of the church is now Lutheran, this beautiful monument has liberally been allowed to stand for the admiration of every sect. It is of stone, sixty feet high, tapering from the floor of the church almost to the top of the choir, and then it turns over in a graceful curve, and thus forms the appearance of a vast shepherd's crook. Within it are several groups, on different platforms or stories, representing, as they rise, the various scenes of our Lord's passion. Thus, the Resurrection is at the summit, where the eye just begins to lose sight of the coarser outlines of the form, a most appropriate position. The whole structure is supported on the shoulders of three stooping figures, which are the fac-similes of the pious artist Adam Krafft and his two assistants, and serve to remind one of their long, incessant labor for five years, and of the miserable pittance of a little over three hundred dollars, which they received for this astonishing work. But the name of all others which is inseparably connected with Nuremberg, and which must ever throw about it a tender and gentle memory, making it a fit spot to be visited by the enthusiast as well as the artist, is that of Albert Dürer, a man of wonderful and varied abilities, superior in intellectual perfections, probably, to every man of his time, and yet bearing in his bosom one of the noblest and truest hearts that ever beat.

I think that Shakespeare is the only character whom I can call more myriad-minded. In every art of imitation or ornament, and in many of the more abstruse sciences, he led the world. That you may have an idea of his personal appearance, I will tell you a little bit of my own experience. In the picture gallery at Munich I stopped with admiration before the portrait of a person. Long golden curls which fell down upon the shoulders, an oval face of noble contour, and deep, unfathomable brown eyes, which beamed with angelic sweetness. I said to myself, that is the most pleasing likeness of the Saviour that I ever saw, and looked in the catalogue to discover the artist, when I found that it was the portrait of Albert Dürer, painted by himself. He planned churches and carved statues, painted wonderful pictures and wrote books on mathematics; and the mighty fortifications around the city, which stood the long siege of Wallenstein during the Thirty Years' War, testify to his skill as an engineer. What a pity that such a man could not spend his life in peace! He was hunted to his grave by a termagant wife. I stood in the cemetery, by his simple slab, and was almost inclined to take a resolution against marriage, for fear of meeting with a similar fate.

Mr. D. has just come in, attired in a long cloak, and looking much like an Italian bandit, and, in accordance with his appearance, wants me to go and read Italian with him. As my paper is about out, I think that I shall accept his offer.

BERLIN, *December* 3, 1857.

DEAREST MOTHER, — I sit down to write my weekly letter home in a much more cheerful, not to say jolly, frame of mind than usual. To this state your last brief but dear letter has much contributed, as it released me from some very anxious thoughts about J.; but now the news that he is well again, and that all is right at home, has filled me with joy, and I fee much like executing some of those ape-like gambols of my youthful days, on which you were wont vainly to attempt to frown.

So you had got that grouty, wormy, miserable, melancholic letter which I sent from Munich. I almost wished that I had not written it, but I was afraid that if I did not write at all, you might be anxious; so with a head-stopping, eye-blinding, idea-clogging influenza, I sat down on an unpleasant Sunday afternoon in that most disagreeable city, and you have obtained the result. You see how slavishly I am influenced by mere outward circumstances and objects, and you must not be anxious or sorrowful, even if I write letters as blue as indigo or as doleful as Niobe. To-day, on the contrary, what spirits I have had! A bright, warm sun, which unfortunately set at about 3 P. M., a delightful bracing air and clear sky, have made me feel as if I could do nothing but shout and sing all day long; and although I have had a good tough spell of horseback riding, and after it two hours more of walking and jumping, which latter amusement has made me somewhat lame, I still feel as light and airy as a bird. Is it a misfortune to have a nature so susceptible to impressions, so easily filled with enthusiasm and bounding hope and spirits, and as easily depressed and darkened with sadness and melancholy? Many perhaps would think it so; but for myself, I would rather live a year of time enlivened by the changing emotions of intense pain and lofty pleasure, than drag out a dozen years in the dead-and-alive existence of phlegmatic insensibility. One of my professors has been lecturing on Human Temperaments, and has classified and arranged them in a very clear and perspicuous manner, so that I have taken much interest in the subject, and we have had considerable talk about it in our little circle. I am composed chiefly of the sanguine and melancholic, with a pretty fair sprinkling of the choleric and a total absence of the phlegmatic. I think a little dose of the latter temperament would not be a bad thing to settle and quiet my other more rampant qualities.

My life here in Berlin contains but little of thrilling interest, as I am in my room much of the time. Although I cannot accuse myself of any very severe study, yet with law and Greek studies, Italian reading, German speaking, and general literature, my time is very fully occupied, and these short days slip by almost before I am aware of it. I am improving quite diligently my opportunities of becoming acquainted with the old Civil or Roman Law, the study of which is much pursued on the Continent, because its rules and principles lie at the bottom of almost all their codes, showing traces even at this remote age of the universality of the Roman Empire, and afterwards of the feudal system. But as England always, from the earliest times, regarded with suspicion the Civil Law, as being of Romish and papal origin, and as opposed to their much cherished Common Law, consequently both for English and Americans, the study of the Civil Law is not so much a necessary or important pursuit, as it is one of scholarship, and one which contributes, by the excellence of its maxims and the depths of its erudition, to the more complete and symmetrical formation of an elegant legal education. Still it is the foster child of tyranny, shaped and managed to suit the will of a single despotic individual, while the English Common Law, which is the foundation of almost all of our State codes, and which is in many of the States adopted bodily, this glorious English Common Law is the eldest-born of Anglo-Saxon freedom, and has grown quietly up from the mass of the people, perpetuating their customs and expressing their wants. But I will turn to a more congenial topic: you told me about a Sunday at home; I will give you some idea of my last Sunday in Berlin. At ten o'clock, A. M., I sallied forth in company with S., and we took our way through the Linden (all the shops in which were closed), to the Dome Church, where the royal family attend, and where is performed the finest religious music in Berlin. It was totally beyond my conception of how nobly simple psalms could be made to sound. The pieces which are generally performed are Mendelssohn's Psalms, and the choir consists principally of young boys, who carry the soprano and the alto, while the bass and tenor are executed by very superior adult voices. The effect is neither strained nor operatic; the voices are too natural to admit of the former, and too numerous to admit any idea of individual display. On the contrary, the several clear silvery voices of the boys, supported and strengthened by those of the powerful basses and tenors, produced a pure and devotional effect, such as I think I never heard in church music. After the music was over we left the Dome Church, and took our way to the English Chapel, where I attend regularly every Sunday, not from any remarkable attractions in the preaching, but because I must hear at least one sermon in the vernacular. Going solely to the German churches may be good enough practice for learning German, but for myself it don't seem to me like going to church, unless the exercises are in English; not because I do not understand German sermons well enough, but because they suggest nothing to me of religious education, or of the worship at home. So to the English Chapel we went. It is a very comfortable little room, nicely arranged, with good seats, an organ, and all the paraphernalia of the English church.

Although there are about forty or fifty Americans in Berlin, they don't come here much to church, or anywhere else I imagine, and the audience is mostly composed of English. Governor Wright, the American Minister, much superior in his moral to his social and intellectual qualities, sets his countrymen a good example in this respect, and is generally to be seen in his pew, with several of his attachés.

The music is led here, also, by a squad of small boys from the minister's, Mr. Belson's, charity school. He, his wife and daughter, have collected quite a number of wild German urchins together, clothed them decently, and taught them English, and the way they should go; they sing old, well-known chants, and I am delighted to be able to shout away on "*Venite exultemus*" and the "*Te Deum*," which are sung every Sunday. The long service being completed, the pastor ascends the pulpit and announces his text. But it is precious little of his sermons that I hear, for while my eyes are fixed upon the preacher, my mind goes wandering off to New Haven, and sits with you, and listens to Dr. C., as learnedly and powerfully he discusses a favorite text, with a good screed of orthodox Calvinism, a slight sprinkling of poetical quotation, and a moving appeal at the close. How different they used to be from the inanities of that man in a black bag, who has at last concluded his mighty discourse. And so from the church to the hotel, and our Sunday dinner; the hallowing influences of the day may be seen translated into Berlin German in the carefully trimmed moustache of the porter, the stiff standing collar and pure white vest of the head waiter, and the nice pudding which forms our dessert on this occasion. I do not doubt that even in Protestant Prussia the Sabbath has, to most, but little more significance than is shown in these trifling matters. Dinner over, the afternoon soon slipped away, and P. and I went to the Dome Church to hear a German sermon. After two hymns, one of them ten verses long, in which the congregation joined with a universality and unction which would have gladdened the heart of H. W. Beecher, the minister, the Rev. Mr. Strauss, the chief Court Preacher, made his appearance and realized to my mind the idea of a court preacher, — his eyes continually smiling, and a manner most soft and insinuating, he seemed to my mind just the man to smooth the way to Heaven for a royal family, allowing no unpleasant truths to clog the paths, and no briers of self-denial to scratch the royal flesh. And his sermon did not bely his outward appearance. His text was Rom. xiii. 12, 13. "The night is far spent," etc. From this he drew a moral which translated into English would read, "You had better be good, you had better be good." Notwithstanding the bad effects of the formality and spiritless morality of the Lutheran Church, it is far, far above the Roman Catholic. The thoughts of the people, though chilled by forms, are in no slavery to confessional and Pope. Still the baneful effects of a too close union between church and state are very perceptible here, and it is difficult to think very highly of a conversion and confirmation which is necessary for admittance to the lowest office, and for license to practice the simplest trade.

BERLIN, *December* 13, 1857.

MY DEAR COUSIN. . . . . Really I must get away from Berlin in imagination, if not in reality, or else the ink in my pen will freeze under its chilly atmosphere; so let us talk together of a region where the airs are softer and the skies bluer than in this Hyperborean city. To Venice! Ah, that lovely place is now for me as well as for you a child of memory, and the tales of its river streets, its merchant palaces, its gliding gondolas and rich relics of Oriental wealth and power, can no longer fill my mind with vague, ill-defined ideas, nor send my imagination off in aimless flights after its as yet unseen beauties, as they used to do in days that are past. Instead of this, I have now, stored up in one of memory's sweetest nooks, a charming recollection which can "never pass into nothingness," but which will always remain in my mind, enriching it with its indefinable charm, and enlarging it with sensations of a beauty at once rich and rare, which it had never before experienced. In seeing Venice, the dreams of my school-boy days were more completely realized than if I had seen even Rome itself; in fact, the city of Sallust and Cæsar, Livy and Horace, always reminded me powerfully of long Latin lessons, and of being kept in after school for not learning them; and Corinne's eternal noise and nonsense gave the *coup-de-grace* to all my youthful interest in the Seven Hilled city. But of Venice all my early impressions were bright and pleasant; she, to me, " was as a fairy city of the heart;" and then what thronging associations the genius of many ages has gathered about her, by the aid of both prose and poetry. I think that Schiller's "Ghost-Seer" struck me as perhaps the piece of literature which was most thoroughly imbued with the spirit of the place; and often when I paced the great Piazza di San Marco late into the night, when the noise of the crowd and the blaze of gas-lights had given place to the silence of the night and the friendly beam of the stars, I would be seized with a kind of superstitious dread, or rather, nervousness, and at such times I would look around, expecting every moment to see the mysterious Armenian watching me intently, or to feel the heavy hand of the still more mysterious Russian laid upon my shoulder. . . . . If I consider Venice aright it is neither the pictures of Titian or Tintoretto, the palaces of San Michele, nor the churches of

Palladio that make it what it is, but the city itself, with the wonderful peculiarities which separate it from every other city in the world. I think that I should have had almost as good an idea of Venice if I had not seen a single picture or entered a single church while there. Not that I did not very fully enjoy the beautiful pictures of Titian. I think that I have as yet seen no paintings which have given me such complete and unmixed pleasure as they did. My two favorites were that gorgeous "Assumption of the Virgin," in the Academy, and that charming votive offering of the Pesaro family, which stands almost opposite to the painter's own monument in the church of Santa Maria Gloriosa. The celebrated "Peter Martyr" I was unable to appreciate very highly, although it is easy to see that it is painted with wonderful skill; but, as I told J. at the time, I had no patience with the situation of the figures, wherein one rather "*scaly*"-looking assassin is represented as rushing upon Peter and his companion, both of them sturdy and muscular men, and killing Peter, while his companion ignominiously takes to flight. Such a state of affairs my own pugnacious disposition is totally unable to comprehend, for from a comparison of the muscular developments of Peter and the assassin, I should think that the saint ought to give the sinner a tremendous thrashing. . . . . . I had a most delightful week in Venice, although at times I was rather lonely for want of a companion. I left her with much regret, and went on to Padua and Verona. After passing through some most charming scenery, I reached Brescia, and spent several very pleasant hours there, most of the time investigating the old Roman remains which were discovered in the temple exhumed there, not a great while ago. . . . . After going through the churches and picture-galleries of Brescia, I went on to Bergamo. I had, that afternoon, from the top of the old Castello, a view of the country round, which surpassed in beauty almost everything that I have seen out of Switzerland. The broad, fertile plains of Lombardy lay before me; in the far west could be faintly traced the outline of the stately Cathedral of Milan, a conspicuous object at the distance of thirty-five miles. Off to the north, the landscape was shut in by the Alps, which enclose and hold in their laps the lovely lakes of Como and Maggiore. To the south appeared in the dim distance the Apennines with cities at their base, while off in the far northwest loomed up the mountains of the St. Gothard, and still further off, Monte Rosa itself, whose name was fully explained by the soft purple and red light which tinged not only it, but the whole range, with the lovely hues of an October sunset, and poured over the whole valley a wealth of autumn glory, such as I had scarcely hoped to see out of our own dear land of the west, the sunset's brightest and fairest home. And I thought to myself, " Give me that western home, with its active manly life, blessed by honesty and upheld by self-respect, and remove far away the pests and plague-spots of this rotten European system ; and if Art cannot flourish under the tree of Liberty, then let Art die " —. . . . . I spent a week at Munich, fairly reveling in Art. What an admirable historical collection the Pinacothek is, for the old German and Italian schools ! . . . . I could talk about these things without ceasing, almost, were it not for two important considerations, first, that I am boring the unhappy victim, and next, the more I say about these things the more I display my ignorance of art, and undoubtedly expose myself to what old Æschylus would called " infinite laughter." But perhaps, after all, my simple impressions won't hurt anybody, and if they interest you, or recall to you pleasant memories of the past year they will fulfill their mission well enough. . . . .

December 19, 1857.

. . . . We had a great excitement at the American Legation last Tuesday, all the Americans in town having been invited there to a *dejeuner*, at which they were to meet that great man, Alexander Von Humboldt. There were so many points of great interest, and also of peculiar ludicrousness, mingling in this affair, that I must give you an account of it.

For myself, I should not have wasted the time to go there, for I had wished to make a separate call on Humboldt, had it not been that Gov. W. had made great promises about sundry buckwheat cakes, mince pies, Indian Johnny-cake, tomato, and many other old friends among the edibles, which, with the help of the ladies, he was going to bring into a state of proper redness. So then I, unable from this Pisgah of expectation to resist this Canaan prospect of American grub, threw down my Gaius, Justinian, and Montesquieu, put on my tail-coat, finished my letter to grandpapa, and pretty punctually at 12 M. presented myself at the Legation, which is in a very nice house, but, alas! up four pair of stairs, which it is a weariness to climb. Considering how lazy most of these Continentals are, it is strange that these four pair do not cause a rupture of diplomatic relations between them and the United States.

In the parlor I found about forty Americans, of whom three were ladies. Of the gentlemen present I need say nothing, except that they looked much as might have been expected. I was not at all ashamed of the New England representation, there being no less than seven graduates of old Yale.

At $12\frac{1}{2}$ precisely, the announcement was made that "Humboldt was coming," and Gov. W., with the assistance of two of his attachés, who acted as aides-de-camp under this trying emergency, arranged his forces to meet the advancing Lion. The disposition of the troops was most admirable; in front he placed the *ladies*, on either side frowned the dark array of black coats, ready to rush to the rescue if the van should falter. The arrangement reminded me of Napoleon's echelon battles, the artillery in front and in the centre, while the infantry and cavalry supported the flank and reserve. Having thus posted us, the Gov. retired, and soon returned again with all his attachés, and also with the venerable object of interest which we had assembled to stare at. The Governor's remarks were very brief, therefore that was soon over.

The old gentleman responded in a few polite commonplaces, which showed that he was much pleased with his reception. Upon being requested to take the big arm-chair, he refused, until the ladies were seated, and then he sat down and began to talk, in a right cheerful and lively way, with the ladies and gentlemen as they were introduced to him, and as they stood or sat around his chair, so I had a capital opportunity to observe him. He wears his years, nearly ninety, with a wonderful life and spirit. He is below the medium height, a frame which seems once to have been compact and strong enough, but which stoops, though not excessively, and seems still to retain strength and vitality. From his eye there still shine remnants of that searching glance which has seen and observed so much more than is allotted to the share of ordinary men, and from his lips still pour the utterances of that wisdom which brought forth "Cosmos," the almost infinite source of universal learning; and upon the ruins of his failing body his soul sits throned, like Lear in the hovel, worn and battered by travel, and tempest, and the flight of years, and labor unending, but yet a kingly soul, before which no living human intellect can refuse to bow in reverential homage, as to a mighty master, who for nearly three generations has lived in close and sweet communion with Nature, and has learned from her secrets which have been hidden from minds less vast and universal. But to return from the spiritual to the material. He was dressed in a button-up over-coat, evidently for the protection of his frame against the winter air, and around his neck an enormous white handkerchief, which reached up to the top of his head behind, and half enveloped his face, so that his utterances seemed to proceed from a white cloud. He talked on all sorts of subjects, principally American affairs at the present day, upon which he was probably as well, if not better informed than any American present. He discussed the Mormon question, and gave it as his opinion, that the troubles which arise in our political world were chiefly owing to our allowing foreigners to vote. The opinion which he expressed upon this subject was such as would gain for him the unanimous nomination and support of the Know-Nothing party, for any office, from President down. He led the conversation in a very graceful and easy manner, and talked more than any one else. He seemed very kindly disposed towards our people, and considering that we were titleless and orderless, he complimented us by not wearing a single one of the numberless titles and orders which have been heaped upon him by many princely hands. He expressed great pleasure, upon leaving, at having met so many Americans. I was so much pleased that I did n't care, although the great American breakfast had turned out a failure. I have thought since, what a grand and noble thing it would be to be such a man, and yet, when I examine myself, I find that my ambition is so wild and foolish, that it would not be satisfied with anything else.

To make a high and clear mark in the world, to leave a name at the sound of which in after days, hearts might thrill and eyes brighten, to do something great, whether in literature, in law, or in active life, something that will live after me, for all this I have deep and restless longings, which, alas, cannot see their way even to a partial fulfillment. . . . .

Among the many benefits which I enjoyed by being matriculated into the University, the greatest is that I have nothing to do with the police, and so when I want to leave Berlin for Dresden, instead of being obliged to get my passport from the police office, and have it *viséd*, I simply procured a "permit of travel" from the University Court, in which it is stated that the "Herr law student, William Wheeler, 5 feet 5½ inches in height, light hair and beard, free forehead, blue gray eyes, regular nose and mouth, oval chin, healthy complexion, has received permission to travel to Dresden and back, the object of the journey being 'For Pleasure.'" This will save me some trouble, for the police at Dresden are said to be very strict, and to conjure with a man's passport abominably, for which conjuring they charge a good fee.

Although Berlin is rather a humdrum and common-place city, yet it has its peculiarities and oddities, and you can easily imagine that I am always on the bright lookout for any such to produce a little laughable excitement. One standing joke, which affords a good deal of amusement, is to observe the manners and customs of the droschky drivers, the droschky being the counterpart of our hack, but the droschky driver has no counterpart in any place that I ever visited.

Very stout in person, somewhat like Old Tony Weller, and protected from wind and rain alike by water-proof hats and enormous overcoats, they sit on the boxes of their carriages, totally regardless of fares or any other sublunary considerations, especially as they generally are wrapt in roseate slumbers. If I were a draughtsman, I could quickly produce a series of "strolls past a droschky stand," which would rival Cruikshank in comicality, and make John Leach hide his diminished head. . . . .

It is rather late in the month to wish you a merry Christmas and a Happy New Year; may you all be preserved in health and happiness through the coming year, and as the year '57 has been for us one of sad parting, may the year '58 behold one joyful meeting; accept this, dearest mother, as my greeting for the New Year.

BERLIN, *December* 21, 1857.

DEAR AUNTY, — I received your kind and interesting letter last Saturday, and you shall have an answer to it immediately, if you will be satisfied with a short one. But I scarcely feel able to write you a letter of sufficient interest to repay you for yours. Since my life has been that of a quiet student, and engaged rather in dry law than in pleasing art, I could give you an accurate account of the laws of the old Roman Republic, or of the Constitution of Sulla, with much more confidence than I could discourse on the frescoes of Kaulbach, the statues of Rauch, or the pictures of Van Eyck or Correggio, although I have by no means neglected art, and the Gallery, which is open free at all times, has been one of my favorite loafing places. It pleased me so much to read your opinions on art and to see that, in a great measure, they corresponded with my own, — and I must acknowledge that I was far more impressed with the interior of the Milan Cathedral than I allowed at the time; but the fact is I had just then grown so in love with Nature's fairest works, that I was scarcely in a fit state to look with proper awe and admiration upon the solemn temples which man had piled in honor of Nature's God. But as I recall in memory its vast dim aisles and glorious pillars, and windows blazing with wealth of art, I can think of nothing which surpasses it but that incomparable building, the Dome of Cologne. May I live to make another pilgrimage to Europe, some twenty or thirty years hence, and see that wondrous structure in a state of completion. But the only one of your criticisms to which I cannot respond, is that upon Titian, "that he is 'of the earth earthy.'" Now I will give up, with perfect willingness, Old Rubens, throw Tintoretto and Giorgione overboard, call *them* earthy if you will, but I can't hear Titian condemned in such a wholesale manner without sticking up for him a little. Far be it from me to place him above, or on an equality with, the spiritual Raphael, who has won my whole heart already by the few specimens I have seen of him, for Raphael's art was surely something divine. But let Titian have a place not much below *him*, and far above the imitators of Raphael, who, like Icarus, soared too high for their waxen wings, and tumbled headlong. The successful painter of the natural surely ought to stand above the unsuccessful representer of the supernatural.

The pictures of Titian's which I enjoyed the most were the lovely "Vanity" in the Louvre, about which I think I have bored you already ; a splendid "Woman taken in Adultery" at Brescia ; and two or three at Venice, especially the "Assumption of the Virgin" and the votive offerings he painted for the chapel of the Pesaro family. To these I can add that charming portrait of his daughter Lavinia, which is in the gallery here, and before which I spend some time at every visit. I expect a great treat when we go to Dresden, among other treasures of art, in seeing his "Christ with the Tribute Money," which is said to be the finest and most perfect among the works of his earlier period. I have been studying up somewhat upon the history of Italian art, for which this gallery affords admirable opportunities. There is scarcely any so rich in specimens of those old pre-Raphael masters such as Filippo Lippi, Vivarinis, Cima da Conegliano, Carpaccio, Andrea Mantegna, Morone, Perugino, Francia, etc., with which formidable array I am beginning to have a dim kind of friendship and acquaintance. In fact, the only way really to enjoy a gallery is to have plenty of time to study it, and let the beauties come upon you gradually.

But enough of art. We received by the *Atlantic* the welcome news that Fernando Wood had been defeated. It was announced by Mr. D., who came in late to dinner with the newspaper in his hand, and the enthusiastic delight of the whole party, Democrats and all, was so great that we immediately had some champagne and drank the health of D. F. Tieman and Pelatiah Perit and the Police Commissioners. It does really seem as if that unfortunate city was now to have a respite from its riots and murders, and was about to lose its reputation of being the most miserably governed city in the world.

December 22. — What an odd day for Pilgrim's day! A mild temperature, drizzling rain, and candles almost all the day long. They don't seem capable of getting up a decent storm here — everything is a mere drizzle, drozzle, and nothing like the weather in which —

"The breaking waves dashed high,
On a stern and rock-bound coast."

The only notice which our crowd took of the day has been to read Bryant's pretty little poem on the subject together, and to wish ourselves at home with unusual fervency. . . .

With love, your affectionate nephew.

BERLIN, *January* 19, 1858.

. . . . During the interval that has elapsed since I wrote, my life has flowed on in such a regular and quiet channel that if I had tried to write before this, I should have been reduced to mere metaphysical discussion or poetical revery, in order to fill up my pages. I am becoming convinced, more and more, that letter-writing cannot be in a high degree conversational. I think that the reason of this is, that a person in a foreign land especially imagines it necessary to have his letters always full of something new and strange and beautiful, and he cannot rid himself of the idea that quiet daily life is a rather poor subject to talk about, after he has been describing pictures, churches, and mountains, and imparting his impressions of the manners of various people. Of this idea I am endeavoring to free myself, but still it is hard for me to think that you can take as much interest in my student experience here in Berlin as I do in the relation of what goes on at home, even down to the most trifling detail and particular. . . . .

The marriage of young Prince Frederic William and young Princess Victoria of England is of course all the talk here now; the city is to be illuminated, there is to be a procession of the trades, etc., and a band of the thirty fairest maidens in Berlin are to receive the princess at the city gates. I do not see where they are going to scare up so many pretty girls as that, for neither in concert, opera, or church, in street or carriage, have I seen a single female who, in our favored land, would be called very pretty. However, notwithstanding all her beautiful portraits in the shop windows, the princess is said to be rather homely, so that there would be a sort of impropriety in her being received by any very charming bevy of beauties.

I have been reading with much interest the proceedings which have recently transpired in the United States Senate with reference to the President's message, and especially the treatment of the Kansas question. Such a piece of flagrant injustice was never heard of, I think, as to force a Constitution upon the people, without giving them the liberty of saying whether they would accept it or not. Especially pointed and full of matter have been the speeches of Douglas; still I am very sorry to see this affair taken up by the leaders of the Democratic party, for I believe that the Free State men will now content themselves with only half-way justice. It would be better to wait longer and struggle more, that in the end the advantages obtained might be more complete and satisfactory. I always look with suspicion upon any change for the better in the conduct and principles of the Democratic leaders; it is almost too much like the conversion of "Reynard the Fox" in the German story, and the subsequent pilgrimage which he undertook.

At the present time, the advantages to be gained by Douglas, in rallying round himself the opposition to the administration, are so great, that they might easily cause the motives and honesty of a much better man to be suspected. His sudden defection seemed to make a great sensation in the administration camp, and Mr. Bigler made a very poor business of it in trying to respond to the little Illinoisian. The poor man seemed as much frightened as the master of a menagerie might be if a lion, whom he had always supposed to be tame and manageable, should suddenly show his teeth and rush at him. . . .

In the last number of the "Weekly Times" there was quite a long sketch of Florence Nightingale, by Mary Cowden Clarke. I was very glad to get hold of something of the sort, as my ideas of that admirable woman had always been of a rather dim and ill-defined nature. Such a charming and noble character, — such active benevolence, with so little show and pretense; so intensely energetic, and yet so retiring; so deeply devoted to one great aim, and yet always so ready to afford sympathy and assistance to any and all of the great needs that touch and move the human heart! To read of such a woman gives a higher and nobler idea of the capacities and powers of woman as woman. I defy any man to rise from that reading without a greater esteem of, and more hearty respect for, the other sex. Another more practical effect of the consideration of such a character must be, I think, to fill many a young man with a lofty emulation to use his powers too — those energetic capabilities, which are the gift of man as gentle sympathy and strong affections are those of woman — for doing good to his kind, and helping, for his part, to bear the burdens of others, which have been laid too heavily on them by adverse fate or unhappy circumstances.

Do you think that the profession of the law is one which allows very many opportunities for doing good? Such, at any rate, is not the generally received opinion; but I hope I may not find, in my own case, that the lawyer necessarily excludes the man of tender and benevolent feelings.

A party of nine of us, all Americans, paid a visit, last Saturday, to the Royal Schloss or Palace. It is an immense building, in the shape of a quadrangle, and equal to a city square at home. The top is crowned by a vast dome, — about the largest one I ever saw, — the top of it being made to resemble the Prussian crown. Some of the rooms within are quite splendid, especially one called the White Hall, which has been newly fitted up within a few years, at an expense of $600,000, — quite a sum to expend upon a single apartment. The whole arrangement of the rooms did not please me nearly so much as that of the palace at Munich, which was built and decorated by a king who had more taste and art in his head than have existed in the thick skulls of the whole Prussian dynasty together, from the Electors of Brandenburg down to the present most gracious king. But nowhere have I seen a palace which looked as if it was built to be lived in, nor have I been in one in which I would be willing to take up my abode for life. I hear that the English palaces are much more inhabitable. Is it then really the case that "comfort" exists, neither in word nor in fact, anywhere save in the Anglo-Saxon nations?

I have driven work at a very good rate since I came back from Dresden, and have managed to accomplish something. I find that keeping constantly busy is an admirable remedy against homesickness, and that azure demon has great difficulty in making an entry. Still there are unoccupied moments, when he gets at me, and seems to make up for lost time by the violence with which he attacks. I am reading, with much interest, Montesquieu's "Spirit of Laws" in the original, to stir up my French somewhat. It is an admirable book, and characterized by great liberality and learning. I should like to arrive at just such scholarly attainments in the law, and to be filled with just such generous and liberal sentiments, as to be able to write such a book.

My principal amusement at present is in attending the concerts of instrumental music, which occur every Tuesday and Friday afternoons. The bulk of the performance consists of symphonies of the great masters, and they are executed astonishingly well. I take my book along and read during the intervals and the performance of pieces in which I take little interest. These concerts cost only twelve and a half cents apiece; and for a subscriber like myself, who buys a large number of the tickets at a time, only six and a quarter cents. My great want just now is that of female society. With the exception of my busy landlady, with whom I hold discourses every morning, as she squats on the floor and makes the fire, I have not spoken to a female for over a month.

To A. W. D.

BERLIN, *Jan.* 28, 1858.

The weather is too important a topic not to be discussed, for it makes a most amazing difference in my whole frame of mind, whether it is a fine day or not. To-day, after a struggle with the clouds, the sun has succeeded in making his appearance, and his beams, covering a large patch of my floor, are extremely grateful. He manages to get up now to a pretty good height above the horizon, and makes a much longer day of it than he did a month ago, when we dined at 2 P. M. by gas-light, and had only about five or six hours of real day. To-day is a sharp, bright January day, one of the coldest that we have had. The snow lies about two inches deep on the roofs, but pretty well worn away in the streets. The broad dirty gutters are frozen up and thus prevented for a time from sending forth their usual rich odors, for which Berlin is famous. The frost has melted off my window, so that I can look out and scrutinize my surroundings, which are not without some interest, although No. 27 Mittelstrasse could not exactly be said to be situated in the most lively part of Berlin. Everybody is walking fast to get out of the cold as soon as possible. An American would be struck by the peculiar head-dresses worn by the German women of the lower classes, for they don't wear any at all, but have their hair very neatly and often very beautifully arranged, and so go bare-headed in the severest weather; otherwise, however, they are generally much more warmly clad than persons of the same class at home. A milk-cart, attached to two large dogs, stands nearly opposite my window. This is one of the regular institutions of Berlin, and dog-carts are to be seen everywhere. The driver of the dog-cart now in front of my window has gone away, and the two poor canine steeds have lain down upon the frozen ground and have gone to sleep. Probably they are now oblivious of their miseries, and have forgotten hunger, cold, and kicks. Doubtless they are gnawing phantom bones in canine dreamlands. An innumerable squad of little children, just returned from school, are busily engaged in hunting up a smooth place in the gutter to slide on, and they make the scene quite lively, with their merry laughter and pretty faces; for German children are pretty, although they get bravely over every tendency of that description before they grow up to manhood and womanhood. Scores of little sparrows are hopping about in the sun, picking up every vestige of food which they can find, and looking as though they considered themselves very spunky in coming out in such cold weather. When the wind blows hard they all sit in a long row, sometimes as many as fifty or sixty together, on the ledge which projects above the windows of a house, and thus find a shelter; but if anything is thrown out into the street which can possibly be eaten, they pop down, just like boys diving off a wharf, one after another, in a very comical way, and the grub is soon disposed of by their busy little bills. Three butchers come out of their shop, laughing very jollily and rubbing their hands; how can they jest so when they have just been depriving a fellow-being of life, for did I not see, a little while ago, a highly-reluctant pig dragged in there, and, doubtless having a presentiment of his fate, filling the air with piercing yells? Oh, ye butchers; what have ye done with that innocent pig? They pass by without answering, and I fear that they do not duly appreciate the enormity of what they have done: probably they were more concerned about the enormity of the pig. A student passes by, with a Chor or secret-society cap upon his head; the colors are black, white, and pink, which shows that he belongs to the Chor known as the Prussians. If he is thinking at all, his mind is probably divided between the number of mugs of beer which he drank last night and the duel which he is going to fight to-morrow; the lives of these society or chor men being made up chiefly, not of "victuals and drink," like "the old woman that lived under the hill," of Mother Goose celebrity, but rather of "duels and drink;" the ambition of the student duellist being to cut his adversary dreadfully with his sword, and his fame measured by the number of needles' lengths which the doctor has had to use to sew up his antagonist's wounds; thus, "five needles" would be a good long cut, reaching from the forehead to the chin, and laying open the whole face.

But hark! from a neighboring court-yard comes a sound which is familiar enough to both of us — the mellifluous sounds of a hand-organ. Now in America I should be inclined to go out and send him away as a nuisance, but here I do not feel so, for probably that poor organ-grinder is an old invalid soldier, who has seen great battles, and whose heart, perhaps, would throb if I should speak to him of Leipsic, Dresden, Lutzen, or Waterloo. It makes me sad to see them, — men who fought like heroes in the "War of Liberation," and gave Germany once more an independent name, when she had been trodden under foot by the French invaders; men who, on the New Year's night of 1814, marching to join Wellington, arrived upon the banks of the great German river, whose waters had been saved to Germany by their exertions, and, with one unanimous cry, rushed forward, and in an ecstacy of successful patriotism shouted, "The Rhine! the Rhine!" Then who, under the generalship of Blücher, arrived upon the bloody field of Waterloo just in time to save the day, and to overthrow the greatest man of the world, — is it fit that such men should go about half like beggars, with a hand-organ on their shoulders, and thus obtain from charity that support which they so richly deserve from a rescued country? After this don't let anybody tell me that republics are ungrateful. Just compare this arrangement with our own. *We* give the veteran soldier a tract of noble land in the West, where he can sit down and spend his life as an independent land-owner, and with the prospect of leaving his children improved property, which will enrich them. *Here* the old soldier, perhaps blind or lame, *receives permission to grind a hand-organ, and for this valuable license he pays a large fee.* It sometimes makes me feel quite enraged, as do many other of the peculiar monarchical dodges which they get up here. . . . .

But now the sounds of the hand-organ are growing fainter and fainter, and as the sun has got behind the roof of one of the houses opposite, I must retire to the other corner of my room, and establish self and portfolio within the genial atmosphere which surrounds my stove for a distance of about three feet on every side. Odd-looking things these porcelain stoves are, and as they stand in the corner of the room, looking so ghastly, they sometimes make me think that probably several years ago there must have been an iron stove there, but it died, and now its favorite place is haunted by its ghost, all in white, sending out also a very ghostly and impalpable kind of heat; I really believe that if we should have any very cold weather I should be found some frosty morning stark and stiff, embracing my abominable German stove, as if to prevail upon it to be merciful and to recall a little of the heat which it used to have when it was alive and a respectable iron stove. . . . . At the risk of repeating what you have very possibly heard before, I must give you an account of our German music here, especially of a series of concerts which come off every Tuesday and Friday, and which I attend quite regularly. In a hall of very large dimensions, without any fixed seats, but filled with small movable tables, with chairs around them, sit a large and highly-respectable audience, the ladies with their knitting or embroidery, the gentlemen with their beer, while upon a raised platform a most admirable orchestra, inferior only to that of the opera, performs beautifully the most classical German music. The programme generally contains two symphonies, three overtures, and one or two andantes and fantasias, and the names of at least three of the six great masters, Mozart, Beethoven, Mendelssohn, Weber, Haydn, and Handel, secure good music enough to satisfy any one. Besides these there are generally a couple of admirable pieces by men of less note, such as Liszt, Berlioz, Cherubini, and Schubert. I enjoy these concerts so much that I can scarcely avoid wasting an afternoon every time one of them comes off. They are so free and unrestrained one can do what he pleases, and I sometimes take a book along and study during the performance of borous pieces.

But my favorite way is to fling my head down on my arms on the table, and, shutting out the glaring lights and the well-dressed people, to listen undisturbed to the sweet music, now so sad, and now so powerful. To me it is beginning to have a deep meaning, such as I was never able to discover in music before. Hark! it is a pastoral symphony of Beethoven. How fresh and clear the sounds rise up, bringing before the mind the pure air and the immeasurable blue sky. That delicate flute-passage reminds of the running brooks and their flower-clad banks, while the soft summer wind gently murmurs in the tree-tops throughout the grand old forest. Now, in merry chorus and with clanging horns, the hunt breaks in upon the solitude, and then departs, fading sweetly, softly away in the distance.

> "Oh, sweet and far, from cliff and scaur
> The horns of elf-land faintly blowing."

And now, the jocund harvest home, the dance after toil, and the song of even-tide, while the sun sinks sadly in the west, and solemn night comes on, heralded by the evening star. How glorious and lovely is Nature! How superior to all Art, since the highest triumph of the latter is to successfully imitate the former.

Or perhaps the piece is an andante by Mozart, and, what is more, a religious andante. Cathedral aisles, with vaulted Gothic roofs and pointed windows, through which streams the richly-tinted light, are the proper places in which to hear such stately music, and the solemn organ should add its voice of power to the noble tones.

Ignorant as I am of the technicalities of music, it seems to me that the first German masters have the power of managing the minor passages beyond all others. Those passages, which when treated by some, are so often harsh, and even discordant, become the gems of German music. Ideas and sentiments are produced by their sad, wild tones which seem beyond the sphere of the major key, and which touch with wonderful gentleness a chord which exists in every human heart — the chord of melancholy. I am afraid that I have not succeeded in expressing my ideas upon this subject very distinctly, but I shall be perfectly satisfied if you understand me, though I am rather afraid that you will laugh at my crude impressions of music. . . . .

I will not bore you with an account of my studies; suffice it to say that my attention is considerably occupied by the interesting writings of a certain gentleman, named Justinian, who lived about 540 A. D. Those highly interesting books of his, the Institutes and the Pandects, I have dipped into somewhat, but as I am opposed to light literature, I have not yet taken up his "Novella." French Law, German Art, and Italian Poetry, manage to give the *coup de grace* to the remainder of my day.

Sunday Afternoon, Jan. 31. — Since I wrote the previous part of this letter, I have been quite gay: Friday night I went to the opera and heard " Der Freischütz " by Weber, and last night I saw Schiller's " Maria Stuart " performed at the theatre. There are many fine gems in " Der Freischütz," especially the overture, about which Jack used to rave greatly, a most charming little evening hymn, which I had often heard sung in church at home, without having any idea where it came from, and the Bridesmaid's Song, " A rosy crown," etc. The celebrated incantation scene was very fine, but somehow I could not help comparing it with the witch scene in Shakespeare's "Macbeth" (which I have also seen here as an opera), and reflecting how much the great poet beat the German on his own ground, although the latter had all the celebrated horrors of the Black Forest to back him. " Maria Stuart " was capitally performed, and gave me a better idea of the customs and costumes of the time, and also of that particularly romantic piece of history, than I had ever had before. The scene in which Mary walks in the garden after having been shut up in the close castle, her enjoyment of liberty to breathe the fresh air, the wishes which she breathed to the clouds sailing southward towards France, and then the following scene with Elizabeth, were admirably done, and the young actress who performed Mary Stuart was received with enthusiastic applause. This I think is one of Schiller's first plays, equal to "William Tell" and "Don Carlos," and only inferior to the "Maid of Orleans" and the "Robbers." I was never so much aggravated by the immorality of the Germans as yesterday. I had been longing all winter to see Meyerbeer's "Prophete" at the opera. Imagine my disgust at seeing it advertised for to-night; of course I did not for a moment think of going, for ever since I came abroad, I have kept Sunday very strictly and scrupulously, as a kind of memento of home; but I can assure you that it was a great disappointment. However my misery was made more tolerable by seeing all my friends in the same condition, and hearing their wrathful growls. It looks odd enough here, to see every one go to church in the morning very devoutly, and then, in the afternoon, to see them out on the skating-ground, or driving round town in their carriages, while, in the evening, a first-rate set of performances is brought out at the theatre and opera. I wonder how the Germans understand the fourth section of the Decalogue. I suppose, however, that this systematic breaking of Sunday is rather political than religious; the government finds it necessary to give the people amusements on their day of leisure, in order to keep them out of mischief; music, public shows, illuminations, etc., divert their minds from politics, and destroy in a great measure their self-respect, and that is just what the rulers want to bring about.

BERLIN, *February* 1, 1858.

DEAREST MOTHER, — Notwithstanding the promise contained in J.'s last, that I should get a letter by Saturday's or

Wednesday's mail, I began to fear that I was not going to get any after all, for Monday passed by without bringing me anything, and Wednesday, when the mail of January 13th was to arrive, seemed to intend to treat me in the same manner. All the others announced letters from home, when we met at dinner, but S. and myself, the two most homesick and letter-hungry men in the whole crowd. Imagine my surprise and pleasure, on coming to my room about 11 P. M., to see a small white object lying on my table, which I was sure was not there when I went out. You can picture to yourself the haste with which I lit my lamp, and the eagerness with which I tore open the packet, to see who the letters were from, and what was the state of affairs at home. . . . . There was something extremely pleasant in receiving such kind letters so late in the evening, and a great relief to my mind when it feared it was about to be disappointed. You will not be surprised to hear that I had a most distinct dream that night, the scene of which was laid in New Haven. It was a lovely summer evening, and I was walking in Hillhouse Avenue ; every tree and house seemed so familiar, and when I got up near No. 10 I could see them through the open window at supper. I hurried by, for fear that they might see me, and make me come in there first, when I wished my first welcome to proceed from you. I turned the corner ; our house looked charming in the summer twilight ; in a moment I was on the front step ; both of the hall doors were open, and you were all walking up and down the hall and out into the back piazza. A. was there with J., and you had one of the children on each side of you. No one saw me, and I was just starting forward to utter a well-known cry, when at the very instant that my foot touched the threshold, I woke up and found that I had kicked off the superincumbent feather bed, and was in a frigid condition, the very reverse of summer. Was it not provoking that I could not dream just a few minutes longer ? . . . . Letters are the only voices we have left us to call up affection's echoes, and to prevent the absent from continually hovering in an atmosphere of doubt and anxiety. I shall be very glad when the time shall come for us to speak no more through silent letters, but audibly and face to face.

Well, the great transaction is finally done, and England and Prussia are now united by the closest of ties. You will of course read all about it in the quotations from English newspapers. In my next I shall be able to give you an account of the performances and festivities which greeted the royal couple on their entry into Berlin, which is to take place next Monday, February 8th. The English ambassador illuminated his house, on the night of the wedding, with a variety of crowns, eagles, and similar monarchical devices; and prominent above all, that highly sensible motto, " Honi soit qui mal y pense." Extensive preparations are going on for illuminations which are to come off next Monday, especially around the equestrian statue of Frederic the Great, which stands in the finest part of the Linden, nearly opposite the University. But I must close for the present.

February 2. — What a day this is! Boreas is out in pontificals, howling through the streets, and now is blowing before him a blinding snow-storm. As I was going to lecture this morning I saw a grand hat chase. The unhappy Teuton pursued for about an eighth of a mile his fugitive beaver, which now trundled on its brim, and now flopped over from side to side; at length he trod on it, and succeeded in recovering it, though in a sadly dilapidated condition.

I await with considerable impatience your answer to my letter in which I asked your opinion with regard to my going to Italy. I recognize the value of the journey more than ever now, since I have more of an idea of the artistic attractions of that fair land, from the histories of art which I have been cramming somewhat. The idea of possibly going to Greece, with such a companion as Mr. D., is almost too charming to be fulfilled. I am in hopes that it may come about, and I take it for granted that you will approve of what will give me so much pleasure and perhaps great profit.

BERLIN, *February* 14, 1858.

DEAR J., — .... I was glad to hear that you took an interest in what I wrote about the Dresden Gallery. I should have said something more about it in my last, if my space had not been mostly taken up with discussing another subject. It is such a perfect treasure-house of art that it would be unjust for any one to suppose that its fame rests wholly upon the few great *chef-d'œuvres* of Raphael, Holbein, and Correggio, which it contains. These form, it is true, its first and highest class, but there is besides these a large number of very beautiful specimens of the best masters, less impressive, perhaps, than the above, but almost equally interesting, although in a less intense degree. The Venetian school is quite well represented, although I scarcely think that its greatest master is seen here to the best advantage. The celebrated tribute-money picture of the Saviour did not please me very much, though doubtless, in mere mechanism and artistic workmanship, it is a masterpiece. The face of the Saviour struck me as unmeaning and soft, the expression being rather an unpleasant one.

The principal Venus, too, has been so severely cleaned that the look of the flesh is anything but natural, and the face has rather an insipid mien, which I have seen in several of Titian's pretty women. Palma Vecchio, a contemporary of Titian, has contributed two or three gems to this collection; a Holy Family, much after Titian's manner, which displays a strange mixture of the rich coloring and brilliant effects of the Venetian school, with a sweet simplicity and a pervading religious feeling such as is found only in the older masters of the school; in the more modern ones, as Tintoretto and Paul Veronese, the religious sentiment is either neglected for, or obscured by, the splendid pageants, rich garments, and graceful animals which appear so universally in their pictures. Paul Veronese's anachronisms amuse me very much. The best of his works at Dresden is that of Faith, Hope, and Love conducting a prominent Venetian family before the

Virgin's throne. The whole getting up of the picture, dogs and garments included, is splendid, and the faces of the three angelic virtues are very lovely. In another fine painting of his, the "Finding of Moses among the Bulrushes," Pharaoh's daughter and her maid-servants are all dressed in what I suppose to be the height of Venetian fashion about the year 1575, A. D. In the Pre-raphaelite works of the Roman and Florentine schools, the Dresden Gallery is sadly deficient, and it does not possess a single specimen of the works of Giotto, Fra Angelico, Ghirlandajo, Filippo Lippi, Leonardo da Vinci, or Michael Angelo, except in copies; and Andrea del Sarto, "the faultless painter," does not appear to much advantage. On the other hand, the collection is very rich in specimens of the Bolognese or Eclectic school, the Caracci, Guido Reni, Francesco Albani, with his charming groups of dancing cupids, Domenichino, Guercino, whose paintings are so soft and sweet. But, although I have a delightful recollection of them all, yet as I took no notes when at Dresden, my account of them would have to be too general to be interesting. But there is one class of painters which I cannot, in justice to my own feelings, pass over unnoticed, and that is the school of the Netherlands, the cabinet pictures of the two Teniers, especially the younger Adrian Brouwer, Van Ostade, Metzu, Mieris, Hondekoeter, and Gerard Dow. The first and last of this list, viz., David Teniers the younger, and Gerard Dow, are my most especial favorites. The feelings aroused by these pictures might be said to be exactly the opposite of those excited by the great works of the religious painters, and decidedly of a lower order; but then it is impossible, or at least painful and unnatural, always to keep one's emotions up to the correct pitch of howling enthusiasm; and it was a great relief to me, after gazing for some time at the Madonna di San Sisto, or those beautiful Correggios, to go into the smaller rooms and exercise the muscles of my diaphragm by having a good laugh at one of Brouwer's horridly vulgar pictures, representing two drunken peasants knocking each other over the head with their beer jugs; or perhaps some subject still more at variance with decency and high art. The subjects represented here are nothing more nor less then the mere simple scenes of every-day Dutch life, and are pervaded thoroughly by that humor, which an unprejudiced by-stander, with keen perceptions of the ludicrous, can find in almost every observation of his fellow-men when gathered in a social way. In this class there are very different styles: Brouwer and Van Ostade give us caricatures; their peasants are inexpressibly coarse and ugly, the combats extravagantly violent, and their subjects abominably vulgar. Teniers, on the contrary, takes the same class of persons, and gives us in a few bold and yet soft touches a most lively and pleasing picture of Dutch life. A capital specimen of Teniers is in the Museum here at Berlin, the "Temptation of St. Anthony," a favorite subject with the Dutch painters, and which is founded on the old church legend. The saint sits at a table in a desert place, with a large book open before him, but from the perusal of which he is somewhat hindered by the delicate attentions paid him by a legion of devils of all sizes and shapes, among whom are portraits of his mother-in-law and his wife, who show the cloven hoof just peeping out from under their dresses. The latter offers him a goblet of wine, which he puts aside with a deprecatory look. The devils display in their number and great variety the inexhaustible genius of the painter. Almost every time that I look at this picture, I discover some new and untried devil, when I thought that I had previously hunted up every one. The greatest charm of all the paintings of Teniers consists in the perfect acquaintance which they show with the phenomena of social life. Perhaps none but artists can tell how such wonderful effects are produced by so few apparently careless touches upon a few inches of canvas, but there is a something in their general result which cannot fail to attract us, although we cannot explain why, for "one touch of nature makes the whole world kin." I think that the life-like humorousness of Teniers bears the same relation to the inspired beauty of Raphael, or the graceful fancy of Correggio, that Shakespeare's comedies do to Milton's " Penseroso," or Sir

Philip Sydney's sonnets. I suppose that Hondekoeter is the most celebrated painter of live birds that ever lived. One of his best is a grand bird-concert, of which a venerable owl is the Max Maretzek, and beats the time with one foot in a most impressive manner. However, there is one small rooster, by Metzu, which beats anything of Hondekoeter's, or any one's else that I ever saw in that line. The scene is at the stall of a game-seller, and the proprietor holds out in his hands towards a young woman this ideal rooster, who sits with a demure air, as if to say, "You see I am obliged to submit to circumstances, but should n't I like to peck?" It seems to me perfectly astonishing that anything so spirited and natural could be represented in so very small a space. . . . . You will be pleased to have heard that I have given up my blue ideas which I had about going to Italy, and also hope to realize a long-cherished day-dream of mine by seeing Athens and Greece.

BERLIN, *February* 18, 1858.

DEAR M., — . . . . I have had, for the past three weeks, a very bad cold in the head, to which has been added a cough and sore throat. The former was aggravated, and the latter brought on, by the coldness of the weather on February 8th, when the young Prince William and his bride, Victoria of England, made their triumphal entry into Berlin. Monday morning opened very fine, and when P. and I sauntered out into the Linden, it was odd to see what a crowd of people had already gathered there. As early as 10 A. M., the companies of the trades were in motion to take their places; for, by an ancient custom, the procession which receives a newly married pair into Berlin is almost wholly civil in its character, consequently the trades, many of them very ancient and venerable, were out in strong force. After some forty postilions, came the Guild of the Butchers and Merchants; the former, according to an ancient custom, performing the part of civil escort, while a couple of troops of dragoons formed the military one. After these had passed, followed the court carriages, drawn each by six horses, containing those interesting developments of human nature known as lords of the bed-chamber, gentlemen-ushers, ladies-in-waiting, maids-of-honor, etc., who find honor and glory in being the domestics of a king, and carrying the lap dogs of a princess. Then, in a splendid gilded coach drawn by eight horses, escorted by the governor of the city and the president of police, came the newly married pair. . . . . But I let the royal carriage pass by, and observe some of the trades and guilds which follow in an immense body 25,000 strong. The first is the Shooters' Guild. Their privileges date from 1548 A. D. They were followed by the miners in their strange dress, as weird as the gnomes and kobolds whose treasures they are employed in plundering. The Guild of Tinners were led by two knights of the olden time, covered, horses and all, with a splendid imitation of the gold and silver plate mail. It seemed to me to symbolize the difference between the present age and the age of chivalry; for the solid iron and steel of those times we have substituted a sort of tin imitation, which can neither stand the thrust of spear nor the blow of sword, but it glitters and that satisfies us. The Fishers' Guild, two hundred and fifty years old, had a very picturesque uniform, and carried a large seine to which bells and other musical instruments were fastened, so that when the net was shaken it produced a most silvery and delightful chime. The Turners exhibited a beautiful set of mammoth chessmen which excited my cupidity. The banner carried by the Goldsmiths, was said to have cost 10,000 thalers. That despised class of men, the Tailors, turned out strong. They are a most venerable body, dating from 1288. How strange it is! empires rise into being and sink into nothingness, a Hapsburg succeeds to Hohenstaufen, and a Stuart to a Tudor, revolutions shake thrones and then are quenched in blood, but meanwhile the Tailors' Guild pursues the even tenor of its way, and now, in the year of grace 1858, turns out in such numbers as assures a plentiful supply of galligaskins to the good city of Berlin for at least a generation to come.

The procession closed with the machine-shop men to the

number of eight thousand, — locomotive and steamboat builders, car manufacturers, and makers of all the conveyances and engines and accessories which mighty steam, the genius of the nineteenth century, brings in his train. They are the representatives of the present age, as the old Trades and Guilds, with their ancient privileges, were of the past.

In the evening the city was brilliantly illuminated. C., P., S., and I went out, and, formed in solid phalanx in the crushing crowd for mutual offense and defense, we had the pleasure of picking up and rescuing an old lady, who fell down in one very bad rush, and stood a pretty good chance of being trampled under foot. I had never seen an illumination before, and so I gave myself up to a kind of childish delight at the swarming crowds, the bright lights, and the happy faces. The torch-light procession, about which there had been so much excitement and bother, did not come off then, but was transferred to Saturday evening, and was a capital affair. . . . . At the palace the committee went in to present the homage of the students to the prince and princess. They gave three cheers; not the glorious Anglo-Saxon hurrah! but a mean-spirited hoch or high, which does n't ring out worth a snap. The most interesting scene of all was the breaking-up place, where they put out their torches and sang "Gaudeamus." I was pleased to see how they do such things here, and I satisfied myself that although their paraphernalia and gettings-up were much better than with us, they did not have half the spunk and spirit of our jolly American students. . . . .

February 19. — . . . The homage I rendered to the picture of the "Sistine Madonna" was neither to the actual picture, nor to the personages which it represents, but to the glorious human mind which called it into being. I have, and hope that I may always have, a heartfelt admiration for whatever is good and noble in the world, whether in the empire of studious thought, of the creative art, or of brave and manly actions. The enthusiasm which I feel upon gazing at a masterpiece of painting, no more deserves to be called adoration than the sensations which one experiences on contemplating the genius of Shakespeare, the gallantry or bravery of Tancred and Bayard, or the virtue of Washington. No, instead of being troubled by this, you ought, on the contrary, to rejoice at anything which tends to develop the reverent sentiments, and to bring the hollow on the top of my head, where the bump of veneration ought to be, up to the level of my other phrenological developments. You know that I am rather given to exaggerate, and I must ask you to make allowances for all that I may hereafter say, in the heat of enthusiasm, and believe that the sight of new lands, new governments, and new modes of thinking, have only served to make me prize more highly than ever my own land and the ideas in which I was brought up. . . . .

TRIESTE, *March* 7, 1858.

DEAR M., — At last we have got in motion again, and after a painful journey of six days, I have once more reached the shores of the Adriatic, and expect to-morrow to be in Italy, I hope, if not to enjoy myself, at least to get warm ; for the history of the past trip down here has been one in which the demon of cold has played a prominent part, and even in this latitude it is bleak and chilly, while the dreadful Boro of the Adriatic sweeps through the city with great fury. On getting up this morning, I heard a confused hubbub, and looking out of the window that faced a large square, saw a most motley crowd of persons of all ranks, ages, and nations, with their varied costumes, making the dreary market-place quite gay. There were Greeks with their white camises, Turks with long cloaks and red fez, dark-eyed and haired nondescripts, whom I took to be Albanians, villainous-looking Italians, while here and there a sun-browned face with brown hair and beard, spoke of the Anglo-Saxon or the Dane. Most of them were sailors, dressed in the odd habiliments which the sons of Neptune get themselves up in when ashore. They lounged around with a rolling gait, and a knowing swagger, which reminded me of my old friends of the *Australia*. On Monday last, March 1st, after the mails had disappointed us all by coming in without any letters for any of us, we packed our trunks, paid our last bill to our landlord, and made our last farewell to our landlady and children, and tore ourselves away from the friendly hand-grasps of J. C. and T. D., and took the train for Dresden. We went to our old quarters, the "Golden Angel." In the morning we sallied out, and made a bee-line of the straightest description for the picture-gallery. We spent an hour in looking at engravings on the ground floor, and I enjoyed very much observing the progress of the child of Painting from its earliest infancy to the present time. It is quite remarkable that, in these old times, the art of the engraver was not an absorbing one, but was rather a companion or adjunct to those of sculpture and painting, so that we find almost all the earliest engravers of any note, such as Wohlgemuth, Marc Antony, Albert Dürer, and Rembrandt, to have been also first-rate painters. We then went up that splendid, wide staircase, to that picture-gallery which, while it falls below the united collections of both Rome and Florence, claims for itself the proud title of being more than a match for either the Pitti or Uffizi alone, or even Vatican. I greeted the two lovely Madonnas of Raphael and Holbein, the beautiful Correggios, thec harming Vandykes, and many others, as dear old friends. It was so pleasant to see again those master-pieces that had so delighted me at first, and which, during the two intervening months, had always been capable of bringing up in my mind fair, and good, and noble thoughts. I think that I regarded the Sistine Madonna with increased admiration, but with less excitement and enthusiasm, than when I first saw it in the winter; but I must, once for all, disclaim the slightest feeling of adoration, either then or now. But for that serene and sweet Madonna of Holbein, I felt, more than ever before, a sort of tender regard and love. The whole scene was such a family one, and so home-like, that it seems impossible to believe that it was a superhuman being who was standing in that room, but rather a noble and powerful woman, who had come to the house of sickness to give her aid, and to fill it with the sweet and holy light. I shall always remember that picture as long as I live,.for to comprehend and enjoy it, one needs only to be a devoted lover of his own mother and his home, which is a quality I am inclined to think that I possess in pretty fair measure. I spent nearly all day in taking a last look of all my favorites, and discovered several new ones with which I was not particularly acquainted. . . . .

We left Dresden Tuesday, at midnight, having fortified ourselves with all the hot things which the restaurant at Dresden could afford. More cheerless, not to say dangerously cold, affairs, than these German cars, it would be difficult to conceive of; and there is not a particle of fire to counteract the cold. What wonder if the unhappy passenger gets gradually stiffened with the frost. After a regular purgatorial ride of three hours we reached Badenbach, the Austrian frontier, where we bade farewell to our old friend, the thaler, who had so long been our stay and support in Berlin, and now shook hands with the Austrian florin, a rather scaly coin, who is considerably larger than his Dutch and Bavarian cousins. By means of packing ourselves together in one carriage, so that we bore a striking resemblance to Cerberus, one body with three heads, we managed to keep decently comfortable during the following four hours before reaching Prague. Just a little while before we reached Prague, the sun rose gloriously, and by dint of scratching a hole through the thick frost which had collected on the car window I managed to see it very nicely. We arrived in P. chilled through, and it took a hot stove and a good hot breakfast to restore circulation, and to bring back the idea that life was still extant in our stiffened bodies. In the expectations which I had formed of the picturesqueness of Prague, I was not disappointed. It lies in a low basin, surrounded by lofty hills, some of them quite precipitous, and crowned on the west side by the imposing mass of the Hradschin, the palace of the old Bohemian kings, — while through this hollow flows the noble Moldau, a broad and majestic river, and, I should think, a rapid one. When I saw it, it was motionless. You can form some idea of the appearance of Prague by supposing a city, full of oriental and splendid buildings, to be surrounded on all sides by a ring of hills higher, and almost as steep, as East Rock, with a broad river flowing through it, crossed by three bridges — one celebrated for its size and antiquity, another a beautiful suspension bridge. The first church we entered contained the tomb of Professor Olmsted's old friend and fellow-laborer in the star-gazing department, Tycho Brahe. It is made of a slab of red marble, and contains his effigy, and above, his motto, which is certainly a very noble one, similar to that on John Dixwell's grave behind Centre Church, — *Esse potius quam haberi* — To be, rather than to be esteemed. Opposite to the church stands the town hall, which retains somewhat of its former Gothic beauty. This building, and the place before it, stand as memorials of the fearful excesses committed, under the guise of religious zeal, by both Hussites and Catholics. It was from the windows of the Rathhaus that the Hussite mob, in 1419, ejected the magistrates who had excited their displeasure, and it was in the square in front of it that the Protestant leaders were executed, after the battle of the White Hill had given the Catholics the unexpected preponderance. The old bridge is the longest in Germany, and is 500 years old. It is decorated at regular intervals with the statues of saints, but the great lion of all is St. John Nepomuk, who was drowned here for his religious opinions, and has, from this circumstance, become the patron saint of bridges all over Germany. The Hradschin is the most immense pile I ever saw, and inclosing in its vast quadrangle a cathedral, chapels, public halls, public offices, seems like a small city, complete in itself. We ascended to the top of the cathedral and enjoyed a view of the city lying beneath us, beyond, the broad plains of Bohemia, while to the west, lay the White Hill, where Frederic yielded to Ferdinand, and the light of Protestantism in Bohemia and South Germany was put out in torrents of blood. One of the oddest things in Prague is the Jews' quarter, which is said without doubt to have existed since the founding of the city. Everywhere appeared ancient Abraham, who looked anxious to do a little business with me. Every window was tenanted by some worthy Sarah, or Rebekah, while in the doorways and middle of the street rolled scores of dirty urchins, whose bird-like probosces left not the shadow of doubt that they were sprigs and cuttings of the vine that was brought out of Egypt. The house of Huss stands in the Jews' quarter, and I took considerable interest in observing the dwelling-place of the great early reformer, although I must confess myself dreadfully ignorant of his more minute history, except that he was called the Great Goose of Bohemia, that he cackled loud and to some purpose, that he was roasted in a meadow near the good city of Constance, which meadow I saw, and finally, that it was with a quill from the tail of this goose that Luther wrote his renowned thesis. I was highly delighted with all I saw of the good city of Prague, and wished the weather would have permitted me to walk out of town, to get acquainted with the whole situation of the place. I left that evening at 7, and in that long nocturnal ride of twelve hours, was in a state of torpid suffering which lasted till I reached Vienna. That night seemed to be equal to several long days, and even now the remembrance of it makes me shudder all over. . . . .

FLORENCE, *March* 18, 1858.

DEAR BROTHER, — Of my doleful ride to Prague, my visit there, and the still more miserable vigil on that freezing night, for twelve hours from Prague to Vienna, I have fully informed mother. I should like to suggest to the Germans, as a suitable motive for a new revolution, the coldness of the night trains in winter. A Magna Charta might be extorted from the sovereign, with the privilege of having the cars warmed with the waste steam, or at least having vessels of warm water for the feet. The Prussians gained less than this by the revolution of '49, the only permanent benefit they acquired by that bloody contest being the permission to smoke in the streets of Berlin. Thursday, March 4th, was devoted to seeing what there was to be seen. My eye was first caught by a Gothic spire, of the richest style of work, towering above everything around. I traced my way to it, and was soon standing beside the Cathedral of St. Stephen, one of the purest and finest buildings of the Germanic style, my own favorite class of architecture. The south tower, which is the only one completed, is a most magnificent specimen of its kind; covered with rich ornaments, trefoils and pinnacles on every side, yet not so as to prevent it from diminishing gradually and regularly as it rises. It mounts to the height of 444 feet, showing in all its course the perfect grace and beauty of the Gothic style, which consists, perhaps as much as anything, in the subordination of the infinitude of small ornaments and highly-wrought, minute devices — (which the eye notices with pleasure as it passes, while it is not arrested by them) — to a grand and symmetrical whole; a gradual lessening and lessening in size, until the cross at the top seems almost to pierce the sky, — such is the spire of St. Stephen's. We had a long, weary climb up that beautiful south tower, but finally reached the summit and were amply repaid for our exertions. We sat down and enjoyed the view, just where, almost two hundred years ago, the brave Count Starhemberg had sat and watched, almost hopelessly, the vast army of the Turks, which was, day after day, drawing closer and closer around the beleaguered city. And from this spot he saw the approaching banners of the brave John Sobieski of Poland, who speedily joined battle with the infidels, and did for Germany, at Vienna, what Charles Martel did at Tours for France. The tide of Islamism has, since then, rather set in the opposite direction. The fire watch lives near the top of the cathedral tower, and has capital arrangements for discovering the exact situation of a fire. The watchman was very polite in explaining his telegraph to us, and when he found out that we were Americans, he insisted upon our coming into his room and sitting down. I found out that he had fought against the Italian patriots in 1849, and likewise against Kossuth in the same year. He wanted to know how Kossuth was received in America. He was full of enthusiasm for his own country and the Emperor, and decidedly down upon Kossuth. It seemed so odd to meet one who had fought for Austria, and to hear the other side as it were. . . . . .

I was much disappointed at the specimens of Albert Dürer

which I saw at Vienna, for I had been led to suppose that his genius shone with peculiar brightness in the galleries there. As yet I have seen nothing of this master which justifies the high and apparently overweening rank which has been accorded to him in German art. . . . We bade good-by to Vienna at an early hour, and soon the spire of St. Stephen's faded away behind us to the northwest. At first the cold condensed the vapor on the windows, and made it difficult to see anything, but soon the warm sun melted off the frost, and we had a fine chance to survey the scenery and the snow mountains through which this railroad pursues its course. It was difficult to know which to admire most, the lofty mountains clad with snow, the precipices, the deep defiles, the tremendous forests, or the wondrous skill and engineering enterprise with which so fine a railway had been conducted through them. At a place called Gloggnitz the railroad runs, by a series of curved gradients, right up the side of what might almost be termed a precipice. Some time after leaving Gloggnitz, having passed over several viaducts and through one or two tunnels, we found ourselves again almost exactly over the same town, but now at a height of 700 feet above it. The effect produced by such a climbing of our ferruginous steed was strange enough. . . . We dined at Gratz, a fine place which I should have liked to visit further. We saw a ruined castle remarkable for astronomical observations made in it by Tycho Brahe. We crossed the Drave at Marburg, and got to Laibach in the evening. I will say nothing about it except to quote from the hand-book a tradition of the place, which appears to me rather beats Banagher. They say that Jason and the Argonauts, fleeing from Colchis, after they had gobbled the golden fleece, sailed across the Black Sea, then up the Danube, and up the Drave to where Laibach now stands. This town they founded, and then went down to the Adriatic, and there embarked for Greece. As the Argonauts could not very easily have dragged their ship over land to Trieste, perhaps a search at Laibach, by some of those grubbing German antiquaries like Lepsius, might bring to light some fragments of that renowned tub the *Argo*. We got into

Trieste late; and now permit me to pass with a great leap from Trieste to Parma, where I arrived Thursday evening, March 11th. I had a good full day at Parma, which I enjoyed more than I have any one day for a long time. There is scarcely a city I have seen that presents more art charms than this old nest of the Farnese family. It has a noble cathedral, its cupola being adorned with the celebrated frescoes of Correggio, said to be the finest work of his genius in existence. The Academy of Fine Arts is not deficient in works of other artists, while in those of Correggio it can easily bid defiance to the rest of the world. The antiquarian would find a splendid library, noted for its oriental treasures, and a museum of antiques which is very interesting.

FLORENCE, *March* 22, 1858.

. . . .
Just think of it,—only four months more, and I shall, D. V., be again at home among you all, and then my absence of fourteen months (how fearfully long it will have been!) will seem like a half-forgotten dream, partly pleasant and partly disagreeable, although I hope that the rougher features will be mellowed down by distance and time, and that I shall be able to look back upon my European experiences with more pleasurable sensations than can be felt while actually passing through them. But I can assure you that it is pretty hard work to be obliged incessantly, day in and day out, to visit treasure-houses and masterpieces of art, and so often to pass by spots renowned in history, or hallowed by memories of great and noble men. This sort of thing keeps the emotions too incessantly upon the stretch, and at last one almost wishes to run away to some quiet place, and let the works of art remain without a single glance of admiration or criticism, the interesting spots without a single rapture or sigh. . . . I wish that I could have time to digest all that I saw, and that after a week of "doing" I might retire into some quiet country place, to read and study and work up what I had seen with my own ideas, making the memory of it my own property, and not dependent for half my recollections upon guide-books and

works on art. But this it is impossible to do, for almost every respectable city has its picture-gallery and its museum of antiquities; so, for example, Bologna, where we spent Sunday and Monday of last week, the 14th and 15th of March, possesses a very fine gallery of paintings, which of course we *had* to see, for it would have been sacrilege to have passed through the city without visiting the fine works of the celebrated Bolognese or Eclectic school, who believed in choosing from each master his best quality, and uniting them all in one picture ; so they proposed to add to the majesty of Michael Angelo and the feeling of Raphael the coloring of Titian and the grace of Correggio. They succeeded better than might have been expected from such a patchwork sort of theory, as the names of the Caracci, Guercino, Guido Reni, Albani, and Domenichino amply prove. Bologna is, as might be supposed, a capital place to study these great masters; but I will not bore you with any further account of my visit to the gallery (as I have enough of such stuff to tell you besides), except to say that I enjoyed them all very well, but liked Raphael's beautiful St. Cecilia more than any of them. . . . . On Tuesday morning, at 4 A. M., we left Bologna by diligence for Florence, and of course for the first couple of hours sat in mortal terror of being suddenly attacked by a fierce gang of banditti ; for these robbers of the Apennines are an odd, lazy set; they have their holes in Bologna, and an hour or so before the diligence starts they leave the city and go up the mountains a few miles, to wait until it comes along; they then strip it, and its passengers, and go back to Bologna to finish their morning's nap, or to eat their breakfast, for which they will have acquired an appetite by this little stroke of business: consequently the worst part of this worst of Italian roads is at the distance of about an hour or two from the city, and when we passed through it, the light, just beginning to grow gray with the dawn, was exactly the right kind for a robbery. The road looked fit for an ambuscade ; and once, when I saw three men in the middle of the road, I felt sure that they must be the scouts of the gang, and expected every instant to hear a whistle and to see black-bearded ruffians start from every bush, like Roderick Dhu's men in the "Lady of the Lake." I now reflected upon my unhappy opera, "The Bandits of the Apennines." How little, when I wrote it, did I think that I should ever be so near the haunts of those much slandered gentlemen, or stand such a good chance of sharing the unhappy fate of my two heroes, Mr. Brown and Mr. Jones! I now perceived the difference subsisting between quietly writing a work in the study and going through the actual experience in real life. However, they would n't have got much cash out of our party, for we were as poor as pilgrims, and I, the treasurer and financier of the crowd, had only one solitary napoleon. For that lonely piece of gold I was prepared to resist to the death; and I have no doubt but that our crowd would have made the only good resistance of the whole party, our escort included, which consisted of four rascally gens d'armes, who rode after the diligence in an old wagon, looking very fierce and valiant, but whose first warlike act, I strongly suspect, would have been to rat over to the enemy with their arms and ammunition, and then come in for the lion's share of the booty. At any rate, notwithstanding our perilous condition, we passed the dangerous spot with our throats uncut and our pockets unemptied, and that napoleon survived to buy me a black vest in the good city of Florence. I had occasion, in quite an odd way, to bring all my philological acquirements into play in quite a short time. Our whole party dismounted from the diligence to walk up hill. When we reached the steepest place in the Apennines, and as we were walking past another party of gentlemen, one of them accosted P. and S. in French; but they passed by in silence, and I was obliged, in order to remove any thought of discourtesy, to pitch wildly in upon "the universal language," although during my stay in Berlin my German had driven almost all my French out of my head. However, I got along pretty well, and tickled the Parisian gentleman hugely with some well-aimed praises of Paris. From the other fellow, who was an Italian, I picked up some information about the state of Lombardy which interested me. They were greatly puzzled to know what countryman I was. Englishman? No. German? Nein. Russian? No. Italian? No. Swede or Dane? No. "Well," exclaimed the Frenchman, "you must come from some other world!" "I do," said I. (Here their eyes opened widely.) "I come from the *New* World." Whereupon they fell into a train of thought which led them to the correct conclusion that I was an American. Upon returning to my seat in the diligence I found by my side a fat and jolly old fellow, who attacked me quite fiercely in Italian, and I managed to pay him back pretty well; for I have a great faculty of going right in on a language, and making the greatest possible use of what I know. This is of course the best way to improve my practice, and already I have got on quite famously in the sweet tongue of Tasso. Well, I mustered up enough Italian to give him a tremendous idea of the grandeur of the American eagle, our free institutions, and the facility with which a man can there acquire land, and raise himself from the position of a laborer to that of a proprietor. Indeed, this last is what interests foreigners more than anything else about our country. Our freedom they think very good, but scarcely understand it; our universal franchise they cannot comprehend, but the fact that either by squatting, or buying at a very low price, a man can acquire a property in the soil, and work it for his own use, and not as a tenant, seems to have a peculiar charm for them, and probably there is nothing which contributes more to form the idea prevalent among many persons here, that America is a sort of Canaan, in which all persons become instantly rich and happy, as soon as they have crossed the Jordan of the Atlantic. My old friend had travelled a great deal in the Orient on business, and told me some very interesting stories of his voyages, and also of two or three shipwrecks, from one of which he escaped with nothing but his life and night-shirt, leaving behind his "best suit of clothes and his cargo worth 80,000 florins."

Happening to hear P. address S. in German, he inquired if I spoke it, and appeared perfectly delighted when I told him.

I did. He was a Swiss from St. Gall, and we had a good talk together about the scenery of that region, with which I was well acquainted, having been through it last August with H. C. So then for a good part of the rest of the way to Florence we kept it up steadily in German, politics, travels, railroads, etc., being the chief topics. As we approached Florence, we went back to the Italian tongue again, and I amused the driver and postilions with sundry delectable anecdotes of the American turf; Trustee's great feat of trotting twenty miles in fifty-seven minutes and a fraction quite astonished them, and I fear that I laid myself open to the reproach of having drawn the long bow. Our scenery all the way was really magnificent, for almost all the innumerable peaks of the Apennines were covered with pure white snow, much of which had probably fallen within a week. We came across at just the right time, for while it was warm enough to be comfortable, there had not been a sufficiently long succession of warm days to melt the snow, and thus both destroy the beauty of the scenery, and make the roads bad. We reached Florence at about 8½ P. M., and were soon comfortably settled in the fine Hotel de New York, which commands about the best view, and is in the best situation of any hotel in Florence, even if its name and low prices were not a sufficient recommendation. We made a very nice arrangement, and got capital rooms, looking right out on the Arno. What shall I say, my dearest mother, of the pleasure, the delight, which I have experienced since I came to this place; from the cold regions north of the Apennines with their snow and chilly atmosphere, from the bleak, dreary plains of Berlin, and the cheerless hills of Prague, to a city where Spring has already taken up her abode, and already begun to scatter flowers over the face of the earth. The warm, balmy air, the bright sun, the blue sky, the green earth, and the busy, jolly city, all make simple existence here most pleasant, while the snow-clad summits of the Apennines loom up in the northeast, to remind us of what we have been through. I have always before my eyes the stream of the Arno, rendered picturesque by its four fine bridges; beyond this the beautiful hills of Bellosguardo and Arcetri, covered to their summits with fine villas; and the latter (Arcetri) made interesting as well as beautiful by the Tower of Galileo, from which he took his most important observations, and in which he extended to Milton a friendly hospitality, when the latter was on his travels. The meeting of two such men, so surpassingly great in worlds of thought, so different yet equally majestic, the contemplation of the actual and the ideal heaven, would be a worthy subject, I should think, either for pencil or pen. Never did two men come together who had done more for the progress of thought and the enfranchisement of the human mind from slavery, whether political, physical, or religious. How noble must have been their conversation! What glorious thoughts must have flowed forth in calm and dignified utterances! What a boon to have seen them seated together: Milton, with his long, flowing locks, and face of solemn beauty; Galileo, with that massive forehead, and firm-set mouth, which said, "But it *does* move." They might be taken as representatives of Poetry and Science, while upon both a still nobler name can be bestowed, for are they not both Apostles of Human Freedom? There are many interesting memories in Florence, but none which interested me as much as this. As regards the endless treassures of art in this city, what shall I say? The bounds of a short letter like this are scarcely equal to the enterprise, and I will try to tell you something about them at length in the first letter I write you from Rome.

March 24. — I paid a very pleasant visit yesterday to Mr. Powers' studio here, and took P. with me; having been previously fortified with a letter of introduction to Mr. Powers from J. C., we had the pleasure of seeing him in person, were received by him very cordially, and invited to his house this evening. His family is said to be a very pleasant one, and we expect to have quite a nice time. We then spent an hour or so in the studio, admiring the statues, some of which are very beautiful. I liked his "California" best of all; it is the property of Mr. Wm. Astor of New York, and will go there as soon as it is completely finished. She stands with the divining-rod (which reminded me of Dousterswivel, in the "Antiquary") in her hand, and at her feet a large mass of quartz crystals, as indicative of the home of the gold ; her whole form and contour was very suggestive of richness and wealth. Allegorical representatives of countries are often far-fetched and hard to understand, but I think that in this statue the idea of the "Golden State" was admirably hit. I was also very much delighted with a "Fisher Boy," listening to the sound of a sea-shell which he holds to his ear ; and a " Proserpina," beautifully sculptured, and adorned with acanthus leaves. To say nothing of Mr. Powers' many other excellences, I think the shape of his heads is more classic, and the arrangement of the hair more graceful than I have ever seen them in any other.

ROME, *April* 2, 1858.

DEAREST MOTHER, — Here I am at last in Rome, and here I have been for nearly a week, but have scarcely yet come to believe that such is the case. It seems so unreal to be for the first time in a place of which I have thought, heard, and read so much, and whose very name is so suggestive of a thousand bewildering and yet most important and interesting memories, that for a while there must be a strange confusion of thoughts and objects in the mind, and, in a great measure, an incapacity to enjoy or appreciate any one thing as it ought to be enjoyed and appreciated. I suppose that the true pleasure derived from the monuments of the past, especially of Rome, consists rather in the remembrance of them in the future than the contemplation of them in the present. . . . . Perhaps it would be a good idea for me to give a day at Florence, that you may know how I spent my day, and also what pleased and impressed me most in that fair city, which is so full of noble art and interesting memories. As we must make a long day of it, it will be better to be up early in the morning, and off before the throng of sight-seers shall fill every place, like the frogs of Pharaoh, driving away by their presence the Genius of the Past, who likes best to linger in lonely places, and to be sought by few though fervent worshippers. In this church which we now enter he is to be found, if anywhere, for along its noble aisles are placed monuments adorned with sculptured wreaths, carved with high-sounding inscriptions, supported by marble mourners. It would seem as though a line of illustrious kings had been gathered to their dust, and we are not mistaken, for these are indeed kings, — monarchs of thought, powerful to sway opinions and feelings and emotions, worthy of admiration from all nations and all ages. Michael Angelo, Galileo, Alfieri, Dante, and Machiavelli, the highest names which Florence can boast in the several departments of Art, Science, Prose, Poetry, and Politics. Dante's tomb, it is true, is but a cenotaph, for his ashes repose on the shores of the Adriatic, at Ravenna, where, he died. If you will take my arm we will pick our way to another church, some distance off, St. Mark's by name. The church we will not enter, but will turn aside and go into the cloister connected with it. Passing now from cell to cell through passage, refectory, and chapter-house, we enjoy an exhibition of the finest specimens in existence of the early Pre-raphaelite art, for it was in these cells that Fra Angelico spent twenty years of his life, and, an artist wholly self taught, surpassed in feeling, spirituality, and sentiment, the first masters of the day. The defect of his style, belonging to what is called the Byzantine school of painting, is more than compensated by the deep sentiment of devotion, the singleness of heart and soul, which fills every pious face of saint, and angel, and adoring mortal. .... A gentle grace, peculiar to this painter, pervades every form, and every face is lit up with a sweet light of love and absorbed devotion.

For some reason, I am much more delighted with expression and beauty of sentiment, than either majesty of form or broadness of coloring. I can leave to sculpture and its friends all the charms of sensuous form and marble reality, — give me the truthful tender thoughts which painting alone can express. I have not time to say much about the cathedral. It is quite imposing, but homely enough, after the Gothic pile of St. Stephen's at Vienna. The dome is the largest in the world, surpassing in size that of St. Peter's. Passing by the cathedral, we arrive at the Church of San Lorenzo, embracing in its cloisters and quadrangle the Sacristy, the Medician Chapel, and the Laurentian Library. In the Sacristy are the monuments of Lorenzo and Julian de Medici. The latter is adorned with two figures by Michael Angelo, representing Day and Night. The Night sinks back in an attitude of perfect repose, and yet it would be impossible to mistake her sleep for that of death. The following, one of the many praises pronounced upon it, I must translate for you. "The Night whom thou seest sleeping in so sweet an attitude, was sculptured by an angel in this stone, and while she sleeps has life, — wake her, if thou believest me not, and she will speak to thee." To this Michael Angelo replied, putting his words into the mouth of his master-piece : " Pleasant to me is my sleep, and still more my existence in the marble stone, for not to see, not to feel injury and sad disgrace, is my great happiness. Therefore, wake me not ; oh, speak low ! " . . . . .

We will turn now to the chambers of the Laurentian Library, — this glorious collection of precious manuscripts, — the most important, if not the most extensive, in Europe, a proof of what enlightened patronage can accomplish, when it exerts itself in the proper channels, and works for the future as well as for the present. Among the manuscripts are several extremely interesting ones — the earliest manuscript of Virgil,— a " Divina Commedia " of Dante ; a Horace, with notes by Petrarch ; and what had the greatest interest to me, as an incipient lawyer, the earliest MSS. of the Pandects of Justinian, brought from Amalfi in the twelfth century, the discovery of which led to most important results, as it introduced the study of the Roman law, and the general practice of that style of jurisprudence, all over Europe, except in England and the Scandinavian nations. It is said that, when first brought to Florence, honors were paid to it as to a holy relic ; tapers were lighted before it, and magistrates stood bare-headed in its presence. I have my doubts whether the same reverence would be paid to any legal treasure in the present day. I think it highly improbable that the printer's devils stood bare-headed before the first edition of even " Blackstone's Commentaries." I should enjoy spending a winter in Florence, with a permit to use this library, and disport myself among the old MSS. as much as I liked.

April 6. . . . . Early on Thursday morning, March 25, we set off on the cars for Sienna, the railway being finished to that city. Rode through a beautiful and fertile country, watered by the Arno, until we changed cars at Empoli, where the road branches off for Pisa. From this point we missed both Arno and fertility, and the remainder of our ride to Sienna was uninteresting enough. The arrangement which I had made with the diligence office at Florence proved very convenient. We found a man at the depôt, ready to carry our baggage. While walking from the gate of the city to our hotel we passed the diligence office. The coach from Rome had just arrived. The passengers were scattered about outside, and directly my eye fell upon a face, and an old cap, which I recollected to have seen occasionally last summer in Switzerland, and after making a desperate rush forward I found that I had made no mistake, and that it was B. L. E. W., of course, was not far off. They were going immediately to Florence; but as the train did not leave till 4½ P. M., we had a good talk together, as touching the passes of Switzerland, the Jungfrau, Interlachen, and our Michel. I believe that W. expressed the sentiments of L. and C., and I know that he expressed mine, when he said those four weeks in Switzerland were the happiest time of his life. We sallied out and *did* several of the notabilities of the place. The Cathedral is a very large and handsome church, and of very decent antiquity, as it was finished some time in 1200, and has several objects of curiosity. The pavement is inlaid with large mosaics of Bible stories, which are funny enough, consisting of gray marble inlaid upon white. A single subject is sometimes oddly represented in two parts, on opposite sides of the church, with another entirely different subject between. Thus, on one side, the youthful David has just let drive from his sling a certain smooth pebble from the Brook Kishon. After passing over considerable space, in which are several other groups, we see the aforementioned lump quietly travelling through the air, and, a little further on, our old friend Goliath of Gath, who, though not yet hit, has a large hole in his forehead, where the deadly missile is about to strike him, — thus proving the truth of that well-known remark, that coming events cast their shadows before. The frieze of the cathedral is the oddest one I ever saw. It is adorned with heads of the popes down to the time of Alexander III. They are fearfully ugly, and are all alike. Pope Joan, the only female who ever occupied in person the pontifical throne, used to be in the collection, but she has been taken away, and one called Pope Zacharias was substituted in her place. I was obliged to view everything very hastily, as the time was so limited, which was quite a disappointment to me, as I had begun to take some interest in the history of early art, and the school of Sienna bears a very prominent place, as being that in which the school of Italy first had an independent existence, apart from the instruction, although not as yet from the influence, of Byzantine artists. The preëminent claims of Sienna above Florence, as the mother of Italian painting, rest upon the works of one Guido of Sienna, who lived some forty or fifty years before Cimabue, and about a hundred before Giotto. His finest, nay, I believe his only work, which I saw in the Church of St. Dominick at Sienna, — a rather colossal Madonna and child, — is somewhat stiff, but decidedly free for that time ; and, considering the age of the picture, the poor light in which it was placed, and other disadvantages, I can but consider it as a very remarkable work of art. It bears date 1221 A. D., so that it must be 637 years old. It is wonderful that it has been preserved at all in a condition capable of being understood.

We strayed around town with our friends, exchanged experiences, discussed all the news of the past year, from the Lecompton Constitution to ———'s engagement, and finally saw them off for Florence. My next labor was to go to the stables of the diligence company and engage a carriage in which to make our descent upon Rome. I pitched upon a very nice light one, and we had nothing to do but to wait the arrival of the fourth member. In due time he arrived; and I had better give you a description of him at once. Tall and stout, chunky face, chunky nose (both red), chunky English whiskers, twinkling eyes, a good-natured mouth. He was an Irishman, — English chaplain at Nice, but full of good humor, bulls, quotations from Horace, and Irish songs, so that close upon each other followed "Video ut alta stet nive candidum Soracte" and "Bryan O'Flynn had no breeches to wear." Imagine us, then, rolling grandly out of the city of Sienna by the Porta Romana, and the passengers busily engaged in smoke-compelling, with the solitary exception of your virtuous brother, who has remained as pure of tobacco as he was when he first went forth, an innocent child, from the threshold of the A. H., to wander in this wicked world. . . . . Our horses carried us splendidly over the ground, and on the first day we accomplished seventy-five English miles. We got that evening to a place called Bolsena, situated on a lake of the same name, a beautiful sheet of water, but as dangerous as it is beautiful, for its shores are desolated by the most fearful form of malaria. You may believe that we felt uneasy about spending the night in such a place. However, I was very careful to shut my window before making my entry into a very suspicious-looking bed; but I was so very tired that neither dread of malaria nor the attacks of fleas could suffice to keep me awake. The next morning we were up bright and early, to enable us to get to Rome before the diligence should arrive there with its load of passengers to occupy all the vacant rooms in the hotels. I was nearly dressed, when I heard a great rattling in the road, and, looking out of the window, saw the diligence tear by with seven horses and full of people. We had our horses put to while we took a hasty breakfast, and then off at a good rate, the postilion inspired with hopes of enormous drink-money before his enraptured eyes. We got ahead with jolly good speed, and, on driving into the third post town, Viterbo by name (celebrated for its handsome fountains and pretty women), imagine our satisfaction at seeing the diligence standing in the road empty and horseless. We got fresh horses, and were soon far ahead. We had passed the last post-station, but were several miles from our place of destination, when, upon reaching the top of an eminence, the postilion rose in his saddle, and, pointing to the southwest with his whip, exclaimed, "Roma!" It was a magical word enough, and ought to have aroused in a young student like myself, not wholly devoid of enthusiasm, strong and pleasant emotions; but, whether I had been disgusted with Byron's nonsense about the Niobe of nations, I did not feel any more moved by my first view of the Eternal City than if it had been Berlin. The thought that occupied me most was one of anxiety lest we should find all the rooms at the hotels occupied, and have trouble. I feel thoroughly ashamed that such should have been my frame of mind.

We spent a couple of hours in looking for rooms without success, till we happened to come across J. C., and we set off together, and succeeded in getting the rooms that had been occupied by T. D. and his party a year ago. They are on the Pincian Hill, right opposite to the Church of the Capuchins, and rendered interesting to me by the story of "The Improvisatore." We are very comfortably situated, and our remoteness from the central parts of the city is compensated by the healthiness and quiet of our district. . . . .

ROME, *April* 14, 1858.

MY DEAR COUSIN, — I can assure you that a letter should have been upon the stocks for you long ere this, had it not been for a peculiar combination of circumstances which prevented it. . . . . This afternoon I have been out of doors for the first time in three days and a half, and you can easily imagine that my spirits are in a condition of most enviable jollity. It is a most lovely evening. Rain has been pouring down steadily all the morning, but now it has cleared off to display a sky of the tenderest blue, strewed here and there with light clouds, which promise to reflect beautifully the gorgeous tints of the approaching sunset. The bell of the Capuchin Church is tolling mellowly to vespers just across the street, and the bare-footed friars go slowly in to prayer, many of them aged and infirm, destined soon to lie, cowled and hooded skeletons, with their brethren in the strange burial vault of the Capuchin Church. The rays of the declining sun light up the roof of the French barracks, and on, beyond, the imposing mass of the Barberini Palace. I can never look upon those walls without thinking of a certain portrait which they contain, and of the melancholy fate that casts so sad and yet so winning an expression over that sweet young face. I have an American friend who thinks, rather profanely, that the face of Beatrice Cenci, as painted by Guido, is more beautiful than that of the Sistine Madonna! At the rear of the house, looking through the entry which connects our magnificent suite of apartments, I see my two friends and *compagnons de voyage* busily engaged in smoking, and hurling an occasional *bajocco* at sundry cats who have taken advantage of the fine evening to disport themselves in the courtyard. Everywhere there is the pleasant influence of the evening, and now, as the sun has sunk beneath the horizon, and the fleecy clouds are all bright with his last beams, I feel that this is really the "Bella Italia,"— an appellation which I had for some time hesitated to give to the snow-covered hills of Lombardy and Tuscany. Excuse this digression into the beauties of nature, but I thought that you would enjoy such a little *aquarelle* painted from my own window, and giving you some idea of my surroundings in Rome. I wanted to catch it with the rain drops and the sunset glow upon it before it grew too dark to write, otherwise I should not have said a word before thanking you for your kind letter of last January. . . . . I am glad to hear that you are getting better contented with New York as a dwelling-place, and allow that there is some good existing out of Europe. For myself, I am rather liable to go to the other extreme, and see a peculiar charm in everything American, simply because it savors of home. Undoubtedly the true course lies between these two extremes, — the nobleness and truth of our free institutions, adorned with the charms of European art, and the higher civilization, in matters of taste, which exists on this side of the water, would, it appears to me, realize the dreams of statesmen, — a more beautiful republic than even the Greek mind of Plato ever imagined. . . . .

The union of the kingdom of Venetian Lombardy with the Austrian possessions proper had to be effected at any cost; and, as the railroad is now completed to Trieste, the once proud cities of Venice and Milan lie eternally at the feet of Vienna and of the stupid autocrat who reigns there. . . . .
I have enjoyed Rome beyond my fondest expectations. The Baths of Caracalla, the Forum, and the Coliseum, would alone be worth a passage across the Atlantic. . . . . I have bought for you the panoramic pictures of the clergy which you desired, also a set of similar pictures of the monastic orders; the old monks are very leathery, but funny, especially the Capuchins. — With much love to all, I am ever your affectionate cousin.

ROME, *April* 16, 1858.

. . . . I have been in Rome now nearly three weeks, and am beginning to enjoy it to the full. The old ruins, the stately churches and palaces, the works of art in the galleries, all begin to wear a familiar aspect, and I know now just what my favorites are, and can go right to them without delay. As my letters to you were shortened by my attendance on the ceremonies of Holy Week, perhaps it would be only just for me to tell you something about them. The phenomena of the Romish Church have an interest to a philosophical mind, as showing to what splendid emptinesses and absurdities the souls of any people can be brought to yield their homage and adoration. The first religious spectacle was the procession to St. Peter's on Palm Sunday, and the blessing of the palms in that church. I saw little, and understood less. The cardinals bobbed to the Pope, and the Pope to the cardinals, — they kissed his toe, and he patted their heads, — then the palms were consecrated and blessed, and sprinkled and mumbled over, and carried from the high altar to the Pope's throne, and from the Pope's throne to the high altar, and then distributed to the happy recipients. On Wednesday, having fortified myself with that most necessary article of clothing in Holy Week, my old tail-coat, I went up to the Sistine Chapel to hear the first "Miserere." The corridor of the Vatican was separated from the Chapel by three long flights of stairs. I put in practice my old habit of going up two stairs at a time, and got ahead finely, so that I entered the Chapel among the first. As the service did not begin until 4 P. M., and the "Miserere" until about 6, I had time to gaze at the products of Michael Angelo's genius upon the walls, and at the end of the chapel, the gigantic Sybils and Prophets on the triangular spaces between the windows. They struck me as being wonderful creations of inspired majesty and grace, and the subsequent visits I have made them has fully confirmed this opinion.

But to the performances. About 4 P. M., the violet-coated cardinals, with their capes of ermine, began to enter, — their trains carried by clergy of the lower orders, who, after they had arranged the trains all right, sat down at the feet of their superiors with an appearance of great humility. At length Pope Pius arrived and took his throne, when began the chanting of the penitential psalms, with lessons interspersed. At the right of the altar stood a tall candelabra, containing fifteen candles. At the end of every psalm a candle was extinguished. The chanting was very loud and boisterous. Once or twice a very beautiful passage was inserted, as if to give a foretaste of what was to come. The series of performances was kept up a very long time, and every one who had to stand was very tired and uneasy. The Pope's guard chattered together, the English around me talked and laughed quite loudly, and I heard of an American family producing a basket of provender, and going into sundry sandwiches. Nothing could have seemed less like a religious service which was being performed on a festival of the most solemn nature, and it was impossible to feel impressed, either by the chapel itself, or the rite which was going on in it. When the candles were reduced to one, the choir broke forth with the "Miserere," — the remaining candle was taken down and carried under the altar, to typify Christ's descending into the earth. Finer music I scarcely ever heard, but it seemed so operatic, and got up, that I was totally unable to connect it in any way with the mysteries of religion. The levity of every one around, the universal sense that it was a mere show, and, more than all, my extreme fatigue, were sufficient to drive away every feeling of devotion, and leave no higher sentiment than that of mere critical admiration, — just such as we accord to a successful singer at a concert. The performance closed with a strange, loud knocking of a stick, said to indicate the descent of Christ into purgatory, and the release of those imprisoned there. On Good Friday I went to St. Peter's, and heard the "Miserere" there. It was a much finer one than that of Wednesday, and far more expressive of religious sentiment, although not as well performed artistically, as by the choristers of the Papal Chapel. The grandest ceremonies of all were those of Easter Sunday. . . . . .

The procession came in all the grandeur and pomp of regal splendor. The Pope was dressed in a long robe of gold and silver, with a tiara on his head that flashed back the light of jewels. He proceeded up that glorious nave, seated himself upon his throne, — then service began. The music was splendid, and one of the best parts of it was the mass, chanted by the Pope himself, the choir giving the responses. The conclusion of the service was the music representing the visit of the Marys to the sepulchre, their inquiries of the angels, and then, after a dead pause, the glad annunciation that "The Lord had risen indeed." This last sounded with thrilling and startling effect from a band of silver trumpets. More inspiring or beautiful music I have seldom or never heard. With magnificence even greater than before, the procession swept out of the church. From the balcony in front the Pope gave the threefold benediction to the vast multitude outside, and the letters of indulgence, on which the benediction is written, were thrown down for the people to scramble for. The guns of the Castle of St. Angelo pealed forth, and nothing now remains except the illumination Sunday night, and the fire-works Monday night on the Pincian Hill. The most ordinary effect produced by these spectacles seems to be a contempt for all religion, when, in the capital of the Christian world, the Christian religion is made such a farce. It is now April 20th. . . . . I have spent days at the Forum, and have made myself familiar with that most interesting collection of ruins, the Arches of Severus, Titus, and Constantine, the beautiful temples, and the palace of the Cæsars, displaying the ruins of the most magnificent dwelling that emperor ever lived in. I have seen the Coliseum by sun-light, moon-light, star-light, and no light at all, up stairs and down, and have risked my neck in scrambling after flowers that grew in its ruined arches. I have spent hours in the Baths of Caracalla, hunting up the localities of that stupendous building, admiring the rich mosaic pavement, which preserves its color to this day as when it was first laid down, going to the vast swimming hall, now to the vapor baths then to the cold baths, observing the library and other rooms for study and luxury with which the Romans surrounded their bathing halls,— a style of institution which does not exist at the present day. I was most intensely interested in the Pantheon. There is a combination of circumstances in it which make it, to me, perfectly irresistible. First, the grand Grecian portico, with its glorious perfect columns, then, the dome within, rising, as it were, from the very ground, and lighted only from above by the aperture through which streams in the sunlight. When first I entered, the sunlight was streaming upon a slab in a side chapel, and upon that slab was inscribed a name dear to every heart not dead to all that is wonderful in art. It was the grave of Raphael.

Austrian Steamer "Dalmatia," among the
Ionian Islands, off Leucadia, May 4.

Once more I am for a season a traveller on the sea. . . . . The long swell of the Ionian Sea jogs our little steam-tug up

and down in such a peculiar way that, if this letter ever is
finished, you must attribute it to a series of fortunate rolls and
heaves of the vessel, rather than to any active volition on my
own part; but I cannot resist the temptation of writing to you
from the deck rather than the close cabin, in the hope that I
may give you some idea, taken from an actual view of nature,
of the light-blue seas, the soft skies, the balmy air, and the
craggy but picturesque islands, redolent of classic fame, with
which we are now surrounded. . . . . I spent the Sunday
after leaving Rome at Leghorn, and the next Monday was
devoted to a visit to Pisa. We visited those four celebrated
buildings, the Cathedral, Baptistry, Campo Santo, and the
Leaning Tower. The Leaning Tower, one of my oldest
friends and acquaintances, I felt considerable satisfaction in,
first, in recognizing it as my old friend, and second, in perceiving that it did actually lean, in a manner obvious to the
naked eye of an ordinary traveller, without the aid of a guide-
book. I took much interest in examining the old Cathedral,
which has so long been a bone of contention among the
critics, which is nearly a century ahead of its time. In the
Campo Santo I was especially pleased with the series of Old
Testament histories; — the grace and charming naturalness
with which those Oriental stories are told, struck me as being
decidedly wonderful for that early age of painting, while the
numerous portraits and Middle Age dresses introduced,
stamped with great distinctness the strange custom of that
period, in mingling their own friends with the patriarchs of
old, and every-day occurrences with Bible history. The Baptistry is a very beautiful building, and contains a most remarkable ancient pulpit, and exquisitely-carved baptismal
font of Greek workmanship. We went back in the afternoon
to Leghorn, and were forced to exchange our large Neapoli
tan steamer for a very small boat, called the *Eden;* but,
alas, its accommodations savored of anything rather than
Paradise. In this small tub, with the seductive appellation,
we embarked for Genoa. The sea was rough and the weather
rainy, and we were tossed around fearfully, making almost

every one deadly sick. P. and I stood on our dignity as old sailors, and succeeded in escaping the demon of sea-sickness. As evening was beginning to fall on the Ligurian Hills, the fair white palaces of Genoa the Proud appeared, lining the hill-side. With this delightful but unsatisfactory view of the grand old city of the Dorias I was obliged to rest content, as, if we expected to be in Trieste by Friday, it would be necessary to take the earliest morning train for Milan, deferring my view of Genoa until my return from Greece by way of Naples. Our ride through Sardinia was delightful. We took third class tickets, and found the wooden seats and open cars very pleasant for a warm day. The lower classes too, with whom we came in contact, seemed to be far more comfortable in circumstances than I had seen them in any other part of Italy. It was perfectly refreshing, after spending a month in wretched, slavish Rome, to find myself once more in a country where the people were not wholly destitute of self-respect, where manufactures seemed flourishing, and where the press was free. As evening came on, I had the pleasure of pointing out to L. the white pinnacles, bright with the setting sun, of glorious Milan Cathedral, and by eight o'clock we were comfortably settled in the fine old Lombard city ; and, as the moon rose about nine, you may be sure that we did not miss the opportunity of seeing the cathedral by moonlight. It really seemed like a spectacle of fairy-land, — the almost endless forest of pure white pinnacles, slenderly projecting up into the blue ether, looked like a luxuriant forest of aquatic but graceful lilies with white stalks, while below spread an expanse of glittering marbles, carved into windows the most quaint, canopies the most rich, borders and ornaments the most exquisite, while from their pedestals and pinnacles looked down many hundreds of statues of saints of the olden time, once persecuted and tortured and put to shame and death, but now gazing down from their marble effigies, clad in white robes and with palms in their hands, as calm and quiet and beautiful as the moonlight which lights them all with her silver glory. I spent a good part of the day I was at Milan in studying its exterior, both below and above, wondering over its immense roof, and sitting, half awe-struck, half-entranced with delight, at the foot of the pillars which overarch its glorious nave and aisles. We left Milan in time to catch the boat for Trieste. We entered the harbor about 1 P. M., and one of the first objects that we descried on shore was the venerable form of T. D., with a most outlandish cap on his head, frantically waving his hands to us, and a few moments more and we were in each other's arms, united again after a separation of just two months. We spent that afternoon in talking, writing letters, drawing money, seeing about passports, etc. Early the next morning we went to the rooms of the Austrian Lloyds, and took passage for the Piræus, and by Saturday afternoon we were off in the *Vulcan*.

May 6. Gulf of Corinth, just off Phocis and Mount Parnassus. — Again I take up my pen to continue this letter, and to tell you how thoroughly paid I feel already for the voyage I have undertaken, by the beautiful and classic scenes which I have seen, the noble natural landscapes which have surrounded me by sea and land, and, more than all, by the fresh and buoyant enthusiasm which, even before we have reached Athens or passed Corinth, fills my pulse with bounding blood, and makes my veins thrill, as we sail through these lovely seas, with ancient cities on one hand and venerable mountains on the other. I have trod the shore and soil of classic Greece, and have had a foretaste of the pleasures of both eye and soul that await me on the classic hills and plains of Attica. But, before I loose wholly the rein of my joyous delight, permit me to sketch my sea-path hither, and give a short log of our voyage. We left Trieste in the *Vulcan*, one of the best steamers of the Austrian Lloyds Co., and soon that trading town of the Adriatic faded from sight, and we ran down the Illyrian shore in the teeth of a stiff breeze, which soon freshened into a fierce gale. We sat down to an excellent dinner with about a dozen gentlemen, Greeks. Of all that party, only five, including L. and myself, appeared at breakfast the next morning, — our venerable mentor, T. D., being among the slain. I never knew a Sunday pass with so little suggestion of its being Sunday. As we could n't go to church ourselves, we sneaked off to the stern of the vessel, near the wheel, and indulged in a quiet hymn or two. The next day we crossed the Adriatic, towards Albani, and ran along beside the Acroceraunian Mountains. True to their old classical reputation, the famous Thunder Peaks got us up a highly respectable storm. A tremendous sirocco blew from the south, having on its wings the parched air of Lybian deserts, raising the waves to lofty surges, before which our good vessel pitched and tossed for several hours without making any headway. But our steamer was very new and strong, and we could in safety laugh the mad waves to scorn, — indeed I should have enjoyed it extremely, had it not been for two untoward circumstances. First, Mr. D. lay in his berth, most pale and miserable; and, secondly, we had an unfortunate *contretemps* at breakfast which deserves to be mentioned. At the *dejeuner à la fourchette*, which occurs at 10½ A. M., we were seated some five ravenous individuals, the unterrified ones, who made up by their rapacity for the absence of the rest. We had had several severe lurches, which had made the glasses rattle; but I, filled with a serene confidence, had just helped myself to some very nice chicken curry, when suddenly a crash on deck was heard, as if a whole sea had fallen upon it, and this was instantly followed by a tremendous roll to larboard, which sent every movable flying in all directions. Those on the starboard side found themselves deprived in a moment of every necessary of life, while we on the larboard were covered with the edible mercies which flowed in from every side. I was perhaps more favored than any other individual, and received in my lap one bottle of wine, two cups of tea, a large amount of chicken-curry, a couple of oranges, and three knives. I met, on the whole, with no injury but such as the steward's wet cloth soon repaired. We on the larboard side repaired to the safer situation of the starboard, and got through our breakfast without further calamity. The storm moderated in the afternoon, and we reached Corfu, but we were deprived of a view of it, as it was 9 P. M., and we were to leave at midnight. Here we left our noble steamer for a much smaller one, *Dalmatia* by name, whose course lay through the Gulf of Corinth to the Isthmus, giving us a better view of the countries of Greece than if we had gone around Cape Matapan. As the factotum of the crowd, I had the extreme pleasure of going on shore at Corfu at about 10 P. M., to see that our transfer from one steamer to another was properly noted on our tickets. I did the business, and congratulated myself in getting out of that den of vile soldiers and sailors without having my throat cut or my pocket picked. We got off at midnight, and, when we woke in the morning, we found ourselves off the Albanian coast, called in old times Epirus, and soon entered the Gulf of Arta, now the Bay of Previsa, and had about an hour to recall our recollections of that tremendous sea-fight, of which the world was the prize, — the contest of Roman with Roman, until Cleopatra fled and Antony followed her, traitorous to his own manhood, choosing for himself an ignominious death, and leaving to his rival the vast empire of the Roman world.

When I commenced writing this letter, we were just passing the fatal rock from which the unhappy Sappho sprang for the purpose of at once putting an end to her life and misery. I should have enjoyed immensely having a few days to roam on foot over Ulysses's rocky island, and identify the localities with those of the Odyssey. It is said that Homer lived some time in Ithaca, and his topography, always correct, is in this island wonderfully accurate. We touched at the principal town of Zante, entered the Gulf of Corinth, touched at Missolonghi, — name thrilling to the heart for its glorious defense. We arrived by noon at Patras, and went ashore, and here our feet first touched the soil of Greece in the old district of Achaia.

ATHENS, *May* 9, 1858.

DEAR J., — . . . . 10 P. M. I have just returned from a very pleasant visit at Dr. King's, where we were all invited to tea. We called there for the first time last evening, where we were very cordially received by the good Doctor, who is truly one of nature's noblemen, and a thorough American to the backbone. Nor did he confine his hospitality to a simple greeting, but immediately invited us to stay to tea that same evening, and, as we were elsewhere engaged, he insisted upon our coming this evening to take tea with the family. This evening he asked us to come to tea to-morrow evening, to meet a few friends. This kindly behavior on his part is not, I believe, unusual. He seems to combine most admirably all the qualities of a patriotic consul and a Christian missionary. His family also is very pleasant, although he himself is the principal attraction. The daughters have been educated in America, and are very pleasing. . . . .

I am so sorry that I wrote such unsatisfactory letters from Rome, — but the truth is, that I did my best under the circumstances. . . . . Some few visits that I made to the studios of artists gave me a glimpse into that life, a mixture of æsthetic delight with frequent physical suffering, — full of beautiful ideas, but too poor to buy the paint with which to lay them on the canvas, or the marble from which to hew them into visible form. Mr. Paul Akers, who sculped Uncle B.'s bust, has a work about completed in the clay. It is called "The Drowned Pearl Fisher," a great attempt, and it was painful to see the excessive interest which he took in it, as it approached completion. I made a call at the studio of John Gibson, who is the greatest English sculptor living. He was engaged on a statue of "Bacchus." The figure had a lyre in its hand. I asked Mr. G. why he had put the attribute of Apollo into the hands of Bacchus, whereupon he regaled me with an interesting account (from Pausanias, I think) of Bacchus with a lyre, by Praxiteles ; and he also mentioned that he had seen a fine old gem which presented a similar subject. Notwithstanding his reputation, I do not think him equal to Powers.

May 12. — The excursions of the past two days, yesterday to Marathon, and to-day to Eleusis and Salamis, have so fatigued me that I should resign my pen and go straight to bed, were I not so brimful of Greek enthusiasm, and anxious to converse with you as much as possible while I am still a breather of the inspiring Attic air, this most pellucid ether, as Euripides has it. On our sail up the Gulf of Corinth, we looked out for Parnassus with peculiar eagerness, and I was afraid lest, like too many of the classic eminences, it might turn out a half ant hill, — but it was not the case. As we approached Salona and the fated plain of Cirrha, grand and imposing did the venerable mountain lift up his lofty head, and superbly clad, on head and shoulders, with an ermine cloak of snow, with a dark cincture of woods about his waist, I was content to admire the grand old mountain from a distance without desiring to climb its sacred sides, with the possibility of being frozen, or the probability of having my throat cut or my nose cut off. We went to the Isthmus of Corinth, and then to the city of Corinth. I must tell you about it. Rising about 5 A. M. we went on shore from the steamer, and made the acquaintance of the vehicle which was to convey us to Corinth, and it needed only a single glance at the four-wheeled abomination to fill us with the most unfeigned horror and disgust. Upon an ox-cart of the roughest description, imagine placed a crate, wide at the top, narrow at the bottom, sans back, sans sides, sans seat, sans cushion, sans everything. The worst lumber-wagon I ever saw would be a princely chariot in comparison. Into this locomotive nightmare we tumbled, and curled our sad carcasses upon what might be called bags or pillows, but which I should denominate emigrant packets for transporting, from one part of the country to another, crowds of Corinthian fleas. Future experience justified this appellation. There we sat for two mortal hours, P. making himself rather comfortable by smoking; T. D. sat perfectly still in speechless agony, but preserving that dignity which was proper for an ex-tutor with two of his quondam Freshmen ; while I gave vent to my sufferings in frequent and long-drawn howls which seemed to win our driver's heart. At all events we had lots of fun, and amused ourselves by imagining the sensation we should create by driving the turn-out of the isthmus up Chapel Street or Hillhouse Avenue, and loud were our shouts of laughter when a peculiarly horrible jolt brought us all together into that state of mixed-up-ed-ness in which Prof. Dana says that the Coral Polyp always exists. The destruction of Corinth by an earthquake, an account of which you must have seen in the papers, has knocked it so thoroughly endways that I doubt if Paul himself would know it, notwithstanding his eighteen months' residence there. The Temple of Minerva, consisting of seven columns with entablatures, is almost the only building that has remained unaffected in some way by the shocks. We had a tough walk up to the Citadel, or Acro-Corinth, a height which commands a glorious view of both gulfs and the country round. You look off to the southwest among the rugged mountains of Arcadia, and to the northeast among the ditto of Attica.

We had a gorgeous sail to the Piræus, with Salamis on the left, Egina on the right, behind the old city of Megara, which still has a very imposing aspect. At 5 P. M. we neared the Piræus, and saw before us the mountains Hymettus and Pentelicus, and, more than all, the Acropolis, crowned by the stately Parthenon. There are a few moments in a man's life which are invested with a peculiar interest to him, and which will never lose their place in his memory, nor cease to have a freshness and vividness of outline no matter how many years pass away. Such a time was that afternoon and evening, to be marked with a white stone. I wish that you could have been by my side, to share what I might call an overwhelming enthusiasm of feeling, which was owing not merely to the sight of the Parthenon, and also of the Theseum, close by which most perfect monument of Doric art we passed on our ride up, but rather to a combination of these, with many other sights and sounds. We crossed the bed of the whispering Ilissus, we drove through streets whose names were classic, and passed shops whose signs looked like Felton's Greek Grammar. The timetable at the hotel pointed out the day (May 8) as ΑΙΓΡΙΛΙΟΣ 25, this being according to old style which still prevails here. The first half hour, nay, the first few minutes alone, after my arrival here, would have been sufficient to repay me for all the time and expense of having come here. With regard to the remains of art in Athens, in my present sleepy state you cannot expect me to say anything particularly bright or original. The Parthenon has been called the finest building on the finest site in the world. I could sit for hours looking at the silent grandeur of these marble columns, the heavy masses of the entablature above them, and their perfect fitness to each other, and to an ideal beauty, although actually so mighty and massive. Whether standing alone, or simply crowned by an entablature or under a complete and symmetrical pediment, they are still, for some inexplicable reason, beyond all praise, and greatly beyond all imitation. I must confess that the glories of the New Haven State House pale before them.

The Temple of Theseus, which is almost as perfect as when Cimon first raised it over the recovered bones of Attica's favorite hero, is a better example from which to draw a full and correct idea of the arrangements of a temple of the best period. Next to the Parthenon and Temple of Theseus I was most struck with the Propylea, or vast triumphal arch, comprising in itself a succession of vast porticoes and temples, through which the solemn processions used to pass on the occasion of the Panathenaic festivals. I wish I could express in adequate language my admiration for these *chef d'œuvres* of antiquity. Rome, with all her massive ruins, has nothing to compare with them in majesty, beauty, and grace.

ATHENS, *May* 18.

DEAREST MOTHER, — .... I cannot express to you in too warm terms the pleasure which I have enjoyed during my stay here. About every thing ancient, there has been a charm of most delightful familiarity, as it were, and where everything modern is something so strange or new, the contrast is most strange and pleasing; and while I can never weary of wandering among the ruins of the ancient city, and the wonders of the Acropolis, the modern city is not without an interest of its own in the strange medley of costumes and nationalities which the streets afford. Greeks in their national dress, with the tall fez, the richly embroidered jacket, the flowing folds of the white camise, the red leggings, which always remind one of the leg armor of ancient times; the Turk, with his stolid face and loose trowsers, turban or tarbouche on head, and pipe in hand; fierce-looking Albanians from the mountains; an occasional Bavarian soldier of the king; in addition to all these, a motley crowd in Frank dress, strangers in Athens, Jews and proselytes, Cretes and Arabians. I find that even the little I read of Homer, of Thucydides, of Demosthenes, and of the Tragic Poets, suffices to throw a most ineffable charm over every scene and antique monument; but there has been one spot which we have visited which is invested with an interest something more than merely classic, — a something which appeals not only to the classical scholar, but to every human heart which can thrill at high and noble deeds, — it is the Plain of Marathon. I must tell you somewhat about our excursion there. Some previous preparations were necessary, as it is quite an expedition; and as we could go only half the distance in a carriage, we had to send horses forward the day before to this half-way station, to meet us there. Our party was increased by the addition of a young American. . . . . Well, at 5 A. M. we were off, well supplied with grub and wine, and rejoicing in a guide named Miltiades, — a most fit person with whom to visit this memorable battle-field. We left Athens, over which the rising sun was just beginning to throw a rosy light, and rode for two hours or more in our carriage, to a village called Caphissia. Here we found the horses waiting for us, and most extraordinary looking creatures they were. A gaunt sorrel specimen fell to my lot, and sorely did I repent, before long, that I had ever got astride of him. We dashed out of Caphissia at a gallant rate, for our horses, as we soon found out, though rum ones to look at, were devils to go. Our path wound round the southwestern foot of Pentelicus, through dense shrubbery, and over waste patches that reminded us distinctly of some parts of Connecticut. But what gave a peculiar charm to the whole affair was, that the region through which we were passing was one of the worst dens of the robbers in all Attica, and as our ears had been regaled at Dr. King's with some choice stories of the course of sprouts which they caused their prisoners to go through, such as roasting before a slow fire, cutting the nose and ears, you can easily imagine that we felt a little nervous when riding through a place that seemed made for an ambush, and where it would be equally impossible to escape, to defend ourselves, or ever to be found of those who might be sent to rescue us. It is in circumstances like these, that a man feels the true and legitimate value of a revolver, — it is a friend in need. One reason, perhaps, why we saw nothing of them was, that only one week or two before, the chief of the robbers in this region, with two or three of his followers, had been killed, and a certain salutary degree of terror had been struck into the rest. Thus through rough woods and scrubby brushwood, and over rocky ridges, we rode for some three hours, now going at a hand gallop down the smoother slopes and through the level valleys, and then painfully climbing up a steep ascent, where our horses could never have kept their footing, had they not had almost the agility of cats. At length our guide, who was some distance ahead, shouted, " From the top of the next ridge you will see Marathon," and put his little black pony to the top of his speed, we all following to the best of our abilities, though at the risk of broken necks. First appeared the mountains of Eubœa across the channel, next the ocean, and then, in all the calm sweetness of a lovely spring day, the noble plain itself. The scene of this wonderful battle — the most glorious, perhaps, in all the world's history — lay there at our feet, and we could, almost at a glance, perceive every familiar locality, the ocean beach in the distance, where the invading army landed, and drew up their formidable array; the two marshes could be seen, one on each side of the plain, by means of which the Greeks prevented the Persians from surrounding them, and into which they drove them when the tide of battle had turned; and from this very slope upon which we stood did that noble little band of Athenians rush down upon the plain, with their thrilling war shout, which they were so soon to change into the pæan of victory. Thus it appeared to the bodily eye, and it required no very great stretch of imagination to people the silent plain with the memories of the Past, to place upon the stage the actors in that glorious drama. Through this plain we had a good ride to the sea beach. Our horses, excited by the fresh sea air, completely ran away with us, and did not stop until they reached the top of a small mountain close by the water. We were on the Tumulus of the Athenians, the brave men who fell in the battle, and who were afterwards almost deified by their countrymen: for when Demosthenes wished to implore the Athenians to be true to their ancient freedom, the most forcible adjuration he could use was by the two hundred that fell at Marathon.

It was on the tomb of Miltiades that we rested our horses, and as we felt hot and dusty after our long ride, we could not resist the tempting look of the sea, which really seemed to invite us to a bath. So, galloping right down to the beach, we stopped and went in, — a most dangerous proceeding, as we afterwards discovered. Such an indulgence so early in the season is extremely likely to be followed by an instant attack of the Greek fever. It was very providential that we were none of us attacked, for soon after, by the ignorance of our guide, we got into a mess which was just the thing to develop the beginning of fever. Supposing one of the marshes to be dry, we attempted to cross it. We had got about half way through when suddenly we found ourselves among deep and dangerous mud-holes, into which our horses sank almost up to their shoulders. T. D. had a sure-footed horse which managed to keep on his legs, but B., our companion, and myself, were thrown violently off several times by the struggles of our horses, — indeed, I almost feared that we might be doomed to share the fate of the left wing of the Persians. My own horse, in particular, was very troublesome. Every time he got into the mud he would kick and plunge frightfully, thus sinking himself continually deeper. The last time he fell he sank almost up to his neck, and in his frantic endeavors to get out, threw himself on me, covering me with mud. After that, I thought it prudent to lead him the rest of the way. At length we emerged, horses and fellows cased in mud. We took our luncheon at the village of Vrana. After dinner we had a trial of skill in throwing stones at the wine bottle. I hit it, and made a decided impression, both on the bottle and the native population. We went home over Pentelicus, up break-neck paths, where we had to lead our horses. Our views of the plains of Marathon and Attica were superb. Examined with much interest the marble quarries; they look very rich. We finally reached Caphissia, where we had left our carriage, almost too tired to get into it. We had had nine hours in the saddle, the toughest work I ever did in my life, too tired even to sleep. To-day we all move about with a gait resembling a lame duck. Aside from these little troubles, I scarcely ever enjoyed an expedition so much in my life. To-morrow I must be off for Naples. I will try to finish this to have it in readiness to mail when I reach that place.

Thursday, May 20. — I am sitting by my open window looking off over the sunlit Bay of Naples to Vesuvius, after a voyage of four days from the Piræus. Of course my first visit was to Rogers's, the banker, where I found a jolly good pile of letters. The time is very nearly approaching when I shall once more fill my place at the table and the fireside, and shall be no more a wanderer. How gladly shall I give up this nomadic life and return to the calm and quiet delights of home and study. Yes, from this old, wicked, worn-out Europe, I am coming home to my country. Every step is now Westward ho! towards dear America, and dearer New England.

Naples is delightful now, the air is not very hot, and seems quite cool after the fierce sun of Athens. I feel without energy, which is chiefly owing to the fact of being entirely alone, but I shall gird up my loins and try to make some excursions to Pompeii, Vesuvius, and Capri. On Sunday afternoon, May 16, we came in sight of Sicily, and the long, sloping sides of Mount Etna. Had I had plenty of time and a good companion, I think that I should have run down to Catania, and attempted the ascent of that famous old mountain of the Cyclops; but, as I had neither, I was obliged to satisfy myself with a distant glance. We got to Messina Sunday evening, and left there at 2 P. M. Monday; passed up through the Lipari Islands and quite near Stromboli. This just fulfilled my idea of a volcano, rising abruptly from the water's edge in a vast round cone, with no land at its base to destroy the effect. When I woke up in the morning, we were gliding just between Capri and the promontory of Sorrento into the Bay of Naples. Everything was perfect; the air was most invigorating; the city of Naples most fair; and the landscape, all around, of a charming variety, from the high, precipitous shores of Capri and Ischia, and the steep hill-sides of Posilippo and Castellamare, to the smiling beauty of Sorrento and the peaceful scenery of Baiæ. Above all these old Vesuvius calmly raised his mighty head, himself the most picturesque and striking object in the scenery, but rolling from his summit a long, gray pillar of smoke, to warn that terror was mingled with all this beauty, — that under this fair and exuberant life was ever slumbering a strange and awful death. An expedition to Vesuvius was planned, which was interrupted by a pouring rain just as we were starting for Resina, so I and two English artists whom I had met with went to Herculaneum, and then I came home. I started by myself to go to Baiæ, and here I met with two Americans, with whom I had a pleasant talk, and they asked me to call on them. .... I received an invitation from them to join their party for a three days' trip to Pompeii, Amalfi, Pæstum, Capri, and Sorrento. It was too valuable a chance to lose.

On Monday morning we set out on our tour into the enchanting environs of Naples. My capacity for speaking Italian felt rather insulted by the presence of a *valet de place;* but my companions had engaged him, and there was nothing for it but to keep a sharp lookout, and see that he did not cheat us any more than was necessary and proper. A ride of half an hour brought us to the station of Pompeii. How it would have astonished the ancient Pompeians if they could have suddenly seen a locomotive with a train of cars come puffing up to their city. They probably would have concluded that the old fables of classic story were being acted over, and that a new fire-breathing Chimera had come upon the earth. A short walk brought us to the gate of the buried town, "The City of the Dead." We entered the Street of the Merchants, and found everything in the shops as it had been left. The temples of Fortune, of Venus, of Isis, of Jupiter, stood there in various states of perfection, but without their attendant priests. The restaurants and resorts of pleasure still preserve the traces of inventive luxury; but their walls no longer ring with the Bacchanalian songs of the most corrupt period of the world. The houses of the wealthy and tasteful are still rich with marble columns and curious mosaics and frescoes, whose colors still shine with a brilliancy not to be equaled. Their chambers are silent now; no fountain plays in the impluvium; no voices sound in the atrium. In the remains of that city we probably see in miniature the remains of the highest civilization the world knew until the genius of Christianity had fully developed itself, — had extended its influence from simple morals to the improving of the entire life.

The houses of Pompeii are mostly small, one-story affairs, containing bedrooms in which it would be almost impossible to lie down, much more to swing a cat, provided the Pompeians indulged in that cruel pastime. A hole to sleep in, and a hall in which to give banquets, seem to have been all that was absolutely necessary for a housekeeper. The house of Diomede was almost the only exception to the one-story, and that is one of the most splendid mansions in Pompeii. We left Pompeii by the Street of the Tombs, which is a volume of interest in itself. But I must hasten on the account of our trip. We took a carriage at La Cava, and drove along the sea-shore from Vietri to Amalfi, one of the most picturesque and remarkable roads I ever saw. The villages were built right on the sides of precipices, the houses being stuck into every imaginable fissure, and the cultivated spots were all made by the most indefatigable terracing. Sometimes as many as a dozen monstrous terraces were made in the side of a single hill, and on these the orange, the vine, and the olive flourished to more advantage than they could possibly have done on a level. We visited Amalfi and its cathedral. I never saw a town more full of rascals, that is to say, inhabitants; of these a swarm surrounded the carriage, clamorous for alms, whether possessed of the necessary qualifications of blindness or deformity or not. I never sustained such a siege in my life. Luckily an organ-grinder with a monkey came along just then, which effectually diverted from us the public admiration. We spent the night at Salerno. I came home from Sorrento to-day, and expect to go to Vesuvius to-morrow.

.... I have not time to tell you about my ascent to Vesuvius, which I accomplished, notwithstanding an eruption had broken out that morning, and had filled the path with hot lava. The view from my window, with the red streams running down its sides in two places, and with a wide red field of flame in the plain where the lava had rested, was most magnificent. I left Naples yesterday afternoon, and came to this place (Civita Vecchia). We shall lie here till afternoon, and then go to Leghorn.

FLORENCE, *June* 1, 1858.

DEAR J., — .... The expedition to Posilipo, Pozzuoli, Lake Avernus, Baiæ, etc., I made alone. I did not succeed in getting up much enthusiastic steam at Virgil's tomb at Posilipo. The truth is, that I had read so little of the great Mantuan since I left school, that his beauties had almost slipped from my mind. The chief associations with which his name was connected were rulers, copy-books, Leverett's Lexicon, etc., so I cut the classical associations, and satisfied myself with admiring the magnificent view of the bay, where

"Murmuring Naples, spire overtopping spire,
Lies on the slope beyond where Virgil sleeps."

Passing through the Tunnel, or, as it is called with more

poetry than truth, the Grotto of Posilipo, I had a delightful ride through a narrow country lane, almost overgrown with most luxuriant vegetation, to the lake on whose banks is the famous Grotto del Cane. On my approach, a man came out of a house with the key of the cave, which is a little hole like a cellar above ground. In a couple of minutes a woman made her appearance, dragging along the reluctant Cane. A combination of the motives of humanity and economy, caused me to forego the Cane. I saw the effect of the exhalation, well enough, upon a powerfully burning torch, which went out instantly. I realized it more fully by putting down my head, taking the vapors in my face, until I had just consciousness enough left to stagger off into the air. I went back to my carriage, accompanied by the reprieved Cane, who jumped around me as if he appreciated that I had saved him from the pangs of death and the pleasures of resuscitation. I have not time to tell you of all that I saw that day, — the Lucrine Lake, once famed for its oysters, — of Lake Avernus, little resembling the entrance to the infernal regions, as the poets imagined it, of the ruins of the ancient Cumæ, of the Bay of Baiæ, and the Roman ruins and temples that line its shores, — of all these things, any of them interesting enough to merit particular descriptions, I cannot speak as I should like to. I will only tell you a little about what interested me far the most of anything I saw that day, which was the Temple of Jupiter Serapis at Pozzuoli. I had often heard of it before, in the geological lectures and in other reading, but I had not noticed where it was situated, but had placed it in the East somewhere, not far from the ruins of Baalbec. Imagine, then, my delight at learning that it was really within my ken and reach, and my pleasure on entering the water-covered inclosure, and seeing those remarkable pillars, forming in themselves a book of geological history. I suppose that nowhere is the chronicle of successive geological changes, elevations and depressions of the earth's surface, written in such clear and unmistakable characters as there, — the long smooth space, from the pedestal to a height of twelve feet, indicating a depression which took place when the column was surrounded to that height by rubbish, or perhaps scoriæ from some volcanic eruption, thus protected from the action of the sea and the boring of marine animals, — then, high in the air above this, nine feet completely honey-combed by the industrious piercing of numberless lithotomites, worn and fretted by the incessant dashing of the waves, doubtless for hundreds of years; above this the smooth portion of the column, which had as yet suffered no wear and tear save that of the atmosphere and time. The mosaic pavement of the temple is covered with water to the depth of several inches, and this will grow deeper as the subsiding movement, which is still in operation, goes on. The day's excursion to Baiæ was a most delightful one. I visited the temples there, saw the Tarantella danced, went down to Misenum, came back to Pozzuoli in a sail-boat, following the same route taken by Pliny when he started out in '79 A. D., on that expedition to see Vesuvius which cost him his life. This sail across the Bay of Baiæ may be called the climax of my day's enjoyment.

I made the ascent of Vesuvius with a gentleman from New York, and I will rush, *in medias res*, into an account of this expedition, before the very vivid impression which it produced has worn away from my mind. You may imagine it was not feeble, when I tell you that quite a fierce eruption was in full fuss and fury when we were upon the mountain. On Thursday morning, May 27, Mr. Y. and I left Naples in a carriage, for the burning mountain. A thick cloud shrouded the top of the mountain, and seemed to portend a shower of rain, but we did not know what had happened in the night, nor what was the nature of the cloud that hung there, almost the only one in a beautifully clear sky. At Resina we engaged a guide, and also a horse for Mr. Y., both to meet us at the Hermitage, a building situated something more than half way up, where travellers leave their carriages, and proceed on horseback, or on foot, to the base of the Cone itself. When we got to the Hermitage, we found the guide and horse awaiting us, and then learned from him that there had been a sharp earthquake in the night, and that several new craters had opened in the side of the Cone, and, moreover, that it would be impossible to ascend to the summit of the mountain, as a small crater had opened in the very path, and had sent out a storm of lava which had just filled it up. He proposed that we should go to see the new craters, without going to the top. I, who had made a vow to look down the great crater, if it cost me my hat and boots, was of course tremendously disappointed, and had a shrewd suspicion that our guide wanted to save his old bones the bother of climbing up the Cone, and yet to pocket the fare all the same. However, we met an Italian gentleman coming down, and, thanks to my Italian lessons, I understood him to say that he had been to the top. I suggested this fact to the guide, and pointed towards the foot of the Cone. Then we began our scramble, the guide first, I at his heels, Mr. Y. some few yards behind, a man with a basket of provisions to eat at the top, and two sturdy fellows with straps, with which they proposed to help the signor up the mountain. Upon our first appearance they spotted him, and I tried to send them away. They informed me that the signor was "*molto grosso*," and that he would have to resort to them sooner or later. Their prediction was correct, and he was obliged to put himself under the boosting and pushing regimen, much as his better nature rebelled against it. For myself, I got along capitally. Our course lay, for some distance, right over the fresh lava of that very morning, which was still almost too hot to walk upon, while half-way up the ascent, in the side of the Cone, the crater which had sent it forth was still smoking away, like Doc Mulford, causing us to feel rather nervous. We reached the crater, which was a little affair only a few feet across. Very near us, but separated from our sight by a ridge, every few moments we could hear a loud roar and swash, as of a heavy surf breaking upon the sea-shore, announcing that a new stream of lava had been cast out. After an hour of pretty tough scrambling, we reached the platform at the top, and could see the crater and the small cone casting out an immense volume of smoke mingled with flame.

We set one of the men to cook some eggs in a ravine, while we ourselves went with the guide and one of the bearers to see the great crater. Our crossing of the platform was neither safe nor pleasant. The earthquake of the night before had rent great chasms, large enough to fall into, and a few feet down we could see and feel the red-hot stream of flowing lava. But what was worst of all was that, from these crevices, came up strong exhalations and thick clouds of sulphur, through which we were obliged to walk, until I was nearly choked, and eyes, nose, and mouth filled with these horrid fumes. I was in continual danger of putting my foot into a crack, and getting it burnt off. I then wished most devoutly that I had your practice in the laboratory, and could breathe those smells as comfortably as my native air. At length we reached the edge of the crater. From the round edge projected a thin shell of incrustations; upon this the bearer got down. The guide refused to, as it was only two or three inches thick. I followed the bearer, and while he held me by the arm, looked down into that fearful abyss. I do not exaggerate in the least when I say that the sight fairly unmanned me. A deep, dull red sea of fire, covered with a cloud of smoke, but tossing in restless agitation, and sending forth a sound like that of the sea when a storm is out, and the winds and waves pout together. Besides the occasional explosion of gases, there was a deep, solemn waving and heaving of the entire mass. Add to this the rolling sulphur clouds, the fierce, bright flashes of flame from the top of the cone, and the ghastly exhalations arising on every side, and you have a scene which it is not in human nature to behold unmoved. For myself, all my strength left me, I became much oppressed, and even terrified, and had scarcely the power to cross the sulphur fields again. I shall never see anything like that again. It was like standing on the burning Sinai. We rested awhile, ate our eggs, cooked by volcanic heat, and salted with volcanic salt. We then made the descent, not over the large scoriæ, where we had come up, but in another place. The ascent which it had required an hour to make, I descended in three minutes. We descended to the ancient crater, which was left when Pompeii and Herculaneum were destroyed. From here we had a fine chance to see the eruption from the new craters. No less than five craters, side by side, were hard at work, especially the one in the centre, in throwing red-hot rocks and molten lava. The stream of fire which proceeded from them was, when I saw it, about twenty feet wide by five to ten feet high. We went right in front of it; as it rolled slowly on we put our staves into the red-hot mass. The guide twisted out portions, and buried coins in it before it cooled. This was as grandly beautiful a sight as the one on the summit was terrible. Just think of a river of fire thirty feet wide! and by the next evening I saw it from my window in Naples, widened to a hundred feet, and coming down the mountain slope in a manner rather alarming to Resina. I place my day at Vesuvius side by side with that of the Jardin, near Mont Blanc, — the two grandest scenes I ever saw or ever shall see, — the one all ice, the other all fire.

I spent a delightful evening yesterday at the house of H. Powers, the great sculptor, the greatest living sculptor, I believe. He is the perfect incarnation of hospitality. My recollections of Florence will always be necessarily connected with his family.

LONDON, *June* 17.

.... I have been very busy in travelling and sight-seeing. I am really ashamed to send such a miserably short affair as this must be, in answer to your nice long ones; but as I shall come myself, as a sort of P. S. to my letter, I think that you will pardon me. You will find that all my improvements and advantages, if so be I have acquired any, which I consider as very dubious, lie under the surface, and are of a spiritual rather than fleshly order, for I have grown into as unprepossessing a young man as you would wish to see. The sun has tanned me to a dirty whitey-brown color, which contrasts badly enough with my light eyes, and my capillary arrangements in general are in a highly scrubby condition, so I recommend you to look not on the outward appearance.

NEW HAVEN, *July* 10, 1858.

MY DEAR COUSIN, — Your very kind and thoughtful letter came in this morning, and pleased me with the thought that you took so strong an interest in my arrival. Well, Europe is with the past, and nothing now remains save to carve out a happy and noble future in America, our own dear native land, — to find as high and true a pleasure in action here as we have done in travel and art-study and observation there. But I scarely think at all of Europe just now. I am all absorbed in the perfect happiness of getting home, and of taking rest, not among strangers, but in the midst of those who are to me the dearest ones in the world. You can easily imagine that last Tuesday evening was a pleasant one to me; they were all on the tip-toe of expectation, and I did n't surprise them much when I dashed in. Mother met me at the gate. . . . .

To L. R. P.

HYDE PARK ON THE HUDSON,
August 16, 1858.

MY DEAR FRIEND, — T. D. handed me your letter just as I was entering into the full whirl of business which naturally comes upon a man in New Haven during commencement week, and especially when that man is Class Secretary, and has a thousand things to look after and provide. That season of toil and turmoil has passed, and I have now some leisure and quiet wherein to consider your very kind and interesting letter, to read it over once more with renewed pleasure, and finally to settle myself peacefully down to frame a reply. I was rejoiced at a number of facts stated in your letter, most of all that you were hoping to walk unscathed through the fiery furnace of Kohl (no pun intended here), and likewise that you had steeled your gentle heart against the seductive advances of Wurst in all its witching forms. Somewhat counterbalancing and depreciating my joy, was your confession and acknowledgment of the soft impeachment of Bier. Alas! sweet Pinckney,[1] I see thee with a prophetic eye pre-

[1] A sort of "pet name," used only by him and his brother.

maturely swelling to those gigantic proportions to which the friends of "Tony Weller"[1] have always looked forward with fear and trembling, and thy otherwise delicate members all distended into symmetrical magnitude. All the kindlier feelings of my nature shudder as I think of you dragging yourself up the Righi, or picture you, like Falstaff, "larding the lean earth" as you walk along some hot and dusty road. Would I could be with you to give you an occasional lift for "Auld lang syne." I cannot exactly analyze, my dear fellow, the nature of my sentiments towards you, but perhaps the best way after all will be to take it on faith, and to consider your friendship as a permanent and well-founded fact, without wondering why it is that we fight so much while together, and like each other so well when separated. When we get past the "squirtish" period of young manhood, probably we shall get along better, and be willing to take each other's opinions and sentiments at par, or even at a premium.

You ask about my return home with interest, and speak of my being "a lion," "a centre," and other bad names. Perhaps I had better proceed at once to inform you of the immense stir which my arrival created. At about 9½ P. M., on Tuesday evening, July 6, we rode together from the station through the elm-lined streets, it being too dark for us to be recognized, but not too much so to see that the city was looking unusually lovely. At the corner of College and Wall Streets I dropped "the Relic,"[2] and with some trembling and anxiety continued out through College Street, crossed the railroad, and was soon landed at the door of the "Ash-Heap."[3] Of the welcome home I received I can give you no adequate description: you will find out what it is yourself before many months are over. Suffice it to say that all home-sickness and absence and longings were fully repaid when I found myself once more sitting by my mother's side. I can send you no kinder wish than that you may be as happy in your return

---

[1] A similar phrase.
[2] A name for the friend with whom he returned.
[3] So he jokingly called his home.

home as I was in mine. For a week I basked lazily in the smiles of home faces, carefully avoiding any meetings with any of my former friends. . . . .

NEW HAVEN, *August* 20. — The woodchuck-shooting, whereof I spake in my last sheet, turned out disastrously to myself and triumphantly to those innocent animals, as I came in woodchuckless, and with a sprained ankle, caused by jumping on a stone hidden among some leaves. I spent the remainder of my visit at Hyde Park upon the sofa, and have now come home to try the same kind of exercise here. . . . . By the way, my young friend, let me remind you that I have emerged from the degraded age of twenty-one, and am now a venerable patriarch of twenty-two years. Infant, where are you now? Don't you wish you were twenty-two? But you can't come it; you are still very verdant and youthful, and I am sorry that the brief space of this letter will not permit me to give you a screed of good advice. But don't despair; cherish hope, and perhaps one of these days you may become twenty-two likewise, although I cannot by any means promise you that you will ever catch up with me; still, there's no knowing what may be done by active exertion.[1] A birthday is generally a day of plans and resolutions, a day of looking on the ground left behind, and gazing onward to the future. For myself, *my* past was too unsatisfactory to me to receive much attention; but I rather settled my plans for the next year or two to come. As you expressed a desire to hear what they were, I will tell you as nearly as I can. I expect to spend a good part of the coming year at home, working on the class report, studying generally, and doing something at the law, probably in a lawyer's office. Next year I shall enter Harvard Law School, and take from that college my degree. If anything favorable then "turns up" at the East, I shall take to that, but if not, then "Westward Ho!" for a life of misery among the stumps of Iowa or Minnesota. . . . . I seem to

---

[1] There was an interval of eight days between his birth and mine. He scarcely ever failed, when that week came round, to remind me of it as above.

find myself considerably changed since I came home from Europe. I am aware of no actual benefit derived from my absence from home, and indeed I doubt whether I derived any; while on the other hand all my ideas have undergone a process of unsettling which makes me very restless and thoughtful, and at times even despairing of the future, so that I am often disposed almost to wish that I had never tasted of the tree of European knowledge, or spent one pleasant year in aimless wanderings over the Continent. On the whole, I am inclined to think that the ultimate effect of travel upon my own mind has been anything but good, without taking into account the wasted year, which might have been well-improved if I had only been content to stay at home. But I won't bother you with any further Jeremiad on this subject; I only hope that you may reap more satisfaction and profit from your residence abroad than I have done.

To L. R. P.

NEW HAVEN, *December* 2, 1858.

MY DEAR PINCKNEY, — My constitution has not yet thoroughly recovered from the shock which it underwent upon the receipt of a letter from you, when, as you well and ably observe, I was myself in debt to you. Is Pinckney also among the letterwriters? Can it be possible that that amiable youth has relinquished his favorite doctrine of non-interference, and has finally given in his adherence to those principles of common decency in correspondence which are generally accepted by the human race? "Representative of two hemispheres, welcome to our shores!" I do hereby extend my full and free forgiveness to you for writing out of your time. If I shall succeed in filling these four pages, it will certainly be a very remarkable feat, and the longest letter I have written since I wrote to you last, — my epistles for the last four months having consisted of a few brief and pointed remarks, chiefly of an interrogatory character. Indeed, I shall congratulate myself if I get safely through without asking you when you were born, and whether you are married, and, if so, when, and how many babies you have at this present. May your good genius, my friend, always defend you from being made a class secretary, or any similar animal, with a penalty attached of hard labor and solitary confinement for a portion of each day for the space of several months.

You speak of your achievements in Hebrew with a certain degree of discouragement. It would be very strange if you did not feel so, for it is a language whose greatest difficulties (always provided that you are only striving after ordinary proficiency in it, and not after thorough scholarship) lie at the very portal. When you have once made yourself familiar with the letters and the vowel points, the conjugations of the verb, and the declensions of the noun, you float along bravely on the ocean of translation, with no subjunctive modes, no ablatives absolute or genitives of cause, no datives of likeness to make you afraid. From the moment that you have mastered the "Birēshith bara Elohim," you feel possessed of a patent right to go it loose and criticise the construers of the Bible, from St. Jerome to Mr. Sawyer and Chevalier Bunsen. . . . . I am deeply interested in Plato's "Phædon," more than I could have thought I ever should be when some nine years ago I was wont to hurl my Sophocles' Greek Grammar against the wall of my study in boyish rage. When you come to read this great story (and when you do, don't fail to read it in the original Greek), you will be delighted more than I can tell you. I am pushing Goethe somewhat; have read "Götz von Berlichingen," "Die Geschwister," "Hermann" and "Dorothea," and a number of his smaller pieces, and have been greatly pleased. But, notwithstanding I derive so much pleasure from these pursuits, they rather hinder than help me in my general professional work. Law is covered over and hidden by these numerous πάρεργα, and I see the problem of making my living as far from a solution as it was three years and three months ago, when I took off my tail-coat on Commencement night. I am looking forward to my next spring and summer at Harvard, when I hope to accomplish something more tangible than I have yet done. But probably it will not amount to

much, and if it should, to what end? I am tempted at times
almost to despair when I think that I should experience no satisfaction even I if should succeed in my highest ambition most
perfectly. Now, don't moralize over this. I will promise beforehand to imagine exactly all you would say. John's dog waxes
in girth, and his paws are more mammoth than ever, while his
futile gambols defy description. The relations between his
dogship and the goodly fellowship of cats are of a somewhat
disturbed nature: he worries them all with the exception of
the sable ancestress of the family, the old *Ur*-cat, who
scratches his nose gorgeously, and makes him howl *peccavi*.
He has better luck with the kittens; and it was only yesterday that, after a brief tempest of bitings, scratchings, barkings, and spittings, I found a bunch of fur in his mouth which
had a strange resemblance to that growing on the back of our
promising young cat named Fanny, who, with a very disgusted
expression of face, was sitting upon the highest shelf of the
dresser, "inhabiting," as Euripides says under similar circumstances, " mansions impregnable by misfortune."

I have written you a very absurd letter, and rather nonsensically long, but I hope that you will respond with an
epistle of at least equal length. Talk about anything, and,
above all, of yourself. I doubt not that J. would send his
love to you if I should wake him up now (2.05 A. M.) and
ask him; but the experiment might be hazardous.

III.

LETTERS OF HOME, AND PROFESSIONAL STUDY AND LIFE.

1859–61.

III.

LETTERS OF HOME, AND PROFESSIONAL STUDY AND LIFE.

———◆———

To L. R. P.

NEW HAVEN, *February* 13, 1859.

.... My conscience has for some time been pricking me about writing to you, and when your kind letter arrived, it nearly took all the hair off the top of my head, being a coal of the first magnitude. I began to put my Report in press about February 1st, and have already got thirty-two pages printed, which is nearly half of the whole concern; but an unpleasant accident occurred last Thursday evening, which will have the effect of delaying me considerably; the attic where Morehouse stores his paper, etc., formerly A. Σ. Φ. hall, when you and I belonged to that institution, took fire and burned partly up, destroying some $500 worth of paper, and the whole impression (500 copies) of the first two forms of my Report. Rather disgusting, *nit?* However, I hope to drive up rapidly and get the thing sufficiently under way to allow me to get off to Cambridge by March 4.

Hebrew languishes rather: we have only four recitations per week now, instead of six as we had last term. We are reading in the Psalms, and find them considerably more difficult than Genesis, which in fact was a little *too* easy. We have been tackling the Messianic Psalms, the 2d and 16th; what is your opinion of the meaning of שְׁאוֹל and שָׁחַת? I perpetrated an essay on the true pronunciation of the word

Jehovah some month or so ago, wherein I indorsed McWhorter, and spread myself generally. How jolly it is to take some good meaty subject, and go into the library and claw over authorities! I wish that I had the prospect before me of being able to do more of it.

I enjoyed the "Autocrat" immensely; it made the somewhat borous ride from P. to N. Y. pass away imperceptibly. I think that the "Allegory of Old Age," the professor's paper, is the gem of the work. The "Chambered Nautilus" also is a real bit of poetry. It is quite easy to see how often and how much Dr. H. has profited by the existence of the "Noctes;" not so much in filching ideas, as in the general management of his talks. In that part on trees, I rather noticed a "skin." The poem on "Æstivation" also tickled my midriff considerably; the "Parson's Legacy" is rather a failure after the "One Hoss Shay." Have just read Kingsley's "Two Years Ago;" tastes rather flat in comparison with "Amyas Leigh;" but I think Tom Thumall a very attractive character, don't you? a regular creation of the present age.

Y. and I finished the "Phædo" of Plato yesterday; the closing passages were full of simple sublimity. . . . . I was invited to Mrs. Dana's last night to meet Professor L. Agassiz; it was a delightful occasion; he seems to be one of the kindest and jolliest of men, and talks on all subjects with equal facility. How small it does make me feel to talk face to face with one whose knowledge is so immense, and whose acquirements so valuable; it seemed to me as if I did wrong in talking to him, and keeping him from thinking or working. Science, of course, was rampant that evening, and the conversation was generally rather steep for me. . . . .

I *do* rather like you upon the whole, and am always yours.

CAMBRIDGE, *March* 7, 1859.

I have at last got fixed here, and before I compose my weary carcass for its first slumber under my own vine and fig-tree, I will endeavor to scribble you a few hasty lines. I reached "Bosting" at midnight; and went to the United States Hotel, just across the street from the depot. After breakfast, I devoted myself to finding L. C. He was not in his office, so I went to Cambridge and had a confab with the Janitor of the Law School, obtained what information I needed, paddled back to Boston, found L., took him to dinner with me, and he and I came back here together and commenced a vigorous hunt for rooms. Success at last crowned our efforts, and we lit upon the house where I now am. The house, which looks as if it might have been built by some of the earliest of the Puritans, is situated upon an open space which rejoices in the appellation of Winthrop Square. It is two minutes' walk from the Law Building. My room will be delightful in summer, as it is open on three sides, and a couple of fine horse-chestnut trees reach their branches up to the window. After we had struck the bargain for the room, we went to the Law School, and L. introduced me to Professor Washburn and Professor Parker, and I entered my name in the book. I shall enter, as I had thought, at the middle of the middle year, but in order to do this, I must have a certificate from the professors of the Yale Law School, that I attended there from September, 1856, to May, 1857. I wish J. to get this for me.

To H. N. C.

CAMBRIDGE, *March* 8, 1859.

You see that I have at last set out on the voyage of life for myself, having deserted the family ark at New Haven. It makes me sad to think of it; the idea of going away for good and all, and always hereafter being at home only as a visitor. Indeed, mother said it made her feel much worse than my going to Europe did ; but I could hardly agree with her in that, for then I was going away to something entirely new and untried, whereas here I have merely been transplanted from one scene of student-life to another, and among students I always feel myself more or less at home. Still I feel sure that I shall be homesick on some of these long afternoons and evenings, when I have studied myself tired, and long for something home-like to talk to and smile at. . . . . .

My landladies had never taken lodgers before, and expressed their great delight at finding their first one of such an orderly and quiet (?) disposition. I wonder what they will say when Linus comes over and spends an evening with me. Cambridge is the most disagreeable place at this season of the year that you can well imagine. Mud and snow lie everywhere, in deep sloughs of despond, which the rays of the sun open to unfathomed depths; everybody, from the gray-haired man down to the infant in arms, wears india-rubber boots. Indeed, I should think that the first question propounded by the medical examiner of a Cambridge life insurance office would be, "Do you wear india rubber boots?" and at the close of the insurance policy might be inserted some such clause as this, "and this policy to become void in case the holder thereof goes out without I. R. boots." I hope to work hard here, and to recover my habits of study, which I have almost lost by two years of idleness, travelling, and half-work. Law shall have eight hours, at least, *per diem*, and that is time enough for any *one* study. What an astonishing difference there is with regard to control of time, between being at home and being away from home. I considered myself fortunate at home if I could find six hours for undisturbed study; here I have no trouble in finding fourteen. New Haven was socially very pleasant before I came away,— too pleasant to allow me to do anything. I enjoyed Y.'s society very much. .... We read Plato's "Phædo" together last winter, and enjoyed it extremely, rather for the picture it gives of the character and life of Socrates than for the intrinsic value of the arguments, which seemed to me frequently to depend on wire-drawn distinctions, and to contain a great deal of solemn trifling. If I had time, I should like to expand at length upon what I thought of Socrates, but I must come to a close.

CAMBRIDGE, *March* 14, 1859.

DEAR BROTHER,— .... I have been surprised to see how heterodox the fellows are on the subject of getting up early in the morning; they are even so base as to approve of 7 A. M. as a proper hour for breakfast, and dilate on the amount of time gained by such a barbarous custom. I can safely say that I never heard such sentiments before from the lips of young students, and I fear that all my attempts at exciting an eight o'clock breakfast rebellion will prove futile. There is really a great deal of earnestness among the law students, although some of it is simply the result of the first shine of vacation good resolutions; already I have perceived a letting down of these lofty determinations, less love for Dane Hall, and more for Boston, and an increased tenderness of feeling for whist and billiards, which were at first spurned with as virtuous indignation as were the spirits by St. Anthony. I believe that there is a great possibility of overdoing hard work and making it distasteful. I intend to avoid this by a careful and philosophical division of my time.

After a couple of hours of hard study at Cruise or Greenleaf, I can take up a Noctes, or Charles Lamb, or Philidor, or spend a half hour at the newspapers in the reading room, and return to work with a redoubled zest. I intend to give about ten hours a day to law, including lectures, and to scatter through these my four hours of relaxation of all descriptions. I shall write letters when I can find time for them, and sometimes shall make time for them, as on this occasion, when I ought to be getting myself up on "hearsay evidence," so as to be able to appreciate Professor Parsons' lectures on that subject.

I have no space in this letter to give you any impressions of the professors, or their mode of lecturing; suffice it to say, that I have not changed my old opinion about the comparative value of recitations and lectures, when employed for elementary instruction, nor do I see any reason to believe that the latter can ever be so useful as the former. So I have managed to combine the advantages of the two, and after taking as full notes as possible, I hunt up all the references, and then Joe J., and a man from New York named T., and myself, have a sort of recitation together, in which one takes the note-books and examines the others upon the substance of the lectures. We are also examining Greenleaf's edition of "Cruise on Real Property," and reciting it in the same way.

It will, I think, prove extremely useful, as everything which is not thoroughly understood is discussed in a colloquial style, until we have not only mastered it, but can talk it off of ourselves. T. is very sober and dignified, and knows a great deal of law; besides, he keeps us from cutting up and wasting time. I shall envy you your meeting in Brush's room. You must not fail to tell me all about it, and if this reaches you before the meeting, remember me most kindly to each and every one of the fellows.

CAMBRIDGE, March 17, 1859.

Well, here I am once more, in a "furrin" land, *i. e.*, in Yankee land, where codfish holds his sway, " every inch a fish," and where the abomination of "shillings," *i. e.*, 16⅔ cents, still is preserved in the manners and customs of an enlightened but degraded population. That you may distinctly locate me in your imagination, suppose, upon one corner of a small street, and facing upon a diminutive plot of ground dignified by the name of Winthrop Square (?), a most venerable house, which was doubtless of a respectable antiquity when Annapolis was just beginning to cut her first teeth. If I were an artist, I would try to send you a drawing of my present abode, though I doubt if I ever could learn to draw badly enough to do justice to its extremely tumble-down aspect. My room is in one of the wings (for this venerable architectural bird has two wings and a tail, and will probably fly away if it ever gets through moulting, which it seems to be doing at present); and being thus in a somewhat isolated situation, has windows to the north, east, and west, promising charming ventilation in summer, and even now admitting freely the pleasant rays of both the morning and the evening sun; and last night the moonlight streamed in at my east window, in a way which affected me with an odd mixture of pleasure and pain — a sense of independence saddened down by a touch of homesickness. The ceiling is low, and across it, in about the middle of the room, runs a heavy projecting beam, which comes down to within a few inches of my head when I stand. An old-fashioned fire-place, a pre-Adamite wardrobe and bureau to match, the very two old brass candlesticks, by whose light Noah and his three sons played whist in the Ark, — these, and sundry other relics of a by-gone age, make up the principal items of notice in my den. Indeed, with the exception of an upstart table and a pair of parvenu chairs, I am pretty much the only piece of furniture that is not bashful about telling its age. . . . .

LOWELL, *April* 3, 1859.

DEAR BROTHER, — In order to save you exclamations of surprise at the above direction, I will immediately inform you that I have *not* become disgusted with the Law, and retired into a cotton factory, but L. having kindly invited me to come home with him and spend Sunday, I very gladly accepted, and having added B. to our number, we sallied forth from the " wenerable" city of "Bosting," and after a ride of an hour in a baggage car, narrowly watched by the baggage-man to prevent our robbing the mails, which hung around in tempting rows, we arrived at this celebrated place, and met with a very cordial reception from L.'s family. So, after having listened to two sermons, and having eaten a capital dinner, I sit down to answer your two most acceptable letters. I should have written you last week, but I was very busy getting up a case for the Moot Court Club, to which I belong. Ordinarily an appointee is allowed two weeks to get up his case in, but both the regular counsel had backed out, and although it was hardly fair for one so inexperienced, the clerk insisted upon my filling one of the vacant places, leaving me to fill the other as best I could. Luckily I managed to get the young man named T., of whom you have heard me speak, to go in with me. I was very glad to get an antagonist as green as myself, rather than some experienced old un, who was up to all sorts of legal snuff. We managed to get up a pretty mild case — an action on a promissory note. Our trial of it comes off in the Coke Club tomorrow night, when I hope that we shall not disgrace ourselves in the eyes of our seniors, and I have a faint private expectation of winning the case. I must tell you something about the school moot courts, and how they are managed. They take place once a week before one of the professors, and the whole school; are tried by four students, two from the senior and two from the middle class, and are about as severe an ordeal for a young lawyer as I can very easily imagine. The speeches are elaborated with very great care, and must require a great deal of time in preparation. I almost shake in my shoes to think of the time when I shall be put through the mill. However, as I am in the middle class, I shall go on as junior counsel, and shall have less than half of the responsibility of the case on my shoulders. All the school attend, and take very full notes, especially of the decisions, and with good reason, for the professors deliver much more elaborate opinions than many judges on the bench. The club courts are entirely different; the clubs are composed of from sixteen to twenty-five members, and meet also once a week for the purpose of trying cases; the members take turns in acting as judge and counsel, and it is so arranged that every man has to act in one or other of these capacities three or four times a term. I belong to the Coke Club, which is the most *recherché* and select; as it has but sixteen members, and professes to require two years' previous study of the law for an election to it, but they made an exception to their general rule and took J. J., T., and myself, without inquiring how long we had walked in the ways of wickedness. I am also a member of the Berrien Club, but have not yet attended any of its meetings. These clubs are solely for the purpose of trying cases, and when business is over, that is at 9 P. M., they disperse without making the slightest kind of a row. In fact, there is no arrangement in Cambridge Law School for cultivating the social element, and I greatly disgusted a crowd of law students the other day, by remarking that all we did was to cultivate the worst part of our intellectual nature. Perhaps after all it is better for me that it is so, as I am rather prone to go into social meetings too extensively, and to waste time therein. . . . .

CAMBRIDGE, *April* 7, 1859.

DEAR M., — .... I have been here now nearly five weeks, and think I shall be able to employ my time to sufficient purpose to repay for absence from home. .... I had expected to find myself very much unaccustomed to study, and that it would be very hard to break myself into work again, after almost two years wasted in travelling and other idleness, but was pleasantly surprised by discovering that I was as fond of study as ever, and could go at it with as great a zest. .... A year ago to-day I was wandering in the Roman Forum, and climbing for wallflowers in the Coliseum. It really seems that there is no part of the world more perfectly familiar to my mind's eye than that spot, and the almost daily walk I used to take to reach it. "Kennst du den Weg?" I am inclined to think you do, and that you would have no objection to treading it again, nor indeed should I myself feel able to refuse an invitation to take a walk with you there to-day. It is a glorious day for seeing ruins, really too beautiful to take for visiting galleries, but one which should be spent in the open air; so let us set off immediately for the Baths of Caracalla. Which way shall we go? Down the Corso, across the Forum to the Arch of Janus and the Cloaca Maxima, and then under the shadow of the Palatine Hill by the Via dei Cerchi?" Or shall we take the route over Monte Cavallo, and past the Forum of Trajan to the Coliseum, and thence through the Arch of Constantine, stopping to take the scene of lovely quiet and perfect peace from the monastic terraces of dear San Gregorio? Then how charming to sit in the long grass to-day in the Baths of Caracalla, drinking in at every breath more pure draughts of true classical feeling than could be obtained by years of reading in the study. And then those beautiful daisies with crimson edges! Well, we can't always do just what we want to do, and I must not forget that 1859 is not 1858. I have troubled you with this nonsense because a fit of longing after Italy suddenly came over me, and I thought that you would be likely to be more lenient to absurdities of this kind than any one else. What a pity it was that we could not have been in Italy at the same time.

April 18, 1859. — I have been feeling pretty homesick lately, and to-day is not one to make a blue man feel cheerful. It snowed in the morning, hailed at noon, and is now raining in the most dreary manner. I have been feeling rather unwell for some days, which has dreadfully aggravated my longing for home, and my disgust for the classic shades of the Harvard Law School. Indeed, I am almost tempted to bid Kent and Chitty and Blackstone an eternal farewell, and engage in some pursuit which is more congenial to my natural disposition. I sometimes picture to myself the amount of success which I might possibly obtain, and then I think what a mere nothing it would be in the abyss of my ambition. I sometimes even envy the lot of those who are condemned to a life of mere manual drudgery, as being happier than that which must ever be the portion of an ambitious and mediocre mind. I am sometimes almost ready to withdraw from all toil and strife, and give myself up to the easy occupation of a reader and a scholar. It is for this reason, and for this alone, that I regret my year in Europe. The pleasant thoughts linked to objects there will be continually recurring, and always at the very moment when I wish to fix my mind most firmly on the dry details of my profession. I really think that a student of law ought not to know of the existence of anything else. To him scholarship, art, literature, the pleasures of society, should be a sealed book, for in them he will see beauties and find delights which can never exist in his stern mistress, Jurisprudence. But I now imagine that I hear you saying, "Every man is born to labor and to suffer, and this is at present your trial period. You do not come into this world to bask in the sunshine like a butterfly, but to work like a man." Yes; but it is hard to love the good for its own sake, when nothing beautiful also attracts. Giving up all my other reading and study is to me, on entering the law, what the loss of her flowing hair and sparkling jewels is to a novice when she takes the vows at the convent altar. I had rather keep my mind and heart fresh and bright and happy, than, when arrived at a withered age, receive some miserable judgeship or political reward, — the price of life-long toil on the legal treadmill.

To L. R. P.

CAMBRIDGE, *May* 1, 1859.

.... Your last blow was well put in, and took me just in the right spot, and only a few moments before I dodged, *i. e.*, removed hither, changing the New Haven mud for the Cambridge mud, and finding a difference of at least three inches in favor of the profundity of the latter. During the eight weeks that I have spent here, I have seen so few sights, heard so few new "loads," and indulged in so few flirtations (their entire number being expressed by the formula $\sqrt{x^3 - 4xy + 4y^2} - x + 2y$), that I feel myself totally unable to communicate to you anything of the slightest interest. I suppose that it would be proper for me to begin by giving you some account of how I am situated, and what I am doing, and having once fulfilled this duty, I can then give rein to my fancy, and indulge in as much nonsense as I think thy highly respectable disposition can stand at one dose. I arrived here on the 5th of March, and became speedily established in a very pleasant room (in which I wish that you were now sitting, right over forenenst me, with a cigar in your old mug), on the second story of a most ancient house, which dates from the Third Crusade, and inhabited by a couple of ladies who probably made their appearance a few centuries later. At any rate they are of the Hard-shell religious belief, and for a few weeks held a prayer-meeting directly under my room, all the fixins of which were extremely powerful, except the time, which was weekly. This interesting devotional exercise has recently dried up, thus completely refuting the statement of Mr. Keats, that

"A thing of beauty is a thing forever."[1]

I take my dinner at the Brattle House, which was formerly

[1] I once heard the line so quoted, and it became a standing joke between us. — L. R. P.

the hotel of Cambridge, but failed to remunerate, and has been purchased by the Law Faculty to afford food and shelter to a large portion of our band of sucking attorneys. "To what base uses may we return, Horatio!" As for my breakfast and tea, I take those meals myself by myself whenever Hopdance cries very clamorously, and I enjoy very highly the perfect independence which it gives me. At 11 A. M. I go to lecture, when one of the professors holds forth for two hours, with a short intermission at noon. The rest of the day belongs to ourselves, and a good deal of hard work is done regularly, much more than I ever saw in college or anywhere else. There is very little dissipation, much less than I could have supposed possible among such a set of young men, and a tone of earnestness and desire to accomplish something is prevalent throughout the whole school. It is this, I think, more than the actual instruction, which makes this institution so deservedly popular. A man can study law here, if anywhere, since it is the all-absorbing topic of interest, and forms the subject of conversation and discussion among almost all the students. We have two lectures a day for five days, Prof. Parsons lecturing on Mondays and Thursdays, Prof. Parker on Tuesdays, and Prof. Washburn on Wednesdays and Fridays. Our professors are as different as they well could be. Parsons, who lectures on Evidence and Kent's Commentaries, is one of the raciest and jolliest old bricks you ever saw; his lectures are full of anecdotes, personal and otherwise, and he treats law much as Prof. Silliman in his best days must have treated chemistry; any person, whether studying law or not, would be charmed with the man, whose literary claims are almost as great as his legal ones. Prof. Parker, formerly Chief Justice of the Supreme Court of New Hampshire, is probably the great legal gun of the institution, and contributes more than any other to give it a name and a fame through the country generally; he is a very sound and reliable lawyer, but has an intensely dry manner, and his lectures on Pleading and Constitutional Law, though valuable, are the least interesting ones we have. Washburn, who lectures on Real Estate, Wills, and Criminal Law, is very enthusiastic about his work, and is never better pleased than when the fellows go up to his room and ask him questions. He makes his subject very clear by repeated and careful explanations, and I think that I obtain more benefit from his lectures on Real Estate than from any other course. Once a week we have a grand moot court before the whole school, over which one of the Profs. presides as judge, and in which four students take part, the two senior counsel being from the Senior Class, and the two junior counsel from the Middle class, — the Junior Class not being allowed to partake on account of their youth and inexperience. As there are about twenty weeks in the term, each member of the Senior and Middle classes has to speak about once a term. As I am a Middler, I expect to go on as junior counsel before a great while. Besides this public moot court, there are some six or eight clubs, of sixteen to twenty-four members each, which meet in the evening, once a week, and try cases, with two counsel, and one of their number as judge. This is perhaps the most improving exercise of all, since, as the number of the audience is so small, there is very little temptation for a man to splurge, and he just sticks to his brief, and makes a simple, straightforward argument. I belong to two of these clubs, the Coke and the Berrien ; the former is the crack club, and, as a general rule, no fellow is admitted to it until he has studied two years ; but I had the good luck to get in without this qualification. I tried a case in it about three weeks ago, and won it ; and next week, on Monday, I shall try another, and on Tuesday shall sit as judge in the Berrien Club; so that you see I have work enough before me. Indeed, I have been trying my best to work hard, and to learn something about Law, although hitherto my success has been very problematical. I feel incessantly how unfit I am for law, and yet my duty seems to point me in this direction, so there is nothing for it but to dig on.

I do not wholly neglect my old divinity, literature and the classics ; I have made a pretty fair beginning at " Electra," and am reading Dante with James Russell Lowell's Italian class, composed chiefly of theologs and undergrads; we recite three times a week, and take two cantos at a lesson, so that we go ahead swimmingly, and the class (though not I) have already finished the "Purgatorio," and since I have been in it we have read sixteen cantos of the "Paradiso," and eight of the "Inferno." Dante is not nearly as difficult as I had supposed, for his great similarity to the Latin makes it easy for one who has studied that language, and the idiomatic forms are not as numerous as in the modern Italian. I am really awed by the power and magnificence of the poem, and think that it is superior in many respects to Milton's great Epic. Mr. Lowell's explanations and illustrations are very pleasant, and his conversation is charming; so that you can easily imagine how I must enjoy these recitations; they are, in fact, my principal dissipation.

As for Hebrew, I find myself almost totally unable to do anything at it, but have read a Psalm now and then, to keep the letters in my memory. I enjoyed the study of it last winter, very much, and should be sorry to lose it all. Prof. Gibbs never introduced us much to your segholate friends, קְטֹל & Co.; I think that his best energies were rather devoted towards impressing on our youthful minds the proper declension of אֶרֶץ and מֶלֶךְ and the conjugation of Ayin doubled, or סָב; also, to the proper placing of the Daghesh forte, and the terrible consequences which might arise from overlooking it. As for the pronunciation of the memorial name יָהוֶה, I will show you the essay which I wrote on the subject, when you come on to N. H., for I think that you would feel much interested if you once began to look into it; if you want to grub it out yourself, the grand fountain-head of all information is Gesenius' Thesaurus, under the word, and from it flow many valuable references; for a compendious and very learned discussion of the question, see Hengstenberg, "Authoritie des Pentateuchs," vol. i. But I have no one here with whom to discuss these matters, and, indeed, I probably should lose caste as a lawyer, if I betrayed my fondness for these forbidden fruits; among these semi-barbarians, Θέμις is the supreme goddess, and neither 'Αθήνη with her blue eyes and stockings, nor 'Αφροδίτη with her flirtations, can seduce her votaries from the delights of the legal tread-mill. Speaking of 'Αφροδίτη reminds me that I do not know a single female in Cambridge, my hochgeehrten Hausfrauen ausgenommen, and am therefore, in an eminently safe and jolly condition. . . .

A year ago this beautiful spring day, you and I were standing together on the deck of the good steamer *Vulcan*, as she dashed down the Adriatic, and Trieste faded away in the distance, while by our side stood a venerable Form, which had then not yet succumbed to the *mal del mare*, though soon destined to lie prostrate in his state-room, utterly reckless of all mundane considerations, while you and I took duckings of the waves as they dashed over the bow, and enjoyed all the fierce battling of the winds and waves in that storm off the Acroceraunian Promontory. And then our change on Monday night to that funny, cramped little cabin on the *Dálmata*, and our cruise up the Gulf of Corinth, and that delightful week at Athens, — don't you wish that you could do it all over again? There must have been a splendid sunset visible this glorious afternoon from the slopes of Hymettus, and the Parthenon must have shone magnificently in the horizontal rays of the sun; to say nothing of the inspiring air, and the sweet perfume everywhere of the thyme and scented flowers. Would it not be grand to spend a month there camping out, Miltiades at the head of the commissariat, the Form presiding over the classical reminiscences, while you and I would devote our attention to getting up small fights for our own delectation and to his extreme disgust. There is a fresh and racy charm about our two weeks' spree to Greece, such as attaches to no other part of my travels, Switzerland coming the nearest to it; and a sort of accompanying halo surrounds the heads of those with whom I went there, for we have in common some delightful mutual memories. Well, probably we shall never get over there again; but if we do not, we have already garnered up enough in recollection to give us many a happy hour in the future.

CAMBRIDGE, *June* 12, 1859.

DEAR MOTHER, — Cambridge was looking very pleasant when I returned after the recess, and seemed to me for the first time like a habitable place. Having been idle for a week or so, I am doubly willing to apply myself to work. Our Italian recitations have come to an end, and much as I regret the closing of a series of exercises which afforded so much pleasure and literary profit, I, as a law student, cannot help rejoicing that so dangerous a temptation has been removed, and that I shall now have at least eight hours a week more for my law. Mr. Lowell proposes to give his Italian class a supper, so that he can have one more good talk with them before they break up. Such a man at Yale would be of immense value in improving the general style of culture, and in weaving something of the beautiful into that practical nature which I think too many of the students carry away from New Haven. I doubt if there be a better place in the whole country than Yale, for fitting a youth for the hard, stern conflict of every-day life, but I cannot help thinking that their culture would be more complete and beautiful, if poetry and the modern languages took their place in the instructions, as well as logic and mathematics. We are so strong, at Yale, in the solid and the useful, that we think the lighter but not less important graces of too little moment. I spent part of yesterday evening at the K. I always enjoy my visits there very much, it seems so like old times to meet members of the Hornet's Nest who remain faithful to the memory of that jolly concern.

June 30. — My epistle must be very brief this afternoon. We are to play our long-expected match game of ball with the scientific students, and as I am captain of the field, I am very much worried for fear that we may be terribly beaten ; beaten we certainly shall be, for our adversaries have played a year, while we have only played a month, but I hope that we shall be able to make a pretty close game of it, and come out not so very far behind.

A week ago last Tuesday, I went to a small affair at Prof.

Washburn's. There was considerable singing, in which amusement there was quite a contest between the Yale and Harvard songs, but our stock was so much larger that we could give them song for song, and come out in the end with a good surplus. I spent last Sunday with K. On Saturday afternoon we had a fine drive through a most charming country. I think that I never saw the face of any country which looked more beautiful; everywhere the most careful and complete cultivation. It would be rather tame for a long sojourn, and I think I should wish, after awhile, to change it for bolder prospects, but in its peculiar way I think that it bears away the palm from anything I have ever seen on this side the water.

To L. R. P.

CAMBRIDGE, *July* 8, 1859.

. . . . . I don't want to appear dilatory or unfair in the matter of correspondence, but the truth of it is that I am a sworn foe of short letters, and many a time I have checked an impulse to sit down and let drive at you, because I have known that I should be obliged, by want of time, to bite off long before I had got thoroughly pumped out (there is a slight mixing of metaphors in the last sentence, but never mind), and my feelings on mailing such a letter would be of the most unsatisfactory description. But now I labor under no such disadvantage, for I have a good long Saturday evening before me, and unless some bore comes in and eats up some of my time, we can manage to have a pretty thorough chat together, and to make it fair and square you shall insert a cigar between your cherry lips while I do all the talking. Where to begin? Here goes first for an account of my studies. They have become more legal and less literary than during the early part of the term.: my Italian lessons terminated about a month ago, and I have knocked off from Greek entirely. Those Dante recitations I shall never forget; we had a well-informed and enthusiastic class, a most charming teacher, whose main object seemed to be to inspire us with that same love and appreciation of our poet which he himself enjoyed, and above all the freshness and glory of the "Divine Comedy" itself, which came to me so "rich and strange" that astonishment was mingled in a great degree with the delight. It had not been hackneyed by daily use, nor had familiarity bred contempt, as is too often the case with many of the greatest poets; we are taught to parse out of Milton's "Paradise Lost," Shakespeare is as familiar in our mouths as household words, we drag through Virgil at school, and through Homer and Sophocles at college, and, by becoming acquainted with them in such a manner, we lose that beauty which they would have to us if we took them up *con amore*, and in their original freshness; so that you can appreciate my happiness at opening up such a mine of enjoyment, when I tell you that it has enlarged the sphere of my thoughts and feelings in a manner which I should have believed impossible by any single work. Lowell calls it a temple into which a man can retire at any time, and be completely secluded from the murmurs of the world outside. While I was in the class we read two cantos of the "Purgatorio," seventeen of the "Inferno," and the whole (thirty-three cantos) of the "Paradiso"; I shall hope to be able during the vacation to do something towards finishing the rest. I do a little German now and then, but not enough to amount to anything; I think that I shall try next term to make arrangements with some of the girls here (whose acquaintance I shall cultivate for that sole purpose) to read German or Italian; I don't see any use in having the *fems* around unless we can make something out of them. Speaking of *fems* takes me back to N. H. and my visit there, of which you express a desire to hear some account: so you may just apply your "instrument for correcting for the parallax," while I proceed to unfold my plain unvarnished tale.

. . . . . The C——s were as kind and friendly as ever; not changed, unless for the better, from what they were in the pleasant old times of the "week teas." I went to a very nice old folks' party there, and enjoyed it very much, as I always do when I get among people of my own age; you, being unfortunately young, would doubtless have preferred the frivolity of a young people's party. . . . . . I was very glad to have you speak of the scene of the present war, and our own connection with it last year, as I have often thought it over by myself, and I have remembered that day from Geneva to Milan with great pleasure. If the Sardinians have n't cut the throat of that Austrian custom-house officer at Magenta, who insisted on hauling my engravings out of their case, I don't see the use of having any war at all; do you recollect my righteous indignation on that occasion, and the "curses, not loud but deep," which I ejected, to the great terror and disgust of our little *conducteur?* And then in the evening, just after sunset, when we approached Milan, and saw the Duomo in the distance, looking like a great white snow-bank? How would you like to be travelling there now? it must be perfectly horrible to witness that beautiful country so completely devastated, and the air foul with the effluvia from half-buried corpses. Pah! I see by the papers that the dead at Magenta were buried so hastily that the air for miles around is poisoned by the pestilential odors; it must be rather more unpleasant than even the passport and custom-house nuisances. It would be right pleasant to renew our recollections of Italy together, but my favorite dream is of a tent-journey through Greece. I'll tell you how we'll fix it; let us hunt up some old cock of gigantic purse, who has two daughters very lovely in person and mind, and likewise furnished with cheerful dispositions and plenty of *dosh;* these charming beings we will marry forthwith, and sail for the Piræus. It would be so pleasant to throw aside Hebrew Grammar and Law Digests, and, forgetting that we had ever thought of such a thing as a profession, spend a couple of happy, listless, loafing years in wandering over the mountains of the mainland, and cruising among the islands of the Ægean Sea, "with the blue above and the blue below." Then, when we had become sated with this Epicurean, lotus-eating life, we could come back to our western homes, and return the old gentleman his daughters, as we should have no further use for them. Did you ever have a temptation of this kind, Pinckney? I have; and it is the fairest and most dangerous shape in which the Old Nick presents himself to me, but there is a little too strong a smell of the dishonorable about it. . . . .

CAMBRIDGE, THE DEN, *Sunday Evening*,
June 19, 1859.

. . . . That is what a letter should be; it ought to convey to the receiver a mental picture of the physical and intellectual state of the writer, and as many little particularities and items as possible should be added, to round out the picture to its proper fullness, and to supply shade and color. Now, by an exercise of my imagination, and that not a very powerful one, I can bring you before my mental vision; but this exertion is wonderfully lightened by some actual description, which sets the whole subject forward as a living reality. . . . . And now, in order to act up to my principles, I will inform you of my own immediate surroundings before going further. It is a delightful Sunday evening, and after having enjoyed the glowing sunset in a stroll, taken with another young reprobate of a law student, I have returned to my lair in the venerable mansion, and am now writing at a long table on which the formidable array of law books and other rubbish leaves just room enough to write.

The trees in the square in front, now full of rich foliage, throw long, sharp shadows; and in a few hours the moonbeams through their leaves will checker the grass below with fantastic streaks, as

"When they fall
Through some cathedral window."

But although this topic of moon-beams is a fruitful one, and doubtless of absorbing interest to a native of the sunny South, like yourself, who are also a bit "frivolous" withal, yet it won't do for me to pursue it, nor any other poetical subject, since I can now give no time to such things, — or to use a forcible but vulgar expression, I have stopped "running with that machine." The Madonna over the head of the bed, and the row of plants in the window, would seem to indicate that the youthful occupant cultivated the æsthetic in a small way, while the grim features of a set of boxing-gloves peeping over the bookcase, show that his admiration for literature is only surpassed by his love of sparring.

Enter, my young friend, and take a chair, that comfortable arm-chair with a cushion, for if I recollect right, you have a most Davenportly fondness for being comfortable. Now I will make you the best cup of coffee that you have tasted for many a day (I have become a regular "*cordon bleu*" at making coffee), and then we will have a good talk upon New Haven matters, which will of course be of greater mutual interest to us than others, for Cambridge is nothing at all to you, and to me it is merely the prison to which I am temporarily exiled.

I spent ten days at home during the last of May, and longed heartily for you, for our city was looking more beautiful than I had ever seen it before, or, at least it seemed so, since it was three years since I had seen it in the freshness of early summer; "the hour of splendor in the grass, of glory in the flower." And there was one friend there that I found perperfectly unaltered, except that she had beautified herself with a new coat of paint, and that friend was the jolly little *Una*. Out of six pleasant days which we had while I was at home, I spent five in her — sometimes alone, and sometimes with J., and one or two others. Her old thwarts received me in as friendly a manner as if strangers had not sat upon them, and she sprang forward under the oars as if no arms but mine had meddled with their handles.

When you come to New Haven this summer, I think that you and I must have a row together in that small tub. Also tramps, moreover strolls out Prospect Street, peradventure excursions to the Rocks, mayhap moonlight walks on the Avenue, likewise forays to Whitneyville after water-lilies; yea, also, and lounges in Chapel Street, eating pea-nuts, as in the days of Auld lang syne; to say nothing of parties, picnics, rides, tea-fights, sprees, hoe-downs, romps, and divers other diversions in which we will indulge, and on Sundays, when you assume the character of "the church-going belle," of which Cowper speaks, I will occasionally expose myself to the dire influences of Episcopacy to accompany you.

December 31. — I sit down on this last day of the old year to answer your last kind letter, to tell you how much I love you, and to wish you a Happy New Year. I spent Christmas up at Lowell, as I hinted in my last that I should. I went on Saturday morning, and got there in time for dinner. There was quite a little party of visitors, one a Miss C. from Tennessee, although a scion from one of those regular old-fashioned Presbyterian families in the South, she, L., and I, managed to keep the family party from moulding pretty thoroughly. On Monday we all went out skating, and had a jolly time. My boot-heel came off, but I skated along just about the same, my object being to have fun, and not to exhibit my skill in skating. Going home from the pond there were seven of us, four girls and three fellows, all packed in a small cutter. We presented quite a show as we went through town, L. standing in front driving, with his closely packed crowd behind. I thought often of you at home, and that I was among strangers at Christmas, but I did not allow the thought to make me too blue, and was as hilarious as any of them. I came down early Tuesday morning, and got to work by half-past eight o'clock. I always enjoy a visit at Lowell. They are all so hospitable and so desirous to make a guest feel perfectly at home.

NEW YORK, *February* 14, 1860.
357 Fourth Street.

DEAR MOTHER, — This is to inform you of my safe arrival and comfortable settlement in this city. . . . . I called upon Y., who was out, and then I went down to Wall Street and saw Mr. M., who received me very cordially. We had quite a talk on the subject of law; and he said that he would give me something to do, as soon as I became familiar with the practice of the courts. He seems disposed to do all in his power to facilitate my progress in my profession. I then went to Fourth Street and found Y., who seemed very glad to see me, and ready to enter into any chumming arrangement. This morning we met again, had a solemn interview with his landlady, and settled the matter. The situation is good, being between Lafayette Place and Broadway, only a step from the

Astor Library, and conveniently removed from almost all the localities I should be likely to haunt.

February 26. — Those snaps that you sent down were very nice, and between myself and my under-tenants, the mice, rapidly disappeared. I have been much bothered by these little rascals, there being a knot-hole in my pantry, which gives them free egress and regress, so I finally determined to go into a crusade and war of extermination against them, and this morning got a trap, baited it with the object so dear to the mural heart, toasted cheese, and have already caught four of these " Wee sleekit, coorin', tim'rous beasties," as Burns calls them, and hope to put an end to their entire race, — I refer to their family, and not their way of racing up and down the walls in the night. I forgot to tell you that I went to hear Cassius M. Clay, the first Wednesday that I was in town. The speech was very sensible, but the delivery was very poor. I met or saw a good many old friends at the meeting, which was very large and respectable indeed. I expect that most of my old *confrères* are now in the Republican ranks. . Being so near the Cooper Institute, we have capital opportunities for hearing all the political big guns.

NEW YORK, *February* 19, 1860.

. . . . Time is passing rapidly by us, dear friend. How fresh to me seemed that letter of yours of which I have spoken above ! So many little incidents mentioned therein, which are as clear before my mind as if they had happened yesterday, and yet it is now just four years and a half since that letter was written. That interval can hardly be a sad one to look back upon ; we have both been developing our powers, growing, in the truest sense of the word, — passing from the epoch of simple impulse to one combined of thought and impulse. No, there is nothing very depressing in recalling such an almost cloudless past; but how will it be, when a period of equal length has passed, and the summer of 1864 *shall be with us ?* . . . .

Fortunately for me, there are still two kind angels left to drive away the demons of loneliness and despondency, — they are Literature and Music. The Astor Library is just round the corner, and the Academy of Music only a few blocks off, so that I shall never be left totally destitute of something congenial.

March 11, 1860.

.... Your letter gave me the first news which I had had of the death of Professor Goodrich. I was much shocked by it, as I did not know that he had been any more ill than ordinary. I think he took a deep, personal interest in the welfare of the students, and this feeling was reciprocated by them to a great degree; very many looked forward to his Bible class with great anticipation, and longed for it as a time when they would hear the great truths expounded to, and impressed upon them, in a manner at once kind and earnest. Last night I went with L. and M. to hear Dr. Storrs preach. We were well repaid for our walk by the sermon, — text, Ephesians iii. 17, 18, 19. It was divided into four heads of Christian attainment; *first*, the indwelling of Christ by faith; *second*, the love principle as the basis of all; *third*, the infinite knowledge and comprehension; *fourth*, being filled with all the fullness of God. Each of these points was set forth and analyzed in noble language and with great fervency. Perhaps he is sometimes rather wordy, but I think that he generally has some great idea beneath the beautiful covering of words, — pearls of thought under the deep river of flowing speech.

April 19. — I am aware that several of my last letters home have been very short, but I have been decidedly busy recently, as the examination is near at hand, and I have been trying to overhaul the dusty pigeon-holes of my mental lawyer's desk, and to arrange the little law I know in some kind of order, so that I may be able to lay my hand on it when subjected "to the question" by the examining committee next month. Our Cambridge crowd do all we can to encourage and help each other on. For the purpose of impressing the "Code" more deeply upon our mutual minds, we have instituted a series of private examinations, of which the first one came off in my room on Monday last. I was the examiner, and having prepared some

350 questions, I succeeded in boring pretty steadily for nearly three hours, and in putting the other four to their wits' end to answer properly. I think that we shall all pass respectable examinations, and sustain the reputation hitherto possessed by the Cambridge students, which has been very good.

May 31. — . . . . I had a pleasant call at the G's. the other evening. It is so jolly to meet some one who knows all my friends, and is familiar with all my favorite localities, with whom I can talk about New Haven people, discuss East and West Rock and the wild flowers which grow thereon, and even touch upon literature occasionally, instead of this ceaseless chit-chat about society or politics, or the last New York excitement. I met D. E. one Tuesday, and we went to Central Park together. I was perfectly astonished at the amount of progress that has been made there. It is the one thing that New York has a right to be proud of. To be sure, it must always look more or less trim and artificial, and not to be compared with a bit of real untamed nature ; but we must be satisfied with what we can get, and not demand the Alps in our back yard, or Niagara across the street. I have my shingle up and my cards out. I send you a specimen of the latter. . . . .

You assault me on the subject of my suit in the Marine Court. Now I must defend myself by saying that I did not go there by choice, but from necessity; as my client was sued and I had to go there to defend him, a catastrophe which might have fallen upon W. M. Evarts, as well as upon myself. I hardly fear much contamination by just rubbing against the shysters, who in that place most do congregate.

TO L. R. P.

NEW YORK, *April* 7, 1860.

MY DEAR CHILD, — A letter to you has for some time been brewing within me, and I think it advisable to tap myself as soon as possible, and give you the freedom of the spigot before my epistolary effervescence has entirely subsided and grown as flat as a mug of lager, "long drawn out." A vile and immoral simile, to be sure, to use to such a sober youth as yourself, but I know that you have a strong head, as witness your performances at the Sylvester Fest, December 31, 1857, at Dresden; and I don't feel alarmed lest you be upset by so slight a figure of speech. In plain language, I have desired to address myself to you, and to hear from you in return, and this desire was rather aggravated than appeased, by what I saw of you at New Haven, especially in that very pleasant call which you paid me just two weeks ago this Saturday evening. *That* I enjoyed highly, and it was that more than anything else which prevented me from calling at your room as I promised to do; a hurried stay at 102 N. C. interrupted by the inroads of Freshmen, and embittered to me by the thought that I was consuming your time, would have weakened the power of the pleasant impression of that evening which I still retain, and therefore, I say cold-bloodedly that I am glad that I did not call upon you. If it could have been in the evening, it would have been *gang anders;* then, after the

> "Tea, and other curious messes,
> Which the neat-handed Pinckney dresses,"

we should have had "divine talk," varying in its subject from Greek poets to the girls, etc. And above all, our brilliant dreams and speculations about the future, whose withdrawn curtain shows you as a penniless parson, myself as a ditto pettifogger; you with a wife and nine small children, like John Rogers, myself in my attic solus, no companion save my pen-wiper-cat, and my attendant δαιμόνιον. Not that I would cast a slur on being poor, or speak of poverty disrespectfully; no, I would rather go to the other extreme and speak of wealth as a crime, for here wealth is thought the only virtue, "every virtue under heaven." I am speaking seriously, sadly now; pray for me, my dear friend, that I may not become tainted with this cursed mercenary spirit which says, "Be rich or you are not virtuous, make money or you are not respectable, and reckon your success as not attained unless it comes freighted with gold." Sentiments like these I hear more or less openly from all people; from strong-minded, earnest people, from refined and pious girls, from intellectual ladies, in a word, from those whom you would expect to be the very last to harbor such thoughts. I shall look to you for assistance always; scholarship, philosophy, theology, anything we can write and talk about to avoid the subject of getting rich. I suppose that if I had come from any other place than New Haven, the contrast would not be so strong, but up there wealth weighs so lightly against the imponderables, thought and cultivation, and the touchstone of excellence is so different, that the shock which I felt when I first began to see how universal these ideas were here, was very great. I amost envy you your studious retirement at old Yale, and your seclusion from noise and turmoil and the "strife of tongues." Do not suppose, however, that I exhaust all my energies in repinings and howlings of this description; I intend to go ahead and do my best to keep away from Blackwell's Island and Sing-Sing, and not to bring a disgrace upon my family; but still I hope that however imperative the demands of business may be, I may always have some " calm and sure retreat," for a short time every day, where peace shall reign, and the noise of business life be softened by the distance, and

"Fall a soft murmur on the uninjured ear."

Does all this seem rather nonsensical to you? Very possibly, but if a man thinks nonsense he must write nonsense, and I am not ashamed that you should know any of my thoughts, for to me they are serious and real. . . . . I am not doing much in which you would be interested; I manage to get a couple of hours for study on the Code, before going down to the office in the morning; at the office I do all sorts of small jobs, keeping the register of cases, drawing easy complaints, copying foreclosure suits, and when not otherwise employed, cramming up the Revised Statutes. Then in the evening I pretend to study some more on the Code, but this does n't amount to much, as I either go out or else get to reading something else which has a less soporific effect. I find that day-time is the only convenient season for cramming law. I am reading Shakespeare when I take my tea, which I find very delightul; my copy suffers considerably by the arrangement, as the teacup *will* dribble sometimes. I have read the "Tempest," "Measure for Measure," "Two Gentlemen of Verona," "Taming of the Shrew," and "Midsummer Night's Dream," in this way, which I have only adopted since I returned from New Haven, last week. I am pretending to read Dante with my W—— cousins, but as they have nothing else to do, they are too busy to study up lessons, and I have to act as "pony," whenever they come to a strange word or hard sentence; of course we don't get on very fast, and this very evening we made an abortive attempt to get through the Fourth Canto of the Hölle; they are as bad on Dante as Y—— on Ajax, or your sweet self on "Electra;" I seriously think of finishing the Electra by myself some of these days. Speaking of reading, literature, etc., have you seen the "Marble Faun," or Mrs. Browning's last book of ravings on the subject of Italy? I think that Hawthorne's work must be rather interesting for us, as he describes Rome and the artists' studios just as we saw them; he speaks of Akers's studio, and his statue of the Drowned Pearl Diver; by the way, that statue is on exhibition here at the Düsseldorf, and you must not fail to go and see it when you come to N. Y.; it is a splendid production. Mrs. Browning's book, from what I have been able to see of it, is like most of her "Casa Guidi Windows," written with plenty of *animus* and enthusiasm, but little judgment, "full of sound and fury, signifying nothing." I don't think that politics are within the sphere of poetry, and this Italian matter is purely political, not exhibiting the spectacle of a nation fighting desperately for freedom, which might be a legitimate subject for a little something in the lyric line. Have you seen the "Cornhill Magazine?" It is really quite stunning; there is a life of William Hogarth, of which two parts have been published, which is chock-full of charming literary scraps, and is, moreover, written with a power and ease not surpassed by Thackeray himself; if you come across it, don't fail to collar it.

I don't see much of the world of nature at present; the most interesting natural object about these parts is a very shaggy donkey attached to the establishment (*i. e.*, fastened to the cart), of a vendress of oranges, on the corner of Fourth Street and the Bowery; and frequently have I been beguiled of my loose pennies, in order that I might have an opportunity of examining him more narrowly. He is a stunted beast, and I should think that he had the consumption, as do almost all donkeys when brought to this frightful climate of ours, were it not that he is too homely and ugly to have so romantic a disease. One great defect in him is that he is mute, silent as the grave; probably he has hung his harp on some Bowery willow, and refuses to sing his native song in a strange land. I gave him a good dig in the ribs this afternoon, λάθρη τῆς προπώλου, but it only elicited a vicious grin and an uneasy movement of the hind legs, so I did n't push the matter. If he *should* bray, what scenes would arise at the sound, as if at a magical invocation! The Lungo L'Arno where that single powerful animal was wont to ring our matins and chime our vespers; the Piazza Barberini with its perennial fount of song, and above all, the Alban Lake, where, like the beacon lights that announced the fall of Troy to Clytemnestra, one jackass took up the note from another, and thence passed it in endless succession; if I might parody Shelley, I would say —

"There the voluptuous jackasses
Are browsing through all the broad noonday,"

but it is really too bad; only just look at the passage yourself in the "Prometheus Unbound," beginning "There the voluptuous nightingales," and see if you don't think that the whole of that semi-chorus would describe that scene splendidly with a little alteration; besides, Shelley wrote his "Prometheus Unbound," at Rome, and probably the passage was suggested by some such asinine antiphonal chanting."

NEW YORK, *April* 30, 1860.

I lost so much time from my work by this illness, that I have recently been obliged to study very hard in order to prepare myself for the examination for admission to the Bar, which comes off next week Wednesday. Till then I shall be fully occupied, but after that, as free as a bird (with its leg tied to a stick and its wings clipped) for the next ten years, at the end of which time I shall hope to begin to have a little business. My plans for the future are not only uncertain, but perfectly *nix*. I have not the most remote idea as to whether I shall set up for myself, or engage myself as a clerk for a year or two, or make a partnership arrangement with some one; probably shall try to do the " clerk " for a while, as it is the way in which almost all young lawyers here begin and acquire a knowledge of the practice. Would n't it be a good joke if I should get plucked! The examination is very severe, and I don't feel at all sure that I shall not. If I go into an office in some subordinate position, I am afraid that I shall not be able to get down to Annapolis this summer, for lawyers' clerks are expected to disabuse their minds of such absurd ideas as summer vacations, and they must sit and roast in the office while the principal goes to Newport and has a good time. I don't object to this arrangement, of course; young men *ought* to work and have a hard time of it for a while, and if they must break out into pitiful howling, it shows what sort of stuff they are made of. Just as Carlyle says, that the most melancholy sight in the world is that of a man asking for work and not getting it, so I think one of the noblest sights is that of a man doing his work cheerfully — " a heart that at its labor sings." But you can't understand this, of course, and you probably think it very stupid of me to consent to stay through all the summer heat in the city, but you must not shake my resolutions, since I am my own worst enemy, and have already too strong a tendency to flee from that which is arduous to what is tasteful and pleasant: the same spirit which made me in college prefer classics to mathematics. There is one bright streak of sunshine on the picture of the future, and that is your projected visit here next month. It was so much too good to be true that I refused to believe it for a while, but now the probabilities seem to be accumulating, and I have given myself leave to hope a little, but not too strongly, lest I should be disappointed. When are you coming? I have a plan that we should make a foray up to New Haven together, and have a perfectly glorious time, wandering through the sweet May woods (they will be almost perfect then) and thinking of "the days that are no more," or rather of the days that are yet to be, for spring is the season of hope, and we will leave memory to the autumn days. Or perhaps in some boat (alas ! not the *Una*), we will rock on the waves of the bay, and the print of a No. 8 boot and a No. — gaiter on the sands of Morris Cove shall tell where we landed to munch and crunch a frugal lunch. . . . . Speaking of the 1st of May reminds me that a Brooklyn clergyman preached, the other day, on the subject of " Moving " as a means of Christian discipline ! I doubt if there be any one thing which is quite as effectual for trying the soul in the furnace of affliction, unless it be " housecleaning," and that can only be considered as a purifying trial to the male members of the human family — the female portion seeing in it only occasion for triumph and fiendish joy. I am here also reminded to tell you that I moved my room last week, or rather moved *from* my room, as it was not sufficiently attractive to induce me to take it with me bodily. . . . . I propose turning gardener in my leisure hours, and raising some flowers in the quite extensive beds in our back yard here. I can't bear the idea of letting the spring and summer pass without flowers, and am willing to work to get them. . . . . I am *so* happy now — the real spring feeling, which I always have about this time, a desire to sing or do something to express my pent-up feelings. , I heard on Easter Sunday some most delicious music at Dr. Hawkes's church, and came home with the full determination of writing you a regular Easter letter, but somehow was prevented. That is the one holy day of the Episcopal Church in which I can join with all my soul, for

"The heavens laugh with you in your jubilee,
My heart is at your festival,
The fullness of your bliss, I feel, I feel it all."

NEW YORK, *June* 1, 1860.

DEAR ——, — You will perceive by the inclosed cards that I am at last married to the bride to whom I have been so long paying my court. The fair divinity of the legal profession has consented to be mine for life, or at least so long as I shall treat her with that attention and tenderness which are her just due. In return she promises to feed me, to clothe me decently, and perhaps give me some reputation.

Somehow or other, though, as I talk about this goddess of mine, she becomes very shadowy and unsubstantial, and now I find it impossible to see her at all, for your face has come between, and Law suffers a disastrous eclipse. Well, for the present, let her disappear. I am in her power only from 9 A. M. to 5 P. M., for at that latter hour I unclasp my hand from her skinny parchment fingers and leave her alone in the solitude of No. 54 Merchants' Exchange, while I make stolen visits to those old friends of mine, Languages and Literature, and occasionally take my pen to have a chat with some dear human friend who is far away.

NEW YORK, *June* 3, 1860.

DEAR M., — .... I must first of all thank you for your very kind letter, and for the friendly wishes expressed therein with reference to my entering upon my profession. Whether I shall attain any degree of success in it is yet to me a very dubious problem. If I can once get my enthusiasm for it fairly aroused, I defy anything but poor health to prevent me from fighting my way up to the first ranks. If I look upon it merely as a means of gaining a living, I shall probably gain a living by it and nothing more, and all my superfluous ambition would expend itself upon such *dilettante* pursuits as languages and general literature. I *hope* that I shall pursue the former course, but must live the life which my powers and tastes dictate, still feeling that it is far better to be a really good lawyer than a mere dabbler in Greek and German. . . . You speak of enjoying " The Marble Faun " very highly. I read it about three weeks ago, and liked some things in it very well, but thought the whole work decidedly a failure for Hawthorne, although any other man might be proud of having written it. The general story, or plot, is unusually fragmentary and pointless, even for him. He introduces mysteries which are entirely unnecessary, and which have the effect of simply lumbering up the story, and nothing more. His descriptions are always fine; but can any word-painting equal the picture which rises before your mind at the very sound of the word "Roma." . . . . Hawthorne is only thoroughly at home in his experiments on the American mind. He does not *know* the English or Italian temperament well enough to draw them so minutely. For this reason I think that the characters of Miriam and Donatello, carefully elaborated as they are, are failures. . . . . The whole tradition of the Faun seemed to me too thin a fancy to be drawn out to such a length, and I think that Mr. Hawthorne must do better than that book, or else let his fame rest on "The Scarlet Letter" and "The House of the Seven Gables." Excuse this lengthy critique, but when I am reading books at the same time with friends, I am very fond of talking them over with them.

I am very glad to hear that you have directed your "meditations" to the subject of "slippers," and I hope that that will not be the whole of it, for if ever there was a case of real want and destitution, it exists in "this chile." So, if you have any regard for the feelings of this unhappy Decemvirate, let the slippers be made the special order of the day. . . . .

NEW YORK, *June* 19, 1860.

DEAR MOTHER, — It is now quite a long time since I have written you anything that deserves the name of a letter. It is so hot, and I have been so lazy. I want to get away very much, but so long as there is anything to be done, I suppose it will be good discipline for me to stay here and do it. I should like to go home and make a long visit, and that is because this is the last year that I shall have a chance to do so for a long while. I went to Tarrytown on Saturday afternoon; spent a most delightful Sunday there; heard H. preach in the morning. In the afternoon the children had exercises in the church. They sang several simple hymns, addresses were made, and last of all Harry made a sort of farewell address, as it was the last time he was to meet them in that way. Just as he finished, an old man came tottering up towards the pulpit, and said he must take his young brother once more by the hand. He was eighty-seven years of age. When he had taken H. by the hand he poured forth his grateful thanks and benedictions, mingled with many tears, and you may be sure that there were few dry eyes in the church. It was such a spontaneous burst of gratitude and feeling, that it seemed perfectly natural, and not at all peculiar. .... I have joined a base ball club, as I find that I am unable to keep steadily at work at the Gymnasium in this sweltering weather. I went to Hunter's Point and played with the club. I played very hard, and was so used up that I could hardly sit straight in my chair, and have been lame ever since. My garden is doing well; the roses have bloomed well; my tuberoses are coming up nicely; and the gladiolas are flourishing like green bay trees.

To L. R. P.

NEW YORK, *July* 13, 1860.

MY DEAR PACK, — I send you herewith a couple of books of the President's which I have kept so long. There is at our house also an "Antigone" in German, "für die deutsche Bühne," which J. will hand you. Don't hook these books for your own private benefit, but return them to Mr. Woolsey, and say to him that I should have returned them before I went to Europe, had not my flitting been so very sudden that I hardly had time for anything. After my return from Europe the books were mislaid and overlooked, and were not turned up until quite recently. This is a poor excuse, I am aware, but it is the fact, and the best I have. I am, of course, very sorry that I should have been so careless, especially about books, as I have a theory on the subject of borrowing books which differs widely from my practice on this occasion.

That "Electra" of yours does not make its appearance. I fear me much that you did not spend the Fourth in getting it up, but rather in some carnal amusement of the genus "bust," species picnic, and have deserted our sad Ἤλεκτρα, ἀεικεῖ σὸν στολᾷ and hair not adorned nor fit for supplication (ἀλιπαρής), for the society of some New Haven Chrysothemis, to whom there is a large picnic basket (πλουσία τράπεζα). Whenever you will send on, this deponent will hasten to reciprocate.

NEW YORK, *August* 17, 1860.

Here in the dreary solitude of the office I take up my pen to write to you, although I have nothing in the world to say, and have not even your last letter by me to answer and refute. It is for me a peculiarly difficult task to write anything but a business letter down here. Instead of my own cheerful little library before me, from whose shelves look genially down the pleasant faces (or rather backs) of Chaucer (your gift), and Spenser, and Tasso, and Kit North, and Charles Lamb, warming up the vacant wall with kindly thoughts and inspiring companionship, I have here the sheep-skin covered Reports, and the Code, and the Revised Statutes, and many other ogres of legal learning, who stand ready to devour any thought not professional as soon as it is born. Writing under such disadvantages, you must pardon all stupidity, and not allow yourself to believe that "Cousin Will" has lost all his decent ideas in the process of becoming a lawyer. If I really had anything to tell you, I could say it as well from this heart of commerce as from my own study, but when it comes to making a long letter "out of nothing and all very good," as our catechism has it, it is *tout-a-fait une autre chose*, for the very inherent practicality of the Merchants' Exchange rebukes the doing of anything for which some tangible result, some pocketable sum in dollars and cents, cannot be shown. Once in a while I rebel against these statutes of the Money King, but he is generally too much for me, and if he does not break my spirit, or make me yield him servile obedience, he yet succeeds in driving away all airy fancies, and in recalling all wandering thoughts to the Now and the Here. . . . . Last Tuesday was my twenty-fourth birthday, and I am now progressing in my twenty-fifth year! So much of life spent, so little done, and that little done so shabbily and superficially! And most of all, the future promises so little more. I am at times tempted to give up all thoughts of honor and nobleness, and turn to grubbing for money with the rest, and live for the passing day. You cannot conceive of the utter self-abasement and self-contempt which I felt on last Tuesday evening, when I took a retrospect of things in general. Thinking is what I can't afford to do; it always throws me into such a state of savage unrest. But when I pass down under these stormy surface waves, I find it all quiet and serene with the recollection of home and mother, and a few other dear friends. Yes, this is my religion, now, the best I have, my sanctuary, for

> "All the babble of life's angry voices
> Dies, in hushed silence, at its peaceful door."

NEW YORK, *September* 14, 1860.

. . . . The very cold and blustering weather, which has been making us all shiver, has passed away, and the days are now really autumnal, though rather more like October than September. In this city, September is a month of reawakening life and activity; the absent citizens begin to return from the four winds, where they have been trying to get a little fresh air during the summer, business revives again, the opera and the Philharmonic tune their fiddle strings and clear their throats, and life begins once more to flow as usual in the old channels. It is quite noticeable, the process called hibernation is exactly reversed in a large city; here we don't hibernate, we æstivate; as the hot weather comes on, the people of passage wing their way to cooler climates, while those who are too poor, or too busy, to accompany them, retire to their holes and relapse into a torpid state, in which they remain until the middle of September. It is true that during the month of æstivation the streets of New York are nearly as full as ever, but not with the genuine New York dormouse; they are animals from farther south, fleeing from their time of æstivation. I only hope that in the harvest of business which the fall always brings with it, this dormouse may get a legal nut or two to crack.

October 27. — . . . . I enjoyed my visit at home very much indeed, although the weather was so unpleasant all the time. After I have been away from home about a month, I begin to feel a very great restlessness, which interferes with my work decidedly, and my thoughts will wander in spite of me, but after I have spent a few days at home I come back to my work refreshed and invigorated, and feeling like a legal game cock.

NEW YORK, *September* 22, 1860.

DEAR M.— . . . . To-day I write, not because I have time enough, for I have not (and I seem to myself to take this time by stealth), but because this day, so bright, clear, inspiring, reminds me of you and all friends in the country, who are drinking in this glorious air like draughts of wine, — not the sparkling, intoxicating champagne, which floats in the air of April, but good old wine of autumn, generous Madeira or Sherry, which strengthens as well as gladdens the heart of man. This is just that delightful weather, between the heats of summer and what *my* poet calls " the melancholy days, the saddest of the year." What glorious weather for horseback-riding, and what good times we could have together at H. P., galloping in trots of discovery through back lanes and cross paths, and now and then through a bit of wood, whose leaves are just receiving the first touch from the brush of that greatest of landscape painters, Autumn ! . . . . I intend to subscribe to the Philharmonic this winter. For a student, like myself, whose days are devoted to work, and whose evenings to general reading, music is the safest and most enjoyable mode of refreshing and diverting the mind ; society, politics, dissipation, all these bring with them excitements and entanglements which do not leave the mind in the best condition for quiet work ; but music exerts no such disturbing force, it merely, " when soft voices die, vibrates in the memory." . . . .

To L. R. P.

NEW YORK, *October* 14, 1860.

MY DEAR BOY, — I don't owe you a letter, I am well aware, as I do not apply that term to the diminutive document which

I received from you two or three weeks ago, but then I hold liberal opinions on the subject of correspondence, and believe in writing when I feel like it, and in not writing when I don't; some people act as if corresponding was a similar affair to a cash account or to matching cents: suffice it to say that this morning I feel like having a talk with you, and, as I shall have all the say, you can imagine that you are talking with some of your lady friends. As I was filing some letters this morning, I happened to look over the older ones, and I chanced upon a letter from you at Berlin, written six days after T. D. and I left Liverpool. It carried me back irresistibly to a point more than two years ago, when I first returned home, and when you were just setting out on Swiss tramps and Belgian sight-seeing. You spoke of many matters which were then doubtful, but which are now settled; of meeting friends abroad who are now quietly at home; of future prospects which are now to a certain extent defined. We were then both of us at the most migratory and unsettled period of life, and it was very natural that changes should take place; from irresponsible, wandering, jolly Burschen, whose sole trade was a kind of literary "Bummeln," we have subsided, you into a tutor, with "Leider, auch Theologie" before you, and I into a briefless shyster "in den königlichen, kaiserlichen Grabzellen zu New York." This retrospect of "two years ago" also reminds me of the old society relations at N. H., and the sad feelings which I had when I came home and found my place filled up; and how absurdly I resented what was only a natural sequence of the passage of time and the constitution of human nature. I ought to have made use of T. D.'s favorite proverb, "Blessed are they that expect nothing, for they shall not be disappointed." *Now*, I have brought down my expectations to a very low notch, and receive thankfully the smallest crumbs of regard from old friends, and this is undoubtedly the most sensible and philosophic view to take of things, but it is impossible for me to pass the sponge over my memory and not recollect how pleasant the old times were, and how often, with Faust, I could have said to the passing moment, "Stay, for thou art fair." One thing, I think, however, has not changed in the past two years, and that is my regard for you, or, if it has, it has been only to grow stronger and warmer from better acquaintance and more matured opinions. . . . .

I have work enough now at the office to keep me pretty busy all day. Mr. M. is the attorney for this " Artisan's Bank," the recent suspension of which has been talked a good deal about in the papers within the last two weeks, and consequently he has spent most of his time settling its affairs, and is not in the office an hour a day; so that I have lots of work, and, worse yet, of responsibility, on my hands. I shall be glad enough when the affairs of the Bank are settled, and I shall be no more obliged to act upon my own discretion in important matters. I think that I am progressing in knowledge of the practice, but I cannot expect to get ahead very fast when I do not give my whole mind to my profession, any more than I am doing at present. Out of office hours I am variously occupied; generally twice a week I go off to play ball with a very good set of fellows; on the other days I try to do some work in my room, but with dubious success. I am reading Wordsworth's "Excursion" now, and enjoy it very much; I don't see how I ever could have considered as dull and heavy, a book which treats the deepest and most interesting subjects in a manner at once so tender and so majestic; there is something inexpressibly soothing and quieting about it, which does my fidgety spirit good, and satisfies

> " The universal instinct of repose,
> The longing for confirmed tranquillity,
> Inward and outward."

I grind away at Mommsen's " Römische Geschichte," and get some good out of it, but it goes into things too deeply, and views matters from a stand-point so learned and philological, that it is rather above the head of my ignorance; the style, too, is involved, and makes pretty tough German to translate; I can't read it very fast. If you know of any first-rate German, that reads pretty smooth and pays the time expended, I wish you would let me know. Have you finished that book of

Schlegel that I saw on your table, and how do you like it? I spend an evening occasionally in the Cooper Institute, looking over the magazines. There is a jolly article in the last "Blackwood" on King Arthur and the Table Round. Do you ever see the "Cornhill"? The series of articles in it by G. A. Sala, on Hogarth, is now finished; the first two numbers were very good, but I am inclined to think that the others are inferior. I hope that you will stir up some more "Electra" soon, unless you are too busy, as I run a great risk of forgetting all my Greek between the batches.

I went to the Prince of Wales' ball on Friday; the account whereof, behold, is it not written in the "New York Herald," so that he who runs (after a newsboy and gets a copy) may read?"

To H. R. C.

NEW YORK, *September* 30, 1860.

DEAR HARRY, — I won't waste half my first sheet in apologies and excuses for not writing before, but will throw myself at once upon the mercy of the court and plead guilty of gross laziness, trusting to the clemency of the judge, and hoping that he will let me know my sentence as soon as may be convenient for him. It seems so natural to get hold of a sheet of foreign letter paper once more, and to be talking with you about foreign parts; you who are so intimately associated in my mind with sea-voyages and Alp-climbings, all of which old times I live over again both in sleeping and in waking dreams, to say nothing of the new imaginary expeditions which I am continually projecting. But you are by this time far beyond the routes of travel, walking in unknown paths, almost as far as those regions which Horace speaks of as

> "Quæ loca fabulosus,
> Lambit Hydaspes."

Don't laugh, now, you rascal, if my geography be pretty badly out of joint, for I intend to brush up ideas and information about those regions, and post myself thoroughly as to the place of your abode. When you write, you must tell me all about your voyage, and how you passed through the Straits of Gibraltar, and whether you thought of me when you did, and how you enjoyed your sail through the Mediterranean, and how you were impressed by your first sight of Turkish soil. I have of course taken the deepest interest in the events which have been transpiring in Syria, and have felt very anxious that the Turkish government should either effectually suppress the revolters, or get itself suppressed. Did the disturbances extend much in your direction? I have found it difficult to understand clearly whether the trouble was entirely confined to the Lebanon region, or whether it was a general and wide-spread plot. It would seem as if the Sultan would have to take his walking-ticket before long, and let the progress of civilization and religion pursue its course. The "sick man" might safely be called a dead man now, and it would hardly seem to pay for the Powers of Europe to galvanize him much longer. I hope that whatever occurs, you may be preserved in health and strength to go on with your labors, and may keep up a good spirit and a cheerful heart. . . . .

The election is of course absorbing much of the public interest at present. Lincoln's chances seem very fair just now; the Democracy is irreconcilably split, and in this State I almost doubt whether all the opposing parties, if combined, would be equal to the Republicans. The news from Pennsylvania, too, is very cheering; but that is a changeable, dangerous State, and it may veer round before the election, and vote the devil's ticket after all. May God speed the right, which is his own cause, and give us honesty and justice in our next administration. It would be hard indeed to bear if after so nearly grasping the object of our efforts and desires, we should again fall back into the darkness and barbarism of another pro-slavery government; the only thing we can do is to work hard and hope for the best. I am glad to say that the campaign this year seems likely to be much quieter, and much less disfigured by absurdities and excesses, than in the days of "Fremont and Jessie." Things about New Haven are much the same as ever. The old Laboratory in front of North College, formerly the President's house, has been entirely torn down, and this change greatly improves the personal appearance of the colleges ; there is nothing now to interfere with the grandeur of that uninterrupted line of red brick.

NEW YORK, *November* 11, 1860.

. . . . This has been a very important and exciting week ; we Republicans have done the deed, and now the great question must be settled one way or the other, and I don't think it makes much difference in which. If the Southerners simply blow, and boast, and threaten for a while, and then acquiesce in the inauguration of Mr. Lincoln, we shall have peace, which is a good thing enough in its way, and the material interests of commerce and manufactures will not be much deranged. If secession does really take place, and hostilities are commenced, so much the better. There will be misery and bloodshed for a while, and all the horrors of civil strife, but it will only hasten on the great result which must sooner or later be reached, only assist to throw more light on the problem which must one day be solved. And then the country will emerge from that chaos of fire and blood, fresh and free, its dross purged away, and its great sin expiated. May I live to see that day.

December 7. — . . . . I began my Bible class yesterday, with about thirty. As they had just received their question-books, they could not answer very briskly, and I had to talk pretty steadily for nearly an hour. I hope they will do their share next time. I had prepared myself moderately well, by about three hours' hard cramming, the night before. I find that my knowledge of Hebrew stands me in good stead, and explains many matters which otherwise seemed contradictory.

NEW YORK, *December* 23, 1860.

DEAR M., — . . . . Since writing the above, I have been to my Bible class. " Your Bible class," I hear you exclaim, — " Where on earth did you pick up a Bible-class ? " The way it came about was this. I was calling on Dr. N., and he asked me if I was engaged in any Sunday-school. I said no, but that I should like to be. He then proposed that I should take charge of the Bible class connected with his church. After some hesitation I said I would, and went over to the church the next Sunday to spy out the land. Imagine my horror on finding that the class was about thirty in number, many of them older than myself! I felt badly stuck, you may be sure, but the only way was to face the music. So last Sunday I prepared the lesson pretty thoroughly, and found it much easier work than I had supposed, but a task requiring impudence, of which quality, you know, I am utterly devoid. To-day I got along still better, and succeeded in getting the class to discuss the lesson themselves, and not to leave the talking entirely to me. Our lessons are in the Book of Judges, and you may be sure that I go it strong on the historical and geographical allusions — and once in a while I venture upon an original translation of the original tongue — leaving, however, the religious teachings to be drawn by the older men. I don't know what effect my way of teaching may have upon the class, but I know for myself that I have become deeply interested in this careful study — the deeper I go into it, the more closely I find it to be linked with other parts of Scripture, which seemed to have no connection when I read them casually. . . . .

I suppose that you have heard all about Thanksgiving Day, and how the "fatal thirteen" sat down to dinner, and how we drank to "absent pardners," for all grandpa's children were there, but not one of their mates. Uncle R. was the star performer on the occasion, in the character of the "Prodigal Son," — though his appearance told no tales of having been nourished on husks, but rather spoke of English beef and humming ale. . . . .

I don't speak of politics, because everybody talks about them, until I am fairly sick of the word. I don't think anything is to be apprehended from the crazy conduct of the Southerners. If the U. S. calls for volunteers to put Charleston down, I think that the law would present much inferior attractions to me.

NEW YORK, *January* 4, 1861.

DEAR MOTHER, — .... I was hard at work all New Year's Day, and went from the Dan of Second Place in Brooklyn, to the Beersheba of Thirty-seventh Street, New York, and did not get through till after ten o'clock, although I made only twenty-eight calls; but then they, especially the Brooklyn ones, were generally pretty long.

I do wish that one that we love would be a little more enthusiastic. I think that enthusiasm is the source of more pure and exalted pleasure than almost any other earthly feeling. It quickens and sharpens the mental eye and ear; it gives a zest to enjoyment; it raises the heart at the sight of God's work in nature, and fills the eyes with happy tears at hearing of noble and generous deeds. Perhaps the old Greeks were not so far wrong in their composition of this word, making it "God in us." ....

January 8. — I went to a performance on Monday night at Mrs. Botta's. It was a reading by Mrs. Siddons, of English Ballad Poetry. The course is to continue throughout the winter. Mrs. S. reads well, and has a charming appreciation of the old classics. I have a card for the course, and shall go now and then.

February 24, 1861. — .... I got two very good views of President Lincoln. I was quite disappointed at finding him a much greater beauty than I had supposed. I had hoped to have a real sharp poignant sensation of ugliness incarnate, to see a man who deserved to receive the fabled jack-knife. He looked very solemn, and I think that he had reason to be so. On his passage down Broadway he looked excessively tired, and did his bowing by means of a string passing down the leg of his pantaloons and fastened to his collar, — this string was pulled by one of his suite at regular intervals, and a bow was the result.

I see by the papers that he cut and ran from Harrisburg, and got to Washington sooner than was expected. I think that he acted right, and that he cannot take too great care of his life, — the intelligence which he received must have been of a kind to justify such a step. I hope that his life may be preserved, and that he may be inaugurated. . . . . If war comes, it will be the holiest and most righteous war the world has ever seen, and will wash us with much blood from our national sin.

March 29, 1861. — . . . . If you will look through the newspaper of to-day you will see that Governor Morgan has at last recognized my modest merit, and granted me the appointment of notary public. This I consider one of the most discreet and proper acts of his administration, and one for which he deserves to be nominated an indefinite number of times. It is a great satisfaction to me to think that my visit to Albany on that dreadful January day was not all for naught.

To H. N. C.

NEW YORK, *April* 2, 1861.

. . . . Take good care of your health, Harry, and don't allow yourself to think that duty demands that you should overwork yourself: your duty really lies in living to make your influence more extended and your experience more complete. You must not forget the means which God has provided to help you, in pressing on too hastily to the wished-for end. Don't think that I am lecturing you; I only want to remind you of the fact that even an active mind, and a zealous, ardent soul, will make themselves more powerfully felt in a community of men, and especially uneducated men, if they are backed up, so to speak, and sustained by a vigorous, active body, whose contributions to the general stock of good are promptness and facility in action, delight in God's visible world, cheerfulness always. I think of you very often, my dear boy, and of what you are doing, and of what items of work your daily life is made up. And once in a while, perhaps, there steals over me a thought that I ought not to be here working only for myself, and doing nothing in return for all the great goodness and kindness which have been shown to me. I am sorry to say that these thoughts of labor and self-sacrifice come but seldom, and are easily dissipated; they pass away and leave me as cold and selfish as before. Still it is better to think, even occasionally, than not to think at all. I hope that in your zeal for the spiritual welfare of the heathen strangers of Persia, you do not forget that of the heathen *friends* whom you have left at home.

You will be surprised, and I don't know whether pleased or amused, to hear that I am the teacher of a large and old Bible class. The way in which it came about was this: A relative of mine, Dr. N., was called last year to Allen Street Presbyterian Church, in New York, and has been working there very vigorously, roping in every one he could get hold of. He asked me one day if I was engaged in any Sunday-school work. I said no; that I had been to mission-schools, and that they had seemed very plentifully supplied with teachers. He then asked me if I would not like to take a Bible class in his Sunday-school. I, supposing that it was a class composed of three or four young men, agreed to do it, and the next Sunday went down to Allen Street to spy out the land, and see what things looked like. Imagine my consternation on finding that the Bible class consisted of all the teachers of the Sabbath-school and some others, ages from forty to eighteen; that they met in the church, and made a pretty formidable show of numbers! I would have fled forthwith, but was seized and ruthlessly introduced to the "committee who had been appointed to get a new teacher," who informed me that I had been appointed teacher on Dr. N.'s recommendation, etc. I thought that this was drawing it pretty strong, but I waited and heard the lesson gone through with. One of the teachers conducted the exercises, and made so many bulls, that I felt sure that I could not do worse. So I asked for a week to think it over, and took counsel. Y. was very urgent that I should take it, and so I prepared the lesson for the next time, and went over there. I got along very nicely, although I had a class of some thirty, and became so much interested in the subject of the lesson that I determined to continue, and have done so ever since, which is now some four months. We use the Union Question Book, and prepare the lesson for the Sunday-school of the next Sunday. Of course the first thing is to properly get up the lesson for the children; but I have endeavored to go a great deal farther than that, and to get some higher good out of it for ourselves. I don't know how well I have succeeded with the rest, but it has given me a great many ideas I never had before, and a reverent spirit and mode of feeling quite new to me. We have finished Judges and Ruth, and are just beginning 1 Samuel. I work like a beaver with commentaries, Bible Dictionary, etc., and when a difficult passage occurs, I frequently find a solution by scratching my head for an hour or two over the Hebrew, which I had studied for several months at New Haven with Professor Gibbs, when I was getting up the class report, and which now comes nicely into play. I take great pleasure and interest in the work, and only wish that the class would do the same. Some of the older men take hold well, but most are either very reserved or very stupid. What do you think of this undertaking? Is it presumptuous on my part? You see I confine myself mostly to explanation of the text and comparison of passages, and manage to draw out some of the elders to make the practical applications. Perhaps my uncle, Mr. D., about hit it, when he said that he thought it was a first-rate thing for me, but that he did n't know how it might be for the class. However, I honestly do my best, and shall give it up whenever it seems that I am getting at all pernicious. I have given you a somewhat extended account of this, because I thought that what I was doing in this way would interest you more if told with particularity. Please to let me know, when you write to me, just what you think about it.

Saturday, April 6. — . . . . I suppose that you listen with great eagerness for political news from home. The day is certainly one of great and stirring events, and it seems to me inconceivable that so many Northern people can view them with indifference, or at most with trembling cowardice. It seems impossible to imagine how a conflict can be avoided in the present state of affairs; but, while I earnestly deprecate the beginning of civil war, I think that there are worse things than war, and that the dominant spirit of money-getting at the North is more corrupting and demoralizing. The North is too much demoralized already: some through interest, some through fear, and a goodly number through a desire to obey law, even though it be weakly wielded. I do not suppose that I am very well fitted for a soldier, but still I have a good deal of fight in me, and think that I shall never see a holier cause to fight for. I shall consider it my duty at least to offer myself if the general government makes a requisition for volunteers. And for the result in the end there can be, I think, no doubt; so, when you hear of the troubles and disturbances here, do not be excessively anxious, for it is really necessary that the country should pass through some such phase of trial and suffering, and then emerge in the clear light of truth and freedom. It has really tended to destroy the distinctions between right and wrong, and to overthrow in many minds a belief in God's government of human affairs to see the system of slavery, not apologized for, but defended and upheld as a sacred and divine institution. This spectacle, together with that of the official robberies and treacheries at Washington during the last year, and more recently at the South, have made every patriotic heart sink with shame and sorrow; and now nothing but blood and much grief and misery and disaster will atone for our national crime. In such a crisis as this, no man who is young and unfettered by domestic ties has any right to withold himself.

I am working into the practice of my profession, and learn quite rapidly. I hope to be able to make an honest living out of it some of these days, or rather years. I am now, by appointment of Governor Morgan, a notary public, which is quite a help to me in a variety of ways, and also brings me in somewhat of "the filthy."

Sunday, April 14. — Well, it has come at last. War is fairly upon us, and April 12, 1861, will be marked as the day upon which began the fiercest civil war of modern times. We are still in a state of the greatest uncertainty as to what has been done, but there is reason to believe that Fort Sumter has been reduced by the traitors. Since the news came yesterday I have hardly thought of anything else, and I am almost sick with excitement and anxiety. What I most fear is that the rebels may also take Washington by a *coup de main*, which would be the climax of our disgrace. I think that the North is now thoroughly roused, and that there will be a loud and speedy response to any call which the States may make for volunteers. Pennsylvania and New York have each voted $500,000 to arm the State, and it is said that each of the States will soon be called upon to furnish its quota of troops. I think that if they get ahead faster in Connecticut than they do here, I shall go up there and enlist. I don't know how wise this course which I contemplate may be, but I can no otherwise.

I hear that you are making capital progress with your Syriac, or whatever the language is that you are studying. Please to tell me something about it when you write, and what it is like.

IV.

LETTERS OF ARMY LIFE AND SERVICE.

1861–64.

IV.

LETTERS OF ARMY LIFE AND SERVICE.

April 27, 1861.

DEAR MOTHER, — I have not written you, because I was so uncertain about my movements. . . . . Now, however, I am fixed, and can give an account of myself. I have felt all along that it was my duty to go, and that it would be disgraceful if I did not. I got a letter to Colonel Stevens, who is in command of those members of the Seventh Regiment who are still in the city, and he put my name down on the roll last Tuesday. All of us who are ready and equipped are to start at the first opportunity. My uniform will be ready to-day, and now I have only my blankets and grub articles to get, and have my hair cut short. The excitement in the city the last week has been fearful; some streets are a long arbor of flags, and recruits march up and down the streets to drum and fife.

To L. R. P.

NEW YORK, *May* 5, 1861.

DEAR BOY, — I was sorry that you were unable to stop on your way through here last week, but perhaps it is best as it is, for you probably would not have found me, as I was not at the office, — my time being divided about equally between military furnishing stores and the drill-room. J. will tell you just what my position is. I will only say that I have joined the recruits of the Seventh, have been drilling for a week and a half, and during the whole of last week was every day expecting to get orders to leave for Washington. But on Friday an order was given not to send on any more troops from this Division at present. This is most vexatious and disappointing, as it places us in a state of extreme suspense, and I am afraid that the choicest part of the scrimmage will be over before we can get down there. However, they promise us that we shall certainly go on at *some* time before long; and I intend to go back to my business, and drill every afternoon from 3 to 6. This delay has its advantages also: the new company will be well-equipped and quite decently drilled before going on, and will be less likely to disgrace the regiment.

I am sorry that you don't like the idea of my going. It seems to me that I could not in decency do anything else. Here I have been for years on the extreme Abolition edge of the Republican party, hoping for the practical assertion, in *some* way, of the rights and honor of the free North, and here is an opportunity to realize all those hopes, — to put those theories into practice. Shall I be outdone in deeds by the very men whom my words have condemned? Shall the Democratic rag-tag and bob-tail go out to war and strike good blows for the right, while we Republicans sit safely at home, and say, "Oh, our lives are too precious to be risked in this conflict!" Have we a right to place an unusual value upon our lives, simply because our advantages have been great; and shall culture and education deafen us to the call of honor and patriotism? Whatever others may say in this strain, I can only reply with Electra, —

Τούτοις ἐγὼ ξῆν τοῖς νόμοις οὐ βούλομαι.[1]

Don't come the Chrysothémis over me at this stirring time. I know that *you* are so situated at present that it would be unwise and almost impossible for you to go; but with me the case is different: I have as yet no professional engagements which cannot be easily transferred; I have no family of my own (wife and νήπια) to regret me peculiarly; I have not even one fair friend to shed a tear if I should never come back;

---

[1] "Not by such rules will I guide my life."

my loss would be in fact rather an advantage, as the noble army of lawyers would be lessened, and a useless, selfish life might be to some extent expiated by a "pro patria mori." But whether I go or stay, whether I get six feet of Virginia soil or a happy return, be sure that I shall love and cherish you always.

THIRTY-SECOND STREET, NEW YORK, *May* 9, 1861.

DEAREST MOTHER, — We are off after all, in spite of what I wrote you this morning. I happened into the drill-room and found that the squad were to sail at 6 P. M., in the steamer *Matanzas*. I rushed to my room, packed up my knapsack and got down to the boat by 5½ P. M. It was announced that we were not to sail until 9 to-morrow morning, and as I was on guard from 9 to 12 P. M., I got the pass-word, ran the guard, came up here to Thirty-second Street, where I sit, the centre of a crowd of sympathizing friends. Good-by, dearest mother; you can have no objection to make this little contribution to the Great Cause. For myself, I cannot see how a life could be more worthily given up, unless it were for God's sake, though is not this God's cause?

God bless you.   Your ever-loving son.

May 11, STEAMER MATANZAS,
CHESAPEAKE BAY, Near the Mouth of the Potomac.

DEAREST MOTHER, — It is now my turn to do guard duty to-day, and as four hours out of the six are spent in the guard-room, with nothing in particular to do, I have a capital chance to let you know how we have got on thus far. I got back to the wharf from Thirty-second Street by 12½, passed the guard safely, by means of the magic word "Gertrude," which was the pass-word for the night, and managed to get some sleep in spite of a tremendous racket kept up by a crowd of youngsters. We got off about 9 A. M., sixty-nine in number, besides Mr. Tyng, in command of the force, and steamed peacefully down the bay, firing a salute as we went, from our enormous armament of *one* small gun. When off Bay Ridge we met a vessel bearing the Sardinian flag. It struck me as an excellent omen that the first flag we should see displayed on our voyage should be the one under which Garibaldi achieved the freedom of Italy, and I led off in three rousing cheers for Italy, which were most enthusiastically returned by the crew. The weather was splendid till four o'clock, when it began to drizzle, and then to rain hard; fortunately for me, my guard duty on deck was over at three, P. M., and I kept dry and got a comfortable sleep. Our vessel is a fast one but very narrow, and rolls terribly. Almost all the men succumbed to the sweet influences of the ocean, and even I had to cave in and cast up my accounts with Neptune. When fairly in the Chesapeake, we were hailed by the steamer *Yankee*, the same one that figured in the siege of Sumter, and the burning of Norfolk. She came alongside and observed us pretty closely, to see if we were all right, and we threw them a sop in the shape of the New York papers, of yesterday, when we separated with mutual cheers.

An English ship has just passed us called the *Union;* we cheered that name with all our might. This I set down as good omen number two. I see it stated in the newspapers that the Secessionists are throwing up a battery on the Maryland side of the Potomac; if so, we may have a brush with them as we pass, although we are not very powerful, having only one miserable little cannon, for arms only horse-carbines. These we shall exchange at Washington for the "Minié" rifles. If we get into Washington in the course of the afternoon we shall go into camp with the Seventh. This whole trip has been a very comfortable one for soldiers. A large number of the men, especially the younger ones, seem to look upon the whole affair as a gigantic spree, and to form no true conception of the serious character of the undertaking. There are some pretty steady fellows along, and we have singing, *ad libitum*. Last night we got out of the rain under a jolly-boat, as it was too unpleasant to go down below, and sang in good style an enormous number of songs, the chorus to each being the same, viz.,

"And the star-spangled banner forever shall wave,
O'er the land of the free and the home of the brave."

One of the guard came in last night pretty sick with a severe sore throat. As he was a mere boy, and had nothing but a lounge to sleep on, I put him into my berth, wrapped him warm, and rubbed his throat with arnica, and he is all right this morning. He is very grateful, and I think that I shall make him show his gratitude by putting himself on a short allowance of oaths. Profanity has been very abundant, but I think that some of us will make a combined effort and keep it under somewhat. Sitting in the guard-room is dull work, I can assure you. They are in decided need of reading. I find plenty of reading matter in the only book I brought with me. The first night out, I lighted on the 63d and 65th Psalms, and enjoyed them very much.

Sunday, May 12. — We had quite a lively time last night. I had gone to bed, and was sound asleep, when the sergeant of the guard knocked on the state-room door with the order, " To quarters." I was up in a jiffy, and dressed and equipped in about five minutes, and got on deck, where the company was rapidly forming in squads. We were informed that a very suspicious looking vessel had borne down upon us; that we might momentarily expect to be fired into. The muskets were handed to us loaded, and we stood ready, like the poor relation in Holmes's "Autocrat," to repel boarders. A few minutes passed along, and the suspicious craft changed her course and stood off, whereupon we returned to our downy couches. It was well to have had the experience of turning out, and we were highly complimented by Captain Tyng upon the promptness with which we mustered. Hurrah! we have just passed Mount Vernon, lowering our flag, tolling our bell, and standing with uncovered heads. It will be a poor story if we do not succeed in getting that spot out of the clutches of the Secessionists.

4 P. M. — Here we are at Washington at last, off the Navy Yard, and 1 must finish this up soon, as the sergeant is going off before long with the letters. We have had a most delight-

ful voyage; we have been fed and housed in a manner more like gentlemen travellers than soldiers. It has been of very little use to harden us, but perhaps we shall have all the more health and freshness to begin the campaign. I expect to bunk in with Tyng, Rodgers, and two or three more of the best fellows in the crowd. We shall have the nicest mess of all. Love to all at home. In best of health and spirits.

CAMP CAMERON, *May* 14, 1861.

DEAR MOTHER, ... We anchored off the Navy Yard, where the Seventy-first Regiment were encamped, and had a foretaste of the joys of camp life, as we saw them going their rounds. Their principal occupations, at present, are to protect the Navy Yard, and to guard the bridge over the Potomac, both very responsible positions. In the evening, before we left the steamer, we had a prayer-meeting in the cabin, commenced by the first mate and a couple of the seamen of the vessel, and conducted by one of our men. I made some remarks on the subject of profanity and decent behavior, and announced myself willing to back up what I said with my influence, both moral and physical. The mate and seamen made some remarks which were very impressive, they seemed so thoroughly to go to the bottom of the matter, and were almost eloquent in their simplicity. We lay all night at the Navy Yard. Captain Tyng went to the camp to get orders from Colonel Lefferts; he returned in the evening and informed us that we were to start the next morning. So at nine o'clock we got our knapsacks packed, and I got my ration-box well filled with grub. We then bade farewell to the steamer *Matanzas* and its officers, and marched off in good style towards the city, having borrowed a couple of drummers from the Seventy-first to enliven us. A march of a mile brought us to the Capital; a couple more miles of marching brought us to Camp Cameron, and up to the house where Colonel Lefferts is quartered. He came out and received us very kindly, and gave the welcome order to take off knapsacks and overcoats, under which we had been sweating for two hours. We were then marched off to our quarters in the camp, which were in a great tent, already occupied by the old members of the artillery whom we came to reinforce. Here sixty mattresses were spread for us, and we tumbled down on them, right glad to reach our haven at last.

Our quarters are intensely democratic and general, but from the great size of the tent, it is much better ventilated and more pleasant than the close small tents of the other companies. Dinner was served at about 1½ P. M., that is to say, we each seized a plate and received a piece of salt junk, a potato, some turnip, a chunk of bread, which soon disappeared under the influence of hunger and open air exercise. Last night was a night of horrors; about 11½ P. M. it began to rain, and I was awakened by a young stream coming gently into my eye, and upon arousing myself completely, I found an inch of water around my head, and gentle rivulets coursing down the mattress. I managed to pull my bed out of the fierce peltings of the pitiless storm, but had to go to sleep again in a very moist state. When I rose, I had to travel off to the spring to wash my face, but the warm sun soon dried me, and I feel splendidly now. We got our arms last night, a splendid Minié rifle with a sword bayonet. I can't say how long we shall stay here; possibly we may come home at the expiration of our thirty days, unless there is some prospect of an active campaign. The Seventh have done and suffered enough already to entitle them to an honorable reception when they come home. That forced march from Annapolis to the Junction has been spoken of by General Scott as one of the best on record. I only wish that I had been with them from the start.

May 19. — Yesterday morning we had a grand parade and inspection, and our company made its first appearance on parade. We got safely into position, and went through the manual for light infantry, at least as well as any other company. We all breathed freer when the parade was over, and we got off so nicely; we took the whole regiment by surprise. On our way back, one of the companies applauded us with their muskets as we passed through their street. On Saturday night there was a meeting of singers at the band quarters, to prepare for Sunday. The band had set the pieces to be sung (Christmas and Autumn) to music, and we worked them up in good style. After that we had some good chanting. On Sunday, service was held in front of the colonel's tent, a desk was placed on the lawn, draped with the American flag, the band and choir had seats at the left, visitors were on the stoop of the house behind, and the men lay grouped about on the grass and under the trees. The sermon was directed against trivial sins, the chaplain saying, that most of his audience knew little of any other. He ought to come down and spend a day or two in our tent, — he would soon be convinced to the contrary. At the close of the service we got small Testaments and Prayer-books all round. I shall always prize this little memento of the campaign. In the evening we had a prayer-meeting in our tent, two or three of our company having previously given notice of it. The attendance was most gratifying; we had about eighty there, and kept it up for more than two hours, singing ever so many hymns (I being leader), and having as many as a dozen prayers and addresses, all short, but most full of fervor, simplicity, and in some cases of penitence. Several fine fellows took themselves severely to task for not having started anything of the kind before, and thanked us so very heartily that we felt doubly rewarded for having set the ball rolling. There is something very striking in hearing a tall, manly soldier confess his devotion to a higher and nobler banner than that of his country. When we got back to our tent we found all our things rained on, and the first part of this letter got badly wet.

CAMP CAMERON, *May* 29, 1861.

DEAREST MOTHER, — I hope my letter to J. will have alleviated, as I hoped it would, any anxiety which might have been excited in your minds by the crazy reports which appeared in the newspapers on Saturday night. By this time you will have learned that there was no engagement after all; that the Virginians fled from Alexandria without striking a blow, and that the Seventh Regiment, after shovelling dirt for three days, like so many Paddies, have marched back in safety to their camp, and are as jolly as ever. They had a pretty rough time of it, and suffered severely from exposure to the rain, and want of provisions. The companies that stayed at home had no sinecure of it either, and we were kept very hard at work all the time ; in fact, I don't feel thoroughly waked up yet, after two days and two nights of steady guard duty. There was a grand battalion parade this morning, and Colonel Lefferts informed us that although our time had expired on the 26th, that it was the desire of the government that we should remain a few days longer, and he hoped the regiment would be willing to do so. A unanimous cry of assent arose, and we shall stay cheerfully through this week. I am not sorry to go back just now, as it will give me an opportunity of returning under better auspices. It seems to me that, with a crowd of good men, I could do and suffer almost anything.

NEW YORK, *June* 16, 1861.

. . . . I find that I settle down to my old life much more easily than I had supposed possible. I feel lithe and active, and ready to work, — just that stock of renewed vigor and activity of which I am always conscious after a week's vacation. And, indeed, it was hardly anything more than a vacation, with a double allowance of hard work, and plain, healthy fare, which made me as springy and elastic as I ever was in my life. In fact, when I went to New Haven, I found that the change was too sudden from camp grub to home living, and for a couple of days after I returned here, I felt very much out of sorts.
. . . . I suppose that I shall be fined for not turning out to parade on the Fourth of July, but my ideas of soldiering are not exactly of the militia type.

Is not Theodore Winthrop's death sad? He left our company a day or two before we broke up camp, to go down to Fortress Monroe. His rank of major was merely a nominal one, as a member of General Butler's staff. The Ninth Company voted to go into mourning for him.

NEW YORK, *June* 21, 1861.

I have just returned from marching, with a part of the regiment, as escort to poor Theodore Winthrop's body on its way to New Haven to be buried. Ours, the Ninth, was one of the companies detailed for the purpose, as he had been a member of the Company, and we acted as special guard of honor. Our men stood guard over the body Wednesday and Thursday nights. At 11 A. M. we started from the armory, and marched up Broadway to Fourteenth Street, thence up Fifth Avenue, to the New Haven Depot, with arms reversed, and at a slow step.

June 30. — I received a very pressing note from M. W. to visit Springwood. I answered it in the same blue strain in which I wrote home last. What should come in last night but a letter from there containing four missives. Of course I could not stand such a battery of rifled remonstrances; the notes dropped into my camp like Sawyer's projectiles, and I immediately sent a flag of truce, saying that I surrendered at discretion, and should come up on Monday evening, when they might send down an ambulance to bring me up from the station. I do not think that I shall be at home before Commencement, unless I have to come up to make arrangements for the Class supper.

October 2, 1861. — Very possibly I may go up the North River to-morrow. I have written to Uncle William to ask him about recruiting prospects in his neighborhood, but have not heard, so I shall go on without waiting any longer. I have not been mustered in as yet; the Major has changed his mind, and says he will be mustered in as Captain, and I as First Lieutenant of the First Battery, but in order to do this we must have eighty men, and we want twenty of that number. I am going into this matter more heartily than ever.

To L. R P.

NEW HAVEN, *August* 15, 1861.

You see I write from New Haven; I found New York utterly unendurable, as there was nothing to be done during the day in the way of business, and then a long evening yawned before me, too hot for study, and yet furnishing no good loafing chances, as all my city friends are disporting themselves in the country. So on Tuesday after receiving from the U. S. Paymaster the sum of $15.45 "for services rendered at Washington," I took the 3.15 train, and rushed into the bosom of my family, where I intend to remain as long as possible. So you see you will have to stop here instead of in New York. .... Yesterday was my birthday, and we had a rather δύσποτμον plum-pudding for dinner. O miserable being, don't you wish you were twenty-five years old? A quarter of a century, just think of it! .... Enough; stop and see me; I will try at any rate to be at the depôt, and "by head and tail" will "hale the groaning" Pinckney (see Tennyson) unto my own abode. *O vieni, vieni.* All send regards. Yours as ever,

WM. WHEELER, Aet. 25.

To L. R. P., Aet. 24.

To L. R. P.

NEW YORK, *October* 2, 1861.

DEAR BOY, — I send you the last heft of the "Electra," and congratulate you and myself on its final completion. I have enjoyed very highly the stolen moments which have been employed upon this noble play, and if I were to be here this winter, I would gladly begin the "Choephoræ" or something else with you, no matter how much law might frown at it. But it seems that it must not be, and when I return from squelching rebels I shall have forgotten all my Greek, and so another link will be broken between us: it is unnecessary for me to say how greatly I have enjoyed this work, and your genial and valuable companionship in it.

You will find my translation but a sorry one, and the notes especially bad; but you will pardon it, as it has been done in the midst of recruiting annoyances and artillery studies, and the slaying of Clytemnestra and Ægisthus has been queerly mixed up with flying thoughts of cascables, reinforces, chases, formations of battery to the right, and maneuvers of mounted cannoneers, so excuse all bulls, and write me as long and as jolly a letter as convenient. Can't you expel a dozen able-bodied Sophomores, and send them down to me?

HEAD-QUARTERS STURMFELS' ARTILLERY, CAMP OF GEN'L BAKER, NEAR POOLESVILLE, MONTGOMERY CO., MD., *October* 21, 1861.

DEAR MOTHER, — For the first time, for more than a week, has it been practicable for me to give you any account of my doings; but I suppose that J. has told you how I was put on duty, immediately upon my return from recruiting on the North River, and kept so almost without cessation until Thursday, when we left the city; in fact I hardly had three hours' sleep any night for a week, and several nights have been entirely sleepless. It was extremely comforting to me to have J. with me during those last two days, when I could not go home to see you, and was too much worried to write. I was sworn in on Tuesday, as second lieutenant, the Major going as captain with the understanding that when the Second Battery was raised I should be raised a peg. The First Lieutenant became so elated at being sworn in that he got drunk, and has not been heard of since, and as the Major is not very well posted on the English word of command, I have had the command of the men entirely, and have had an immense amount of work and responsibility thrown upon me.

On Thursday afternoon, at about 3 P. M., we got everything in readiness, and went up to the quarters, and ordered the men to fall in. They utterly refused to do so till they had received a part of their month's pay, which had been promised them. After some talk and expostulation, I got them marched out of quarters, and on the Eighth Avenue cars, which took us to Barclay St. Then we marched to Pier No. 2, and took the Perth Amboy boat. We reached the secesh village of Baltimore about 8½ A. M. I stood on the platform and managed the brake nearly all the way.

At Baltimore the Union Defense Committee gave us a good breakfast; then we had a dreary ride to Washington, occupying eight hours in going forty miles. At Washington we put our soldiers in barracks, and there we were visited by the Sanitary Commissioners, who took several of our sick men up to their home, where they were so well cared for that we took away six with us the next morning. After breakfast we marched out to Georgetown, where we embarked on a canal boat, on the canal beside the Potomac. We voyaged on that rapid vehicle, and anchored for the night about two miles from Washington. We started again Sunday morning, and soon came in sight of the secession pickets on the opposite side; however they did not pepper us, as that matter of picket shooting has been discontinued by mutual consent. About 3 P. M. we reached Edwards' Ferry, where we disembarked, and found a very warlike state of affairs. Our men had two batteries in position, and behind the rise of the hill were some 1500 or 2000 infantry and cavalry. We were marched off to Poolesville, a distance of about four miles, and then found that General Baker's camp was five miles further off. We stumbled up there in the dark, and at last saw a vast array of lights, marking our destination. They seemed to cover every hillside, and to be without number. Soon we were among them, and cordially received by General Baker. Luckily we did not have to sleep in the tents that were put up for us, for the head wagoner was a German, and invited the men to bunk in, in his covered wagons, which were filled with straw. The Major and I occupied the tent of the quartermaster of the Brigade, but we were badly off for blankets, and I spent a night of sleepless misery on account of the cold. . . . . Our men have been hard at work to-day, hewing wood and drawing water, fetching rations and fixing tents, and building kitchens. I have had it all to superintend. We are miserably fitted out in all things.

CAMP OBSERVATION
NEAR POOLESVILLE, MD., *October* 23, 1861.

DEAR COZ, — Somewhat contrary to my own individual expectations, I *did* get off from New York the same week that I left H. P., but fortunately did not go on Tuesday, since then I should have been in a melancholy state of unpreparedness, and fit only to be an officer of the rag-tag and bobtail cadets. I was mustered into the U. S. service on Tuesday, and got my uniform the same day. I was on duty pretty constantly from the time of my return to New York until Thursday afternoon, when we departed, about ninety strong, by way of Amboy, Elizabeth, Harrisburg, and Baltimore, to Washington, which we reached after a tedious journey of twenty-six (26) hours. The hills were covered with camps, but as we did not pass to the southward, we saw nothing of the great army of the lower Potomac, which is under the supervision of General McClellan in person. . . . . . We are encamped on an elevated breezy situation, so breezy in fact, that at this present moment I am expecting, every instant, that my tent will come down on my head, and close to us are encamped the four regiments of the Brigade, viz.: Baxter's Philadelphia Zouaves, Owen's Irish Phila. Regiment, Morehead's Twenty-eighth Pennsylvania, and the First California Regiment, or rather the remains of it, as its first battalion was almost entirely cut to pieces in the bloody and disastrous fight at Conrad's Ferry the day before yesterday. Of course you must have read an account of it in the newspapers, but you can form no idea of the disheartened feeling which such a piece of criminal mismanagement infuses into soldiers. It is pretty well understood that the troops were thrown across the river with the full knowledge that they could not easily be withdrawn, and with the probability that they would be attacked by the enemy in force. The result is that our Brigade has lost about 350 men, killed, drowned, wounded, and missing, all being of the First Battalion of the First California, our crack regiment; the Fifteenth Massachusetts has also suffered dreadfully, and the Twentieth Massachusetts and the New York Tammany Regiment have been badly cut up. Last, but not least, we have lost General Baker, and almost every one of our best officers who were in action, is either killed or wounded. At Edwards' Ferry I saw General Banks, who had come down with a large part of his Division, and was busily engaged in throwing troops across the river. I very much fear that the tragedy of Conrad's Ferry may be repeated on a larger scale. I can assure you, my dear *Coz.*, that we feel right in the midst of things, and I am disgusted that the want of our horses and guns prevents us from taking an active part. This is an entirely different thing from Seventh Regiment soldiering; it is actual, bloody war, and this fact is impressed upon me very strongly by meeting officers one day in courteous society, and seeing them on the next, mutilated or dead. This is emphatically a war deadly to officers, and I have fully made up my mind never to see any of you again. Major Sturmfels went away to-day to Washington, and I am left in command of the company, so I feel in quite a responsible position, as I am determined to keep everything right and straight until his return. . . . . We have plenty of secessionists all around us, and we are obliged to keep a sharp look-out, as I am convinced that all of them are a set of rascals, and that they keep their co-rebels in Virginia constantly informed of our movements. Many of them in this vicinity belonged to a cavalry troop, which was raised to assist the South, and although some of them have been disarmed and have taken the oath of allegiance, yet I am sure that they would rise and cut our throats, if they saw the enemy cross the Potomac in force. In fact, while I have been writing these lines, an order has come to me from Colonel Owen, commanding the Brigade, to permit no person in citizen's clothes to pass the lines; this is no more than what *our* Company has been doing before, as Major S. has European ideas of strictness and regularity in these matters. I expect, if I live, to pass a tedious and painful winter; already it is getting too cold to sleep much at night, and unless we take some large city and winter there, I fear that there will be a great deal of suffering. Our men as yet have no overcoats, and their blankets are of a very poor character, and insufficient to keep off the winter's cold. I shall think of you often, and of L., and all New York and New Haven friends, and of music and study and society, and shall hope that I shall not be forgotten here in camp.

CAMP OBSERVATION, MARYLAND,
October 30, 1861.

. . . . Everything is quiet in this neighborhood now. Occasionally we hear firing or cannonading from our pickets, but this shooting across the river does not amount to much. Our own camp lies in full view of the enemy on the other side, and we can see just where their encampments are, in the hollow of the hill, but they keep very shady in the day-time. They might shell us if they had any long-range guns in position, but I imagine that they are hardly well enough off in good ammunition to be able to indulge in that kind of target-shooting. I wish that we had our guns. If the enemy, who is said to be in heavy force at Leesburg, should attempt to cross the river, and there should be a general engagement, there would be nothing for us but to retire to the rear with the camp followers.

. . . . Major S. has been absent from the company now for a week, and during that time I have reigned supreme in our little encampment, and have communicated directly with Colonel Owen, the commander of the Brigade, as if I were colonel of a regiment. I am sorry that the state of my foot does not permit me to drill my company as dismounted cannoneers. I have been found lying on my bed most of the time studying. I got hold of Monday's Herald yesterday, and found in it a comparatively correct account of the conflict of Ball's Bluff, only it places the numbers engaged, and the loss, rather too high. I was informed by the brigade surgeon that only 1200 were engaged in all, and of that number all but 500 had already reported themselves; so that number will cover the total loss. . . . . The weather for the last few days has been really delicious, perfect October time, and the sunsets over the Virginia hills are golden curtains, let down in long waves of blue and purple, and I only wish that I were more free from bodily ailment, and could enjoy more the peaceful Indian Summer. When evening comes on, our little company street resounds with songs. Last night we had a regular German concert, many of our men being old campaigners in Faderland, and very beautiful are some of the soldier songs they sing, noble too in sentiment. .... My oven works to a charm, the draught is perfect; in token of the excellence of my fire, I have written the whole of this last page by its light. My only fear is that my chimney (made of beef barrels) may catch fire some cold night, as this is not an uncommon catastrophe. .... I should like a few sheets of blank music paper; I want to copy out the bugle calls for my bugler.

CAMP OBSERVATION, *November* 8, 1861.

..... Captain S. has now been absent from us two weeks and a half, during which time we have heard nothing from him, but supposed that he was doing for us all that was necessary to equip us for the field, and now it appears that he has not even taken the preliminary step of reporting himself to the head of his department, and that we are not recognized as existing in the service at all, and that our men will not get their pay when the paymaster comes, in spite of the pains taken by the orderly and myself to have the muster and payrolls all properly made out, and sent to the Department at Washington. Besides this, our requisition for overcoats has not yet been responded to, and yesterday, at the instance of General Burns, I made an entirely new one, on my own responsibility, which I think will bring the articles, and nothing was ever more needed. I am surprised that we have not more men on the sick list than we have. When half of them are in the hospital, and a few frozen to death, perhaps we may get what we want. Then, too, the brigade quartermaster has been changed, so that it is hard to draw supplies, for either officers or men, and we have to scratch hard for our grub. In spite of my ankle, which is still sore and lame, so that I cannot wear a boot, I have to run about all day, now to the

General, and then to the Commissary, to see that we do not get cheated, now to settle some dispute among the men. I think it is not impossible that I may go down to Washington to-day or to-morrow, to report to General Barry in person, and see what can be done for us. I myself feel full of courage and hope, and shall take the company into my own hands, if the General thinks fit, and use my own influence to get it into the field. I only wish that my foot would heal. The doctor says that it is improving nicely, and if I must go to Washington he will send me to Poolesville in an ambulance, and from there I can go by stage to Washington. What a terrible gale of wind, and rain storm, we had last Saturday. I wish we could hear something about the Great Expedition. I have prayed fervently for its success, and have lain awake on these windy nights thinking about it. Robert Edwards' regiment, the Forty-eighth New York, is with it; this adds to my interest. I wish I was with him.

CAMP OBSERVATION, MD., *November* 11, 1861.

DEAR M., — Thanks for your promptness in answering my last letter. Yours was the first received after reaching this camp, and I was saved a disappointment when the mail came in, the night of that stormy Saturday. . . . . It is a showery, drizzly afternoon, and the men and I equally rejoice at it, for they get off drilling, and I am at liberty to write this letter, and you may be sure that I gladly embrace all such opportunities, when I have them, for when we get on the march there will be no time to sit quietly down and place ourselves *en rapport* with dear friends, but a hasty, hurried scratch must be sufficient to satisfy those at home of the safety and health of the absent one. I am sorry that you got the idea, from my last letter, that I was in poor spirits; true I then had poor accommodations and food, slept cold at night, and the responsibility of taking care of the company weighed upon me somewhat, yet I have never allowed myself to be depressed; the thought of being once more armed for the cause, and of having a chance this time to strike a blow, makes me very happy and elastic; the picture I gave you was one of *physical*, not *mental* condition. Now, however, I am very much more comfortable in my way of living; I have had an oven built in my tent, of large stones, with a flue running out for some distance behind the tent, covered with stones and plastered with clay; the chimney is made of two beef barrels, placed one on top of the other; the draught is generally very good, except when the wind blows from the east, and early in the morning my boy comes in, just after reveille, and lights up a good fire, so that when I rise, I find the edge taken off from the morning frost considerably. These stoves, of this simple construction, are all the rage among the officers in the camps here, and they are a grand institution; only some of them are unable to get beef barrels, and build their chimneys of sugar barrels, which are liable to catch fire, and cause a great deal of disturbance and fun in being extinguished; the Philadelphia Fire Zouaves, the nearest regiment to us, recall their former days, and run "with the machine" to put out the officers' chimneys. *Grub*, too, has manifestly improved; we have a man who waits on our mess who is a great forager, and scours the country round for provisions, wherewith to vary the daily bill of fare, of government salt horse and hard biscuit. Not unsuccessful is his scouring either, as that excellent leg of mutton which we had for dinner yesterday, and that loud-clucking hen in the next tent might testify. A rumor, too, has been blown hitherward, of sundry turkeys in a farmyard not very remote, and I think it highly probable that we shall celebrate the New York Thanksgiving day, by fleshing our teeth in a secesh gobbler. Now that we have learned the ropes, we live as well as anybody in the camp. It is now more than three weeks since we came here, and Major S. has been absent nearly all that time, and our pieces and horses have not yet been sent to us. I have ruled the Company in righteousness in the meantime, have seen to it that the Quartermaster and Commissary did not cheat the men, have maintained their rights, and made known their needs to General Burns, the new General of the Brigade, and, still more, I have mustered the Company for pay, and sent the appropriate muster and pay rolls to the Department at Washington; this last was a great labor, and a sort of job entirely new to me, but after about three days' solid work I made it out, and now the men will get their pay, I hope very soon. We expect the Major back in about a week, and I hope that he will bring our full equipments with him, so that we may be in condition to march across the river with this Division, if it goes. I hope that we *shall* winter in Virginia. It is very cold here, and they say that the snow lies four feet deep on these hills. I am full of anxiety about the Great Expedition; my friend Rob. Edwards is with it as a lieutenant in the Forty-eighth New York. I suppose that by this time you have full accounts of the landing, etc. Our newspapers are few and far between out here. We have pretty lively times in the evenings; the Germans of my company get together and sing very sweetly, and I try to join in with them. I send you a copy of one of their songs, called "Morgenroth;" it is simple, but very sweet, I think, and shows a reflection and elevation of sentiment, to be found only among the Germans. . . . . We are no longer "General Baker's Brigade," but the "First Brigade Corps of Observation, Camp Observation, Md."

November 19. — . . . . You will be anxious to know about my health, after what I wrote in my last. Well, the first dose of restoring physic was that batch of letters on Sunday; they quite set me up. On Monday my trouble, which seems intermittent in its nature, came on again, and after being out for an hour or so, attending to some business at the adjutant general's office, I was obliged to go to bed with a very bad headache. The doctor came in and said that my system required to be stimulated, and prescribed quinine and whiskey. But the real cordial came in another shape. About dark, one of the men came in, and said a gentleman was inquiring for me. Upon asking his name, Mr. W. was brought in. I jumped out of bed, ran out doors in my stocking-feet, and there were Cousin M. and Mr. W. in their carriage. They quickly transferred themselves to my tent, and also a champagne basket full of various goodies ; in fact, a little magazine of provender, which will make our larder rejoice till that box from home arrives. The horses were taken from the carriage, and put in a rustic stable, which my men had built of straw and branches ; we got up a good fire in the oven, and at supper time a table, completely set out for us, was brought into my tent, and I had an opportunity of showing my guests that we did not starve in camp. We sat and talked for a while, and then escorted Cousin M. to Mrs. Fisher's, where she succeeded in getting very comfortable quarters for the night. Mr. W. spent the night with me in my tent. He took breakfast with me, Cousin M. with General Burns and the brigade surgeon. Then they started for home, having given me a great deal of pleasure by the visit. How kind it was for them to come so far. I hope Cousin M. will not send you an exaggerated account of my condition, so as to make you anxious. Mr. W. is a good Union man, and up to the times. It must be a thorn in the flesh of these secesh Marylanders, to have a gentleman among them who takes the "Tribune" regularly, and who advocates the making of Maryland a free state.

The news from the South is most cheering, and I think that every one will rejoice that South Carolina should receive the just reward of her iniquities, and that, too, when she thought that she had removed the noise of war and tumult far away from her borders. I hope that you will all have a good time on Thanksgiving Day this year. I shall think of you as eating turkey together, and shall try to put myself *en rapport* with you in that respect, if such a " bird of loudest lay " can be had.

THANKSGIVING DAY, *November* 28.
CAMP OBSERVATION.

. . . . I received a very substantial epistle last night, in the form of the long expected box. Everything arrived in good order, except in one instance. Please to give my thanks to every one for the torrent of good things poured upon me. I had hoped by Thanksgiving Day to have announced myself as quite recovered, but it goes very slowly, and there are steps backward as well as forward. We had a rousing turkey for dinner to-day, but I had to content myself chiefly with looking at him, while the others made play at his gigantic proportions.

We are still in utter ignorance of what we shall do, but are prepared to stay here for some time. General McClellan may turn out to be timid and temporizing. Will not the use of the Naval Expedition be thrown away, if a simultaneous advance is not soon made?

CAMP OBSERVATION, *December* 9, 1861.

DEAREST MOTHER, — The visit of Uncle R. and J. was most kind and cheering, and brought me up quite a peg. For two or three days after they left I improved, and then began to settle down again. I feel well enough, generally, but am liable to fall into fits of brown study, lassitude, in fact. I received, on Saturday last, a telegraphic despatch from S., ordering me to meet him in Washington, I suppose to make an effort to fix things straight. I hope to get a pass this afternoon, and to start early to-morrow morning.

WASHINGTON, *December* 11.

I reached here last night, after a day of unmitigated torture. I walked over to Poolesville early in the morning, to take the stage, and was forced to ride to Adamstown in a fearful springless wagon, which jounced me almost to pieces, then by rail to the Relay House, and so to Washington, which I reached more like a dead man than anything else. I succeeded, through the courtesy of an officer, in getting a room in the Ebbitt House. When I went into the breakfast room, I was so light-headed that I should have fallen, had I not heard a voice exclaim, "Why, Mr. Wheeler!" I looked round and saw Mrs. R. She took me in the doctor's carriage to the hospital, where her son is sick. The doctor examined me, and insisted on writing me a certificate of disability from duty on account of weakness, and sent me down to General Williams's office. My pass is to be extended to ten days.

ANNAPOLIS, *December* 27, 1861.

MY DEAR MOTHER, — I write you to say that I am daily improving in health and strength, and coming up rapidly, under the combined influence of careful treatment and phosphates. Anything is better than the despondent indifference in which I was at camp. The only thing that worries me is, that I have not yet got my new leave of absence, and my old one expired several days since, so that I have been a sort of deserter. A furlough was written for me, by an old army surgeon, but it was drawn so incorrectly as to be of no use, and was sent back. I then got a proper certificate from Dr. Douglas, of the Tenth Connecticut. This went on to Colonel H., but he had gone to New York, so that my application has lain unattended to, and I am thinking of going directly back to camp without waiting for the leave. We had a pleasant Christmas here. R. was longed and sighed for.

December 31. — I suppose you have been kept informed about me by letters from uncle and aunt, but I will recapitulate a little. I spent the afternoon of December 11 in Mrs. R.'s room. She made me lie down on the sofa, and tucked me up warm. In the evening, the Misses W. sent their man in with a tray covered with nice things, first-rate tea and toast, which went right to the spot. I made a call on them later in the evening, and saw Mrs. H. and Miss J. The latter I had never met, but Mrs. H. I had seen long ago when I was in college. At 3 P. M. I took the train for the Junction, and reached here about eight o'clock. I have improved very rapidly ever since I came here. If my leave does not come, I shall have to go back to Camp Observation, as soon as I am fit to travel. If I get right strong and well, I shall report myself for duty when my leave runs out ; but, in the present disorganized state of our Battery, it does no harm to the public service for me to be absent. If we were ready for active operations, it would be a different thing, and it would be something to be absent a day longer than I could help.

WASHINGTON, *January* 24, 1862.

DEAR MOTHER, — I have finally found rest for the sole of my foot, to a sufficient extent to take pen in hand and to tell you how I am situated. I left New York at 7 A. M. on Tuesday, and after the usual tedious ride, with the pleasures of a chilly storm superadded, I reached Annapolis and received a warm welcome from the friends there. I made a short call on Lieutenant W., who has just returned, and had resigned some time before reaching Annapolis. I really could not help feeling sorry for him, but still I hope that the government will give him his due, by sending him to Fort Warren, and not permit him to go South and assist them in organizing that branch which they so much need — a Navy. I came on here on Wednesday afternoon, and, at an early hour, started for our camp. Some time before I reached it, I could see a long line of evergreens, worked into rustic sheds, and through them flamed out numerous red blankets, showing that at least one essential requisite for a battery had been obtained, and upon coming into camp I found that we had about one hundred and ten horses, and that we were to fetch the guns the next day. I suppose that by this evening we shall have four pieces at camp. As the tents were all full, and as I was not quite ready to do full duty, Captain S. gave me permission to go into Washington for quarters.

We have orders to cross the river, and to join General Blenker's Division, so that very possibly we may be away by Monday. I see that A. R. has turned up as Captain of the First Connecticut Battery.

CAMP DUNCAN, WASHINGTON,
January 26, 1862.

DEAR M., — Sunday has brought with it a sufficient degree of leisure and quiet to permit me to sit peacefully down and tell you how I am, and how I found matters in the Company after my absence from it. . . . . On Wednesday I came to Washington, and found the Company where it was two weeks ago, and that it had received an increase of members, but that entirely on four legs, — we have now one hundred and eight horses, nearly our entire quota, and shall go to the arsenal tomorrow to fetch our guns, — they are said to be iron six-pounders, of Prussian make, warranted to burst, I suppose, at the fifth discharge. Although our Captain is absent, I am not in command, for a German lieutenant is promoted over me, and, as I am not ready to resign, I must e'en submit with a good grace. Besides, this lieutenant is said to be an accomplished artillery officer, and I don't want to push myself above those who are really my superiors. But, what is most unpleasant to me of all, is, that I have to live with these men, to eat their onions and drink their lager, and very rarely to hear a word of musical English from American lips, as I am almost the sole specimen of a Yankee in the Company. There are plenty of Irish, it is true, and their "rich brogue," and a river of talk well supplied with dam(n)s, can be heard at any time in the camp. Now do not think that I make an unnecessary fuss about these things, for a soldier's life has in it enough of hardship and trouble, without adding the mental agony of continual uncongeniality and disagreement of modes and habits of life. I do not "bate one jot of heart or hope," and I am far more determined, now, to see this war out, than I was when I first entered the service.

CAMP DUNCAN, WASHINGTON,
January 28, 1862.

The noises and rows, which always accompany pay-day, have subsided to a sufficient extent to permit me to take off my sabre and pistol, with which I have been prowling through the company street, "a terror to evil-doers," and although I have had a very busy and fatiguing day, and it is now half-past eleven, yet I feel much more like having a good talk with you than like going to bed. How curious the moods of letter-writing are! They are not the same as with that faculty of conversation which enables one to express himself in easy and yet correct words. Conversation is more readily carried on; for then the presence of the friend stimulates and excites, while the *imagination* must assist the letter-writer, to call up the absent face, and to hear the well-known voice in reply, and the laugh, often shared together at a stray flash of humor. I think that if people would give way to their imaginations more, when in a kindly vein, their "winged words" would be more beautiful and would nestle more warmly on the hearts of absent friends. I frequently feel like saying to my correspondents, — "Be more frivolous, describe little things more carefully, and don't touch upon great things, — if you must, do so superficially and say no more than every one else and the newspapers say."

. . . . We, in the field, will bear the hardships of the camp, and you, at home, will bear the anxiety for us, and will give us your prayers; only let the war last until the question has been thoroughly decided, even if it cost the lives of all now in the field, and let our institutions be founded upon a basis of real stability, which no selfish oligarchy can shake at their pleasure.

I think that already some gleams of light are apparent in the South. May the Dayspring soon visit us, and may it really be a Dayspring from on high. Since I have been here, I have not had a single sensation of homesickness, nor any of regret. My lot is cast in with this matter and I will see it out. Courageous and patriotic words from dear and loved friends like yourself, *ma chère*, go right to the soldier's heart, and give it warmth and strength to beat with full pulses in the storm.

But upon my word, I supposed that I was going to be frivolous myself this time, and lo, I have entered into a didactic oration on the first page; please excuse me, and don't take any of it to yourself, but write me just as frivolous a letter as possible, in revenge for my harangue. . . . . I had to sleep in the same room with a monster from Illinois, of the chestnut-worm species (slightly roasted) of mankind; I suppose there are plenty more of the same sort there, but, though they may be very decent people, they are loathsome to look at. He was a peaceably disposed monster, and beyond the little singularity of going to bed in full dress (I am not so sure about the boots), behaved quite creditably. I took him for a hog contractor, but he may have been a member of Congress. . . . .

I was quartered in the city until Saturday, when Captain S. went to New York; since then I have occupied his tent, and have done full duty. When I arrived, I found the company supplied with one hundred and eight horses, nearly their full complement; and I now begin to see how intricate and extensive a matter the charge of a battery of artillery is, when the mere cleaning, feeding, watering, and physicking of the horses is so much of an affair. . . . . We were all paid off to-day, and I rode down to Washington with my pockets full of money-letters, to send by Adams' Express for the men. I am willing to take a good deal of trouble in order to do this; since it both relieves the families at home, and also removes the men from temptation. I called on Miss W. and Mrs. H., dirty boots and all; but as they are "doing" the soldier life, they said, they gloried in my muddy boots.

To L. R. P.

CAMP DUNCAN, WASHINGTON,
February 7, 1862.

DEAR FRIEND,— It is a long time since I have written to you,— not, I think, since I sent you the last heft of the "Electra,"— and I feel ashamed of myself for my long silence; but yet I must plead the shadow of an excuse. Your scholarly, quiet, and decorous life seems so far removed from the dirty and commonplace existence of us here in camp, that hardly more than a faint echo will reach your ear when I speak, and you cannot be expected to take much interest in my stories of drill and guard duty and muddy misery, when in any newspaper you can read accounts far more thrilling and exciting about soldier life. People in general are, I imagine, pretty well disgusted with the subject of the war, and we have to content ourselves with exciting an interest for us in the family circle and no farther. But I feel a very warm interest in what you are doing and studying, old fellow, even in that absorbing Sanskrit, although I am hardly prepared just now to undertake the translation of the Vedas or Hitopadeça (is n't that the cove's name?) with you, after the manner of Electra. I can't quite give up the old classical boys even now; I have a Leipzig "Horace" on my table, and find an occasional ode right jolly reading for odd snatches of time. . . . . My fellow officers get letters from their wives, and read me extracts about their little boys, and their naïve inquiries after "father," and then, when their faces soften and their eyes glisten, I know that my life is very barren and incomplete, and that I have a great mystery to learn and as yet no one to teach it me. . . . . Come with me to our camp, three quarters of a mile east of the Capitol, and let me introduce you to our officers. Captain S——, the getter-up of the Battery, with whom I tent, is a very queer specimen of humanity; jolly, hasty, practical, unreliable, philosophic, childish, and, worst of all, addicted to rising at abominably early hours, and punching me in the ribs until I follow his example. At any rate, an educated officer, and one who seems to enjoy a pretty good reputation for experience among other German officers. (You observe that this paper looks a little greasy; probably the captain has been using it to enfold a Schweine-bifstek, as I constantly find that favorite dish of his in all parts of the tent.) Next, Lieutenant M——, an officer from the General Staff of Würtemberg, well-posted in military matters, but so thoroughly attached to European tactics as to be quite unfit to manage American troops; he is likewise conceited enough to shipwreck the best man that ever lived. Then, Lieutenant Carl von L—— (I only give his first name, as his intermediate names are legion, and would occupy too large a part of my letter), a hohe Herrschaft, and husband of the Gräfinn somebody, and feels it all over, as is seen at first glance. He drinks vast lager, rides pretty well, as he was a cavalry officer before, knows no English, because he is too lazy to learn, consequently is of very little use to us, and is in all respects " ein echter Schwab." Then, Lieutenant S——, a watchmaker from New York, about forty years old, and of rough, harsh appearance, but a real good, kind-hearted fellow, entirely reliable and unpretending, and one who stands up to his work like a man ; the stables are especially under his care, and it makes me laugh to hear him rush out of bed at night whenever any disturbances arise there. . . . . But then, we have such floods of German grub : Schweins-bifstek, Sauerkraut, Brat und Leber-wurst, Zwiebel und Knoblauch, Urisokohl, and all these washed down with plentiful potations of Lager-Bier, Rheinwein, and Schnapps. Add to this that the cooking is all done in our tent, and you " square the awful product "[1] immediately; the consequence is that a strange confusion of goods takes place, and, though I do not, like poor Tom, have "ratsbane in my porridge and halters in my pew," yet I often see a string of Wurst laid on my portfolio, and poor "Horace" has a bunch of Knoblauch on his cover, spite of his protest, —

> "Parentis olim si quis impia manu
> Senile guttur fregerit,
> Edit cicutis allium nocentius."

I think that before long I shall myself become a good German plain cook, and will be able, when I come home, to turn you out abominations of all kinds, gentle reminders of the Hotel Bellevue. This morning three of us started off before sunrise for a ride and trot-practice. On our way home we visited the market at Washington, and I was deputed to do the marketing. We then dashed up Pennsylvania Avenue, I with two fat chickens, slung one on each side of my saddle-bow, like John Gilpin's bottles, "to keep the balance true." Alas! my fate was as sad as his, for suddenly the connecting link between the birds broke, and they plumped down deep into the mud, whence they were extracted by a small boy whom I hired to dive for them. (Fine chance for a parody on "Wer wagt es, Rittersmann oder Knapp, zu tauchen in diesen Schlund!") You would revel in the constant opportunities for speaking German which are afforded here. I go right in and talk, utterly regardless of mistakes. It is pretty hard to make explanations of military matters in German, as I had to do yesterday with an awkward squad of gunners in the "school of the piece," as the technical terms are different and often peculiar; but I go fearlessly ahead. Our pieces are 6-pounder 3-inch rifled guns, beauties for maneuvering, as they are quite light, and I think that they will turn out well in action. I already feel an affection for them, and they be to me as a sweetheart, yea, as many sweethearts. We have had marching orders for some time to cross the river and join General Blenker's division, but the weather has been miserable, and we may not go for two weeks.

[1] A quotation from a sermon we heard together in Rome.

CAMP DUNCAN, *February* 1, 1862.

DEAREST MOTHER, — As I understand that there is very general distress among the people at the North, and as my soldiers are pretty generally sending their money home, I follow their good example, and send you —— by Adams' Express, hoping that it may help to keep the wolf from the door. . . . . The thought of doing something for you, who have done so much for me, dear mother, almost makes me wish that you were indeed dependent on my exertions, and that I could show you, by faithful labor and self-denial, that I am not ungrateful. This money I send home because I am afraid that I may lose it here. I feel a redoubled interest in the service now that we have our guns, horses, battery, wagon forge, and everything complete, and, as I conduct the simpler maneuvers, the more difficult ones begin to become plain to me, and I have a good hope that my daily exercise and drill will constantly explain the study of tactics which I pursued quite industriously in that hillside Camp of Observation. Of course I do not expect ever to be a really good artillery officer, in the proper sense of the word, but still I may be able to do something in the service, and accomplish more than if I were merely a lieutenant of infantry. Yesterday I went down to the arsenal with the caissons for some ammunition, and as I had hardly any officers with me, I felt quite a weight of responsibility upon me. I was continually apprehensive lest one of them might fall into some unfathomable mud-hole, from which our young, untrained horses would never be able to pull it up. Then, at the railroad crossing, I was again very nervous, for on the day when we brought up the pieces, the cars came along close to us, and the horses of one carriage got tied up in a hard knot. But no such accident happened to me, and I brought my charge back all right. This getting on horseback seems to put new life into me; and although I have no horse of my own, I can get along with one of the company horses until the government receives some animals more worthy to be straddled by officers than those now in their stables. Last

Thursday was pay-day, and we had a terrible time with the men for two days after. I won't dilate upon the disagreeable subject, but only say that I almost lost my faith in human nature, so many of the best and most reliable men proved wholly bad and unreliable under the influence of drink. I am sorry to be obliged to inform you that our living here is very bad. The mess at Camp Observation was luxury compared with it. There is no system; each picks up what he can find, and then sits "silently apart gorging himself in gloom," — I would not say gorging, for that presupposes an amount of food not easily attainable. Captain S. is anxious to get across the river to Virginia, so that we may be settled, and have things decent and comfortable. . . . . As soon as I get comfortably quartered I shall be quite content.

CAMP HUNTER'S CHAPEL, VA.,
GENERAL BLENKER'S DIVISION, *February* 23, 1862.

. . . . Sunday is a day of work as well as any other, but we do not drill or undertake any lengthy job likely to take all day. This morning I was hard at work for four hours unloading ammunition and packing it in our caissons. This was decidedly a work of necessity, for the stuff had come up from the arsenal three or four days ago, and ever since then it had been too wet to venture to unpack it. To-day the weather was very fine, so we took advantage of it to get our precious ammunition stowed away, and I was handling canister, shells, and case-shot, instead of going to church. I intend to take my horse next Sunday and ride over to General Franklin's Division to see Jo. J. and go to church with him. He is about three miles and a half from here, in the Alexandria district. The sight of a single friendly face would be a great treat to me here, but I have to make duty take the place of friendship, culture, and most other desirable things. I am now decidedly the laboring oar of the concern, for domestic ties impair the efficiency of two of our officers, for the wife of Lieutenant V. L. is at Washington, and he goes there as often and stays as long as he possibly can. The other afternoon who should appear in camp but Madame S., with three fat, flourishing images of the illustrious captain. He quartered them in a house near by our encampment, put himself on the sick list, and has gone up there to stay with them, and left me to have command of the battery. This keeps me very busy, but then I can manage matters according to my own ideas of what is right, and the responsibility is honorable and exciting. On Washington's Birthday our Battery went out for inspection and review; but that is a long story. I feel still the same delightful state of uncertainty about my daily food; but who cares much for such trivial things when every newspaper brings such delightful, reviving news of the success of our arms in every quarter. I think I could have lived for a week on the news of Fort Donelson alone. How you New Haven folks must rejoice in the success and glory of Captain Foote, who, it seems to me, stands out more prominently than any other commander, as distinguished for his gallant conduct and cool bravery. . . . . Still, the great battle will yet take place in Virginia, and we shall be ready to be in it, for our men are ambitious and quite enthusiastic. Having guns and horses to take care of, and duties of both interest and difficulty to perform, seems to have transformed some of them from drunken wretches to eager, careful workers. After all, no arm is like the artillery. I never could have stood the monotony of infantry service.

CAMP HUNTER'S CHAPEL, VA., GENERAL BLENKER'S DIVISION, February 28, 1862.

Your right kindly and "frivolous" letter, dated February 1st, was duly received by me at Camp Duncan, although directed to General Blenker's Division, for, as you very sensibly suggest, the movements of so celebrated an officer as myself are too well known for my letters ever to go astray, and General McClellan was, at that time, in the habit of daily calling on the Washington Postmaster, and saying to him, "Lieutenant Wheeler is still at Camp Duncan;" so that it was through this considerate behavior on the part of the Commander-in-Chief that I was spared the agony of having your letter delayed. I was much amused with the whole epistle, and thought it a right jolly production for an unhappy being with headache, toothache, bad cold, etc. You can't be too frivolous in a letter. One laugh at some comical idea warms the heart of the reader towards the sender more than a page full of endearments, and you say in your heart, "He must indeed love me if writing to me inspires him with such gladness and lightness of heart." The necessary labors, accompanying the receipt of our guns and ammunition, and the preparations for moving out to this camp, kept me so busy at Washington, that I got no chance to write you, and since we have been in Dixie my time has been still more fully occupied in the arranging of our new camp, and with drills, etc. And now, as I am going out on picket to-morrow morning with my section, I cannot refrain from writing you a few lines (perhaps the last I may write), to let you know that I am well and think of you, as I may not have facilities to write again soon.

We broke up at Camp Duncan on the 12th of February, and marched down to Washington, through Pennsylvania Avenue, across the Long Bridge into Virginia, and then through much mud to this camp, where the Teutonic element has its head-quarters, and revels in endless streams of lager, infinite plantations of sauerkraut, and strings of small but seductive sausages. We selected our camp on a very fine piece of elevated ground, the dryest in the neighborhood, near to the main road, and with good springs of water handy. And now after two weeks of steady hard work; after building a brush stable, also a kitchen, fixing up all the tents nicely and comfortably with board floors, and getting generally settled down, — lo and behold, the order comes that the whole Division must hold themselves in readiness to march at two hours' notice; and so, all our toil will be for naught. I start for the extreme outposts to-morrow morning with my section (the first, containing the first and second pieces), which is the best in the Battery, and I think it very likely that the rest will follow soon; so that you see we are likely to get a pop at your friends the seceshers after all. My whole heart and soul have been wrapped up in my battery, especially since we came out here. I have drilled the whole six pieces at once, and find that it is the only way in which thoroughly to secure the fruits of my study. We turned out on Washington's Birthday for inspection and review by General Blenker. There were three batteries of light artillery, sixteen pieces in all, and we fired a salute of a hundred guns. Although our horses had had very little drill, I succeeded in conducting them and the men through several quite difficult maneuvers, and was very much relieved when I saw the horses stand the firing without running away and tearing everything to pieces.

The thing that gives me plenty of spirit and enthusiasm is that I am extremely well mounted. My horse is a beautiful dark bay, with a sort of metallic reflection in his skin, has a jolly little head, and is, in all points, nicely and strongly put together. I call him "Barry," after the Chief of Artillery, and pet him enormously. He will follow me like a dog, eats sugar out of my hand, and rubs his head on my shoulder when I caress him. You shall ride him too, one of these days, if you will be a good girl, and not *secesh* too much.

CAMP HUNTER'S CHAPEL, *March* 9, 1862.

DEAREST MOTHER, ... My letters to and from home are my only means of communication with the outer world. I am always in camp and have not been to Washington once since we have been out here. When my isolation is interrupted by letters from the dear friends, I feel repaid for all discomforts, and prepare myself to endure all that is endurable, and in my case the unendurable has not been reached yet. I think that there must be something in the free and out of door life that hardens and strengthens me to bear what is inharmonious and incompatible in my mental and social existence. . . . . If there is anything like a general engagement, they will need all the guns they can get, and I think that our greenhorns can drive, load, and fire well enough to take part. My heart is full of anxiety when I think of that final struggle, not on my own account, that may come when we go to the field, but for the almost indescribable greatness of the interests at stake. A born coward ought to fight well for this once, as such another opportunity will never come up in the world's history, to inspire courage and noble daring. . . . . Where do you suppose this letter is being written? Has it any peculiar smell, like Michael's boots, for example? For I am writing it in the stable, sitting on a camp-stool, in the nice clean stall with my horse, General Barry; in fact it is the pleasantest place in the camp; for such occupation my tent is too warm, this lovely spring day, but here, with the sweet branches of pine and hemlock trees on every side, protecting me from the wind, and with the clear blue sky all overhead, I can write my letter, and yet not lose all the calm and happy influences of God's light and air. The General is very inquisitive, and has several times smelled and bit at my paper; he is a regular nibbler, and the other day walked behind me and ate up half of a Herald, which I had under my arm. He is now quite lame, his foot is adorned with a fine bran poultice, which I hope will bring him all right in a day or two. I sympathize with him in his trouble, and pay him several visits every day, with a little sugar or salt to tickle his equine palate with.

March 15, 1862.

DEAR AUNT E.,— . . . . Perhaps my next will contain something more interesting than dull descriptions of camp life in this great lazy army of the Potomac.

A move is to be made very soon; troops from all parts are concentrating in this neighborhood, and even the brigade to which we were attached in Maryland, General Burns's, has just marched in and gone to Bailey's Cross Roads. The whole Division received special notice, on last Saturday, that three days' preparation would be allowed to get into perfect marching order. I think that the forward move would have been made to-day if the weather had continued good. . . . . The winds play the very mischief with us, in our somewhat exposed situation. A violent southwester, a week or so ago, proved fatal to most of the tents in our encampment; at first one Sibley tent broke from its moorings and collapsed, then another and another, then the tent of the orderly sergeant went by the board, and the fields around were whitened with official documents of every description. Then the captain's rose and made a graceful pirouette on one pole, and subsided on the ground. I expected every minute to see my tent follow its example, and, for the whole day, my tent-mate and I took turns in sitting on the fly, to break the force of the hurricane. I did not sleep a wink, and the tent rocked like a boat on the waves; but morning found us all right.

In summer this must be a lovely place for an encampment; beautiful ranges of hills, crowned by forts bristling with cannon and abattis, and between them fine level spots for drill and parade, with excellent streams of water all around. The name of the camp is taken from a homely red wooden building, erected by a farmer of the name of Hunter, and used as a place of worship; it has been degraded from its former high use, to serve as a magazine for quartermaster's and commissary's stores. This Division is called the German Division, and the officers at head-quarters have to do business in a polyglot fashion. I greatly outraged the assistant adjutant general by refusing to recognize a German order which was sent to me, when I was in command.

Every moment is precious to us now, as we shall have to go into the fight with the others, and it would be desirable for us to be able to do a little more execution among the enemy than our own men. I am endeavoring to interest the men in the subject, as much as possible, and to call out their latent enthusiasm. They take hold very much better than I could have dared to expect, and there is considerable emulation among the different pieces, to see which shall be best drilled and best maneuvered. I rode over to General Franklin's Division to see J. J., and found that he had been ill at home for some weeks with a bad fever. On my way back I inquired for Fort Richardson, and found that it was within a gun-shot of our encampment, and that I had been three weeks so near to the Fourth Connecticut, and to my friend T. T., who is the adjutant of it. The regiment is a wonder of neatness, and was pronounced by General McClellan's committee of inspection to be the finest regiment in the volunteer service. How splendidly Commodore Foote has borne himself. He and Lyon are, to my mind, the heroes of the war so far. Connecticut has no reason to be ashamed of her sons.

I am in excellent health and spirits, and am growing fat, in spite of hard fare and poor accommodations.

FAIRFAX COURT HOUSE, VA.,
March 19, 1862.

I have at last a moment of leisure at my command, and my trunk has just come up from camp, so that I have an opportunity to drop you a line, — a baker's dozen of artillery officers are sitting in the room. Our head-quarters were formerly the parlor of a very decent house, and there is a perpetual clatter of tongues disputing about horses, points of discipline, and other military matters, while now and then a beer glass comes down empty in a very emphatic manner. But I have found it necessary to make myself very often deaf and callous to these things, otherwise my life would be very hard to bear. My last letter to J. was written from our last camp, Taylor's Cross Roads, and just before I got it finished, a hurried order came to march; I thrust it into my pocket and rushed off to make preparations, Captain S. being absent. In less than an hour we were off on the road to Fairfax, and a heavy rain, which seemed to follow us on our marches like a tutelary genius, poured pitilessly down. The road was at first pretty good, but became ever worse as the Division advanced, and at last the mud got so deep as to give us much trouble. My section went through everything without a halt, but two or three of the other carriages were not so fortunate, and I had to halt the column and send back teams to pull them out of the mud. In consequence we were a long time on the road, and when we reached this place, I was as thoroughly soaked as if I had been dipped in a pond. Then we had to find quarters for men and horses, especially the latter, and this was no easy matter, as the cavalry had come in before us, and horses' heads peeped out of school-room windows, and the ferrule gave way to the cowhide. Many of the inhabitants had fled, and their houses were generally taken possession of for officers' quarters; in smaller houses were some families remaining, and some of the old campaigners in our Company managed to billet themselves there in very comfortable quarters, and about sixty of our men took up their abode in the Court-house where "Old John Brown" was tried and condemned, and immediately constituted a court, and proceeded to reënact the scenes of November, 1859.

We expected to have to march off the next day to some point in advance, but the plans seem to have been changed. . . . . The soldiers have behaved very well; to be sure the fences have suffered somewhat, when firewood was not elsewhere to be had, and a stray pig or fowl may have mysteriously come to an untimely end; but no houses have been burned, and the inhabitants and their property have been treated much better than rebels deserve. We have not been idle since coming here. We have had two or three very good drills, both in section, battery, and battalion, and yesterday we took part in a grand review of General Sumner's Corps d'Armée. At least 40,000 men must have been there, and they were drawn up in two lines of battle, and a reserve. We were in the second line of battle, and I had the honor of commanding the Battery. General Sumner is a rather elderly man, with a shrewd and pleasant face, a squeaky voice, and gray hair. He was enthusiastically cheered as he passed along the lines. It is on occasions of this kind that I feel the want of my jolly little horse, which is still at Hunter's Chapel. The animal I now ride is excellent for mud work, and very sure footed, but unfit for a show occasion.

I think of you very often in my mental and moral loneliness, and try to make old family and home memories supply the place of present good influences.

GENERAL BLENKER'S DIVISION, SUMNER'S CORPS D'ARMÉE,
FAIRFAX COURT HOUSE, VA., *March* 26, 1862.

When I wrote to you last, I was not at all in the mood for it, and simply intended to throw you off a few lines as a bulletin of my condition and prospects, and with the expectation of soon having an opportunity to write you again, when I could really commune with you in spirit, as many times before, but have been so busy and active with preparations, marches, bivouacs, and drills, that the favorable moment could not be seized. And I had promised myself the luxury of a talk with you this very rainy morning, when Captain Schirmer, commanding the light artillery, ordered a court martial, and detailed me as judge advocate of it; so my pen had to deal with melancholy facts of drunkenness, insubordination, and disobedience, rather than serve as interpreter of kind thoughts and wishes from me to you.

But while I was deep in charges and specifications, and the piles of paper around me were growing decidedly Alpine in their character, one of the officers came in and handed me three letters. I glanced at the beloved crow-tracks on the outside, and broke one open, when the president began to look impatient, and the member next to me said in German, "put up your love-letters, and attend to business." So I thrust them into my breast-pocket, but that one glance was enough to show me that they were far more worthy to be called "love-letters" than those which usually bear that name; for one was from Aunt E., one from L. R. P., and one from yourself. . . . . After having convicted three or four unfortunates of various military offenses, and sentenced them to such pleasant little amusements as "Guard duty four times a week," "Hard labor for a month," "Reduction to the ranks," and "Loss of pay," I set myself down to a greedy devourment of my letters, all of which were most kind, and made me ask myself what right a poor devil of a soldier had to have such good friends, and that they should continue to take such a tender interest in him. Letters like these pierce the thick rhinoceros hide of insensibility which the soldier must wrap around himself. So, this morning I was reckless enough, and thought of nothing but blood and wounds and fried secessionists for breakfast; but now, I can't help feeling "low" and soft, with glimpses of a home-life somewhere, and a strong touch of nostalgia under the ribs; and when I go down stairs to go to bed (we go down to bed here, and up-stairs to work), I know that I shall not have spunk enough to kick out the fellows, who, I feel sure, are lying with their dirty boots on my mattress.

We came into this pleasant village, through which the tide of retreat and advance has so often ebbed and flowed, a week ago, having marched here from Taylor's Cross Roads in a tremendous rain-storm. The place was full of soldiers, and men and horses were quartered in the court-house, in churches, private houses, and wherever they could make a lodgment, but only the deserted houses were taken possession of. In cases where the inhabitants had the sense to remain in their dwellings, no soldiers were forced upon them against their consent. We artillery officers, some fifteen in number, have a very respectable house to ourselves. It belonged to a man named Jackson, who is said to be a near relation of the man that shot Ellsworth. (N. B. That Jackson must have a large family connection — at least five hundred Jacksons have turned up in this war who were said to be his relations.) It was not at all disagreeable to get a roof over our heads once more, after bivouacking for a week. Sleeping in the open air is not unpleasant, when you have the blue sky and stars overhead, although the ground may be hard and damp, and the wind cold and stiffening, — *that* one can stand, but when it rains and soaks you through, and you have no dry clothes to put on, but must act on the principle of "Every man his own clothes-horse," ugh ! then the fun ceases to be perceptible, even with my very excellent field-glass. . . . . You ask me what I think of General McClellan and the "Tribune" attacks. I must say that I have lately given up thinking as an occupation, but whatever ideas I may have of the conduct of the General in a military point of view, as a soldier, I have nothing to do but to hold my tongue and do my duty. At the same time you know my opinions on the subject of slavery, and that this matter will never be finally settled until the root of the matter is cut up. Too much blood and treasure have been expended by the North, to permit a mere temporary soldering up of the affairs, — to break out again worse than before.

MANASSAS, *March* 27, 1862.

DEAR M., — For nearly three weeks I have been moving from one bivouac to another, except during the time that we were at Fairfax Court House, and then there was such a bustle and constant excitement, that letter-writing was quite out of the question. Perhaps it would be better for me to give you a little account of our marchings and counter-marchings, as it will enable you better to follow me. On Monday, March 10, we moved out of Camp Hunter's Chapel, and went as far as Annandale; then by a very bad road to Taylor's Farm, where we were encamped for three days. Up to that day, we had very fine weather, and the two nights which R. spent in camp with me were just adapted to an amateur bivouacker, but the next day set in dark and misty, and at night we had a hard rain which knocked away all traces of romance about sleeping out of doors. At eleven A. M. a very sudden order came to march, and we were soon on our way to Fairfax Court House in as heavy a rain-storm as I want to see, unless through a window-pane, and the roads being very bad, halts were numerous, and we had to sit still on our horses and take it. Still we were much better off than the infantry, or *dough-boys* as they are called in army parlance, and one of my men told me that he saw a foot-soldier lying stark dead in the woods from cold and exposure. At Fairfax Court House we stayed for a week, had drills and inspections when the weather permitted, and were reviewed once by General Sumner, who now commands this Corps d'Armée of the Army of the Potomac. It consists of three Divisions, Richardson's, Sedgwick's, and Blenker's, and counts from thirty to forty thousand men. I commanded our Battery at the review, and had the honor of answering some questions put by the General. On Monday last, as we were at battalion drill, we received orders to march, and were off in little more than half an hour; had a splendid night march to Centreville over a first-rate road. We had a very cold bivouac; in the morning I examined the fortifications, and saw the famous wooden guns, painted black, which you must have read about in the papers. The earthworks are not very formidable in their character, but on account of their position, at the head of a long slope, something like a garden-lawn, which furnishes very little protection to besiegers advancing, it would be hard to take it in front without very great loss. Early the next morning we again took up our line of march, and after some hard pulling through the mud came to Bull Run. It was much larger, I should think, than it was last summer, — quite a respectable creek, about three feet deep at the point where we crossed it (Blackburn's Ford, I think), and not more than fifty or sixty yards wide. I sat on my horse in the middle of the stream, the water reaching just above my feet, and directed, and managed until the whole of the Battery had crossed over, and as I sat there, my mind would revert to that day in July last, when our troops crossed it in flight, and to that dreadful Monday when the news reached us at the North, and we thought that all was lost to the Republic. Then as we advanced further, the beautiful blue mountains beyond Manassas showed their heads, in some places covered with snow, and soon we struck upon the railroad which was so serviceable to the rebels in the campaign of last autumn. And so we emerged upon the plateau of Manassas, a fine bit of almost level ground, with woods on two sides, and mountains beyond; an admirable place for a camp, and the secessionists had improved its advantages very decidedly, by building camps of log-huts, in spots sheltered from wind and storm. These huts are shingled, and plastered with mud, and must have been far more comfortable than the tents in which we spent the winter. We encamped on the further end of the plateau, and then, yesterday morning, the Division moved off towards Manassas

Gap and Winchester, to effect a junction with General Banks. Our Battery and the Sixty-fourth New York were left behind to guard this place, an arrangement which did not please me greatly, until I was assured by Captain Schirmer, who commands the Battalion, that there would be no fighting, and that our horses would be much more able to do severe duty, if they could get a day's rest and plenty of forage; so I was pacified, and moved up and took possession of some of those nice secesh huts to await further orders; if there should be a battle, we shall have to go right forward, and if a retreat, we will have to cover it. I am sorry that I asked of you so great an undertaking as I fear the getting up of that flag must be. .... Even if we never carry it into battle, I shall feel most deeply grateful to you for the kindly and tender interest that induced you to make it, and shall look upon it as a proof of the love you bear towards me, and also towards that cause which is so mutually precious to us all. ..... I have not yet heard it positively stated that Blenker had been removed from his command. At any rate, I saw him yesterday at the head of his staff, moving with the Division. I would give a good deal to have Sigel for our commander, as then we should have plenty of hard work and tough knocks, with a clear assurance of victory at the end; but Sigel, if he should take any command here, would have a Corps d'Armée and not merely a Division.

MANASSAS, *March* 30, 1862.

MY DEAR SISTER T., — I received your very nice and kind letter the other day, just after our arrival at this place, and with it the *carte-de-visite*, which looked at me so truthful and natural. I was at first almost startled, and could hardly realize that it was not my little sister herself, who, in some mysterious manner had pasted herself on a card. I am now sitting in a quite comfortable shanty, one of those which the "Secesh" built last winter to accommodate their troops. They are quite substantial, built of logs, and plastered with mud; the roof is made of shingles, and keeps the rain out, except when it rains very hard. ..... We have pretty hard times to get anything to eat, as most of the supplies have gone further on. After drinking sugarless coffee for a few days, we have no coffee at all, and no water fit to drink. Of course, under such circumstances, the hen-roosts and barn-yards of the rebel folks have to suffer considerably. I have now in my cap the feather of a guinea-hen, from one not a thousand miles away. Of her untimely end I will say nothing, except that she was extremely tough, and that I shall abstain from guinea-hen in future.

PRESCOTT HOUSE, WASHINGTON, D. C.,
April 9, 1862.

DEAR J., — You will be somewhat surprised at the heading of this letter, but a little wind of business has blown me here, and I take advantage of a little leisure time after breakfast, before assaulting the departments, to answer your very jolly and refreshing letter, which I received at Warrenton Junction, just as I was coming away. It was just the kind of letter that I like to get, — a picture of home and New Haven matters, with a good dose of peppering thrown in. General observations and reflections in a letter between intimate friends are generally "nichts nutz," unless made in a way that illustrates the character of the person making them. It is the neat little touches thrown skillfully in, that make the home picture glow with life, and make the heart of the absent member beat warmly as he looks at it, — the one is like the bland, unmeaning allegorical pictures of the French school; the latter like the homely but delightful interiors of Teniers and Dow. I had some hint of the dissipation in which N. H. was indulging from T. D., who also spoke of you as "pars fui" thereof, but I had no idea of the extent to which you had been engaged in it till I heard it from yourself. . . . . To let you know a little about myself. I spent nine days altogether in the shanties of Manassas, and lived in plenty and prosperity, drawing the necessaries of life from Uncle Sam on the one hand, and on the other foraging for double rations of corn and hay, and occasionally picking up stray horses, oxen, sheep, pigs, and poultry of every kind. My horse-stealing experience was neither very pleasant nor successful. I got two old " clams " from a deserted farm-house, which got played out on the very first march, and two good horses from the sheriff of Prince William's County, whom I had heard to be a vile secesh, but who turned out to be one of those Union men who are now getting to be so plenty in the South, and I had to fork over the animals or run the risk of a row with General Sumner, although I needed them extremely to move my battery. You may be sure that I felt much as Robin Hood did when the sheriff of Nottinghamshire got the head start of him, and made up my mind not to meddle with sheriffs in future. On Thursday last our rest was broken by the arrival of a troop of the mounted rifles, to cover us on our march to Warrenton, and the next day General Sumner came through and ordered us to depart immediately. So I set off with my detachment, being the largest one I had had command of, with half the cavalry in front, the other half behind our wagons, and two at my own back as *garde d'honneur*. We started late in the day, and marched to the Jersey settlement near Bristow, where we encamped for the night on the farm of Major Snow, a Northern man. We took supper and breakfast with him very pleasantly, and did not despoil him, except a few oats for our horses, and a king-bolt for one of our wagons. The officers slept on the floor of his very handsome parlor, and I napped it gorgeously on the rug before the fire (*more antiquo*). It rained in the night, and in the morning the roads were very bad, and we had a journey of extreme difficulty and fatigue. We had to cut roads, ford streams, and dig out the wheels of our carriages with shovels from the putty-like mud. I was constantly in the saddle for some fourteen hours. At last we reached Warrenton Junction, the camp of the Division, and the men lay down in the mud perfectly fagged out. I had to lead the way myself in order to start out a wood-chopping party, and, after cutting down a good sized oak, I too was not sorry to succumb. Early the next morning the Division had orders to march; but Captain S. said that our horses were not fit to go, so I sent only one section with Lieutenant Singer, and was ordered myself to Washington to get some new horses. I started off immediately, had two days of rough travel in this horrible snow-storm, and got here last night. I fear that I shall not have much luck, but intend to try everything to get them, as it is miserable to be so close to the enemy and yet constantly impeded by the want of the means of moving.

I enclose a couple of secesh shin-plasters for J. The S. C. is rather interesting.

To L. R. P.

WASHINGTON, *April* 12, 1862.

. . . . Your very kind letter reached me safely at Manassas, having ridden the stormy waves of Bull Run, and then having been carried all the way out to Warrenton Junction, where the rest of the Division was lying, and brought back again to me. From these experiences it suffered nothing, except perhaps a slight stiffening from getting wet and being dried again, and a faint odor of "Limburger," from being so long on the person of the Division P. M. Unfortunately I have it not with me, and so must answer it from recollection, and not *punctuatim et seriatim.*

Your account of your work shows me that you have not at all taken my advice in regard to secluding yourself, but have grown worse, if anything, rather than better. Far be it from me to say that your time is ill-spent in making yourself a thorough scholar, and in going to the sources of language for a firm foundation ; but is it not a species of refined selfishness for you to give yourself wholly to this self-accomplishment? and do you not forget that, whether as a teacher or a preacher, your work is to be done, and your influence put forth in the living, breathing Now, and that if your fairest life is in the Past, you cannot know and appreciate the Present as you should? These scholarly pursuits are the most beautiful in the world, if they are kept subordinate to the great aims of duty and daily labor, and made co-workers in attaining some great and noble end ; but when made an *end in themselves*, their life is gone, and the more the mind gains of knowledge, so much the more does the soul lose of freshness and working power. Look at the scholarship of Dante, of Milton; deep, grand, and beautiful as it was, how it was transfigured by the heavenly light of religion and patriotism, till the student was quite forgotten. But this is certainly a queer sermon for a rough soldier to be preaching to a scholar, and forgive me if it be not applicable to you; but it is what I have often thought you wanted, and I know that you will pardon me for speaking out. The life I lead myself is just the opposite. Everything is intensely practical, just what lies before our feet, and in the immediate horizon; to keep the men and horses alive and healthy; to drill and march them well; to manage provision and forage carefully; to be always ready for anything that may occur; to have everything about the guns and equipments in perfect order; and for us officers to ride long, eat hearty, watch well, sleep sound, — this is our life, and a most sensual and beastly life too, if it were not for a few sparks of duty and love of country, that keep the heart aglow in the wildest night-storm, sustain the body through fatigue and privations, and even make our rough campaigning "bright, with something of an angel light." Since we came into the field I have been so well in body, and so glad in spirit, that I have felt almost exultant, and my feelings have been just those of the cove in the "Two Voices," who " sang the joyful pæan clear," etc., q. v. . . . . In my present life, and especially in our Division, there is very little to help serious thoughts. Sunday passes unobserved and often unknown, and there is not a single soul in the whole camp with whom I can walk, talk, or sing in sympathy on that day.

ALEXANDRIA, *April* 29, 1862.

. . . . . I came to Washington for the purpose of getting some new horses, and after I had them all picked out, and was ready to march with them to Warrenton Junction, Captain S. took it into his head that it would be very dangerous for us to march over the mountains to join the Division, and that it would be better for the Battery to come by rail and go by way of Harper's Ferry, — an idea involving much expense to the Government. But as he insisted upon it, I had to leave the horses and go out again by rail. When I reached Warrenton Junction I found that one section of the Battery had been sent out, with other troops, on an important reconnaissance, to the Rappahannock, about ten miles off. At the same time, pretty steady firing was heard in that direction, and soon a message was sent, asking for reënforcements. A company of the Maine Cavalry started off immediately, and I accompanied them. We rode and rode, and at last were almost in the enemy's claws, when an orderly overtook us, and told us that the reconnoitering party had accomplished its object and had retired. The force we had engaged consisted, in all, of about sixteen hundred infantry, two hundred cavalry, and eight pieces of artillery. They regularly surprised the enemy as he was mounting guard, silenced two of his forts, and blew up his magazines, but the force we had was too small to permit of their crossing the river and capturing the forts, so they withdrew in good order, with very little loss. On Sunday, April 20, we broke up camp, put our pieces and caissons on the cars, having left Lieutenant M. with the cannoneers in charge of them. I took the drivers and their horses and marched to Alexandria by the road. We had two days of incessant rain, and several broad and swift creeks to swim, but we made a rapid march, and got to Alexandria Tuesday afternoon, where we found everything all right, except battery wagon and forge, which were to come on the next train, but which had been kept back by the destruction of Bull Run bridge by the freshet. This kept us in Washington several days; at last they have arrived here, and I have come over with horses to bring them to Washington; tomorrow we are to go on to Cumberland and so to Romney.

FRANKLIN, *May* 15, 1862.

DEAR MOTHER, ... The reason why I did not write while at Washington the second time was that I was in a state of chronic disgust at the way in which Battery affairs were going on. I was the only officer who was willing to do duty at the barracks where our men were quartered, and was constantly there during the day-time. We had got some new horses, and as we had no proper stables, they were continually running away, and causing endless trouble and anxiety. The men were very hard to keep in check, and would get off into the city and get drunk and neglect their duty, and then I used to get the credit of all the damage they did, and all the rows they kicked up. At last we got orders to go to Harper's Ferry. After twenty hours of very disagreeable travelling, we reached Sandy Hook, east of Harper's Ferry, and there learned that the bridge had broken down, and we had no safe means of getting across. So we were obliged to go to work and unload our horses, which had been standing, closely packed in the cars, for a day and night, and the poor things showed evident marks of biting, rubbing, and other hard treatment. We waited at Sandy Hook two days for the bridge to be completed. It is a lovely situation, on the Potomac, surrounded by high and abrupt hills. One of these I climbed, and found on the top the Observatory which Colonel Geary had built, to watch the enemy from. The view is as fine a panorama as could well be imagined. On the one side the long, pleasant valley of the Potomac, lying between ranges of high rolling land ; on the other the abrupt bluffs, through which the river forced its way in some period long gone by, leaving the cloven promontories standing out, like the two halves of a broken stone, fitting into each other. Off to the west lay a beautiful stretch of level farm land, sleeping in the warm sun of a May Sabbath, the grain fields just beginning to wear a lovely green, which made a fine contrast with the deep verdure of the pine and oak forests, which clothed the uplands. The same afternoon we received orders to prepare to march, so we packed our horses into the cars, and put all the men on board, in order that we might be able to start off as soon as the bridge was finished. We had to spend the night in the cars, after all. Passing over the bridge was no joke, as a train of coal cars which had passed just before us had caused it to sink two feet, and our train consisted of more than forty cars, very heavily loaded. Very few remained in the cars while crossing, but I thought it hardly fit for a soldier to bother himself about such things, so I confided in the loyalty and good management of the B. & O. R. R., and rode peacefully over. We got to Martinsburg in the evening; but it was too late to see very much of this outpost of secesh. Early the next morning we reached our place of destination, New Creek, which is now the principal depôt of supplies for the Army of Western Virginia. There we unloaded the cars, and got everything in marching trim. *We*, means Lieutenant D., now in command of this Battery, and myself. He has been in command about five weeks. He does his duty right up to the handle, and it is a pleasure to work with and under such a man. I do not feel at all disturbed at having him put over me, as I certainly have not experience enough to fit me properly for a Captain of Light Artillery, and used often to be worried in my mind as to what I should do in doubtful circumstances. From New Creek we marched to Burlington, remained there a day, and were joined by the First Brigade of our Division, under General Stahl. The next morning we marched out of Burlington for Petersburg, twenty-nine miles distant; after making fifteen miles the Brigade went into camp for the night, when just as we were getting supper ready, an order came on from General Fremont to hurry on all the available cavalry and artillery to Petersburg, by forced marches, so we had to harness up again and go forward, fully expecting to see the enemy by break of day. In this we were disappointed, and went into Petersburg right peacefully, about two A. M. There we found General Fremont and a few troops. Our absent section of two guns, which marched from Warrenton Junction early in April, came in with more Artillery. They had endured all the privations and dangers of that very rough march. I went down the road to meet them, and rode up with the section past General Fremont, who stood on an eminence receiving the troops. As soon as we had passed, I was accosted most heartily by my friend S. from New York, who is on General F.'s staff. I dined with him that day, and met Colonel

ARMY LIFE AND SERVICE. 331

Albert, Chief of Staff, Fazougi, who made the great charge on Springfield with the body guard, and others whose names are inseparably connected with the " Hundred Days in Missouri." Early the next day the whole concern broke up at Petersburg, and marched, post haste, in this direction to support Schenck and Milroy, who were opposing, with seven thousand men, a force of sixteen thousand under Jackson. We made about half the distance the first day, and the next were rejoicing in the prospect of a fight, as our Brigade was in the advance; but, after advancing a few miles, we learned that our generals had repelled the enemy, and retreated successfully, awaiting our arrival to drive the enemy back again. You must pardon the uncircumstantial and somewhat careless character of my letters, but my fingers have got more accustomed to the bridle rein than to the pen, and my life is so unsettled that I have hardly a chance to collect my ideas before it is hurly-burly, march off again, and perhaps not another opportunity to sit quietly down for a week.

FRANKLIN, VA., GENERAL FREMONT'S CORPS,
May 23, 1862.

MY DEAREST M., — All right, the flag has arrived in perfect safety, and my heart is full of the warmest gratitude to you, for the kind interest you take in me and my men, and the noble sympathy with us in our work and suffering for the cause. You will not regret one toilsome hour spent over that beautiful work; indeed, not one stitch can be looked upon as taken in vain, when you think that it has filled rough commonplace soldiers with a sort of patriotic inspiration, and now they feel a sort of *chivalry* when they think of their flag and the fair stranger who loved their aim so well as to send it to them. The motto is exactly what I would have chosen if I had been wise enough to think of it, "Loyal till Death;" may we ever be so, upholding the truest and noblest of laws, our Constitution, and yet not merely with modern obedience and good-citizenship, but with true old-fashioned *loyalty*. And for our German boys the motto speaks with a friendly voice, and not that of an utter stranger, "Treu bis in den Tod," is the same motto, only slightly veiled by the change of language. When I first saw the flag, my heart smote me for having imposed upon you a work so toilsome, elaborate, and costly, and had you been almost any one else I should have been sure that it had been executed with some hard feelings towards me, but I know well the true and faithful love you bear our cause, and that when you go into a thing you do it with a whole heart.

The presentation should have taken place that very evening, but we were disappointed about getting some "Lager" or other liquid in which to drink healths to you and the banner, so I had it nicely fixed on the staff of the guide-flag, and it marched at our head to this place closely veiled, and so the company have not seen it yet, for, on account of almost incessant rains and other *contretemps*, it has been impossible to find a day proper for such a *festa*. But it shall be presented very soon with appropriate ceremonies, and then you shall hear both from me, and the jolly little standard-bearer, whom I have mentally selected for the honor. I hope that Mr. T. will in reality carry out his promise of getting us a staff from Mount Vernon, as that would make the whole matter very complete. . . . .

I opine that the day of retreating in this region has for us gone by. A depôt will be established here for forage and provisions, and forts are being built to protect them; we shall then press on to Staunton, repair the railroad, and from that point ever on and on. At present we are tied hand and foot by our want of food for ourselves and our horses; we are seventy miles from the nearest depôt, and everything must be brought by teams, and cross swollen rivers. You will be shocked to hear that, for four days, some of the infantry regiments had not even hard bread, and some of the men were so hungry that they paid two dollars for an ordinary loaf of bread. This very day, while writing this, I have seen a crowd buying large ginger cakes at a dollar a piece. Our Battery has been better off than most other corps, but unless provisions come to-day, I expect that we shall all go hungry to bed. Our Division has had it pretty hard ever since we marched out, having been without tents for two months and a half, and we feel pretty well posted as far as *exposure* goes, but this starving is another phase of soldier life to which we must also accustom ourselves. For myself, I am in pretty good health, and fortunately have not much appetite, so I don't mind much. We lie in the very heart of the mountains, and our marches are often through right picturesque country; the chief drawback is that it rains almost every day, and when it does not rain, it is very hot, and then we have a thunder-storm in the afternoon.

General Fremont's head-quarters are quite near us; I have several acquaintances on his staff, and have received much politeness from them. .... You must tell L. that this letter is for her, too, and that my thanks are equally hers for her interest and assistance. The work seems to go on nobly both in Virginia and further south; I had hardly hoped last fall that we should make such rapid progress. Just a year ago I was in camp at Washington, but it was queer soldiering compared with this. Now we have the genuine article, all but the fighting, and God grant that we may have that too one of these days. ....

FRANKLIN, VA., *May* 25, 1862.

DEAR J. .... I saw in the "Tribune," yesterday, a speech by Parson Brownlow in which he speaks of the miserable condition of the Union men of East Tennessee, and the confidence that he felt in speedy succor from Fremont's Corps. I fear that he trusts in a broken reed, for, at present, that army corps (not so very strong either) has its hands full enough with Jackson's force, and it is in a somewhat desperate condition, being unable to go either back or forward, and standing a fair chance of starving if they continue to lie here. There is no depôt of provisions here, and in fact none within seventy miles, and there are plenty of bushwhackers between here and New Creek to cut off our trains. All the infantry regiments, until yesterday, were without bread or crackers, coffee or sugar, for four days, and many of the poor fellows came over to us and begged for a piece of cracker to satisfy their hunger. We were better off, and by careful management succeeded in holding out until yesterday afternoon, when the train arrived, with thirty barrels of crackers for 15,000 men! Even that was attacked on the road by guerillas, and three or four of the covering party shot. Our poor horses fare worse; they have not had a proper feed for twelve days, and not four rations of grain in all that time. They manage to keep themselves alive by nibbling a little grass, but that gives no strength. We send out wagons every day into the surrounding country, but the country is so poor, as a grain raising district, that they come back with the poorest mockery of a few ears of corn. I am afraid that our men do not confine themselves to the legitimate object for which they are sent out, for various articles make their appearance which not even the largest stretching could bring under the head of forage. My own quarters became adorned the other day with a set of blue cups, plates, and saucers; a large milk pan and a coffee mill turned up yesterday, and I strongly suspect that the very comfortable bench on which I write, was once the ornament of some Methodist or Presbyterian house of worship. Sitting on this bench is the nearest approach I have made to going to church for some months. M. W.'s banner reached me in safety. I have not presented it because no beer has been attainable. The banner is really exquisite, the richest and most elaborate one I ever saw: on one side a wreath of oak and laurel, with crossed cannon and U. S. inside; on the other, a magnificent eagle, with a scroll and Excelsior on it in his mouth; underneath the motto in German characters, "Loyal till Death," above the number 13. The Generals of the Division have seen it, and pronounced it superb. I am afraid it was a very borous and expensive undertaking, but the effort is fully appreciated.

THE BATTLE OF CROSS KEYS.

MOUNT JACKSON, VA., *June* 12, 1862.

DEAREST MOTHER, — After the passage of about ten days I write you from the same place from which I wrote to J., but you must not think that this interval of time has been spent in rest here. On the contrary, we have made forced marches in the direction of Staunton, have fought a battle, and have made a rapid retreat, and reached this place at about noon to-day, a thoroughly used up set both of men and horses. However, I managed to snatch a little sleep this afternoon, and feel quite wide-awake this evening, so I eagerly seize this opportunity to let you hear from me, not knowing what the morrow may bring forth, nor how suddenly we may have to march again. . . . . Be sure that I shall take good care of my health, and shall not expose my life except when duty demands it, and if I fall in the performance of that duty, you will know that it so pleased the Director of all events, and will not sorrow unduly at my dying in the noblest way, and for the highest and best cause. You will wish to know something about our recent movements. About eight days ago the pontoon bridge over the Shenandoah at this point was finished, and our army moved across and marched rapidly after Jackson, who was still but a short distance in advance of us. If we could have saved the bridge and if the rains had not raised the river too high to prevent our immediately rebuilding it, we should have caught this prince of bushwhackers, together with the train and prisoners which he took from Banks. But the elements seemed completely against us, and we lost him by about a day. The second day's march brought us to Harrisonburg. Here we shod our horses, and got everything in readiness for the approaching fight. On Saturday night our cavalry made an attack on the Rebs, but were met by a much larger force than they had expected, and were driven back with loss. On Sunday we marched out in full force to beat up his quarters; the women gazed at us, as we marched through the town, their eyes streaming with tears, for it was their own husbands and sons and brothers that we were to meet in mortal combat. By 10 A. M. the heavy thunder of the cannon showed that the work had commenced, and that our advance was engaged, and soon the rolling fire of musketry told us that it had come to closer quarters. General

Schenk's Ohio Brigade had the extreme right wing; then came General Milroy's Virginia, then our First Brigade in the centre, then the Third Brigade, and lastly our Brigade, the Second, on the left wing; this was our position in the afternoon. Our right wing pushed their left wing back; in the centre the fire was very hot, and Blenker's own regiment, the Eighth New York, suffered dreadfully, being exposed to a galling fire from a whole brigade under cover, while they stood out in a wheat field; still they maintained their ground gallantly and were well supported by Schirmer's Battery, which did great execution. On the left the Third Brigade was just going to charge the enemy, and were aching for, the encounter, when they were withdrawn and we were ordered up at double quick to support them. We had got into a piece of meadow among the woods, and were about to clear the woods and turn the enemy's flank, when our Brigade was also withdrawn, not having fired a shot. Our Battery had no orders to retire, so we stood still while the infantry drew to the rear. For a little while we were in great peril, — we were between the fire of one of our own batteries and the enemy's infantry, — still our men were very cool and collected, and only wanted a chance to do something. Towards night the firing ceased, and we encamped on the border of the battle-field, our Battery covering the left wing from the top of a high hill. The enemy sloped during the darkness, and in the morning was " non est inventus," so we, who were in the extreme advance, lost the chance of distinguishing ourselves. It was a pretty equal fight. Our loss in killed and wounded must have been six hundred. That of the enemy could not have been less than one thousand, as our artillery cut some of his regiments up badly. Had our two brigades, which hardly fired a shot, been allowed to go into the fight, the result would have probably been far different, and our victory would have been thorough and complete. Still it cannot be denied that this Jackson is a man of decided genius, and that very few in our army are fit to compete with him. Thus on Tuesday he fought our army and prevented our further advance, in the night he crossed the bridge, which he burned after him to prevent us from following, and, having received reënforcements under Longstreet, beat back Shields who was advancing on the other side of the river. On Tuesday his combined force returned against us, now treble our number, and we were forced to retreat. Our Brigade was the rear-guard, and I had the honor to cover the extreme rear with my section. The road was about the worst I ever saw. When I had got about six miles I found several of our heavy caissons almost hopelessly bemired; the captain told me to send my section on, and gave me the pleasant task of fetching on those caissons. It was an awful job, as you may imagine. As the horses had had no feed for two days, they were very weak; but I persevered, and marched through Harrisonburg at three in the morning, with everything safe and sound. A rest until 8 A. M.; and then we marched again, luckily on a good road, or our poor horses would have fallen dead; here we hope for rest and feed and food and reënforcements: it is also said that General Sigel is to take command of the Corps. If he does, I feel the most perfect confidence that we shall end this doubtful campaign with brilliant victories. I will not harrow up your sensibilities by speaking of the horrors of the battlefield. It was bad enough to have seen them without repeating. I had an opportunity, during a halt, of tending a whole barnfull of our wounded soldiers, some of them with three bullets in them; one poor fellow pierced by seven, and yet not seriously injured. They all agreed in the statement that they had been very kindly treated by most of the enemy among whom they fell, — a few acting barbarously, but the most with tender and delicate humanity. This makes me feel more kindly to our erring brothers than before. Would that we could join hands and be friends once more. I am in excellent health, but have not known what it was to be dry. At night I have flung myself down by the nearest fire without blankets and have slept sweetly, regardless of deep mud or pouring rain. I love you all as much as ever, if I am a shabby, muddy soldier, worn out with hard work, and unable, from sheer fatigue, to write you an interesting or satisfactory letter.

GENERAL FREMONT'S CORPS D'ARMEE.
MOUNT JACKSON, VA., *June* 15, 1862.

. . . . As usual, my first thought on reading your letter, and the pleasant accounts of social life and family life which it contained, was, How strange all this is! And can it be possible that I shall ever again be civilized, and take my place again among old friends and dear relations, who have never had this primitive nomadic life to live. But in one point I can sympathize with you thoroughly, and that is in love for outdoor life, and for the fresh, young, bride-like earth, dressed in the robe of this loveliest of seasons. I find great difficulty sometimes in realizing that anything is awry or at war here in this beautiful valley where all is so green and fair and bright. For many days we had almost incessant rain, and life on the march was not highly agreeable, especially as at night we had to lie down in mud or water. But now the rainy season seems to have come to an end, and the summer has fairly set in, with wild flowers in the woods, and fragrant clover in the fields, and beautiful starry skies at night, so that it is a pleasure to lie out of doors night and day, and feel with the German poet, "How art thou still so fair, thou wide, wide world!" A nomadic, gypsy sort of life it is, even the luxury of a tent being only allowed when we camp for several days, as at the present time.

. . . . I should have greatly enjoyed being with you at the Easter festival, to see the flowers and hear the anthem, and join with all my heart in the service of the day. I spent Easter Sunday at Catlett's Station in a pouring rain, putting the Battery on the cars, to be taken to Washington, and on Pentecost Sunday we were fighting all day at Cross Keys. In fact Sunday is *very* seldom a day of rest with us, and it often comes and goes without our being aware of it. When peace comes again, I shall appreciate Sunday more than ever.

ARMY LIFE AND SERVICE. 339

CAMP IN THE BLUE RIDGE, PAGE CO.,
July 23, 1862.

MY DEAR AUNTIE, ... If I could succeed in looking upon this whole campaign as a sort of summer excursion or jaunt, nothing could be more pleasant and enjoyable. I have seen some of the finest scenery in the country, and that in sunshine and storm, at midnight and at sunrise, have lived always in the open air and in perfect health, spite of privations and exposure to rain and dew; have had the additional spice of a little danger occasionally, and the sensation of a bold, free life, and yet there has always been something which came in to spoil my enjoyment; it may have been the rough and reckless men we have under us, but more than this was the feeling that we were invaders, laying waste a fair and blooming country, and that our opponents were men fighting to save their firesides and their homesteads. It is by no means agreeable to deprive farmers of their grain and hay, and to carry off favorite horses amid the tears and supplications of the women folk; and you can yourself imagine how hard it was when we came back from Cross Keys, to see in Harrisonburg and New Market the women dressed in black and weeping as if their hearts would break. I cannot help mentally transferring the whole trouble to the Northern country, and thinking how I should feel if the "Louisiana Tigers," or some such notorious corps, should have a chance to march through Connecticut. Indeed I am sometimes in danger of forgetting the real reason and object of the war, because my mind is constantly occupied with the superficial losses and miseries which are daily before my eyes, but which "endure but for a moment," and which, when we succeed, will bring for us "a more exceeding weight of glory," in a preserved Constitution and established laws. Just at present our prospects are not as good as they were, and unless the North responds promptly to the President's call for more troops, it is not unlikely that the Union men now in Virginia may be crushed and driven back by mere weight of numbers. The size of our army has been greatly overrated, — all the men in hospital, in garrison, and in camps in the Northern states having been counted to swell the number, while the Southern force has been correspondingly underrated. . . . . This is a superb region as far as scenery goes. Right above us is a ridge crowned by a natural fortress, with towers and bastions as complete as can be, undoubtedly one of the highest points in Virginia. On every side there roll off beautiful deep valleys, full of orchards, and farmhouses, and fields of grain; and on the higher slopes are countless blackberry pastures, just like those in which my soul used to delight among the Catskills. Children seem to be the greatest wealth of this region; the soil is not first-rate and farming has scanty products, but you can hardly see a house which does not swarm with children of all ages, from the little lisping toddler to the dark-eyed boy of sixteen, not quite old enough "to go with Jackson." If animosities are transmitted to the next generation we shall have a good crop of rebels in this region. . . . . I think of you all at home a great deal, especially just this week, Commencement, when the old college friends are coming together at New Haven, and another class goes away from its classic home.

CAMP AT SPERRYVILLE, VA., NEAR MIDDLETOWN,
GEN. SIGEL'S CORPS, *July* 29, 1862.

. . . . As we are lying quiet here, enjoying both rest and fine weather, I cannot resist the temptation of answering your last most kind letter, as I do not know how soon the orderly may come dashing up with orders for us to be ready to march in two hours. The last installment of letters was a very pleasant one to me, only my pleasure was considerably diminished by the news that J. was also coming out to fight, and that in the Infantry. The fatigues, exposures, and dangers of that branch of the service are so great that I am very anxious lest he should find himself unable to bear them, and what would you all do at home if anything should happen to him? I think that when you all have only two boys, and no one else to lean upon, the most self-sacrificing patriotism could not call upon you to let us both go. I have spoken more at length in my letter to him, but I suppose that he has too decidedly put his hand to the plough to think of turning back. . . . . The North must hurry up and send down those three hundred thousand new recruits, or else the rebels may succeed in making a dash at our broken and reduced columns, forcing their way through and perhaps seriously menacing Washington and Baltimore. . . . . If our armies in Virginia are defeated, the apathetic people of the North may have the satisfaction of seeing the reckless Southerners in their streets, and the farmers in rich New York may see their grain taken to feed the cavalry of Ashby and Hampton. I should greatly dislike to hear of their camping on the green at New Haven, and cutting down the elms to make their fires. . . . . Strange to say the premonition I expressed on the first page has come true. An order came a few minutes ago for us to be ready to march at 6 A. M., to-morrow morning, with one day's rations, probably to support our advance posts, which have been attacked and driven back. It is nearly midnight, but there is a stir of men dressing rations, and a light at the fires where they are cooking them. I must close this letter now in order to take a little sleep, before the toils of to-morrow. Think of me as healthy and hearty, and as loving you all with all my heart.

CAMP NEAR RAPIDAN RIVER, CULPEPPER CO., VA.,
August 17, 1862.

DEAR GRANDFATHER, ... Just now we are having a quite unexpected rest. I had supposed that, after our long sojourn at Thornton's Gap and Sperryville, we would go right on when once started, and not stop until we should be absolutely compelled to do so, but there seems recently to have been a change in the war policy, and McClellan is retiring from Richmond, apparently to concentrate upon us here, as Burnside has already done. . . . . I suppose that you have already seen full accounts in the papers of the battle of Slaughter Mountain, as it is called, and properly so, for it was a slaughter of General Banks' troops, and nothing else. We were stirred up at Sperryville with orders to march forthwith, and at 6 P. M. we were in readiness, but did not get off before 10 P. M. We marched all night and all the next day, through excessive heat and dust. As we approached Culpepper Court House, we heard very heavy cannonading and musketry fire, but did not push on to the battlefield, because it was already too late to do any good, and the troops were excessively fatigued. The next day we arrived, early in the morning, at the field, having marched again in the night, and found that General Banks had substantially maintained his position, but that his troops had suffered dreadfully from a contest with such overwhelming numbers as had been poured upon them. Had they retreated to Culpepper Court House, they would have met the advance brigades of our Corps, and the enemy, if he had dared to follow, would have been thoroughly whipped. The loss of life that occurred in so short a time is almost unparalleled in the history of war, and it must have been one of the hottest engagements of the campaign. I see that the Fifth Connecticut suffered severely, and that my friend E. B., Major in that regiment, was wounded and taken prisoner. I wish that we had been pushed more rapidly forward, in spite of heat and fatigue, and then should doubtless have succeeded in sparing many valuable lives to the country. Sunday, the day after the battle, was excessively hot, and very little was done beyond scouting and skirmishing. Monday was devoted to bringing off the wounded and burying the dead, hostilities having been suspended for that purpose. Our men and the rebels mingled freely together on the battlefield, and conversed; many found old friends and school fellows, and even relatives, in the opposing forces. The piles of dead men and horses, in all possible forms of mutilation, made a horrible sight, and it was not until late in the evening that the dead soldiers were all interred. I think that General Pope's official account is quite fair and impartial, and that the rebels lost the most, though not perhaps very much. We lay near the battlefield, and then marched a few miles to this place, a couple of miles from the Rapidan River, in the midst of a beautiful country, which rolls and undulates like the waves of the sea, and is finely wooded with superb oak forests. . . . . I am much disturbed at J.'s move in the recruiting line. I do not think that the most ardent patriotism could demand more than one from our family, and when both are gone who will look after mother and the girls, to say nothing of you and Aunt E. ? It is a thing that may easily happen, that neither of us will ever come back. I think that very few of the army now in the field will ever see their homes again ; the new conscripts will win the glory of finishing the war, and will carry home our banners in triumph. But the work must and will go on in spite of all temporary considerations and family ties, and the sooner the good people of the North come to see and acknowledge this, the better. . . . . I sometimes find myself indulging in most unpatriotic wishes that I was under the dear old elms once more, if only for a little space. I am only pretty well ; but I take the best care of myself that I can, and hope soon to be better.

CAMP NEAR RAPIDAN RIVER, CULPEPPER CO., VA.,
August 17, 1862.

. . . . Your letter was such a nice, kind, jolly one, that it put me immediately into the writing vein ; and besides my opportunities for writing are so few and so widely separated just at present, and the chances of continued life and ability to talk to you are so uncertain, that I have adopted the principle of writing whenever I feel like it, without any regard for retributive justice. And especially should I dislike to go down to Hades with your letter unanswered on my hands ; my ghostly form would be continually revisiting "the glimpses of the moon," and vainly endeavoring, with a phantom hand, to indite a shadowy epistle to one, still most substantially in the flesh. All that you told me about New Haven, the Commencement festivities, the boating party, etc., was intensely interesting to me, in spite of the frightful aggravation I experienced inwardly at being unable to be there with you and help you.

Oh, for an oar in my hands once more, a crowd of the old

sort following my stroke, and a few ladies, also of the old-fashioned sort, to make a good, solid boat-load worth the pulling of *Atlanta, Thulia,* and *Una* men? Just one pull with such surroundings to South End, a lazy day spent in pleasant talk, and watching the long sun-lit ripple rolling in from the Sound; a moon-lit row back to the dear old city, with plenty of songs, and the next day you may put me, like Uriah the Hittite, in the forefront of the battle, and let me take my chance. . . . . .

You interested me very deeply with what you said about what you had seen and heard in the hospitals. I shall be curious to hear from you some of those stories, — write them down, if you think there is any danger of your forgetting them. And, my dear child, I felt so very grateful to you for the interest you felt in our poor, wounded boys; it is the cup of cold water to the disciples and supporters of our great cause, and it shall by no means lose its reward. . . . . .

I have had some queer times foraging in this part of the country. The soldiers interpret General Pope's order "to subsist on the country they pass through," in the most liberal manner, and I have had the pleasure of knocking several such extensive raids on the head, and driving off these self-made "quartermasters" and "commissaries of subsistence." At one house I interfered in favor of a sheep, some bee-hives, and the potato-patch, and was rewarded by being invited into the house, where I met the prettiest girl I have seen in Virginia, — a real stunner, with light brown hair and perfect features, and an arm like the Venus of the capitol. I grieve to say that I was quite enthralled by this she-rebel, and the next night, being out foraging for hay, I stayed to supper, and came home so late that I found a party just saddling to go out and rescue me from the bush-whackers. The captain gave me three days on guard, but I think that it was worth it on the whole. Then, to cap the climax, being sent down to Culpepper after stores, I stopped there yesterday morning on my way back and took breakfast. If we have occasion to retreat, I shall manage to get wounded near that house, and have "sweet

Maud Muller" (I don't know her real name), take care of me. Joking apart, I have nothing in the present to interest me, and nothing in the future to hope for, except an honorable ending for myself, and the full success of the cause. My immediate surroundings and associations are very, very hard to endure, but I shall hold on, praying at least for health, if not for happiness. . . . .

I picked up a letter on the battle field the other day, from a young married lady in Georgia to her two brothers in the army, and it might have been from you, so pleasant and naïve was the style. She chatted about her little baby, and how it resembled its young uncles, etc., and my heart smote me when I thought that perhaps their life-blood had soaked the very ground where I stood.

CAMP NEAR FORT ETHAN ALLEN,
September 14, 1862.

DEAR COZ, — . . . . It is extremely aggravating to me to think that I shall not be able to be present at your wedding, but if I am there, it must be either as a cripple or an invalid, for my battery is *my* plighted bride, " until death do us part," or until peace do see us once more an united land. To tell the truth, I have not the slightest idea that I shall ever see any of you again, and I endeavor always to banish from my mind the pleasant picture of a reunion with the family at New Haven, for when I dwell on it too much, it makes a feeling of regret sometimes arise, and that always interferes with duty; no, I prefer to accept the belief that I *must* fall, and if I *should* survive, it would be so far a pleasant disappointment. The days are looking very dark now, our arms are meeting reverses in every direction, and it requires no prophet to announce that many toilsome marches must be made, and many more battles fought, and thousands of brave men yet fall, before this quarrel shall be settled on the permanent and righteous footing that we seek.

I will not trouble you with any account of how we marched down to the Rapidan, and then how we marched back again; how we shot at the rebels across the narrow Rappahannock, like boys fighting across a handkerchief, and how the artillery of our Corps held the many fords of that river against the overwhelming numbers of the enemy; then how we marched in post haste to Manassas, when we found that the wily Jackson had got in Pope's rear, and was threatening his communications; how our Corps bore the brunt of the battle all day Friday, and covered the repulsed left wing on Saturday night, and were ready to renew the fight the next morning, had we not been ordered away; how we marched back, full of wrath at leaving a field that we had twice won, and were still able to hold, and took our gloomy march to Centreville, Fairfax, Vienna, and at last came under the shelter of the forts on Georgetown Heights, where we now are; all this is not pleasant to repeat, but as an offset, I can assure you, that it was all done without haste or panic, and that "Battery No. 13" stood gallantly by its flag, served its guns under the hottest fire, with coolness and skill, and finally, in spite of loss of men and horses, brought them all off the field, not without words of praise and commendation from our idolized Sigel. We had it the toughest on Friday afternoon, when we were sent by General Sigel to hold a hill from which several of our batteries had already been driven; here three rebel batteries of excellent guns, and finely served, rained shot and shell upon us; a section of a regular battery by our side was silenced and compelled to retire, and then the whole fire was concentrated upon us. I can assure you that I had no idea of ever coming alive out of that *inferno*.

J.'s regiment is in Washington learning drill and discipline; last week he was on guard at the Long Bridge with his company. I knew that he was there, and determined to see if he would know me after our long separation, so I pulled my hat down over my eyes, rode up and gave him my pass, as if I would go over the bridge. He looked at it, said it was all right, and was just about to pass me, when he gave one look at me, and then sprang forward like a mad creature. It was a happy meeting, and we spent the afternoon together. His regiment makes a fine appearance, and I think that he will become a first-class officer. May he be spared to the end!

Written immediately after the second battle of Bull Run.

HEAD-QUARTERS 13TH N. Y. BATTERY,
NEAR CHAIN BRIDGE, VA., *September* 5, 1862.

DEAREST MOTHER, — I take the first opportunity offering itself to give you intelligence of my entire safety and welfare, if it be only a few lines. I was in the hottest of the fight all day Friday, and all the afternoon of Saturday, and exposed myself considerably to keep our boys up to the scratch, but got nothing except a slight scrape on the top of the head from a piece of a shell, and a bruise on the cheek from a canister ball; both of these little wounds are almost quite well, and almost without medical assistance, and I sincerely recognize the protecting hand of God in my preservation. The Battery did right gallantly, though I say it that should not, and were highly praised by General Sigel. As soon as I get the chance I will write again. This must suffice for the present.

Very much love to all.

ACCOUNT OF THE SECOND BATTLE OF BULL RUN.

CAMP NEAR FORT ETHAN ALLEN, VA.,
September 10, 1862.

DEAREST MOTHER, — Your welcome letter has just come to hand, giving me assurance that you had got my hastily-penned note, and were relieved from all immediate and harassing anxiety on my account. I did the best I could to communicate with you, but on account of our being so constantly on the move, officers always in the saddle, and horses in the harness, it was impossible to call the next five minutes our own; so I could only send you a pair of words. I think you can hardly fail to be interested in my experiences for the last three weeks. My last letter to N. H. was written to A. from the banks of the Rapidan, and in that I remember I spoke of the speedy advance of our forces in the direction of Gordonsville; how ignorant I was of the state of affairs was proved by the fact that the very next evening we had orders to be ready to march to the rear in an hour, and before the sun went down our long, slow-moving trains were drawing off in the direction of Culpepper Court House. Our Corps, which had the post of honor in the rear, drew out into the road, and lay there all that night, and a good part of the next day, waiting until the enormous trains and the Corps in front of us should have reached the positions assigned to them. We passed through the foul region of Slaughter Mountain, with great offense to eye and nose; the men had all been buried, but the pile of slaughtered horses still showed where batteries had stood in the hottest fire. We passed through Culpepper that afternoon, and, by dint of steady marching, came to the Rappahannock in the night. Here we took up a position to cover the passage of the river, and stood to our guns until about noon the next day, when we, too, passed over, and the bridge was burned behind us. Thence on from Jeffersonville to White Sulphur Springs, — the Saratoga of the South; but the place of the summer loungers in the streets was filled with soldiers, and the sick men lay in the great hotels which had, two years before, been so full of "dances and delight." Here we hoped for a day's rest, so much needed by both men and horses, but we were allowed only one good sleep, and then off again, after breakfast, to the Rappahannock, along whose banks a fierce, long-range artillery duel was to be kept up for about a week. The first day our four rifled guns came into action, my six-pounders being kept in reserve as too short range. One of our gunners made a splendid shot that day, at over a mile, and dismounted a secesh gun, but this feat was ascribed in the papers to Captain Schirmer's Battery, as have half a dozen things that our Battery has done. The only loss that our artillery sustained that day was Captain Buell, commanding the reserve artillery, and just the man that we could worst afford to lose. A shell passed through his horse, wounding him in both legs, and then the horse fell on him, and caused internal injuries, of which he died that same evening. He was really a charming fellow, quiet, gentle, yet firm and active; his whole Battery loved him to devotion, and I enjoyed his society greatly, ever since we came under his command at Sperryville. For the next two days we had plenty of marching, but little fighting. The next day we were separated from the reserve artillery, and sent to General Milroy's, and ever since we have been connected with this king of the bush-whackers. We have not had occasion to complain that we have been neglected, in getting our full ration of fighting. In fact, before we had been with him two hours he had the rifled guns in full operation on a hill, while I crept forward with my two pieces towards a hill well in the advance. We were well covered by our own pieces until we reached the brow of the hill, and came into battery in an apple orchard; we drove the enemy's cavalry out of the woods, but could not do much to the enemy's battery, which was too long range for us, and their balls and shells tipped the trees about us in a lively manner. The chief of artillery saw that we did not reach them, and ordered us down the hill again; pretty soon Sigel came along and saw my section standing idle, and inquired the reason; upon hearing that Captain Schirmer had sent me back, he said, "Take your section up on the hill again and fire away;" so up I went to a part of the hill more directly in front of the enemy's batteries. Instead of stopping on the summit, I had my guns run down the easy slope towards the enemy, by hand, and thus advanced until I was several hundred yards in front of our line, and had brought the hostile batteries completely within my range; then we went to work, and, by keeping sharp look-out, succeeded in shutting up every gun which the Rebs planted in front of us. Once they ran a gun well up before a bank and masked it, so that it fired three times before I could exactly find it; when I did, I laid my two guns right for the muzzle, and it assumed a dignified silence. By afternoon our Brigade moved further on, and we had no more work of importance till the evening before Friday's battle. Then we shelled the woods where the enemy lay, just at nightfall, and the shells with their burning fuses made a beautiful firework. That night each cannoneer slept at his post by the gun, and we all snoozed soundly, for we knew that we should have plenty to do the next day, and having seen Jackson's handiwork at Manassas, were right anxious to go on and catch the old Valley Fox, whom we had been so long hunting. Alas, it turned out too much like the story of the man who caught the Tartar. Up early, placed our Battery in a commanding position, and engaged a hostile battery for an hour or two, until we drove them away, and then advanced to their position. (N. B. This credited in the newspapers to Schirmer's Battery.) Beyond was a high ridge, on which the enemy had many batteries planted, and a large part of his force concentrated to attack this. Milroy now advanced with his Brigade, and our Battery alone, being only supported by long range fire from batteries on the ridge we had left. He entered a piece of open ground, behind the woods which sheltered him from the batteries on the hill, and throwing skirmishers and a regiment into the woods on the right, tried to carry the railroad embankment in his front. The Battery was not placed in position, but just stood close behind the infantry in column, utterly useless, and itself in danger. After a sharp fight in the woods, our men had to retire, when suddenly a couple of rebel brigades came swarming over the railroad embankment, and our Brigade had to beat a hasty retreat. We did not move until the enemy were pretty near, and then we went back through the opening, the bullets flying in great abundance. Just as my second piece had passed the opening, a shot brought down one of the pole horses, and stopped us short; my first thought was, "The piece is lost;" my next, "It shall be sold dear," and I sprang down, and with the assistance of one man, unlimbered it. I seized the rammer, and we had one shot fired before the other officers knew that we were in danger. The other cannoneers came up, but I held on to the rammer, and did Number One in pretty lively style. The other pieces came into battery on a hill behind us, and opened fire; then the batteries above us began to operate at short range, and between shells, canister, and musketry fire, we had it hot enough. But we soon drove the infantry back to the embankment, and gave our infantry a chance to halt and reform. A reserve horse had been brought up with harness, and was hitched in under the hottest fire; when all was ready, I had the piece limbered up, and followed the rest of the Battery to the opening in the fence. Just at the opening, the reserve horse was shot two or three times, and I had to cut him out of the harness and carry the branch myself for some distance. While acting as Number One, I was struck on the cheek by a canister shot and thought I was hurt, but it swelled two days and then passed off. A splinter of shell struck me on the head, cutting three little holes, and burying itself next the bone. This grew very sore, and the doctor, after taking out a piece of my felt hat, which was driven in also, tried to extract the metal, but could not do it. However, I have poulticed it, and it has healed up entirely. (This exploit of ours, which saved the Brigade, is attributed in the newspapers to Hampton's Pittsburg Battery. I don't care a cent for newspaper praise, but it comes hard for the men to have others steal their well-earned laurels.) In the afternoon we were sent to an important position, from which the rebels had already driven two or three of our batteries. They had got the range exactly, and threw every shell right among us. However, we held the position until our ammunition was exhausted. The fire was really infernal, and we lost several men killed or badly wounded, and many horses. I was astonished to find that the idea of danger was so little present with me, even in the hottest of the fire: but I suppose that it was because I kept myself occupied and worked hard at my duty. A shell struck the piece I was working, and ploughed a great furrow down it; but I hardly noticed it at the time. In fact, I think that the extreme front is the safest as well as the most honorable place. I have seen many a man knocked over by these bounding shots, when he thought he was all safe in the rear. We are hoping soon to get into Washington to refit, as we have lost many horses, and want some of our guns mended. In *our* General (Sigel) we have the most entire confidence, and his corps will follow him anywhere. I suppose you have heard from J. about our meeting at the end of the Long Bridge. It was truly a delight, and a joy inexpressible to me, after these many months, during which I have seen no friendly face, grasped no friendly hand. I felt proud of the old fellow, looking so neat in his fatigue uniform, and doing his duty in so prompt and business-like manner. He seems to have a fine company. What a startling contrast they would make, if ranged alongside of my poor travel-worn, battle-weary ragamuffins. I need rest greatly, and to recruit my health. I would rather stand by my post, and trust to time and rest to heal me, than to go into hospital. I am afraid this egotistical letter may have wearied you.

CAMP NEAR FORT DE KALB, *September* 19, 1862.

DEAR GRANDFATHER, — Your very kind letter reached me a few days ago in the first regular camp we occupied after the battle, and it was very welcome to me, both as showing the kindly interest you cherish in me and my welfare, and also because it informed me that you were freed from anxiety on my account. I have written to mother, giving an account of our retreat from the Rapidan and also of the battle on Friday, in which we largely participated. . . . . I was as thoroughly used up on Friday night as I ever recollect being in my life, for I had some severe hard work all day, as a cannoneer, and then the cessation from the excitement of battle caused a sudden reaction which produced both mental and physical fatigue. However, I managed to sleep pretty well, on ground which we had won from the enemy in the morning, and at break of day proceeded to hunt up the ammunition train and to replenish our exhausted boxes. Then we marched out of camp, and proceeded to the Stone Hospital, of which you will have seen frequent mention made in the newspapers. Here we lay in reserve, waiting for the moment when the eye of our sagacious leader, General Sigel, should see where to push us forward with most effect in the line of battle. Past us filed the long lines of the corps of McClellan's army, comparatively fresh after a rest of a few days, and who had not been engaged on the previous day. Some of the regiments, as for example the Brooklyn Fourteenth, the New York Fifth, (Duryea Zouaves), looked quite full, but the bran new uniforms, and fresh unburned faces showed that the ranks wasted by battle and disease, had been to a great degree filled up with recruits, men as yet untried. I saw quite a number of friends among these regiments, among them Col. Wm. Wainwright, formerly Major of the Twenty-ninth New York, with which we were long brigaded. By the Hospital we lay, listening to the roar of the cannon and the sharp rattle of the musketry, and watching the course of the battle, which began with greatest intensity on the right of the centre, and gradually worked round towards the left wing, where the rebels got some batteries in position, and thus established a cross fire on our troops. Just about this time, when our troops in the centre were falling back, and the hills and fields to the rear were covered with stragglers and attendants on the wounded, our Brigade, General Milroy's, was ordered to the left wing, and we went joyfully onward, hoping to do our share to redeem the battle, which seemed in danger of being lost. At the same time, a fresh body of troops had gone up to the centre, and I there saw a bayonet charge made, by at least a whole brigade, which I shall never forget. Steadily the long line marched on, the banners rising and falling as they passed over the undulating ridges, but still going steadily forward, under a murderous fire from both infantry and artillery. The enemy fall back, and take refuge in a wood, where they are reinforced and make a stand, — still our men pass on, and it seems as if the opposing lines were within touching distance. At last our line staggers under the infernal fire bearing upon it; the wounded are seen first brought to the rear, and finally our men retire a short distance, and resign a part of the ground they had so gallantly won. Now our Brigade marches up on the left, and plunges into the woods to clear them ; our Battery takes up a position on the open ground, and proceeds to shell the woods, over the heads of our own men. As we advance nearer to the woods, we improve our range, the fire becomes hotter, and the rebel sharp-shooters creep up as close as they can, and pick off our cannoneers. The noise of fighting in the woods comes closer, and it becomes evident that the enemy are driving our men back, so I take one six-pounder and go, through a shower of bullets, to that part of the woods where our men are just emerging, closely followed up. We come into position, wait until our own men are well out of the way and the gray jackets are already beginning to swarm out, when we let go a few rounds of canister at one hundred yards' distance, and back they go again in a great hurry. We then retire with the retiring infantry, but only about fifty yards, and then again unlimber and fire, until a fresh regiment comes up and enters the woods. I then rejoin the Battery and we take position on a hill and wait for orders; no orders come, and night comes on, and all is quiet, except occasionally a few volleys from the extreme left, which General Reno is holding, and nothing whatever is seen of panic or disturbance on the battlefield, which we now hold.

. . . . At last an aid from General Sigel comes up and orders us to Centreville, and we proceed thither in perfect order. Of the panic we saw little or nothing, as it occurred mostly in the rear among the stragglers, teamsters, and ambulance drivers. Why we retreated I cannot say, but I feel sure that we would not have done so if Sigel had been in Pope's place. Of what has since happened you know more than I. I have been miserable in health since the battle, caused by cold and exposure; but cannot take time to rest, as one officer is wounded, and one is on detached service. We are now being repaired and refitted. . . . . I have seen J. and his regiment; they are quartered near Washington's Monument. He makes a fine looking officer, and bears himself well among his men. You must miss him greatly in New Haven. May he never know the hardships and perils which I have gone through the past summer. I can hardly venture to hope that we shall both ever be reunited with you at home. For myself, I thirst for active service, and am miserable when lying in camp, as at present.

CENTREVILLE, VA., *September* 28, 1862.

DEAREST MOTHER, — Your letter, dated September 23, reached me late last night at Fairfax, to which place I had made a night march from Fort Ethan Allen, where I had been

detached on picket for a week. . . . . I am, in truth, a very
unsightly object to look upon ; I wear the same jacket and the
same vest that I did when we marched out of camp last February, and they bear spots acquired in half the counties of
Virginia ; still I cannot cast them away without a feeling of
regret, thinking on how many a cold night march they have
kept me warm, how often soaked by the May showers and
dryed again, how often brushed up to make a martial appearance when passing triumphantly through secesh towns, and
how often carelessly rolled together to make a pillow for my
bed on the ground before the bivouac fire ; indeed, so many
of my best thoughts and most ardent labors are associated
with those weather-beaten garments and faded epaulets, that
I cannot believe they look so badly as my friends say ; and
yesterday I went quite coolly in them to drive with General
Abercrombie, and after dinner did the agreeable to a couple of
fair damsels visiting Fort Ethan Allen. My week on picket
was every way a pleasant one, except that I was sick part of
the time, having got badly chilled on one of those cold nights,
as I had no tent and had to sleep under a tarpaulin. . . . .
Then one of my Corporals, a nice young Englishman, took
his blankets and fixed up my shanty to keep the cold out, and
built me a good bed, so that I managed to keep warm and did
not get any worse ; still, I lay in bed for three days in much
pain, and my bones all felt very sore. Joseph S. and young
A. from the class of '63, both on General Abercrombie's staff,
were unremitting in their attentions, brought me doctors, and
books to read, and looked after the material wants of my men,
and were in general so kind that I felt quite sorry yesterday
afternoon when the order came for me to rejoin the Battery
at Fairfax ; and General Abercrombie, too, did n't want to let
me go away from his command, but was obliged to, as General Heintzelman countersigned General Sigel's order to that
effect. We packed up and got off about dark, and a pretty
tough march of some fourteen miles brought us to the Court
House by midnight it was a hard pull for me, as I could not
sit my horse, got chilled again, and did not sleep when I en-

sconced myself within my tent; and worst of all, the Battery was ordered on to Centreville early the next morning. But I have succeeded in getting here more comfortably than I had expected, and shall lie quiet and take all possible care of myself, as I have no idea of becoming useless for the Fall Campaign. I thirst for active service, and hope that we shall soon get a chance to take part in a decisive battle in favor of the Union cause; the mere thought of Bull Run (and the battlefield lies even now stretched out before my eyes as I write), Harper's Ferry, Mumfordsville, makes me sick; why, Colonel D'Utassy with the Garibaldi Guard, from our old Division, could have held the fort alone for twenty-four hours, and been rescued. The rebels are welcome to my somewhat attenuated length of five feet ten, but not with any vitality in it. I have read General Milroy's report, and it is in many respects true, but still a picture of the General's excited state of mind, and it is evident that he hardly knew half the time what he was about. A braver man never lived; he seems to drink in excitement and intoxication from the sound of the bullets, and to be perfectly happy when in the very tempest of battle, but he knows nothing about the object of artillery or the way to use it, and I am heartily glad that we are to have nothing more to do with him. General Sigel's report is soon to appear, and then I hope that our Battery will be spoken of more scientifically and judiciously. I see that I have been unusually egotistical in this letter, but do not believe, dearest mother, that my thoughts are not with you on this calm, beautiful Sabbath afternoon; I feel quiet and very happy, and picture you to myself as you go down to church among the falling elm leaves, and sit in your pew with J. and T., but no raven head of hair at the end; I pray ever most fervently that I may be allowed to meet the dangers of battle alone, and that he may be spared them. You cannot well lose us both. . . . . To me this contest and cause are the same that the quest of the Holy Grail was to Sir Galahad.

"To me is given
Such hope, I know not fear."

To L. R. P.

CENTREVILLE, VA., *September* 30, 1862.

I feel a little inclined to grumble because you confined yourself to one small sheet, and passed over many topics of interest with a bare mention which aggravated me very much, just as with a child to whom one is showing pictures in a book and passes over the prettiest with a turn of the leaf. But you must do better next time, and expand more on those little matters which constitute the filling-in touches of life; if necessary, have a pigeon-hole in your desk, labelled, "Wheelerisch Memoranda," and lay in these hints from day to day for future letters. . . . . I will not weary you by expanding on the subject of the battle of Bull Run, as it has already been set forth at full length in the newspapers. . . . . What surprised me greatly was that so very faint an idea of danger was in my mind at the very hottest of the fight; I was so thoroughly occupied with working my pieces to the best advantage, that I hardly noticed the bullets whistling and shells exploding around, and even some of the most revolting sights of bloodshed and death seemed to me very natural under the peculiar circumstances. I have also observed the truth of Horace's assertion, —

"Mors et fugacem persequitur virum,
Nec parcit imbellis juventæ
Poplitibus timidoque tergo,"

for nothing was more usual than for a shell to strike in the Battery, cut a furrow alongside my foot, and then making a high ricochet in the air, come down several hundred feet to the rear, and cut some cowardly skedaddler right in two, a fate which he would probably have escaped if he had stood up to his work. Well, our men retired, but, I am convinced, wholly without sufficient cause; indeed, I believe that if Sigel had not had positive orders he would have held the field all night, which in fact he did do until late in the evening. And for our Corps and our Battery I have the consoling consciousness that we did our duty fully, and obeyed the order to withdraw with the greatest reluctance. There is a radical defect in the formation of our Army; its regiments, brigades, divisions, and corps, especially the latter, are too small to be thoroughly serviceable and manageable, and there are too many officers of high rank, each possessing a sort of half-cut independence; these corps are not much larger than divisions eight months ago, the divisions have sunk to brigades, and many brigades cannot show a full regiment of fighting men. Now what could Sigel do with his handful of men, perhaps twelve thousand in all? What he *did* do is pretty generally known; what he *might* have done if he had had a full corps of twenty-five thousand to thirty thousand men is aggravating to think of. And now, newspapers are inquiring "What is Sigel doing?" What can be expected of him, with a small corps that suffered far more than any other in the late fight (and yet did not lose a gun or a flag), with his best brigade (Milroy's) detached and sent to Western Virginia? He has now some five thousand men, a superb command with which to fall upon the enemy's rear and cut him off, as seems to be demanded by many! How can the government expect to succeed while they ignore the men who mean *fight*, and give everything to softly warriors like McClellan, who are afraid to hit the enemy too hard? But the chief cause of the present deadness in affairs is the neglect of the Governors of States to forward their quotas; six hundred thousand men look very big on paper, but so long as they are not raised they do us very little good in practice. New York State alone owes yet forty thousand men, and the day of drafting will be delayed until the time for autumn fighting is past, until the roads here become again unfathomable, and the secesh call out their last resources, and gather strength for next year's struggle; so we are always a month or two behind, and the enthusiasm and spirit of our troops evaporates, under this system of timidity and delay. A section of our Battery has just returned from an expedition with the cavalry, in the direction of Warrenton, and report that the cavalry captured there, and in the neighborhood, some sixteen hundred secesh; how true this is I cannot tell. I should have commanded the section on the expedition myself, if I had been well enough to stand the march, for as senior Lieutenant I have always the right to demand the privilege of being detailed, and it is customary for me to do that sort of work with my section from the left wing. But I am now very much better than I have been.

CENTREVILLE, *October* 9, 1862.

MY DEAREST MOTHER, — I answer your most welcome letter with expedition, in order to quiet any anxiety on my account, and also to reassure you as to the probability of my being engaged in any actual fighting when you are assisting at M. W.'s wedding. I was very miserable when I first came here, my complaint having been greatly aggravated by long continuance and want of rest and care. By lying quiet in my tent, and the almost magical effect of the pills which you sent, I soon began to improve, and now am as well as ever, and have an appetite like a wolf whenever I do a little extra work. We were paid off on the 1st, and the Captain went off on the 2d, which was pretty hard on me, as I was thus left to stem the tide of drunkenness and quarrelling almost entirely alone. However, the boys behaved much better than could have been expected, when they had been four months without pay, sent home a great deal to their families, and paid off their debts exemplarily. There was of course noise, and fighting, and trouble, but less than ever before on pay-day.

On Sunday I started off with a picked party and a loaded wagon, to turn in a lot of old horses and useless harness to the Quartermaster in Washington. It was extremely doubtful whether we should succeed in getting all of the old creatures over the twenty-five miles, but by starting on Sunday afternoon, and going that night to Falls Church, resting there and going on the next morning, we arrived at Washington Corral with our full freight of condemned horse-flesh.

I was in the city a day and a half, ordered a neat uniform, and had a *carte-de-visite* taken of my head and shoulders, which I think will be good. Then I came out by the Long

Bridge, and found Company G, Fifteenth Connecticut Volunteers, on guard on the Virginia side. Lieutenants G. and F. were there, but the Captain was in camp, so I rode on to Camp Chase, and found the respected fraternal about a mile from where we lay last winter, at Hunter's Chapel. I sent my men on to Fairfax, and took off my things, to stay to tea. I saw a nice dress parade, enjoyed an excellent cup of the home English Breakfast, and then we talked together till it was quite late, and he got for me the countersign, and then I had a splendid ride under the full autumn moon, and through the soft airs of Indian summer, back to Centreville, which I reached at 1 A. M. . . . .

J. was looking very well indeed, and seems to enter into the spirit of his work admirably, especially in his longing for active service, which there does not seem any very great probability of his getting in the Fifteenth C. V. Nor am I sorry for this. I am a much greater coward about him than myself, as I have seen how numerous the casualities among the officers of an infantry regiment are, especially among those that expose and distinguish themselves. I am very much afraid that we shall lose our General of the Eleventh Army Corps. It is stated positively that he has tendered his resignation, and as the Government does not seem prepared to give him satisfaction they can hardly avoid accepting it. . . . .

FAIRFAX, VA., *October* 30, 1862.

. . . . I thought of you all a great deal on the 15th, and took pleasure in calling up the familiar faces of every one present at the family assemblage at Springwood. On that same day I was starting out with my section on a reconnaissance to Chantilly with the cavalry. I was so weak, that I could hardly sit in my saddle, and my toes trembled in the stirrups, but I had already missed two such expeditions (being on my back in bed) and thought that the excitement might do me good.

We went out on the road towards Aldie and Middleburg, came into battery on a commanding hill, and the cavalry went ahead to scour the country. We remained there that afternoon, watching the skirts of the distant woods for any traces of rebel cavalry, and then bivouacked under the open sky by our fires. The night was cold and frosty, and I could hardly say that I was fairly asleep all night ; but it did me a great deal of good, and when the next day we were relieved, and went into camp, I felt fifty per cent. better. The same evening Captain Johnson's Battery arrived at Centreville to relieve us, and the next morning we bade adieu cheerfully to the exposed and dusty wind hills of that region, and marched to Fairfax Court House, where we are now encamped on the northeast side of the town, in a well sheltered spot on the edge of a wood, and on exactly the same place where the Battery stood when being reviewed by General Sumner last March. This does n't look as if we had made much progress since then, and we have slipped down three stairs for two we have got up. But I have great faith in the army which is now coming into the field, and also in the firm determination of the people and the President, to treat the war as a serious matter. The rebels have been serious ever since last spring, and we see the results. . . . . For myself, I am not satisfied at sitting down now, and allowing these golden days to slip away unimproved. . . . . I am as comfortably fixed as if we were to stay here for months. I have a nice army cot, which folds up, a writing table, a neat little stove, with a first-rate brick chimney on the outside, (put up by a mason in my section from bricks brought from a ruined house near by), and good boards over a good part of my tent floor. I made my calculation that if we stayed ten days, I should get the worth of my money, and if longer it would be so much gain. When we do make winter quarters I intend to make myself thoroughly comfortable if it be any way possible. The two Divisions of our Corps went a few days ago, and indulged a sham battle, skirmishers thrown forward, battalions deployed, artillery placed in position, and pushed forward from height to height, and bayonet charges made by full regimental line. We maneuvered with Steinwehr's Division, which is mostly composed of new regiments. The fresh troops did remarkably, especially the Twenty-sixth Wisconsin and Thirty-third Massachusetts.

CENTREVILLE, VA., *October* 9, 1862.

MY DEAR M., — . . . . I can assure you that the regrets which I had experienced before at being unable to be with you in "the dreadful hour," were deepened and made more poignant by the array of attractions you present to call me thither, and by the warm-hearted steadiness with which you insist that I *must* be there. So pleasant a child of hope it is too hard to stifle with one inexorable word, "impossible;" and yet that word must be written; and, to show you wherein that impossibility consists, I inclose a copy of "General Orders No. 28," from the head-quarters of our Corps, and what our General sees fit to order, that I must obey without grumbling or discontent. Or, perhaps, we could represent the affair as "urgent official business; but then the rub would be to state it in the application in such a way as to make it *seem* so to the powers that be. I think that the only resort left will be for you to make a direct application to the President, and support it by all the influence of our *powerful and illustrious family*. Surely, if you and L. and R. should unite in making up a Round Robin to the Executive, I am sure that the stony-hearted Abe would relent at the sight of so much beauty and worth in tears, and he would immediately dispatch the Fifteenth Connecticut Volunteers to bring me my leave of absence for ten days, with, however, this important condition, that I should not fail to bring him (ye said Abraham) a hunk of the cake.

No, there is no help for it; and I will not further aggravate myself by thinking of my own misfortune in losing so pleasant a family reunion. I will rather think of you and your happiness, ——'s resignation under affliction, of the talks gotten up by our mothers and aunts and uncles, of the harmless fun perpetrated by the "young fry," — in all of these, except of course the last, I shall be with you in spirit, and you can imagine my old jacket and shoulder-straps as lending variety to the toilettes of the guests actually present. . . . . This golden Indian-summer time is just the season for marching and fighting, and I chafe at our present inaction. Why don't they send us on troops enough to move with, or, if we have troops enough already, why don't we "pitch in?" There are mysteries about the conduct of this war that puzzle and almost disgust me, but I manage to keep my faith in "something" alive, although I can hardly say what that "something" is. At present it is mostly confined to the sturdy determination of the people of the North to bring the war to a just and honorable termination.

The 15th October is an anniversary for me too, as on that day I was mustered into service, and shall then have been a United States soldier just one year. May the first anniversary of your wedding day see the country reposing in perfect peace.

GAINESVILLE, VA., *November* 6, 1862.

Your last most welcome letter reached me the day after I wrote to you, and must have passed mine on the way. I can hardly undertake to respond to you in a worthy manner, for it is late at night, and my toes are very cold, besides, we are to march to-morrow morning, and if I expect to rise betimes I must see that I turn in before long. The dreams of winter quarters at Fairfax, in which many of the men indulged, were all dissipated on the first of the month by an order to march early on the morning of the next day: which order pleased me hugely, and I set to work and put the ammunition of the whole Battery in general, and of my section in particular, in tip-top order. The next morning, at the appointed hour, we were all packed up, and horses hitched in, but could not move, as the road was occupied by General Heintzelman's corps, on its way to Centreville. By noon we got off, and reached this place. Our road lay exactly across that part of the battle-field where we had struggled so hard on Friday the 29th, and, strange to say, we stopped at noon on the very hill on which our Battery had stood for two hours in the afternoon in the most infernal fire. This gave us an opportunity to examine the locality with some care. On the back slope of the hill were some ten or fifteen graves of our men, among them that of young Hutchinson of my section, whose poor mother I had the pleasure of consoling with a letter, giving an account of his gallant bearing, and his glorious but almost painless death. . . . . Many of our poor horses were lying on the slope, shriveled to skin and bone, and the meadow beyond was sown broadcast with missiles of every pattern and calibre. I then rode over to the valley where M. came so near leading us in to our destruction, and I saw my two pole horses, one on the hillock where we first unlimbered and fired, the other by the opening of the fence leading into the road, where I played his part for a number of dangerous rods. The space near the railroad embankment, where M.'s men had been driven back, and where the rebels had in their turn been forced back by our canister, was covered with graves poorly dug, and scantily covering the miserable forms within. I was very much depressed by the whole sight, but not shaken in my old resolution to see the end of the matter, or be like these poor men. Some of our men, who were on the hill occupied by the rebel batteries which annoyed us so, state that the graves were in great long trenches, and that the dead horses fairly covered the hillside, showing that the enemy had not passed unscathed through that Gehenna of balls.

In the afternoon we came through to this place, which is a small village of a few houses on the slopes of the Bull Run Ridge. The Manassas Gap Railroad is completed to this place and beyond. The locomotive has a friendly and civilized appearance, and our boys always cheer it. General Sigel arrived here in person to-day, and to-morrow we are to advance, probably to Warrenton, and no one knows what may happen.

I am very well indeed, don't mind sleeping out of doors these cold nights, but prefer a bed in a warm tent decidedly. I am fully prepared to stand a fair share of hardship for the next month.

CHANTILLY, VA., *November* 25, 1862.

DEAR AUNT E., — . . . . Our Corps has, by the new arrangements and division of the Army of the Potomac into four parts, come into the Reserve, and thus we are lying at present in a disagreeable state of "betweenity," neither having the comfort of winter quarters nor the compensating excitement of active operations in the field. I am hoping that Jackson, who is said to be still at Bunker Hill and Charlestown, may make a dash in this direction, in the hope of getting to Washington in the rear of the main army, now down on the Rappahannock. But I think that would be a little too hardy for the Shenandoah Valley Fox.

I do not wish to triumph over the fallen, but I must say that I consider the removal of McClellan as just and necessary. He has been tried, and found wanting in those qualities of swiftness, energy, and ready talent which are absolutely needful in a leader who would successfully combat the genius of Lee, the dash of Stuart, the daring rapidity of Jackson. Whatever else we may say of the rebels, we must also confess that they have managed to pick out their best men, and have put them at the head of their army. The material of the bulk of their army is certainly inferior to the mass of ours, and our artillery is much the best, while we allow only a slight superiority to their cavalry. But material is nothing so long as it is not rightly moulded and put to use. With the prospect of victory when advancing and impunity when retreating, the dirty, half naked, ill-fed white trash of the Southern army will march twenty miles a day, and fight days on empty stomachs; and, with the enthusiasm inspired by such leaders, our boys would do and suffer as much and more. I have had an opportunity to see it proved, that officers who are willing to expose themselves, and lead their men on intelligently, will never lack support. The material of our Battery, for example, is by no means first-rate, and they do for the most part answer to the description of "hirelings;" but I doubt if there are many places so hot that they would not follow their officers into with cheerfulness. In fact, so all-important are the virtues of courage and firmness out here, that one has a tendency to forget that any other virtues are worth practicing; but I have succeeded in keeping alive one more, Faith, — faith in the soundness of Northern hearts, and in the honesty of the President; faith in the approval of the Ruler above, and in the consequent success of our cause. In regard to religious matters, I have thought at times that I had grown entirely callous; but when I have heard a piece of hymn-music, or read a few tender lines of admonition from mother, or ridden out in the pleasant autumn afternoon among the woods and thought; or listened to our colored servants singing some old camp-meeting tune, in a minor and melancholy key, by their fires at night, I have felt that it was not so. I suppose that Thanksgiving Day will be the day after to-morrow in New Haven, and I deeply regret, as ever, that I cannot be home upon that day. It is the festival above all others which I have always been accustomed to spend at home, and now I am again absent. I know that you will remember J. and myself when you sit around that family table, and you may be sure that we will be thinking of you. I have cause for gratitude that this year I am in excellent health, while on last Thanksgiving Day I was so sick that I had merely to look at the gigantic turkey, but could not touch it. I have already projected a foraging expedition for to-morrow, to procure a gobbler to be sacrificed to St. Thanksgiving, and it will go hard with any secesh farmer who refuses to hand him over for a reasonable compensation in greenbacks. We have been going into geese pretty extensively lately, as our cook gets them up in a most palatable manner. The other day I rode several miles with two live ganders slung one on each side of my saddle like holsters. .... I have a first-rate darkey, rejoicing in the name of Glenmore. He has been with me nearly four months, and has kept my horses in first-rate condition. He is a ludicrous object, having a nose like the pyramid of Cheops, with orifices in it like the secondary craters of Vesuvius. He is a great favorite with most of the men, who call him Chocolate, and he has the jolliest and most infectious laugh you ever heard. I feel quite attached to him, and should be very sorry to lose him. . . . .

CHANTILLY, VA., *December* 9, 1862.

DEAREST MOTHER, — Your letter, dated December 2, was duly received, and gladdened my heart in the midst of this bleak wintry weather like a breath of spring, and I take advantage of this pleasant sunny morning, when it is possible for me to inhabit my tent, to answer you. In the first place, that turkey, with the fixings, etc., for which the collective mouths of our officers' mess have been so long watering, and which was to be the Phœnix, or pattern bird, of our cook-house, towards which all future poultry was to strive, and whose virtues should be emulated by geese and chickens yet unhatched, this noble animal, I say, with all his seductive surroundings, is by this time very unpleasant both to look at and to taste of, and indeed it would be too much to expect of him that he should remain more than two weeks on the way, and yet preserve his original sweetness ; in other words, the box has not yet arrived. But although I could not eat the turkey, I thought of you all day long, as in church, but in a pew which had two vacant seats ; then the Thanksgiving dinner, at which I *know* that J. and I were missed ; and still more in the pleasant, quiet evening, when you sat together and talked. I think that never before in my life had I personally so many reasons for being thankful ; a year ago this day I was setting out for Washington, doubtful whether I should ever reach it, and with my whole system thoroughly on the verge of dissolution ; for my recovery, I have, next to God, to thank Uncle R. and Aunt H. ; then I am very thankful for having been able to see you and my other friends once more, and to strengthen my heart with the assurance of your love and sympathy ; then brought through the hardships and exposures of the march and the camp, and the dangers of the battlefield, I find myself now in perfect health, and with a frame to some extent inured to bear everything that may occur in an ordinary campaign. If I were not deeply thankful, I should be indeed ungrateful. The cause of the country, it is true, has experienced no such improvement in the last year, but still we hope ever for a happy and righteous ending, in spite of the mutterings and threats of some members of the Democratic party at the North, and the unfriendly attitude of France.

About what I said on the subject of being awakened to religious thoughts by passing circumstances. I think that you must have received a very incorrect idea, and one which I would not wish you to entertain. The state of the case is this: as a general rule, the chaplains here in the field either wholly neglect their duty, or else so perform it, that they might far better have remained in their tents, and others are talkers who are utterly without any conceptions beyond their pay and their position; now, I have been brought up to consider religion and its exercises and meditations as something serious and awful, and since I have thought at all, I have thought that in this matter a man must be sincere and honest above all things, so if I pray, I cannot avoid placing my whole being in a position of the greatest humility before Him to whom the prayer is offered, and at the same time the greatest earnestness and eagerness in demanding help. But an attendance at church which is merely habitual, a reading of the Bible which is merely mechanical, and a way of praying regularly, but with the mouth alone, these things blunt the religious sense, and satisfy a man's soul with what is really nothing. For these reasons I will not attend the ministrations of chaplains which do not edify me; but whatever I *do* say on this subject you can thoroughly believe.

I have heard nothing from J. directly for a month and a half, and feel very much worried by hearing that he is ill. I have written to him since we came here, but have received no answer. If he gets well over this trouble, and gets nicely toughened up, it will have been a great advantage to him. I should have gone in to see him, but my duty here has been quite constant, and it would have been hard to get away.

The weather has been very trying most of the time since we

came here. About seven days ago we had a furious wind storm, that lasted three days and nights, and ended in snow, which fell to the depth of eight inches. It was utterly impossible to keep warm in my tent, and the only way was to lie and take it. It was especially hard upon our poor horses, which seemed to lose in two days all that they had gained by three weeks' good feed and care. Yesterday my section went to work and built a nice evergreen stable, big enough to hold all our horses (thirty-three), and more too; my little mare Jenny has the warmest corner of it, and it is entirely protected from the wind. In former years, about this time or a little later, I have also worked in evergreens; but then it was to deck churches, or to fix and trim Christmas trees for the young ones. I think that our present work for our poor, irrational, dumb beasts is just as pleasant, and as much a labor of love as the other. And now, just as we have the job completed, comes an order to be ready to march at a moment's notice. You can imagine that those who have built log huts, and got themselves nicely fixed, are not very amiable at the prospect of moving. I feel very glad of it, and hope that we may yet do something before the roads become impassable. I should greatly enjoy a few days at home this winter, but it does n't look much like it just now, and the orders are very strict that no one receives a leave of absence on doctor's certificates, unless it is absolutely necessary for the preservation of life or health; and I am glad to say that I am not a candidate for any such certificate. Captain D. is encouraging a nascent rheumatism, which he thinks will bring him home at Christmas as it did last July; but I unfortunately have no pet malady which appears so conveniently. If a month or so later we take up winter quarters, the matter will doubtless be different, and in that hope I live, for I so long earnestly after you and the girls.

I received a charming letter from Uncle W. the other day; so long as the folks at home write such patriotic, hopeful, cheering letters, they may be sure that their representatives in the field will fight well. The violets in your letter were delicious, and the whole of it was as fragrant and sweet to the smell outwardly as to the heart within.

STAFFORD COURT HOUSE, VA., *December* 20, 1862.

Your last kind letter, date December 15, came to hand this morning, and filled me with thankfulness, in hearing that you were all well at home, and also relieved me to some extent from the excessive anxiety I have felt about J. for the last fortnight. I have not heard from him directly now for nearly two months. I was afraid that he might be so rash and unwise as to march with his regiment, to scenes of hardship and exposure which he was totally unfit to encounter; so you can imagine how glad I felt to hear that he was still at Washington, and was contemplating a further trip to Annapolis, which we can now call the "Convalescent Hospital" for our family, as well as the army in general. Judging from my own experience, I think that he could hardly be in a better place than there, with Aunt H. to nurse him, Uncle R. to judiciously supervise and starve him, and A. to amuse and couster him up as soon as he came down-stairs. Still it must have been extremely trying for him to have to lie still while his regiment marched off to active service, though I do not really know where the Fifteenth Connecticut went to, or what battle they were engaged in. As for our Corps, we have had a very rough time of it indeed. We marched from Chantilly by the way of Fairfax C. H. and Fairfax House; came to the Occoquan River. Up to this point our main trouble was the slippery condition of the roads, on which our horses were frequently falling, with great danger both to man and beast. But this was decidedly a minor evil, compared with what came later. A succession of warm days thawed the frozen ground, and for five or six hard marches we struggled over hills and lakes of mud, and through ravines of putty-like soil, such as can be seen in perfection only in Eastern Virginia. At the passage of the Occoquan we found some fine forts, one above the other, like a terrace, which if defended would have been very costly to take; but they were deserted, and there were no signs of their having been recently occupied. On Sunday we were at Dumfries, near Quantico Creek, and then we had three days of the toughest sort of work to reach the high ground on the left bank of the Rappahannock, near Falmouth. There we learned that the attack had been made without us, and had failed, and as there was danger that the enemy might throw himself on our line of communications, and cut off Burnside's supplies, we were moved back to this important place, to guard the railroad, and our whole Corps is now assembled here. In some respects the march was more trying than that of last May and June from Franklin to Harrisonburg. It is true we we did not have the night marches or the thunder showers, but then we had mud *ad infinitum*, eight days' marching without rest, scarcity of provisions, winter nights, and the depressing thought that we could not march as fast as the infantry through the mud, and that we must sometimes call upon them to help us to extricate our bemired wagons. Several times was I indebted for a lift to the stout hands of the Fairfield County boys of the Seventeenth Connecticut Volunteers, Colonel Noble, who were for several days in the same brigade with us. What was worst of all was, that when we got to Falmouth, we came the day after the fair, and had no fight at all, and had to take our caissons back as full as we brought them. Still it was very acceptable to get a rest here. Bivouacking in the middle of December is no fun, and we should have suffered most severely if the weather had not been unusually mild. At Dumfries, the team wagons were left behind without my knowing it, and so I came off without any blankets, except one on my saddle, and I had to make fatigue and a good fire supply the place of them. In fact, one night I was so used up that I slept in my jacket, without blanket or fire, and felt no ill effects. One night, however, I caught it, — it was the night before we marched to Falmouth. When we lay down around the fire, the stars were shining brightly, and all was serene. Towards morning I woke up and found the rain dashing in torrents in my face, — a cold, driving winter rain, — still I was too tired to seek a shelter, even if there was any to be found, and went to sleep again. Unluckily I lay in a too level place, and when I awoke in the morning I was the "Gentleman of the Lake," and soaked to the skin all down my back. To add to this, by noon it cleared off bright and cold, and the piercing winds made me shiver in my wet clothes. I hardly thought I should get to camp. However, I arrived there safe, and slept dry that night, and by the next evening got the chill out of my bones. But you must not be at all disturbed on my account, when I tell you these things; fatigue and exercise are potent antidotes to cold and exposure. I am twice as buoyant, and hopeful, and happy, on a hard march, as when vegetating in camp. One goes through almost as much on a hunting tramp or a skating party, and who would complain of a little extra privation with our motives before us? I hope you do not feel discouraged at Burnside's partial failure. I continue full of hope till all is gone. This letter must be your Christmas box from me; very, very Happy Christmas and Happy New Year to you, dearest mother.

STAFFORD COURT HOUSE, VA.,
Christmas Eve, 1862.

It is Christmas Eve, when "Peace on earth and good will toward men" is the text, and although nothing is said of good will toward *women*, yet I suppose that they are included, and so will pardon your long silence to-me-ward, and will do my best to spend this evening with you in thought and spirit, at least, if not in person, as in very many happy years in the past. . . . .

Nothing among us here indicates the time. The country is too poor to furnish us with a turkey to diversify our pork and crackers, even if we had the money to purchase one, and we are even without a glass of wine for toasts, as several of our sutlers have been captured on the road. I determined, however, to do the best in my power, so I went out into the woods, and got a most beautiful little *holly-tree*, with splendid leaves, and full of berries, which we planted at the foot of the flagstaff. There are a pair of symbols for you! Above, the emblem of equality, free thought, free speech, justice to all men ; below, the emblem of respect for what is old and reverend, the ornament of this great festival of faith and religion. No freedom can be dangerous that is so rooted and grounded.

And while I am speaking of this, I would further say, that there are very many now fighting in this army, who have apparently lost sight of all early training, and have given up all religious habits, and who seem to think of nothing but their military duties ; that is, you see, at first, only *the flag*, but if you could search deep down you would find the holly tree there too.

. . . . It is beginning to rain, which is a very improper proceeding for the weather on Christmas Eve. I am officer of the day, and when I make my midnight round by the stable, I shall have a fine chance to verify the Catholic legend that at midnight, on Christmas, all "beasts of the stall" go on their knees. I have seen plenty of horses do that in the day-time and irrespective of church festivals.

I need not tell you that we had a tough time of it, marching down here, as the newspapers all speak, "ad nauseam," of the mud and other hindrances. The roughest part of it all was to hear Burnside's cannon when we had only reached Dumfries, and were, still, two long days' march from the scene of conflict. It was also vile in the extreme to reach Falmouth, after seven days' incessant marching, and then to have to turn round and march straight back again. This being on the outskirts of battles, hearing the guns, and meeting the ambulances filled with wounded, I have had enough of, and I long for the excitement of another good hot artillery fire, like that on Friday afternoon at Bull Run. I almost long (I am almost ashamed to confess it) for my quietus ; not that I despair of our success ultimately, or have any doubts of its completeness, but why should I live when so many better men are falling. Then, too, my anxiety for the cause, and my restiveness under my uncongenial surroundings, would be forever quiet. A real good, honorable death might perhaps give some brightness to a dull and useless life. Do you think that I am too sad and gloomy? But what else can you expect of a man who is about to wash down with cold water a Christmas dinner of bean-soup and crackers?

STAFFORD COURT HOUSE, VA.,
December 29, 1862.

DEAREST MOTHER, — Your letter, dated December 24, came safely to hand with the inclosed draft, which I was glad to dispose of to our sutler for something less. . . . . It is very lucky for me that he did not attempt to follow us in our march from Fairfax out here, as he would probably have been captured at Dumfries with the rest, and my things would have shared his fate, and fallen into the hands of the rebel cavalry. A new way of sending things to camp is by mail! I know one regiment in our Corps which receives three pair of boots at least by every mail, and some of the regiments with Burnside had their Christmas turkeys sent on in this way. If you could send me one it would be a regular treat on our mess-table, where we have the unvarying round of crackers and coffee for breakfast, soup and meat for dinner (with potatoes when we can get them), and coffee and crackers for supper. Bread is not to be obtained anywhere, as the sutlers find that it pays better not to bring out anything but whiskey and tobacco. . . . . Christmas Day passed off very drearily; the day before I went out and got a little holly-tree, which I planted at the foot of the flag-staff, where it looked very pretty, and quite lighted up the place. . . . .

I had a pleasant call from young H. of the class of 1859, and Captain Wm. L. of the Seventy-ninth New York, "the Highlanders," who have been in almost every hard fight since the first Bull Run, except the Peninsular battles, a rough experience for such a slight, delicate boy, but in spite of it he looked well, and bright, and hopeful. When J. comes back from camp I intend to make a day of it down in Burnside's army, and to refresh myself with a sight of the cheerful, undesponding spirit which prevails there, in spite of all their reverses.

To L. R. P.

CHANTILLY, VA., *December* 30, 1862.

.... And even now you must not allow yourself to fall into the error of supposing that I have anything particular to say: I only palm off my worthless goods on you, in the hope that you will think rather of the writer than of the written, and send me back a letter telling of yourself, of New Haven and my family, of mutual friends, and their sayings and doings, and dispatches from that dear old student world from which I am now sometime an unwilling exile. You can really form no idea of the peculiar feelings I have towards that college time, and everything connected with it; classmates, friends in other classes, our lady friends of the period. "Hornet's Nest," and even such actual and living realities as my mother and the rest of the family, our house, the elm trees, all partake of a certain vague and shadowy beauty and excellence; it is my "Lost Bower." It is true the loafer within me says, "Recall that vanished time, dwell again in that Bower," but the worker says, "No, you have much more real duty to perform than that;" and so, although I cannot boast of much energy or success in action, I have yet a little too much of the earnest man in me to settle down into scholarly idleness. Still I love to hear about the old times, and the old friends, and you cannot interest me more than when you tell me all the New Haven gossip, what mischief T. D. is about, and the last joke indulged in by B. .... Of our late movements I have but little to say, except that between November 2 and November 19 we made a circumbendibus from Fairfax Court House, through Centreville, Painesville, and Aldie, round to this place, which is only six miles from "the point or place of beginning." At Aldie we had a superb place for winter quarters; our pieces in fine position, plenty of food, forage, and game in the neighborhood, and pretty girls sown broadcast over the land, whose charms were rendered still more piquant by their attitude of fierce but harmless defiance. In fact we had arranged ourselves nicely for a long stay; had plundered the church and schoolhouse of their stores, and even carried off the superb gilt candelabra with a marble bottom, from the pulpit, as likewise the preacher's chair; my Captain (who alone was the sacrilegious perpetrator) remarking pithily about this last article, that it was a real benevolence to the poor people to remove it, since the parson would not preach so long if he had to stand up all the time; or at any rate, as I suggested, he would have to effect "a change of base" à la McClellan. As if to punish us for our evil deeds, Burnside did change his base, and Sigel's Corps having been put in the reserve, he moved his head-quarters to Fairfax Court House, and we moved to Chantilly. Why they put Sigel in the reserve I can't imagine, unless it were that they were afraid of a dash in the rear from Jackson, and considered our Flying Dutchman the only man fit to look after him. I don't know what our Corps amounts to now, as we have a large number of new regiments which are perfectly untried, and which don't promise much; but the old crowd, which fought at the Rappahannock and Bull Run, were as compact and serviceable a little body of men as you could find in the army. Even here, we accomplish more than the Grand Army before Fredericksburg. You will undoubtedly have read in the papers about General Stahl's reconnoisance to Berryville and its results; it was a most successful affair, and our men behaved excellently, using their sabres only, and gave the enemy "tüchtige Hiebe." The prisoners were not a bad looking lot, and kept their pluck up finely, considering the circumstances; the Pennsylvania colts, stolen by Stuart and now recaptured, made a truly beautiful show.

The brigade we are now attached to, the first of the First Division, commanded by Colonel von Gilson of the De Kalb Regiment, and a first-rate soldier to boot, is much more jolly and sociable than any we have before been connected with; and every few nights we, the artillery officers, get a solemn order to "report ourselves at such or such a regiment, where there is Bier; cheese and bread will also be furnished; gentlemen will bring their own cigars, or pipes empty." The Forty-fifth New York is the jolliest, and has moreover a stunning Sing-Verein, which it is a delight to hear. Still, the German, when he gets jolly, is somewhat beastly, and you hear far more coarseness than with *any* crowd of young Americans; I infinitely prefer the quiet supper with a chosen crowd, as we have had them together, and then a sensible chat over the apples and Madeira until the small hours. My Captain is a regular character; he is about forty-five years old, is as gray as a badger, and has a queer, thin profile; he has a way of putting himself in a passion, which would be terrifying to the uninitiated, but which has come to serve me only with amusement. He cannot speak English at all, and is not disposed to learn it, so we have to communicate entirely in German, and this has been of very great service to me, as he speaks very correctly, I might almost say classically, and often corrects me when I make a mistake. But, whatever his faults and failings may be, he has one virtue which outweighs them all: he is truthful and reliable, and is one of those men who believe in keeping a promise, even when lightly made, at every risk. You can imagine that with such a man I have no trouble in getting along well.

To H. A. Y.

STAFFORD COURT HOUSE, VA.,
January 15, 1863.

I have been very much troubled to hear of your ill-health, so long continued and so severe, and have often wished that I could give you of my own superabundance, for I have most of the time been so healthy as to get extremely restless and uncomfortable when lying in camp, and felt never better than when marching all day and sleeping soundly in a mudhole. I had to go through a toughening process at first, it is true, and J. is undergoing the same now; but after that is over, it seems as if some steel had been imparted to the constitution. I hope most earnestly that you may become so restored as to be able to work once more with all vigor on your chosen way; but if it should not be so, you must not grieve overmuch at this enforced inactivity, remembering, that "God does not need either man's work, or his own gifts"; and that "they also serve who only stand and wait"; this last thought has comforted me more than once when I have heard the noise of battle at the front, and we were standing in impatient idleness in the reserve. My dear boy, in every battle in life there must be a reserve, and he who directs these battles will know when to bring it into action.

I have travelled the upper half of Virginia pretty thoroughly since last spring; under Fremont, we starved in Franklin, marched down the Shenandoah Valley, fought at Cross Keys, and came back to Winchester; then, under Sigel, we explored the Suray Valley, crossed the Blue Ridge again, went viâ Culpepper and Cedar Mountain to the Rapidan; then, under Pope (Sigel being still our corps commander), we made a good retreat across the Rappahannock, fought a week up and down its banks, then two days' hard work at Bull Run, where our Corps did and suffered pretty much all that was done and suffered, except the skedaddling; and since then we have been moving about Fairfax, Aldie, Chantilly, etc., until we came down here to support Burnside, and, fortunately, arrived too late to be victimized at that slaughter by Fredericksburg. Such is a hasty outline of my movements; a large part of the time has been spent among the mountains of the Alleghany and Blue Ridge, healthy, free, and glorious, where we foraged, and went fishing, blackberrying, and cherry-picking, and where at times it seemed more like a charming summer picnic "long drawn out" than anything else; the want that I have experienced most has been of that which your wife places as second in her list of 'temporal blessings,' viz., friends; and for months I have gone without seeing a single face which was really dear to me, and without meeting a single person with whom I could talk about anything more deeply interesting than duty and the probability of our catching Jackson. Indeed, at times, I have become very much depressed by this want of intercourse and sympathy, and nothing but the outdoor life, spent in the saddle, and the healthy excitement of the march and the bivouac, has saved me from being very miserable. It is when we are lying quiet in camp for some weeks that a man gets to feel how hard this life is to bear; no books, no friends to exchange thoughts with, no flowers, no gentle woman's society, no music except when the Brigade Band gives us the "S. S. B.," or when some poor boy is laid in the stranger earth of Virginia to the solemn chords of Pleyel's Hymn. And this last consolation we all have, that if our soldier-life is very hard, it is also short, and our death is honorable, and we ask of the passer-by, not like Archytas the "pulvis ter injectus," but rather three simple words of praise and kindness.

I enjoy the artillery service very much; it is the only arm in which intelligence is needed in every rank, and an officer of artillery has really a fine wide field for study. I have in my own section fine young sergeants and corporals, whom it is a pleasure to bring forward and perfect in the elements of our branch, and who fully answer the description which Victor Hugo gives of the sergeant of artillery, in the fifth volume of his "Les Misérables": "Of fair complexion, with a very mild face, and the intelligent air peculiar to that predestined and formidable arm." I regret very much that I did not get with our Battery the chance which that "Captain Wheeler" did at West Point, to distinguish himself, although, even when all is done, a corps gets no praise unless it has a newspaper correspondent in tow, who is stuffed and flattered and deceived. At Bull Run no less than three splendid feats achieved by our Battery were ascribed to others by newspapers, while the dry details of General Milroy's report did us justice; but the romance is always read by more than the history.

January 18, 1863.

. . . . Yesterday we received positive orders to stand ready to march this morning at break of day, and had made all our preparations to do so; but last night the order was countermanded, and so we have a quiet Sabbath after all. . . . .

The idea of marching and having something to do put me in good spirits, and I have strong hopes that this time we shall accomplish something. What we want is a good fair contest of army against army, followed by a decisive victory. If we obtain this, I don't care much whether I live to see the results of it or not. The day for any individual to distinguish himself by single acts of daring has gone by, and the utmost devotion and bravery are now merely a part of every man's daily duty. It is now no compliment to say "brave officer," "brave soldier," but it is a disgrace to have anything else said. You will not, of course, think of sending anything edible to me by mail, especially as we are about to march. The fact is, we lived too well at Chantilly, and when we came here on hard tack we felt the change, though I am now quite reconciled to it.

To L. R. P.

Brooks' Station, Va., *February* 22, 1863.

My dear Boy, — The era extending from the second of February (date of your last letter), to February 22 (date above), is a very much smaller one than that from December 3 (date of *my* last letter), to February 2, and this would perhaps be, to a right mind, convincing of the fact that you did not yet deserve to hear from me; but when I reflect what an unpleasant state of affairs it would bring about if we should all get what we deserve, I think it better not to introduce this principle, and prefer to go it after the G. R., and write promptly to others as I would have others write promptly to me. It is true, I doubt very much if I shall receive my reward directly from you, but the grand principle of compensation *must* be obeyed, and doubtless the recompense will be manifested in an extra and unexpected epistle from my cousin A., or perhaps another pleasant little reminder from the Philadelphia doves, who are not only "harmless," but Ys. . . . . I was not a little interested in your account of the Philological Society, and your paper on the Prometheus question. I should greatly enjoy looking in upon one of your meetings, and sitting in reverence at the feet of some of those distinguished philologs while they enlightened the world on "Anaphora and Chiasmus," or similar important topics. The truth is, I have not the patience nor the industry to pursue these inquiries into the dryer recesses of language ; I prefer to take the results of others' labor, as furnished in grammars, etc., and then to read the classics for the thoughts they contain, as a part of the general treasure of Thought contained in books, whether ancient or modern. That careful industry by means of which a student so thoroughly elaborates a language as to make the ring of its words and the turning of its verses as familiar to him as his own tongue, that capacity of becoming a Greek with Sophocles, and a Roman with Horace, is given, it seems to me, to a very chosen few, and can hardly be sought as an object by any but the professional student. You and I may become excellent German scholars, but Goethe's " Der Fischer " will never sound to us as perfect as to German ears, and however enthusiastic we may be for Dante's "il tremolar della marina," and the ἀνάριθμον γέλασμα, which are sweet to us because half translated into the universal language of similar sound which is shared alike by all, still it is not like English to our ears, not like Shakespeare's " Full fathom five thy father lies," or Byron's " Tremulous silver of Euphrates' waves." But your essay on the subordinate part played by Zeus in the " Prometheus " was something higher than mere scholarship, and I should like very much to see the whole paper, rather than the few hints of it which you gave me. Did it occur to you to look at Shelley's " Prometheus Unbound," in connection with your work, or do you despise the moderns entirely ? I think it is his finest work, and well worth studying for the exquisite melody of many passages ; he seems to adopt the view which you combat, and makes Jove bear all the odium of having inflicted an unjust punishment upon the suffering Reformer (for Prometheus is certainly the original of that species, the first Protestant), and also to get the worst in arguments with him, and to be blackguarded unmercifully, while behind all rises a dim shape called " Demogorgon," who is evidently the chief cook and bottle-washer, and who indulges in certain prophecies of Delphic obscurity and generalizes worse than the "Declaration of Independence" according to Choate. It seems to me that the question narrows itself down to this: injustice had been done to Prometheus, if not by the mere fact of punishment, then certainly by the manner of it, and the unseemly taunts with which it was accompanied. Now we can look upon Zeus, either as a form of the Supreme Being, or as an executor and prime minister of the orders of Fate; that he is not the former, appears everywhere in Æschylus, and it would certainly be impiety to impute injustice to the Supreme Being. That he is the latter, appears to me in "Prometheus" just as much as anywhere else, and his subjection to some higher power is shown by his terror about the mysterious marriage which he was to contract, and which was to be his ruin. All this he would have known and prevented if he had not been a deity "zweiter classe." The whole, in fact, illustrates the "Responsibility of Prime Ministers," leaving no trace of wrong upon the character of the mysterious king upon the throne behind. . . . . With regard to the state of the country, I think it is not by any means so unfavorable as many of our friends at home seem to suppose; we have made great advances in our opinions upon many subjects, such as drafting, arming of the negroes, etc., and I hope to see the campaign carried on in the spring with a vigorous policy and to a successful issue. The army will obey every properly issued and communicated order from head-quarters; so long as the President and the Secretary of War are all right, Congress may blow, legislatures may resolve, and knots of rebel sympathizers may make a show of resistance, but it will amount to nothing; if violent resistance be made to the enforcement of the draft, we can easily spare a couple of veteran regiments who would enjoy nothing more than to drag out concealed rebels and stay-at-homes, and make them bear their share of the burden. In fact, I should have no objections myself to be sent to New York with my section; there is a fine position for artillery on Broadway below Canal street, commanding the street as high as Eleventh, and the balls would ricochet splendidly on the hard pavement. No; the army may as a mass have dim ideas of principles and rights, but they *do* know that they have been working and fighting in this cause, and they do not propose to give up and own themselves thrashed, just because their friends at the North are unwilling to make some slight sacrifices also. I believe in the North's being made to *feel* the war, which she has not yet done as a nation, and to really offer up something to win this great, almost infinite good. Among the articles in the stupid Atlantic Monthly of this month, is one entitled, "The Law of Costs," which has some good ideas, though uncouthly and obscurely worked up. The more we undertake to do this matter cheaply, the longer it will remain to be done. The guns are even now echoing from hill to hill, and across the fields of snow, as the batteries are firing salutes in honor of Washington's birthday. I hope that the next anniversary will see this question nearer a happy solution.

BROOKS' STATION, VA., *March* 14, 1863.

DEAREST MOTHER, — I had hoped to be in New Haven by this time to-day, and to have spent one Sunday with you at home, after my fourteen months' absence. My application for a leave has not yet been heard from. I think it not unlikely that the pleasant weather of the last two or three days has suggested ideas of marching, and that in consequence, no more furloughs will be granted. Perhaps this is for the best, after all. If I should go home, the parting would be most painful, the crust of insensibility and of absorption in my duty would be cast off, — I should be like a soft-shell crab, who had cast his shell prematurely, and had come out of his retreat tender and shivering among his hard-shell companions.

I thought that I had been constant enough in duty to deserve so much consideration, and had looked upon my furlough as sure to come in a day or two. . . . . You must not look upon me as if I were only a first lieutenant of infantry, for our service is so interesting, and at the same time so valuable, that I would not exchange places with a field officer of infantry. Perhaps I may get my battery one of these days; if I should not, you must not think that I am by any means thrown away. I came by accident into this Company, and have now done my duty for eighteen months without much cessation, and if promotion should come to me I would accept it, but I would not seek it.

[The leave of absence having been sent, he was at home for a few days.]

BROOKS' STATION, VA., *March* 30, 1863.

.... I am once more back again in camp, settled down to my old work, and am able to look back on my hurried visit home; although everything passed so rapidly as to make the whole seem like a dream, hardly more vivid than many dreams of home which I have had in camp and bivouac, yet there was an inexpressible satisfaction in meeting you all face to face once more, before entering upon the distractions and occupations of the spring campaign.

[After a few days spent in New York, he went to Annapolis for a day, and then on to Washington.]

I left the Ebbitt House at Washington on Thursday, for the 8 A. M. boat. By 3 P. M. I was at Brooks' Station, the Captain having come to the cars to meet me, while in the background stood Glenmore with the horses, and I felt that I was once more in the traces, and must buckle down to work. The next morning an accident happened which might have resulted seriously, if it had occurred in the night time, and as it was, it came near destroying all our worldly goods. Shortly after breakfast, as I was talking with the Captain, I heard a great shouting and yelling, by our quarters, and looking round I saw the tent occupied by Lieutenant Carlisle and myself in a blaze. In a moment, a half a dozen men were cutting at the tent ropes, pulling up the pegs, and tearing away the tent, to get the burning mass away from our beds, and trunks, and clothes; in this we succeeded entirely, but I burned the fingers of my left hand considerably. We immediately set to work to get a new house over our heads; men were sent off to cut trees, and horses to drag them, and by night a stately edifice of logs had arisen, and by spreading a fly on top, we made a shelter for our goods from the rain, which was beginning to fall. The next day the house had its chinks stopped with chips, and plastered with mud ; a mason from my section took the contract for building the chimney, which, with a foundation of stone, and a continuation of brick, would shame that of many a farmer's house in Virginia. A nice frame door of canvas stretched on boards was made. We moved into our new residence last night, and found it far more roomy and airy than the tent had been ; roof twice as high, and a nice, open fire-place, which gives out far more heat than the old stove had done, so that we do not repine at all at the conflagration. I shall not be sorry to get on the move soon. Our present camping-ground was excellent for winter, but it is too low and marshy for spring, and will be unhealthy before long. Since I began to write this letter, I have been called off to look after one of my corporals, who had been taken suddenly ill. I brought him to the Division hospital, where the doctor told me it was congestive fever, and kept him there.

BROOKS' STATION, VA., *April* 11, 1863.

Here we are still lying, lapped in inactivity, waiting for fine weather and roads practicable for artillery-carriages and team wagons, and in the meantime fretting our very hearts out with *ennui* and spring restlessness, which can find no outlet nor object upon which to exert itself. But I know that you will be kind and considerate enough to make allowances for the stupefying influences of idleness and winter quarters, and will not refuse to accept a commonplace letter, made up out of nothing, just as you would one setting forth the "moving accidents" of march and bivouac, and picket and foraging, and "hair-breadth 'scapes in the imminent deadly breach." The actors now are languid officers wearing new uniforms, drinking wine and making visits; lazy men with decent jackets, clean buttons, and washed faces ; horses fat, guns polished, carriages painted, harness cleaned ; the epoch of reviews, inspections, ladies in camp, soft bread, commissary whiskey, and furloughs to New York. I wave a bit of paper containing the magic words, "March-orders," and, presto! change. You see, on a spring evening, our Battery coming into camp, after a long day's march, and I can imagine that you ask, "Are those dirty creatures on horseback the same with those fine officers whom we saw last winter? Are those wild and ragged animals those well-clad soldiers? And what made them exchange their horses for these meagre brutes?" You then see, further, how, after a most scanty meal, both on the part of men and beasts, they all lie down on the bare ground, and sleep most soundly, perhaps in mud and rain, until the bugle blows the reveille at sunrise, and then again to the road; or perhaps they "take position," and have a fight. And yet, strange as it may seem, the latter kind of life, with all its privations, is infinitely superior to the former, comfortable as it may be; for one who has youth and health, and an animating principle of action within, it is full of zest and interest, and I do not know when I have felt a more joyous elevation of spirits, than when riding through Virginia oak woods, on some lovely summer morning, a good horse under me, the music of birds above, and below, the creaking of caissons, and the ringing of "jingling bridle-reins," and the inspiring prospect of a conflict with an enemy a few miles ahead.

My first day in camp was celebrated by the burning down of my tent, from which I had great difficulty in rescuing my clothes and books. Some of my friends hinted that I had got my house insured when I was at New York, and had then set it on fire to get the insurance, but, probable as this hypothesis might seem, I am myself inclined to think it became ignited from a spark falling upon the canvas, which was already as dry as tinder. However, I did not repine at my loss, but set the men of my section to work, house-building, immediately.

So now we have a shanty, put up in two days, far more comfortable than a tent, and have so far had two weeks enjoyment of it; next winter I intend to put up such a house as soon as we go into winter-quarters. Perhaps you think that I am mistaken in saying "next winter," as if I had no doubt of our still being in the field; I reply that I can hardly hope for such decided successes, before that time, as to permit of a reduction of the army, and my maxim is to be provided for the worst, and above all things *not to under-estimate our enemies*. It will take all the men we can bring into the field, and all the energy those men possess, to make a decided impression on the rebels this year; I believe in not being elevated or thrown off our guard by success, and not unduly depressed by the want of it, but to keep steadily on at our work, until it is finished. And even then it will be better to be joyful, than boastful or triumphant; this war will bring *one* advantage at least, if it cures us of these disgusting qualities.

President Lincoln reviewed our Corps yesterday, and I, for one, did not feel ashamed of our old Eleventh Corps, and I doubt if the President has seen, in the whole Army of the Potomac, a hardier or more soldierly looking set of men. He rode past on a splendid black horse, followed by his two little boys, on ponies, and then came an enormous and splendid cortège of at least two hundred officers. . . . .

The weather, after great changefulness, many an unseasonable snow and rain storm, has at last apparently settled down fine, the roads are rapidly drying up, and we may look for marching orders shortly now. The air is delightfully soft and mild, and the grass is sprouting. I send you a little sprig of trailing arbutus from near our camp; it does not grow here in the same profusion as in Western Virginia, where I used to pluck it in long streamers, and twist it round my hat.

BATTLE OF CHANCELLORSVILLE.

BROOKS' STATION, *May* 14, 1863.

DEAREST MOTHER, — Since we came back to this camp, I have been very much occupied with reports, inventories, and other matters which are necessarily attendant upon a great battle, and so I just dispatched you a line on the 6th. I have felt very much depressed in spirits, and hardly equal to having a good talk, even with you. But I have to-day received your letter, dated May 5, and I feel impelled to let you know all about it at once, that you and the friends at home, who are the only ones whose opinion I care much for, may not be led by newspaper stories or prejudiced reports, to do injustice to our Corps, whose misdeeds are now in every one's mouth, and upon whom is cast the entire weight of blame, that belongs in higher quarters.

I do not know that I can do better than tell you about the whole affair from the beginning of the march on, as you may take an interest in what is already beginning to be historic. The first "eight days rations," which we draw in the expectation of making our attempt, about the middle of April, were quietly consumed in camp, as a series of violent storms swelled the streams, and made moving impracticable, but on Sunday, April 26, we received a renewal of the same order, which was speedily complied with, and soon after came the order of march, which was to begin at $5\frac{1}{2}$ o'clock the next morning. At about midnight who should turn up but our Paymaster, and as the rolls were all signed, he made a quick job of it, and paid the Battery off in just thirteen minutes; this added to the excitement of breaking up winter-quarters, drove away sleep from the camp, and the hum of conversation and laughter was heard until the bugle blew reveille, and we prepared to bid farewell to our pleasant winter-quarters, little thinking that in ten days more we should be re-occupying them again, broken but not beaten. Everything was packed up, six days forage was fastened on the pieces and caissons, and on the off horses, shelter-tents were distributed among the men, while our comfortable wall tents and stately Sibleys were left standing, for the benefit of the Hospital Department, a branch of the service destined in a few days to surpass all others in importance. Our march was at first rather slow, as the Second and Third Divisions, which lay more towards the front, had first to get their unwieldy lengths in motion. Everything not absolutely necessary had been curtailed; one ambulance accompanied each brigade, but not a team-wagon was to be seen in the whole line of march, the trains being all in the rear, and arranged in the order in which they were likely to be used, viz: ammunition, ambulances, supplies. Every man had eight days rations and sixty rounds of ammunition, and thus provided, we could afford to have our teams in the rear and to move on in light marching rig.

The first day we reached Hartwood church, a distance of about fifteen miles; but even this march, though not a long one, tried the infantry very much, as they were soft from the long idleness of winter-quarters, and their haversacks and cartridge-boxes were unusually heavy.

At different points on the road we were joined by the Twelfth Corps, General Slocum, and the Fifth Corps, General Meade, which fell in behind us. The next day we reached Kelly's Ford early in the afternoon, and went into camp, preserving the utmost silence, all orders being given by word of mouth without drum-beat or bugle signal, and the men were not permitted to show themselves on the bank. The value of these precautions was shown by the fact that we took the enemy entirely by surprise; a detachment from Steinwehr's Division crossed the river, drove the enemy out of the rifle pits, and occupied the opposite shore, and then, with great dispatch and success, the engineers laid down the pontoons, and, under cover of night, our whole Corps passed the river and gained the heights about half a mile back. This was a pretty hard job for the artillery, as they sent us no guide to take us through the level swamp lying between the river and the hill; and we floundered about in mud and mire until nearly daybreak; two hours sleep, on a plank taken from a fence, and a wash in a dirty pool, quite refreshed me, and by six o'clock we stood in readiness to renew our march, now upon the south side of the Rappahannock. The Twelfth Corps crossed at daybreak, and filed past us, taking the advance, and the Fifth Corps followed us in the rear. We marched steadily on, the roads were good and we were in high spirits, and everything looked well. Before long we struck upon the Fredericksburg plank-road, and when approaching the ford over the Rapidan, at Germania Mills, the artillery of our Corps was ordered to pass through the infantry of the Twelfth Corps at double-quick, so as to take position and drive away any hostile artillery that might dispute the passage. While trotting over this road, which was a good deal worn and full of ruts, we had a chapter of disagreeable accidents; a caisson, in the first section, broke in the middle from a sudden jolt, and two men sitting on the rear box were thrown violently to the ground and seriously injured, one having his ribs broken and his hip put out. Almost at the same time a man was jolted off from a caisson, in the second section, and the wheel passed over his leg, cracking the bone. I had ordered my drivers not to go quite so rapidly and had no trouble. Our arrival at Germania Mills, on the Rapidan, was so sudden that a body of rebel infantry and cavalry had scant time to get across the river and escape, while a company of pioneers and engineers, who were engaged in building a large bridge over the river, and had all the timbers ready collected and shaped for that purpose, were made prisoners, to the number of about eighty men. It would seem from the building of this bridge, that Lee had the intention of making much the same movement that we were making, — going to one of the upper fords of the Rappahannock in order to cross and flank us, and thus we had anticipated him in his own maneuver. Our own engineers took hold of the bridge timber, and laid down enough of the string pieces to enable the infantry to pass over dry shod; in the meantime the artillery had to ford the river, which was no small undertaking, as the stream was deep, the current very swift, and the bottom full of large stones. A line of cavalry, standing over their girths in water, showed where we were to pass; but the violence of the current was so great, and the footing so uncertain, that I felt almost sure that some carriage would be swept away; but nothing of the kind happened, and, as our ammunition chests were pretty water-tight, we managed to "keep our powder dry." I did not succeed in doing the same by my own person, as my horse had to swim once, which necessitated a very wet seat to me; and the Captain's horse went headforemost into a hole from which I never expected to see him emerge. There were some ludicrous incidents; one of the pack-mules, loaded on each with a box of rifle cartridges, walked deliberately off the string piece into the river, saying, probably, with Hamlet, "Who would fardels bear," etc.; once in, a few desperate plunges freed him from his burden and he swam ashore and rushed off friskily, switching his tail as joyously as if he had not just been a four-legged caisson, the slave of an ordnance officer. When the Eleventh and Twelfth Corps were all safely over the (Fifth Corps had crossed at another point) the bridge was destroyed and our guns were planted along the banks to prevent the enemy from coming up in our rear from the direction of Culpepper or Gordonsville, and disturbing our peaceful slumbers, which we enjoyed that night in a pouring rain. The next day, April 30, we continued our line of march on the Fredericksburg plank-road, passed through the small village of Wilderness, and advanced nearly to Chancellorsville, where General Hooker had his head-quarters. General Howard established his head-quarters near the intersection of the Orange Court House road, or Plank Road, with another road running about northwest; and our Division head-quarters was at a farm-house upon the last-mentioned road, about half a mile from the intersection. Close by this farm-house our Battery went into camp, and General McLean's Brigade lay all around us, the Seventeenth Connecticut to our right, the Fifty-fifth, Twenty-fifth, Seventy-fifth, and One Hundred and Seventh Ohio behind us, and to the left of us. The point of attack indicated to us was the front, viz., towards the Plank Road, which came converging from the southwest, and upon which, the theory seemed to be, the rebels were sure to make their attack; the idea did not seem to occur to the generals that the enemy might go a little further to the west and northwest, and attack our right wing on the flank and rear. Friday, May 1, came, and the infantry commenced entrenching themselves in the road, front as before to the Plank Road, by digging rifle pits and banking the earth up on the fence, securing it with fence rail and strong pegs. In the evening there was considerable firing to the left, with some musketry; we sent off our first section, with Colonel Gilsa's Brigade, to take position on the extreme right and protect the flank; a very good precaution against an enemy of moderate force, but not much against forty thousand men.

The next morning we received an order from General Howard to carefully measure the distance from our Battery to a clear elevated spot in front, near the Plank Road, on which it was apprehended the rebels might endeavor to place a battery and shell our position, and we were told that "we would find it of the greatest importance to have an accurate knowledge of the distance," thus showing that still the attack was expected in front, and a heavy flank attack not dreamed of. In the meantime Jackson was silently massing his army in front of the First Brigade, and on its flank, and yet with such perfect secrecy and skill that the miserable scouts we sent out reported three or four hundred dismounted cavalry, and nothing more. Lieutenant Bohn, thinking that dismounted cavalry were getting too numerous, threw a couple of shrapnels among them but was ordered by General Devens to stop, as he was "shooting our own men." About this time General Hooker rode down through our lines, seemed well satisfied with the state of affairs, and returned; and yet at the very moment when he cast his approving glance over the right wing, the enemy's swarms were closing in upon it, unseen but sure, and there was not a single cavalry vidette to bring us certain information of this deadly snare. Frequent intelligence was sent both to Howard's and Hooker's head-quarters announcing the heavy massing of the enemy on the right, and yet no reinforcements were sent, and no orders to retire to a more favorable position. Perhaps they thought that our weak Divisions, of about 4,000 each, were going separately to withstand the sudden onset of ten times their number, and that in a position most unfavorable, and where the intrenchments, built against the front, were nothing but a weakness when taken in flank. Noon came, no information of an attack, and still we kept our guns trained on the clear spot in front. At 3 P. M., all was still; suddenly the silence was broken by the shots of skirmishers, then sharp volleys of musketry with rapid firing of canister from the right, where Lieutenant Bohn was with his section, and almost at the same moment our Battery was enfiladed from the right by the enemy's shells which fell and burst with most fatal effect. The first shell struck two pole horses in Lieutenant Carlisle's section, then burst, and one piece cut in two the pole of my first piece, while another went on and killed a lead horse on the second. The next two shells were almost equally destructive. We endeavored to place our pieces in the new direction, but before we could do so, the First Brigade came, forced back on McLean's, bringing Bohn's section with it, and it was impossible to fire for fear of killing our own men, who blocked up the road. So we had nothing for it, but to retire to the first hill, where we could take position and accomplish something. I limbered up my first piece with the limber of the caisson and then got both my pieces off safe, retiring quietly. I was just about to mount my horse when the attack began, and gave him to a cannoneer to hold while I unlimbered the caisson. While he was holding him a bullet hit the poor little Frank on the haunch and he broke away and ran past the Battery which was now moving on ahead, giving the Captain and the men the idea that I had been shot from his back. Well I got my piece off all right and followed on foot; as I came a couple of rods further where, through a depression in the ground, the pieces had passed from the field into the road, I found Lieutenant Carlisle with his whole section in a sorry plight, all the horses on one gun had been shot, and all but the pole horse on the other, together with two or three of the drivers, and in a fit of desperation C. had ordered his men to unlimber and fire canister. But the depression was so deep that no sight could be got of the enemy who were on the plain above. I took hold of the third piece and tried to help run it up the bank, but we could not do it. I then sprang to the other gun and told Carlisle that the only possible safety was to cut out the dead horses, limber up the gun and take it off with the pole horse alone. It had been great folly to unlimber then, in the first place, and though he was brave as a lion the predicament rather puzzled him, as well it might. The sergeant cut out the lead and middle horses, and the corporal raised the trail to limber up the gun when a shot struck him, and he dropped the trail on my toes, at the same moment the rebs rushed over the hill and poured a volley into us at very close range, severely wounding poor Carlisle in three places. I don't see how I escaped. I suppose I owed it to the fact that I was on foot. I then made rapid tracks to catch my section ; the first hill was full of artillery in position, and firing, and our Battery had found no room to take position, and so was compelled to go further back. At the Third Division breastworks I amused myself in rallying our infantry, but they could not be held.

The vehemence, energy, and desperation with which the rebels came on was really superb, and the numbers were so overwhelming that a brigade or division line of battle made no show at all, but was immediately flanked and enveloped on both wings. The Third Division, commanded by the celebrated Republican orator Schurz, did worst of all ; it vanished like the dust of the balance at the first assault, and gave no support to McLean's gallant Brigade which did its best to keep back the tide of gray backs, but in vain, and Steinwehr's First Brigade was too weak to stand up against the refluent wave of Schurz's runaways. I don't tell you anything now from hearsay, but what I saw with my own eyes, for as I knew that my section was not in position on this hill, and was in safety on this road, I felt some curiosity to see how the thing went and so I took it pretty easy, keeping as near the enemy's front and our rear as I conveniently could.

All at once I heard my name called, and saw at my side Major Fineauff of the One Hundred and Fifty-third Pennsylvania Regiment, of whom you have heard me speak as my fellow student at Berlin, one of my few friends out here on the field. He had been on General Devens' staff, and was wounded in the leg, or rather lamed and severely contused. I lugged him along for some distance, resisting his frequent requests to me to lay him down and leave him. I gave him a drink of whiskey which gave him life, and at last had the satisfaction of leaving him with a party of his own regiment who brought him safely off. Arrived at the foot of the hill leading to the plateau on which General Hooker's head-quarters stood, *i. e.*, the village of Chancellorsville, I found the Twelfth Corps hastening to our relief, and across the crest of the hill a large number of batteries, mostly brass twelve pounders, medium range, placed in position, while most of the rifled long range guns had been sent further to the rear. I spent some time in searching for our Battery, but without success, and then went back to the hill and served as cannoneer in Dilger's Battery of our Corps, during the whole of the fierce attack of the rebels that ensued. It was queer that the officer in whose section I served, had within a fortnight been a trembling candidate before a board of examination of which I had been secretary, and where I had put him through with all sorts of questions. At the foot of the hill was a wood, which was held partly by the rebs, and partly by the Twelfth Corps ; the enemy made several attempts to drive our men out, and the steady roll of musketry was really appalling. Once they succeeded, but then the batteries on the hill opening drove them back with great loss, and our men retook their position. The next (Sunday) morning I found my section in the right, in the new line, with the First Corps, General Reynolds. The rest of the Battery was at the United States Ford, to which place most of the long range artillery was sent, as being of little use in such close hand to hand bush fighting. Here I was ordered to report to General Reynolds with two guns of Schirmer's Battery and my own section. General Reynolds sent me to General Wadsworth, who commanded one of his Divisions, and he placed me in a fine position, above his Division, who were splendidly intrenched, and I got the regiment which covered me to throw up a breastwork before my gun, high enough to cover the bodies of the gunners. While reporting to General Wadsworth I had the pleasure of meeting young Carrington of the Class of 1859, who was on his staff. There were ten pieces of us all together on this hill, and I longed for an attack, as we had capital infantry with us, and could have repulsed almost anything. But nothing did turn up then, and towards evening I was ordered down to the United States Ford, where we lay for a day and a half, and then, on the 5th, crossed the river in a dense fog, and marched back to our old camp, arriving here in a rain and hail storm which was the most extensive one I ever saw. The hailstones being in some instances, actually larger than hen's eggs, and knocking men off their horses. So, here we are, after an absence of eight days, in the old camp again, having lost two guns, three caissons, twenty-five horses, one officer, and thirteen men, having not had the smallest chance to accomplish anything valuable. In fact there was far too much artillery in that fight, and too many rifled guns which were of no use at all. If a battery was not very well supported by infantry, it might be taken in one desperate rush, as there was no good opportunity to retire. With regard to the conduct of the Eleventh Corps, I have heard some say that they would not fight because they did not have Sigel; this is absurd, and yet allowance must be made for the great influence on the men, produced by their losing the man on whom they leaned unreservedly, and whom they would follow to the death, and getting in his place a person unknown, peculiarly uncongenial to the German mind, and considered by them as a parson in uniform. But any Corps so scattered, and strung along an extended line, could not have failed to be overwhelmed by the force brought so suddenly against it; and a most steadfast bearing to the enemy would have brought with it annihilation, without staying their progress; would have doubled the lists of killed and wounded without having been of benefit. I know that the regiments by our Battery, viz., McLean's Brigade, fought as well as men can fight, and only fell back when further fighting was madness. The fact lies in this nutshell. General Hooker allowed General Howard to scatter his corps along too great a line, and then allowed the Corps thus scattered to be flanked, and now it seems to be the fashion to throw the blame of this mismanagement upon the conduct of the Corps, which seems to me most unjust. Well! enough of this vindication; if any of my friends ask what I have to say about the "flight," "panic," etc., of the Eleventh Corps, you can show them this. Both of my horses were hit, but neither severely. Jenny got a spent ball right on the side of her nose, but the wound is now entirely healed. Frank got a ball on his haunch, but the wound was improving finely, when, what should he do the other night but commit suicide, by hanging himself in his halter; in the morning he was quite dead. He was a beauty and a fine trotter. I felt miserably about it. My poor darkey boy took it so much to heart, that, after burying him with many tears, he could not bear to stay any longer about the place and decamped, which was even more painful to me than losing the horse, as I had taken much interest in him and was really fond of him. We were afraid that we might lose Lieutenant Carlisle; he was shot in the arm, the leg, and the side. What troubled him the most was the loss of his section, and when he became delirious he was crying cannoneers to do this and that and not to desert the gun. He is better now and has been sent off to Washington with a fair prospect of recovery. Mdst of our wounded are doing well except the Corporal who was shot at my side; he will probably lose his leg. As to the whole affair I do not feel discouraged. I am sure that the enemy received greater loss than he inflicted, and that he cannot stand many such blows, while we on the contrary seem, like Antæus, to gather strength from our falls. The death of Stonewall Jackson is a great misfortune to the rebels, but I do not feel like exulting over the grave of such a brave, wise, and energetic antagonist — "peace be to his ashes." You must make this long letter do for sometime now, as I have a great deal of writing to do.

To L. R. P.

BROOKS' STATION, *May* 19, 1863.

MY DEAR FRIEND, — Although I have several debts to pay that are older than yours, and you stand by no means near the top of my list, yet your last letter dated April 23, but which I did not receive until about May 9, came to me so pleasantly upon my return to this camp, breathing so much quiet, and peace, and happiness, after my hard marching, and bloody fighting, that I feel peculiarly impelled to send you a few words in reply; and these words shall be, if you please, not at all about the war and the late battle, but mere chat and friendly talk. If you would like to hear about our march to Kelly's Ford, our passage of the Rappahannock, and then of the Rapidan, the battle at Chancellorsville on Saturday — with an explanation of how the misfortune of our Corps occurred, — I would rather have you ask my mother to read you that part of my last letter to her, than write it all over again myself. Suffice it to say, that I stayed with another officer's section in the face of the enemy, and tried to help it to get off until I was the only man on the spot unhurt, two corporals being shot down at my side, and the officer receiving three bullets; I probably escaped by being on foot, and did not think it my duty to stay behind to rally the infantry, that not being a branch of my business. I hate to brag, or to talk about what I did, but it becomes necessary sometimes, when the corps to which one belongs is charged by the newspapers with having indulged in a universal panic and flight. I only know that if I had one of the reporters for those sheets in my tent for a brief half hour alone, one of us two would have a badly punched head. But enough of this.

Your letter treating of music, and pictures, and children, was to me indeed "humanizing," and I could not help asking myself how it was that my nature had not become more brutalized by my life of "murder and rapine," as the "Richmond Enquirer" would call it, but on the contrary, became as sensitive as ever upon your mention of those tender and beautiful objects; I think that when a certain love for them has become a part of a man's nature, the absence of them, and the want of a cultivation of the corresponding tastes, does not really diminish this love, but rather, other ruder tastes are etched away by the influence of time and use, leaving these in bolder relief. I don't know whether this be correct metaphysics, but it is true as far as I am concerned. What you tell me of this book of "Mendelssohn's Letters," interested me much, and if you really can part with the book, without hope of ever seeing it again, I should be much obliged to you for sending it to me. By my hand lies a very jolly little book entitled "Reisehumoresken; auf einer Wanderung durch die Schweiz und Oberitalien," which has to us here a peculiar interest from its being an only memento of a very gallant officer, Captain von Mensel, of General McLean's staff, with whom I had a pleasant talk half an hour before the sudden attack, in which he disappeared mysteriously, just like Ed. Blake at Cedar Mountain, and we cannot learn whether he was buried promiscuously on the field, or whether he perished in that burning hospital. These genial little books of travel are to me very delightful, and it requires very little imagination for one to place himself in an Italian vettura, or on the bow of one of those ridiculous little "Dämpfers," on a Swiss lake, and to listen to the homely humor of the German, the gabble of English girls, and the ignorant impudence of their companions.

I sometimes like to take a retrospect of the years that are just past, and never more than just at this time, and in this month; in 1857, I was a week out of New York on the *Australia;* in 1858, I had just left you and The Form, at Athens, and had gone to Naples; in 1859, I was gnashing my teeth over a certain ——; in 1860, I was being admitted to the bar; in 1861, I was sporting a gray jacket at Washington; in 1862, I was supporting a starving officer's mess at Franklin, Virginia, among the mountains, with the fruits of my angle. And, after this "roaming with a hungry heart," I also share Ulysses' determination, "to strive, to seek, to find, and not to yield;" every defeat of ours puts the end farther off, but makes our work more sure and thorough, and the final peace more deep and noble; the longer we work upon the laying of our foundation stones, the more pains we take with the selection of our site and the nature of the ground we build on, the more beautiful and lasting will be our edifice, which we can then entrust to the religion of coming centuries to complete, and it will shine from its rocky base to the pilgrims of the future, as the Parthenon did to us five years ago, beautiful, golden, when we sailed up to the Piræus. And yet home, friends, genial society, books, music, all these are so delightful, that I do not dare to think of them much; the only way is to keep the nose steadily down on the grindstone of duty, and then you don't bother about anything else. I like to hear from you very much, for you have such a straight-forward way of going at things that I feel perfect confidence in all your utterances, and take them all as gospel, feeling at times almost willing to "lay my sweet hands in yours, and trust to you."

What comes hard for me to stand just now, is going to the hospitals; I am not exactly right well, and the sight of so much suffering among gallant boys who never wavered on the field, is often too much for me; and yet I try to go, for our poor fellows feel pleased when their officers come in often and inquire about them. The other day I went to see a corporal of our Battery, one of the two shot down at my side; he was on the field and in the enemy's hands several days before being sent over, and his wounds had been neglected. He was a very fine-looking young Irishman, with a good organization and deep susceptibility to both pain and pleasure; one of his wounds had affected the nerves, and the pain came in great wrenches and spasms that made him gnash his teeth and beat his feet on the bed in agony. I became so sick that I could hardly get to the door. The other corporal, who was hit within half a foot from me, received a bad shot in the foot, and came so exhausted to the hospital, that the doctor would not take his leg off; to-day they have given him up, as mortification has set in. When I see these things, I am perfectly astounded at the capacity of delicate ladies, like Miss S. W. and my Cousin A., to go through the scenes with composure, and yet to be benign and helpful at the same time. I never appreciated before the greatness of the service and the sacrifice. But still these acts of devotion and self-sacrifice are not without their stimulus and reward, too; I have never seen anything that went more to my heart than this; after I had sat down by the bed of a poor mangled hero from the ranks, had spoken to him words of praise for his conduct, sympathy for his pain, and offered to do what I could for him, to see his eyes watch me as I left the tent, and to hear his grateful "'Thank you for your kindness, Lieutenant." I intend to try to overcome the prejudices of my sensitive Wheeler nose, and to do something more in this way. . . . . Think of me as in pretty good health, and remembering you with constant affection.

To H. N. C.

HEAD-QUARTERS 13TH N. Y. BATTERY,
BROOKS' STATION, *May* 21, 1863.

The immediate toils of battle are over; the wounded are either agonizing and dying with their painful and mortifying wounds in the field hospitals, or where their hits were slight, are hopping around on sticks and crutches, and looking eagerly forward to the time when they shall be sufficiently restored to exchange the half-rations of the hospital for the full fare of the camp; and the uninjured, having fairly rested themselves from fatigue and excitement, are beginning to feel ennui and fatigue much more severely than from the hardest march, and to wish that Hooker would hurry up again and make another "reconnoisance in force" across the Rappahannock, but this time with fuller results. I hope that you have not allowed yourself to be so prejudiced by the newspapers, against our Corps, the Eleventh, as not to be willing to hear a word of explanation. One very great disadvantage under which we labored was, that shortly before the march, our well-trusted Sigel was replaced in the command of the Corps by General Howard, a stranger, and one in whom we had no confidence; and still further, our Division commander, McLean, who was greatly beloved by his troops, was superseded by Devens, also an utter stranger, and one who brought with him mostly a new and inexperienced staff. The disposition of the Corps in the line of battle at Chancellorsville was also very faulty, it being stretched out over a long line, a mile away from the Twelfth

Corps, and connected with it only by a few pickets. Then there was no cavalry to scout on the flank, and the consequence was, that while we were expecting patiently an attack from the front, the wily Jackson had massed his forces on our right, and even thrown part of them into our rear, thus completely enveloping our Division, and exposing the men, some of whom were raw troops, to a fire on three sides at once. The enemy's attack was in great force and most fierce, his men advancing steadily at a rapid walk, loading and firing as they came, and our First Brigade narrowly escaped being taken prisoners *en masse*. There was no " coign of vantage," no advantageous position, at which to make a stand, as the breastworks and rifle pits had all been constructed with reference to an attack from the front, and consequently were enfiladed by an attack from the right. In fact, we had no chance ; and the men who, at Bull Run, under Sigel, kept the heights of Groveton for a long summer's day, against the desperate assaults of Longstreet's whole army, finally driving him back, and who came the next day to the rescue of the fugitive and demoralized army of the Peninsula, would not rally under a general whose arrangements had proved so futile and deceptive, and to rally under whom would have been to meet repeated defeat and disgrace, without profit. I am sorry to say, that General Howard, on his first coming to the Corps, made himself conspicuous by his zeal in promoting religious observances, and in showing his respect for the Sabbath, to say nothing of a somewhat ostentatious display of personal piety, and now his religious character has to bear the burden of his military errors, and it is said pretty generally, and that with justice, that he obeyed only the last half of the command, " Watch and pray." Don't suppose now, that I look at this in a flippant way at all ; I think that no characters are more admirable than those of men like Havelock, Hedley Vicars, or our own Commodore Foote, who, being once soldiers, did their duty and their work as such with all their might, and yet were none the less thoughtful, earnest, and pious men. But with regard to our General, I feel very much as Cromwell did about that cavalry officer who began to pray aloud in his saddle just as the Ironsides were about to charge at Marston Moor. I hope that he will be removed from command before we go into fight again, for hardly a man in the Corps has the slightest confidence in his ability or capacity, and if he is to lead us, the greatest disasters may be expected. . . . . In this fearfully hot weather which we are having just now, I often sigh for the mountains of Western Virginia, in which we were campaigning a year ago, and at times my thoughts go still farther back, to the deck of the old *Australia*, six years ago ; do you remember, at about this date we had got well free from the storms and head-winds of the Gulf Stream, and were making good time before a fine southwest wind, and after the hot day was over, doubly enjoying the cool evening walk on deck, and many a homesick talk about the friends who had been for a fortnight under the western horizon. That summer and autumn which we spent together, and during which we learned to know and love each other better than before, has always had to my mind and memory a peculiarly rosy and pleasant hue, and I look forward to no greater pleasure than that of sitting down with you at some future day, and, armed with our respective diaries as books of reference and suggestion, wandering through the Louvre once more, visiting Belgium and the Rhine, and clambering over Switzerland with our Alpenstocks. This has all been brought very freshly before my mind by a jolly little German book which I have been reading, called " Reisehumoresken," a vacation ramble through Upper Italy and Switzerland. The author, who was formerly correspondent of the " Cologne Gazette," is a keener observer of peculiarities and eccentricities in his fellow-travellers, than of the marvels of nature, or rather, he seems to restrain the expression of his enthusiasm on this latter point, leaving it to be inferred more from hints than from glowing descriptions, but still, what he says about the Monte Rosa region, which occupies almost half of a volume, made me feel more regretful than ever that we did not diverge from the Rhone Valley when at Leuk, and take in this superb mountain. If I recollect right, we had a battle royal on the subject, but it was finally decided to abide by the original plan, unchangeable as the laws of the Medes, which we had laid down with remorseless pencil on Keller's map, in the fourth story of Meurice's. It is rather aggravating to think of those delightful days, out here where there is no genial society, nothing to read, and where we vibrate from the stagnation and ennui of camp, to the absorbing care and fatigue of the march, and the excitement of the battle; in this too

"A sorrow's crown of sorrow is remembering happier things."

For this reason I was glad that my furlough did not allow me to remain longer at home, and thus get used to comfort and to find the presence of friends a necessity. As it was, my visit was so fleeting and short, that it seemed just as unreal as some visits home which I have made in my sleep and from which I have been summarily recalled by the sound of the reveille bugle. I am in for steady work now until we go again into winter-quarters, that is, if my life be spared so long, and if I do not before that time receive some disabling wound. I am, of course, not insensible of the very great disadvantage, to a professional man, of losing several years at the very commencement of his career, of breaking away from his books and papers to the rough and demoralizing life of a soldier, and you may be sure that I would not do it if I did not consider myself called to it by the voice of most sacred and imperative duty. It astonishes me that any young man in the north, who has his health and is bound by no family ties, can fail to feel the same. It is a great work which will be done, and then how shameful for a man to have to tell his children in after years, "I looked on, while others braved the dangers and wrought the deliverance." And yet, at the same time, I show my own weakness and inconsistency, by my anxiety about my brother, J. who is with General Peck at Suffolk, and whom I would give my life to see safely at home again; I don't believe that my mother worries as much about him as I do.

BROOKS' STATION, *May* 31, 1863.

.... There have been important changes in the Battery since I last wrote you. Captain D. has sent in his resignation and General Howard, the next day, sent for me to report to him personally. I did so, and he received me very kindly, asked me how long I had served with the Battery, whether I had ever commanded it, whether I could drill it, etc., and how we did in the late battle, and then dismissed me, apparently well enough satisfied, for the Captain's resignation was returned the same evening approved — accompanied by a pass to Washington — and the next morning my nomination as Captain, by the Chief of Artillery, went on to Governor Seymour at Albany, so that, unless something unusual happens, I shall before long receive my commission, and shall then have the Battery in which I have so long served, for my very own. You will believe me when I say, that while I feel very glad at the prospect of receiving this promotion, this feeling is decidedly overbalanced by the hope of making the Battery more useful and efficient, more capable of doing something for the general cause. And this I believe that I can do. The captain of a battery has a very independent position, and it lies with him almost entirely whether his battery is a good and serviceable one or not.

.... Please tell J. when you write that it is not impossible that, in a few days, he will not have to lower his rank by writing to me as Lieutenant any more.

BOONESBOROUGH, MD., *July* 9, 1863.

I eagerly take the first breathing moment to drop you a single line, to let you know that after all our fatiguing marches and hard fighting I am still preserved for more service, and am also in most excellent health. We have had unparalleled hard work, marches daily of twenty to thirty miles, and are all pretty well worn out. I won't attempt just now to tell you anything about the battle of Gettysburg, except to say that my Battery was hotly in action on all three days of the fight, and did very good service. We were most of the time on

Cemetery Hill. On the 1st, when poor Reynolds pushed us all forward so rashly, we were in the extreme advance, and I had one piece shot all to pieces, and when we fell back I was obliged to leave it, but on the 5th, when we took possession of the battle-field, I went out and got it and tinkered it up and brought it off. Besides this I picked up an abandoned twelve-pounder gun, belonging to the Third Corps, and thus came out of the affair with five guns, while I went in with only four. Since the battle we have been marching day and night, — last night's was about the first sleep I have had for a week. Worse yet, it has rained incessantly, and I have hardly known what it was to be dry. The battle was a splendid success; all talk about it being a drawn battle is absurd; prisoners were taken by the thousand and the rebel loss was fearful.

But I have no time to write more; my pieces are in the advance, in position, and we look for work.

I write sitting on a cracker-box on a caisson.

BATTLE OF GETTYSBURG.

WARRENTON JUNCTION, *July* 26, 1863.

DEAR GRANDFATHER AND AUNT, — You at home will I think begin to wonder where I am, and why I have not written home before, but if you had known how hard we have been at work and how constantly we have been marching, your wonder would change into surprise and thankfulness that I have not been used up entirely and that I am still able to do duty. As I am indebted to you both for letters, I take this opportunity to write you a double-barreled one, not knowing when I may have access to pen and ink with enough of quiet leisure to compose my ideas. From Boonesborough I dropped a line to mother, informing her of my safety up to that point, but was not able to give her any account of our doings and sufferings during the days of the battle of Gettysburg. I will now give you some description of those scenes from my point of view. After we had been quite refreshed by our halt in the pleasant camp on Goose Creek, and had, most luckily for us, got our horses into condition again, we marched, on June 25, to Edwards' Ferry, and the next morning crossed the river on our pontoons, and marched up through Poolesville and past our old Camp Observation, where I had had my first real experience of a soldier's life. The streets of Poolesville were full of people, almost all of them wearing the real old secesh scowl, and I did not see a single United States flag displayed. The artillery took a road for itself that day, in order not to be encumbered by the infantry, and we made a march of about thirty miles to reach Jefferson City, where we camped in long wet grass, exposed to a heavy rain storm. The next morning my Battery marched with one brigade to Burkettsville, which lies at the foot of South Mountain, and was the scene of the battle of that name in last September, at which the heroic General Reno lost his life. Here we lived on the fat of the land, which is always one of the perquisites and advantages of going off with an independent force. The army had neither eaten out the country, nor raised the prices extravagantly, consequently spring chicken, fresh bread, milk, and butter were the order of the day. This pleasant state of affairs lasted only a day and we had to rejoin the Eleventh at Middletown, from which we marched, the same afternoon, for Frederick City. Both at Middletown, and along the road, were numerous instances of enthusiastic and outspoken patriotism, which went right to our hearts, and made us feel full of fight ; here a party of young girls and children stood and waved handkerchiefs and tiny flags ; there a hotel or public building displayed a good expanse of red, white, and blue bunting ; there a good old lady stood at her door with her servants, and dispensed cups of cold water to every thirsty soldier, while the gray-haired husband stood by her side, his eyes half filled with patriotic and sympathizing tears, and "Good luck to you boys, God bless you." Our whole march in the fertile and beautiful county of Frederick was delightful ; indeed its prosperity and richness, the "peace on earth and good will toward men" that reigned there, seemed to us all to be a type of our bountiful and happy Union, while the devastated crops, the deserted homesteads, the bitter and hostile faces of Virginia which we had just left behind us, represented, not less truthfully, the hideous and destructive nature of Secession, as well as its results. The spirits of the whole army were superb. When we passed through the towns flags were displayed, music struck up, cheers rang along the column of march and when camp was made, after a toilsome march, singing was heard from the quarters of the weary, footsore soldiers.

We passed through Frederick after nightfall, and did not see the place; the next day we marched to Emmettsburg and rested there, preparatory to the approaching conflict. Early on the 1st of July we started for Gettysburg, about eleven miles distant. I was ordered to report with my Battery to General Steinwehr's Division, and thus got ahead of the other batteries, which were in reserve with the First Division. We were marching along, thinking of anything but an approaching fight, when suddenly one of General Howard's aids came galloping up and ordered me forward at double-quick. The roads were very stony, and my wheels were in very bad condition, but ahead I went; the gun-carriages rattling and bouncing in the air; feed, rations, kettles and everything else breaking loose from the caissons, the cannoneers running with all their might to keep up, for the road was so very rough, that I was afraid to have them mount, for fear of the repetition of the accident which befell us while trotting to Chancellorsville. For at least four miles the race continued, and I brought my whole Battery safely into position on the right of Gettysburg, but luckily did not have to fire immediately; my breathless cannoneers made their appearance one by one, and soon each detachment was full. On the left, and in front of the town, there was brisk fighting going on. Reynolds (who was in command of our Corps and his own, the First) had pushed his men forward through the town, and was most rashly trying to drive a much superior enemy from the opposite heights. After passing through the town, we came into a hollow, consisting of farms, orchards, and ploughed land, completely commanded both by the Gettysburg heights and by those in the hands of the enemy, and it seemed to be fated that whoever ventured into that hollow was sure to be defeated. We tried it the first day, and Johnny Rebs the second and third days. Captain Dilger's Battery of our Corps was in front of the town, hammering away at a secesh battery on the heights; but, as he had only smooth bores, he was no match for his opponent and was getting cut up badly, so I was ordered forward to help him. I limbered up and went through the town at a trot, the ladies waving their handkerchiefs, and giving us *all* possible cheer and encouragement. I came into battery on Dilger's right, and soon showed the enemy that they had a three-inch rifled battery to contend with, and they had to shut up entirely. At about the same time the First Corps, which was on our left, succeeded in driving the enemy along the slope of the hill, and we scared them well as they ran. At this moment everything looked auspicious, and Captain Dilger told me that he would move his Battery, under cover of mine, about five hundred yards further forward, in order to give his guns better play, and then that I should follow him and support him. This he did, and as soon as he got into position a dreadful fire was opened upon him, and I had the chief benefit of this as I moved up after him; all the shots fired too high for him fell into my Battery; one struck a driver of a gun and swept him and his two horses right away; strange to say, while both horses were killed, the driver only lost a leg! As we came near the place where we were to take position, we came suddenly on a very substantial fence which the men could not tear down, and we had to wait, under a very heavy fire, until axes could be brought from the caissons and a hole hewed through the fence. While waiting here, I saw an infantry man's leg taken off by a shot, and whirled like a stone through the air, until it came against a caisson with a loud whack. When we got into position we were again too much for the opposing battery, and were getting along finely, when suddenly, on our right, there issued from the base of the hill two great gray clouds, which moved steadily forward towards the infantry of our Corps. At the same time the advance of the First Corps along the face of the hill was checked, and they were driven back. A fierce infantry fight began on our right; our men held a small wood, near the poor-house, with determination, and I turned one section of my Battery to the right and fired canister into the columns of the rebels, taking aim at their red battle-flags, which we knew only too well after the fight at Chancellorsville. This lasted for awhile, but the enemy had massed their infantry too heavily for us, and after losing tremendously our men had to withdraw. We held our position until the rebs had got almost in our rear, when we withdrew with our batteries to another position on the road, where we fired a few more canisters and then retired into the town. While crossing the fields, one of my guns was dismounted by a shot, and, after making the greatest efforts to get it off, I was obliged to leave it on the ground; but on the 5th of July, when we took possession of the entire field of battle, I went down with my blacksmith, mended the carriage, and brought the gun off in triumph. We did not get into the town a minute too soon, as the enemy were there almost as soon as we were, and shot some of our men in the street. We passed through the town and took position on Cemetery Hill, which is a high bluff above the town, at the termination of its principal street. There was a lively musketry fight in the lower part of the town, which ended in the enemy's getting possession of several cross streets below, while our men held on to the upper part; and during the whole of the next two days there was a constant skirmishing from doors and windows. From the tops of some of the houses the rebs managed to get an aim at Cemetery Hill and picked off many a man from the batteries there. The sun went down on the 1st July, leaving us where we were in the morning; that is, having gained the Gettysburg heights and having been repulsed in an attempt to gain the other heights; while General Reynolds had fallen a victim to his own rash attempt, and both Corps had been very seriously cut up. During the night our much needed reinforcements came up; the Second and Third Corps on our left and the Twelfth on our right, and we took a good night's rest, preparatory to the next day's work. The next morning there was brisk skirmishing all along the front, but only desultory shots from the artillery. At about two o'clock in the afternoon the artillery of the Second Corps became hotly engaged on the left, and our boys all stood on tiptoe to watch the contest. Just then General Howard rode along and said, "Never mind the left, boys; look out for your own front"; and sure enough, a few minutes afterward, we saw puffs of smoke, — which we knew well enough arose from the hills opposite to us, — then the boom of the guns and the bursting of the shells among us. They soon got an answer from us; we had nine three-inch rifled guns in a row there, from Hall's Second Maine Battery, Wiedrick's Battery, and mine. Beside these, there were the brass guns of Dilger's Ohio Battery, and "G" of the Fourth Regulars, although they were of more service at close quarters. We did not fire very rapidly, but every shot was aimed with deliberation and judgment, as my corporals were cool and skillful. The result was that in half an hour the enemy's fire slackened, as they had to move their batteries to get out of our fire. Soon they opened again, more fiercely than ever; but we quickly got their new range, and punished them severely. They placed one battery of very long range on our right flank, and completely enfiladed us; luckily for us they did not get the range for some time. A twenty-pounder Parrott battery was brought up from the Reserve, and this kept them very quiet. By $4\frac{1}{2}$ P. M. my ammunition was exhausted, and Major Osborne, our new Chief of Artillery, relieved my Battery with another, and sent mine back to replenish; at the same time he asked me to remain with him and assist him in his very arduous duties, as he had charge of all the batteries on Cemetery Hill, and his regular adjutant was completely used up. This exactly suited me, as my blood was up, and I did not like the idea of going back with my Battery. Until nightfall I was hardly out of fire once, and I was raised to the highest pitch of excitement; the danger was so great and so constant that, at last, it took away the sense of danger. I placed several batteries on the hill, under the

Major's orders, and at length I went back to the Artillery Reserve to bring up a supply of ammunition. While proceeding down the Taneytown road I was a witness of the tremendous attack upon the Third Corps, and of their breaking and fleeing, after a fierce conflict. As this Corps held our extreme left wing at that time, my first thought was that all was lost, and that the enemy would push through to the Baltimore Pike and cut off the three Corps at the front; but I had underrated General Meade's capacity of husbanding his reserves and massing his forces. Hardly had the broken fragments of the Third Corps crossed the pike when the firing was renewed in the woods, and on the crest of the hill, where the whole Fifth Corps had been thrown in to reinforce the left wing, and a few minutes later, as if to make assurance doubly sure, I met the First Division of the Twelfth Corps going at double-quick for one of the cross-roads from the right to the left wing; and in case this should not prove enough, I saw a little further back, among the woods, the dark masses of the Sixth Corps, the strongest corps in the army, waiting to be moved to any point. However, the dose administered by the Fifth Corps proved sufficient. Our line of battle was almost in the shape of a horseshoe, with the reserves on the inside, and these had to march only a short distance in order to reinforce any point threatened. I went back to the Major, and hardly had I got there when the enemy made a most desperate attack upon our extreme right, where a portion of the Twelfth Corps was intrenched. This fight continued a good part of the night, and was renewed at daylight; but the point having been well reinforced, the enemy was repulsed with terrible loss. Late at night, I went down the Baltimore road, to the camp of the Artillery Reserve, to see that my Battery was put in shape for work early the next morning. Our Chief of Artillery, and all of us who commanded batteries, felt a little pride in keeping Cemetery Hill manned by Eleventh Corps Batteries as constantly as possible, although there were thirty batteries which had not fired a shot. I had a great hunt for ammunition, and even then did not find what I wanted, or what suited my guns; but I managed to get about fifty rounds apiece, (I should have had two hundred), and went back to the hill again. As on the previous day, it was brisk skirmishing along the front, some hard fighting in the town, and desultory artillery firing; but at about 1 P. M. Lee's one hundred pieces (I believe that he had more in position), opened all at once, and, as far as noise went, it was the most terrible cannonade that I ever witnessed, and the air was literally alive with flying projectiles, from the six-pound solid shot, which looks like a cricket ball, to the long Whitworth rifled shot, which has probably given rise to the story of the rebs firing railroad iron. My pieces stood in a peculiarly bad place, as they were at the foot of the hill, and got the fire from all three sides; but the enemy's artillery practice was not as good as it used to be, and the situation was not as deadly and dangerous as on Friday afternoon at Bull Run, or on Sunday morning at Chancellorsville. In this place I lost some horses but no men. The fire was still at its height, when a request came from General Hunt, Chief of Artillery, to Major Osborne to send him a battery for General Webb of the Second Corps, who feared an infantry attack. The Major handed me the order and off I went to the hill where the Second Corps was, just above General Meade's head-quarters, and reported to General Hancock, who showed me the position I was to take. As I came up and unlimbered on this crest, the rebels were within four hundred yards and were making a charge across our front upon a battery which stood at my right. Luckily for us, they did not see us until we had got into position, and had poured a couple of rounds of canister over the heads of our own infantry, who were lying behind a stone fence in front of us. Then they turned their attention somewhat to us and a battery of theirs opened very fiercely upon us, and made things very hot; but we paid no attention to their battery, and just kept the canister going into them. Once a double round of canister struck close to their flag, and I saw a dozen of them drop, and the whole column wavered and halted; but the standard-bearer waved his flag and they moved on again, but in a weary and spiritless manner. Just at this moment what should the infantry in front of us do but get up and leave! The Battery seemed lost, but I got hold of some of them, told them not to let the Eleventh Corps' boys laugh at them, and in this way, first a squad, and then the whole regiment, was rallied and got back to the fence again, and about every reb who came up on to that hill was either killed, wounded, or captured. We then went back to our Corps and soon the fighting for the night was over. I went over a part of the battle-field that night, and did what I could to make the wounded comfortable; but very soon this seemed a hopeless undertaking; our wounded were removed in ambulances as fast as possible, but the rebel wounded, who were almost all of them in our hands, received extremely little attention, and lay scattered over the field in groups of twenty, fifty, or even a hundred, trying to help each other a little. Our men could not help it; most of them were too much worn out to raise a hand, and the regular Ambulance Corps could not begin to attend to our own wounded boys. I was glad to do a little something for them, even if it were only to turn them on their side, and give them a glass of water. Utterly as I detest a living active rebel, as soon as he becomes wounded and a prisoner I don't perceive any difference in my feelings towards him and towards one of our own wounded heroes. I suppose this is very heterodox, but I can't help it. I found a Colonel of a Mississippi Regiment shot through the breast, a man of stately bearing, and a soldier of his regiment told me that he was Judge of the Supreme Court of that State. Now here was a man, evidently one of the real old original Secesh; but I forgot that, took him into a barn, made him a straw bed, fixed a pillow for him, got him a cup of coffee, and ignored the fact that he gave me no word of thanks or farewell when I left him. The scenes of the battlefield were very rough, and I will not trouble you with any description of them; I will only mention a rencontre which I had with General Meade on Friday afternoon. I was with my Battery at the foot of the hill, waiting for orders and expecting to be called upon to relieve one of our Corps batteries, when an elderly Major General with spectacles, looking a good deal like a Yale Professor, rode up and asked me if I had a full supply of ammunition. I told him that I had as full a supply as I could get on the field, having been to the ammunition train with an order from Major Osborne, but without success: whereupon he got excited and said, "You must have ammunition; the country can't wait for Major Osborne or any other man; go immediately to the Artillery Reserve and order General Tyler to send up a wagon load." Now I might have told him that there was not a round of three-inch ammunition left with the Artillery Reserve, as I had been there myself shortly before; but something in his face warned me against answering back; so I put spurs to my horse, and got round the corner of a wood, where I stayed until he had left the premises and then came back, to learn that it was General Meade himself. And so the battle closed. We had repulsed the enemy at every point, with very great loss, had taken an immense number of prisoners (I saw several thousand with my own eyes, besides the wounded ones), and had remained in possession of the field, to say nothing of pursuing the enemy from the 5th until this day. I am sure that the importance and decisiveness of the victory cannot well be overrated. I have no time to tell you of our forced march back to Emmettsburg, Middletown, Boonesborough, and Hagerstown. The enemy's crossing under our noses, at Williamsport and Falling Waters, was a masterly maneuver, but I do not think that Meade is at all to blame for it. Our marches since then have been severe, and the men are getting sick with bilious fever on all sides. Thus far I have borne up splendidly and have not been off duty for an hour. I hope and pray that I may continue as well. Major Osborne has forwarded a new demand for my commission to Governor Seymour, and accompanied the request with expressions of approbation, both toward me and the Battery, which have made me feel very proud. I have enjoyed the Major's society greatly. He is a gentleman and a soldier, a most energetic and gallant man, and he contributed greatly, by the management of his artillery, in restoring their lost prestige so brilliantly to the Eleventh Corps. I am now entirely without officers. I have applied for a commission for Henry Miller, my Orderly Sergeant. I hope in a month or two to get everything fixed up in good shape and to get two more guns. .... The time may vary a few months, a few years, or even a few decades, but the job will be settled and that all right too. I am, in this matter, like St. Paul's Charity, ready to bear, believe, hope, and endure all things for the cause, knowing that if we do so, we also, like Charity, shall never fail. This has been a most egotistical letter, but I know you want to hear about me, and not about the army in general or anybody else.

CATLETT'S STATION, VA., *August* 4, 1863.

.... If we rest here for some weeks, as there is talk of our doing, I hope to get track of Sunday again, and at least to have some music. There is a good piano and melodeon at Mr. Catlett's, where General Howard has his headquarters, and as I have been introduced to Mrs. Catlett, a lady of intelligence and refinement, I shall go up there pretty soon and try to beat up a crowd to sing, out of the General's staff.

.... I spent a pleasant Sunday, about two weeks ago, near Waterford, just after we crossed the Potomac. The artillery made a very early march and got into camp by 11 A. M. Somehow, I got into a farm-house, close by my quarters, which was a regular fine old homestead, belonging to an old gentleman named Pierpoint, and he had a pleasant wife and three pretty daughters. There I spent pretty much the whole of the day, tried to get the girls to sing with me out of the "Carmina Sacra," had a good dinner, and successfully resisted all efforts of both General Steinwehr and Schurz, to get me out of the house. I never saw such perfect idyllic simplicity as prevailed in the family. They belonged to the Society of Friends, and one of the girls who had been as far as Alexandria, and had once seen dancing, was looked upon with wonder by the rest. The youngest, however, who was a little mischief, after

T. U. style, declared loudly that if *she* got a chance *she would* dance, *too;* she did n't believe it was so very wicked. I did not bother my head much about the trouble in New York ; I only wished that they would send me with my Battery to the city for a couple of weeks, to enforce the draft. I would much rather fire canister into those drunken Irish rowdies, than into the secesh brethren, who, although deluded, are worth all the Paddies that ever had a brogue. . . . . I try to do my duty fully, and then look to results, not heeding if the material is used up in the process. My own life I reckon no dearer than the rest, if I can win the end. You see, dearest mother, this war has become the religion of very many of our lives, and those of us who think, and who did not enter the service for gain or military distinction, have come more and more to identify this cause for which we are fighting, with all of good and religion in our previous lives, and so it must be if we are to win the victory. We must have an impulse, made of patriotic fire and a deeper feeling, which takes its rise in the thinking soul. If we have this, then we can bear our standards and our military pride high up, for they will have a foundation. I am and have been in good health, almost without intermission, even when so many were falling sick about me, but I think that that putrid swamp would have done for me, too, as well as for the others. Did you hear whether R. E. came safe out of that attack on Fort Wagner? I saw that his regiment was badly cut up.

CATLETT'S STATION, *August* 9, 1863.

Indeed, when I allow myself to think of the quiet delights of home, — the libraries, music, the refining and humanizing influence of dear friends — glorious Sabbath evenings like this, not spent in seeing horses groomed, or in repacking ammunition, but in singing " Tallis," and " Solitude," and " Bemerton " with you, and mother, and the girls, and Aunt E., with my hand clasped in somebody's, I can assure you that a half feeling of regret, and a whole feeling of longing, comes over me, so that it requires a really painful effort to repress it, and to reach forward to those things that are before, even if I do not forget those things that are behind. Sunday evening is my regular time for this sort of Lot's-wife longings and lookings back, partly because the vacant time allows them, and the day suggests them, and partly because the duties of the next day will cure any undue homesickness. Now we are to have a big drill to-morrow morning at 5 A. M., and I rely upon that to do away with the evil effects of my this evening imagining myself sitting by mother, and listening to you singing "When gathering clouds." ....

You will be shocked at hearing that I indulged in another of our favorite menagerie "loads" in the heat of the battle at Gettysburg. It was on the first day, when General Reynolds pushed us through the town, and made an offensive (more to us than to the enemy) attack upon a superior force in a superior position. My Battery and another were in the extreme advance, and were fighting hotly with some rebel batteries, when the rebels massed their forces, threw out three heavy columns, and very soon drove our infantry back, and enveloped the batteries in a dangerous manner. I did not wait for this state of affairs, but immediately left the rebel batteries the whole talk, and began to try to break the rebel columns with canister. The captain of the other battery, Captain D., would not believe that they were not our own men at first, although their blood-red battle-flags were plain enough in sight, and at last he asked me, "Wheeler, which *are* the rebels and which are our men?" Whereupon I retorted upon him with the same answer as that with which the showman so triumphantly crushed the "little boy." "You pays your money and you takes your choice." Somehow or other I felt a joyous exaltation, a perfect indifference to circumstances, through the whole of that three days' fight, and have seldom enjoyed three days more in my life. ....

When I was in Maryland, I did not cease to admire the beauty of the county of Frederick. I really think that there is hardly a piece of ground in the country, equal to that rolling land just east of the slopes of South Mountain. The fields so undulating and yet so fertile, with charming buildings nestled out of the way in so many hollows, the stretches of golden wheat, bending under the blessing of the sunlight, and the soft, delicious, purple-blue of the mountains, ever near at hand, which seemed, like many plain, generous people in daily life, to say, "We are not very high above you, and don't pretend to anything great, but we watch over you constantly, and we send down pure perennial streams of water to cheer and bless your fields and meadows."

CATLETT'S STATION, *September* 5, 1863.

I am beginning to emerge in some degree from the state of torpor and indifference in which I have been lying for nearly a month past, and to feel some interest in what surrounds me. I don't know what has been the matter with me. I have been fully able to do my duty, have drilled my Battery every day to their hearts' content, have sat on court martials, boards of examination and survey, and have felt lively enough as long as I had any excitement, but when this had passed by I was all down again, — my appetite was (and is) most capricious, and, above all, a feeling of unconquerable lassitude, which I could only shake off when some matter of great and pressing importance came along. . . . . . You will be able to form some idea of my state of apathy, when I tell you the news of R. E.'s death, which reached me first through your letter, failed to move me as I should have expected. I know that I felt it most deeply, but I could not shed a single tear. I could only feel a desire to avenge him, and think that such a noble, glorious death was well suited to his gallant, enthusiastic nature, and a fit close to his generous, self-sacrificing life. I cannot help looking at it as a soldier ; we have death so constantly before our eyes that it loses its terrors, and the question with us is not so much whether we shall die or not, but how we shall die and among what surroundings. And the highest, most desirable type of death for the infantry officer, is that met on the enemy's ramparts, with the colors in his hand. It is true, a life of devotion and usefulness is suddenly closed, the hearts of friends are torn with anguish, because they will never see his flashing eye and active form again, and because that home will always be desolate; but was not the event ordered by a higher power, who said "I will take this beautiful soul to me *now* in its bloom of youth, and he shall be spared the evil days to come." And if in this struggle death is to come to me, may it come as it did to Young Crosby, " among my guns in battery," and successfully resisting a hostile attack, dying of a mortal stroke, —

"What time the foemen's ranks are broke."

Dear J., from whom I received a most affectionate and cheering letter yesterday, warmed my heart by speaking of R. in such a kind, appreciative way. He expressed what I wanted to express, only my heart was too full, and my frame of mind too gloomy, for me to find the proper utterance. My daily prayer now is, that it may not happen to my brother. I really believe that I am much less unselfish and patriotic than you are, for I think more of his safety than of the service he is doing the country, and wish it were possible that he could be safe home again. I know, dear mother, that you will not be wearied by this expression of my affection for him, as it is only a proof of my love for you, for that you know is the greatest of all. J. seems in splendid trim and spirits, and to be enjoying his staff life very much. I am glad that he has a place where he can keep himself clean and comfortable, and have decent associates. For myself, and I have seen considerable of all arms of the service, I prefer my own position to any other. I like to have the command of men, and to say, like the centurion, "Go! and he goeth;" and then as Captain of a Battery, I am as independent and as comfortable as a Brigadier. We were reviewed by General Howard the other day, and he praised my horses very highly. We did not get a chance to drill before him, which was a disappointment to me, as it is pretty generally acknowledged that my men are the best in the Corps at the manual of the piece. I have made several small raids out into the country around here, and have got acquainted with several families in the neighborhood of Greenwich. Last Sunday, Lieutenant Mickle (who is a noble, Christian fellow) and I went out to old Rev. Mr. Balch's, a Presbyterian clergyman, and spent the evening. The family consists of the old gentleman and his wife, his son, and two daughters, all grown, and are of the real old-fashioned Presbyterian sort, keeping Sunday like the C.'s. The old gentleman is a graduate of Princeton College and Seminary, and talks about the churches in Cedar Street, and Wall Street, and Drs. Romeyn and Mason, in a way that would interest you very much. He seems to be a sort of chronicle of the last fifty years, and says things that are really quite striking and interesting, such as, " I was present in the Senate when Josiah Quincy began this whole matter, and spoke the first word of secession." From this you can perceive that he is a rebel of the most virulent type, and his two daughters are just as bad. But after the political discussion had waged for some time, we opened the piano, and we had some of the old hymns after the old style, "Ariel," " Greenland's Icy Mountain," " Italian hymn," etc., which did me good, and then we stayed with them to evening worship. He expects to preach to-morrow, and Lieutenant M. and I are going to lend a hand at the singing, and to stay to dinner. It is strange that opinions and sentiments about the war can be so violent one moment, and the next, all the disputants have their heads close together about one hymn book, or are kneeling at one family altar. Religion is the only thing that can lend any humanizing influence to this war. These good people are instant in good works, and, after giving a soldier a good dinner, they will put some nice, simple little book into his hand, which, for sheer politeness, he will not be able to refuse. Just at this moment one of the men is singing some hymn about the " Lion and the Lamb," to a rough, sailor melody.

CATLETT'S STATION, *September* 25, 1863.

. . . . I really shall have to make a formal defense of myself for visiting in the families of natives of this region, as you seem to think that I am failing in devotion and loyalty to the cause in which I am engaged. Now I think that you look at the thing in too theoretical a light, and this is owing to your distance from the scene of operations. I know you too well not to be sure that, in spite of your thorough patriotism and hatred of all that is hostile to our cause, you would yet be the first to help the wounded and destitute, even though rebels, and to feel sorry for families desolated and ruined, even in Virginia. For myself, while I will yield to no man in the obstinacy of the fight and the endurance of the march, still, when a man is wounded or a prisoner, when a woman is lonely and distressed, they rise in my view from the position of rebels to that of our common humanity, and as men and women, I treat them with kindness, though rebels. And do not think for a moment that I sympathize with these people in any of their ideas, or that I allow them to suppose that I am anything but an extreme Emancipationist, determined on seeing the end of the secession movement and of slavery, provided it is granted me to live so long. We talk about books and persons, sing, play games, eat melons and peaches, and in the course of the evening we usually manage to treat them to the "Star Spangled Banner," and a few more of the national airs, which ought to do a secessionist's ears a great deal of good. (Strange to say, since writing the above, a circular from General Howard has come in, in which he observes that it has come to his knowledge that officers in the Corps, and especially the artillery officers, are in the habit of visiting at the houses of rebel secessionists, and recommending that it be stopped: quite an argument in your favor, but I will not back down from what I have just said.)

Lieutenant Carlisle returned about a week ago, quite well, though not very strong, but able to fill my place. When absent yesterday, my First Sergeant, Harry Muller, now promoted to a Second Lieutenancy, came back from New York to be mustered in as an officer, so that I have no longer the whole concern on my hands, and feel much less anxiety. He used to attend on me at Camp Observation, and took such good care of me when I was sick there. He has passed through the successive grades of corporal, sergeant, and orderly sergeant, and after distinguishing himself in several battles, has now arrived at an officer's rank, which he well deserves. The defects of education (which he is daily overcoming, as he is thirsty to learn) are greatly overbalanced by his real manliness and stamina, his fidelity, willingness, and pluck; if I tell him to take his section into a position and keep it there till I relieve him, he will do so, if not a single man comes out alive, and that is the kind of officer I want to have under me. We had a superb review of the corps artillery here last Saturday, before General Hunt, Chief of Artillery of the Army of the Potomac; all the fine batteries were drawn up in a single line by your humble servant — as Major Osborne had charged me with the duty of forming them for review, and I can assure you that the muzzles of the guns were in a bee-line from right to left. General Hunt told the Major that the artillery was as good as any in the army, and the horses were the best he had seen. He spoke with particular praise of my Battery horses. My school is in a flourishing condition; the boys built a table and desk, with forms, out of split logs, and set it up under the shade of the trees, and every day at 2 P. M. the schoolmaster, an old corporal whom I detailed for the purpose, fetches the spelling-books and the writing materials, and sets his classes their lessons. You would be pleased to see the eagerness with which men from twenty to forty years of age seize upon this opportunity for repairing the defects of their early education, and the progress which they all make is most encouraging. The attendance is not compulsory, but the schoolmaster has more than he can attend to. I can assure you it does me good to see that patient row, sitting at the rough table which they themselves had hewn out of the hard oaks of the forest, rough, wild boys, many of them, but every eye softened and brightened by the feeling that they were learning something higher and better than card playing or whiskey drinking. Certainly, Victor Hugo was right when he said, " that what was necessary to purify and cleanse the subterranean abysses of the lowest class, was Light;" and this purification is greater in proportion to the nature of the light admitted, the greatest is obtained when "the entrance of Thy Word giveth light."

I am hoping that very few of the men, if any, will have to call upon the officers to sign their names for them on the next pay-roll.

NASHVILLE, TENN., *October* 8, 1863.

MY DEAREST MOTHER, — I suppose that you have gleaned from the papers some information about the flitting of the Eleventh and Twelfth Corps from the Army of the Potomac. Nothing could have been more sudden than our departure from Catlett's Station, or more at variance with the arrangements which were being made there. Orders had been given to the Corps to take a strong position on Cedar Run, to cover the railroad, and several strong forts were ordered to be built, defending the post, in a large semicircle, from the Cedar Run bridge through General Howard's head-quarters round to the station. These forts were to be constructed with care and elaboration, and were to bear the names of Eleventh Corps heroes who fell at Chancellorsville and Gettysburg. The construction of Fort Dessauer, which covered the railroad bridge and was the most important point of all, was intrusted, said the order, to the Thirteenth New York Battery, and the Twenty-seventh Pennsylvania Regiment, under supervision of Captain Wheeler. I had got my digging parties hard at work, and the bastions and platforms for my guns had already begun to rise, when suddenly we were ordered to suspend operations, lay in rations for a month, and have everything packed up, and the same evening saw my guns put on the cars, and my horses marching off towards Alexandria. We made a very stiff march, leaving Catlett's Station at midnight, and arriving at Alexandria at three o'clock the next day, — a distance of forty-five miles. The guns of all the batteries were sent on immediately, over the Baltimore and Ohio railroad, and each battery commander followed with his horses, as fast as he could get them loaded into the horse-cars. I will not weary you with a detailed account of our most fatiguing journey. Suffice it to say that both men and animals were more distressed and pulled down by it than by the severest forced march. I enjoyed the scenery of the Baltimore and Ohio railroad exceedingly, and rode on top of the cars all the way, while crossing the mountains. We passed through the superb region from Piedmont to Grafton in the splendor of a delicious autumn, which showed all the gorgeous coloring of the infinite stretches, and under the mysterious lights and shadows of a perfect moonlight autumn night. The few inhabitants seemed intensely Union, and confident of being able to guard the mountain passes leading to Wheeling with very little aid from Government. At Benwood we struck the Ohio river and crossed to Bellaire. Here another shipment was necessary, and a day of misery was spent in accomplishing it. My horses went out in the first train, together with those of Captain Dilger, whom I found a pleasant companion. We passed through Zanesville and Columbus, Ohio, and at daybreak found ourselves at Richmond, Indiana. Here began a perfect ovation. The good Quakers, by whom the town is mostly settled, took our poor hungry boys into their houses and gave them breakfast, and many a kind word of cheer. At every town in Indiana, great crowds of ladies came to the cars, with baskets of bread and cake and pie, cold meats and chickens, sourkrout for the Dutchmen, and doughnuts for the Yankees, and pressed it upon the men, without distinction of rank, in the most charming manner. Our reception at Centreville and Cambridge City beat everything in this line. Besides the articles mentioned above, the ladies gave us clean handkerchiefs and towels and pieces of soap, most welcome gifts to men whose eyes were half blinded, and whose faces and hands were grimy, with the dust of a week's railroad journey. I am sure that they will not fight the worse, for having seen how dear the cause is to the best and most beautiful in the land. At Indianapolis we reshipped again for Jeffersonville, where we crossed the Ohio again to Louisville, Kentucky. I was delighted with Louisville, which is certainly one of the finest cities in the country, and indulged in a glorious bath, etc., which will always be fresh in my memory; and at the St. Charles Restaurant I built up the inner man with some first class grub. Once more we put our poor nags into the cars, and came on to this place, where we seem at present to be at a dead-lock, as our namesake, General Wheeler, the rebel, has been burning the bridges on the road to Chattanooga, like a naughty man, and we can obtain no transportation by rail. Very possibly we shall have to take a bare-back ride over the mountains to Rosecranz, as our guns, harness, saddles, and baggage have gone on before us, and are probably, by this time, with the Army of the Cumberland. My baggage now, consists of my sabre and overcoat, and I don't know whether I shall ever see the rest of my traps again. Nashville is a dirty, disagreeable place. I am now staying at the Continental, as I want rest.

STEVENSON, ALA., *October* 20, 1863.

I send you another bulletin to report progress, since I wrote you at Nashville. I do not pretend, in these short notes, to give you any clear idea of what I have been doing and seeing on this tedious and yet hurried march, but try merely to let you know that I had got thus far, and that my health was yet preserved. Perhaps I may get an opportunity to write more at length, when the long winter days come, and I have more comfortable quarters, and my own writing materials. Well, we had a week's rest at Nashville, where we were waiting for the quartermasters to get their trains fixed up; and a miserable week it was. The hotel afforded no decent accommodation, although charging enormous prices; the city was filthy, and the specimens which we saw of the men and officers of the Army of the Cumberland did not make me feel very proud of our new associations. The expedition, consisting of about four hundred team wagons, one battery of artillery, all the artillery horses of the Corps, the officers' horses, a regiment of infantry of the Twelfth Corps, and a large number of stragglers, were to leave Nashville on Saturday morning, and Major Osborne wanted me to take charge of the artillery, and go as second in command of the train; but I declined, both on account of feeling so unwell, and also because I did not wish to go before two senior captains, and suggested that Captain Dilger should have the command, which suggestion the major followed. However, as an attack on the train was expected from Wheeler's Cavalry, I did not like to leave the expedition, and told the Major that I would go along and give any aid I could in case of such an attack. The train was not ready to start on Saturday, because many of the teams were to be composed of green, unbroken mules, running loose in the corral, and it took a long time to get them caught, harnessed, and hitched in, and even then an immense amount of persuasion had to be applied before they could be got to move on. It was a most ludicrous sight, and numbers of people rode out from Nashville expressly to see it. The "Norway rabbits" would stand straight up, and paw furiously, and jump over wagon poles and chuck their darkey drivers in the most alarming manner, and then, as f by agreement, would all lift up their voices in a most pitiful hee-haw. On Monday morning most of the teams were in marching order, and we started off on the Franklin Pike, I having charge of the rear-guard. We marched fifteen miles to Lavergne through pitiless rain, halting for hours to get refractory mules subdued and to repair broken wagons and harness, and came into park in a mudhole after nightfall. The officers in the advance had been discreet enough to hunt up good quarters on their arrival, and I found Colonel Long, the commander, and the artillery officers comfortably ensconced in the parlor of a very fine house, making themselves agreeable to the ladies of the house, and listening to the superb singing of the daughter, Miss Ellen Harris, who gave Union songs, and secesh airs, darkey melodies and opera morceaux with equal facility. I went into the bedroom where there was a fine blazing fire, and dried myself a little, and then joined the party in the other room, where I spent a very pleasant evening. Miss H. was a very handsome girl with magnificent eyes and decidedly the quickest and sharpest young lady I ever saw in my life; a little too much like a flash of lightning. I slept that night before the fire in the spare-room, and felt much better, in the morning, than when I left Nashville, as then I felt hardly fit to mount my horse. Rough marching and field work bring one to health quicker than any medicine. We marched that day to Murfreesborough, passing over the bloody battle-field of Stone River, fought on the last day of 1862. The trees were filled with bullets sometimes as high up as sixty feet, and the trunks in some cases were bored through with shells. We saw a monument of stone, partly finished, which is being raised over the dead of General Hazen's Brigade, who are all buried in one sad inclosure. The fortifications at Murfreesborough are the finest field-works that I have seen anywhere. Here, as elsewhere, we reap the fruits of the engineering labors of the rebels. This place is guarded by some of the Twelfth Massachusetts. We went to bed thoroughly wet, and it rained all that night and all the next day, upon which we had a most fatiguing march to Shelbyville. I was half dead when we got there, and was glad to rush out of the rain into the nearest house where there was a light; it proved to have been deserted by its owner, and was occupied by some refugees. We halted at Shelbyville to await the arrival of the train ; it is a pretty thrifty looking place and known as the " Yankee town," two-thirds of the inhabitants being Unionists. In the afternoon, having dried ourselves and brushed off the Tennessee mud, Lieutenant Mickle and I went out to study the natives. We first went and bought a turkey, and left him to be roasted ; then we got up a pretext for calling at the house of Mr. Bob Matthews, the head secesh in the place, whose three daughters were keeping house alone, the old man having thought it better to leave for Southern parts. You see we were pretty well posted on the Virginia rebs, and wanted to know if the Tennessee variety resembled it. We had a very pleasant call, and then went to Mr. Cowan's for our turkey. Mr. C. took us into his parlor, before a delightful fire in an open grate, and had some of the most agreeable conversation that I have had since I left home. Mr. C. is a canny Scotch Irishman, and thoroughly understands the whole question of the war, and is a strong Union man in his judgment, but does not believe in ruining himself by any premature demonstrations. He suffered enough the other day, when Wheeler's Cavalry entered the town and carried off about all the goods from his store, besides plundering the town. It was a premature union meeting that drew down the rebel vengeance on the place. We stayed to supper, and Mrs. C., a pleasant, motherly lady, the very counterpart of Mrs. I. W., gave us some most excellent tea and muffins, which went just to the right spot. The next day was more propitious and we marched to Tullahoma moving the wagon train behind us, and thus being able to advance with greater speed. That evening at Tullahoma was most superb, like the most perfect weather of our Indian summer. The next day we marched through Deckerd, over Elk River to Cowan, at the foot of the Cumberland mountains. The rain set in again, continued all night, and in the morning we were half soaked before we began the ascent of that most rough and rugged of mountains.

It was worse than the Alleghanies or the Blue Ridge, as the road consisted merely of slabs of smooth rock, sometimes standing on end, and deep gullies between them. I hardly expected that we could get over at all, but we had all the batteries at the summit before noon, and by two P. M. were at Tantallon Station, at the base of the principal ridge. There we found the pickets of our own Corps, and felt somewhat at home.

We left the Battery, Captain Wiedrichs, at Tantallon, to be brought on by its own horses, and pushed on twenty-five miles further, to this place. We reached it after dark ; in the morning we discovered that Lieutenant Muller, with my four guns, and the cannoneers, were in the fort, and we made all speed to join them, leaving the others to go on to Bridgeport. I was very glad to get my men all together again, and to find that every one was well. I expect to march to Bridgeport with my guns to-morrow. I myself am greatly in need of rest, and when I got here yesterday it seemed as if I had a heavy weight on my brain and could not keep still, sitting or lying.

I am better to-day, and hope to escape any serious illness, if I can only get this cold out of my bones.

LOOKOUT VALLEY, TENN.,
November 8, 1863.

MY DEAREST MOTHER, — .... This is Sunday, and yet you would hardly call it a day of quiet or leisure. I have to-day commenced building two forts, on two separate hills, using for that purpose all my cannoneers and fifty infantry men, not being able to escape by the plea that it was Sunday, which I artfully put in. So that, with fort building, working hard on our horses to keep them in condition, and being in readiness to get up and move house at a moment's notice, you may imagine that my thoughts are not in that serene and unruffled state that I would have them for a Sunday talk with my dear mother. .... The service here is not like that in Virginia, and here the war has few, very few, of the softening features which it there possesses. The country is exhausted beyond conception, and so defective are the means of transportation that the army has to struggle with the citizen for his mouthful of corn. The people of this region are, many of them, on the very border of starvation, and swarms are fleeing from it to the happier North, their children in their hand or following in a mournful train behind, their few household effects in a broken wagon, drawn by a miserable horse, and upon their faces a strong, fixed looked of despair, which it makes me sick to think of. And indeed I do not allow myself to reflect upon the necessary and collateral accompaniments of this war, as it would make me too miserable. Thanks to this expedition of General Hooker, the whole army is now moderately well provisioned, and yesterday our men got whole rations for the first time since we came here, having had half and even quarter rations before. Bragg's army must be in a most deplorable condition; deserters are coming into our lines continually, by squads, and even by companies, who declare that they could not stand it any longer, with no blankets to cover them and with nothing but a small ration of parched corn to eat. They also say that if it were not supposed by most of their troops that they would be forced into our ranks if they should come over, the army could not be held together. The nights lately have been intensely cold, so that under several blankets my feet have been like ice. If we suffer this with our complete clothing and camp equipage, what must be the state of the thinly-clad rebels. Speaking of clothing, you must have laughed at my ill-luck with regard to my baggage, and my apparelless condition. I am not at all uncomfortable, as I have an excellent pair of artillery pants, a government shirt, socks, boots, and drawers, but my appearance is not stylish. I shall fight against ennui this winter and shall look to my friends to help me, both by writing me long letters and sending me anything readable. My Catlett's-station school under the oak is suspended for the present, as my cannoneers are all fort building, and my drivers are out foraging for their horses nearly every day; but if we make any permanent winter-quarters I shall try to get a log school-house built and set it running again, if I can raise the necessary stationery.

LOOKOUT VALLEY, NEAR CHATTANOOGA, TENN.,
November 12, 1863.

. . . . Here the infantry throw up rifle-pits and build corduroy roads, while the artillery have to construct their own forts as well as defend them, and besides this go foraging for their horses outside the pickets, at the imminent risk of being tickled by the guerrillas' rifles; and all these duties have been You will laugh when I tell you that, one day, your poor cousin, whose appetite is famous for its power of renewing itself three performed, until a day or two ago, on quarter and half rations. times daily, was obliged to satisfy said appetite by making his faithful steed divide his scanty dinner with his master, and by dining sumptuously off a handful of "maize au naturel."

Don't think that I am at all bothered by these little inconveniences. I am in good health, lively spirits, — am eager for something to do, and ready for anything that may turn up; and, if you could be transported here by magic for an hour or so, I don't think that you would consider me particularly "mouldy." The fact is, the longer I am engaged in this war, and the more I see of the South, and the more I learn of the plans, views, and principles of our adversaries, the more am I contented with my own course in joining the army; and now I do as a matter of the most positive duty, what I undertook, partly from a spirit of restlessness and love of action.

I have felt the deepest pity for the miserable condition of the poor whites of the South, and I think that, at the hands of the so-called chivalry, a heavier reckoning will be demanded for these people, than for their black bondsmen. That, in the aggregate, the condition of the negro has been improved, and his moral and intellectual faculties developed, by his connection with the white man, cannot, I think, be denied. But what has the dominant class done for the poor white in their midst? They have closed the doors of industry upon him, their own brother, thus keeping him poor; they have refused him education, thus keeping him ignorant; and they have encouraged him in all the vices that spring from idleness, thus ruining body, mind, and soul,— and all this, in order to keep him as a tool for their political and, now, for their military purposes. They have been fatally successful on this point, and have so thoroughly committed their fellows, by the actual facts of war and invasion, that, in very many cases, the poor whites, alive as they now are to the game that has been played with them, have yet had their combativeness aroused, and like all men are ashamed to back out or own up whipped. Here, at the foot of Lookout Mountain, our pickets converse daily with those of the enemy, and sad stories are related of privation and suffering in their ranks. These bear their fruit in the numerous squads of deserters which come into our lines, at the rate of over a hundred a day. No army could stand such bleeding as that very long. I met a band of about forty to-day, headed by an officer, and asked them where they were going. "Home," they replied; "this is our last march in the army." And others said, "If our whole Brigade only knew that you would neither imprison us, nor conscript us into your army, they could not be held together a week." Just think of a half a pint of corn-meal per day, and nothing else, not even fresh meat, — and a thin cotton jacket and pants, without overcoat or blanket to keep off the cold of these frosty nights! Human nature cannot endure these things, unless sustained by the conviction of performing a sacred duty, or being actuated by noble principles ; and these they have not, to sustain or actuate them. It is the dread of being shot or hung that is the cohesive power of the Southern army. Only to-night, I heard a sad story, from a young man, of how his brother attempted to make a Union speech in the midst of his regiment, and succeeded, by dint of great spunk and a drawn revolver, in doing so, but was afterwards hung for it. . . . . My cry this winter will be for "something to read," and if you have any nice book that you don't want any more, just mail it out here to me, "among the gloomy hills of darkness" referred to in the Monthly Concert Hymn.

To L. R. P.

LOOKOUT VALLEY, TENN.,
November 19, 1863.

My intentions were most certainly virtuous with regard to your first letter (written from Long Branch during that mystic period in which you were a year younger than myself, but I grieve to say, displaying very little of that old-fashioned reverence once paid to superior age), but in this instance old Dr. Young's "Procrastination," usually the thief of time, descended to petty larceny, and gouged you out of a letter. Suffice it to say, that in the midst of our gay and festive times at Catlett's Station, the place we had chosen after the toils of battle to repose our wearied virtue, while we were eating and drinking, building forts, and entering into boarded tents to dwell, and warming our hands at cunningly-devised fireplaces, suddenly the order arrived to pull up stakes and depart, and when we got time to breath again we were under the shadow of Lookout Mountain, with plenty of rations and sutler's goods dealt out to us daily, provided we could make an eatable dish out of a 20-pound Parrot shell, or could substitute Whitworth's shrapnel for canned pineapples. And by the first mail that came to our hands in this place, I received another letter from you, dated New Haven, September 26, which had, indeed, as you said, wandered after me, but with better success than you had feared. . . . . It is so pleasant, after a long time in which I have hardly had an inducement to think, a time spent in giving orders and laying down rules of discipline, in caring for bodily comfort and speculating on military events, in cracking small jokes and discussing horses and generals, to meet such a one as yourself, though only on paper, and to pass with him at once into that other world, so beloved by me, of thought, and truth, and principle, and remembered happiness, which is all summed up in the words "Yale," "New Haven."

"Soul-like were those days of yore
Let us walk in soul once more;"

and, indeed, you will think that I have got paper enough for a pretty long walk, but there is absolutely no other to be had, and I rummaged Chattanooga yesterday, for this very *Zweck*, and was unable to raise a single sheet of the orthodox rectangular equilateral style. . . . . I should undoubtedly have been doing my duty to my country if I had come out as private in this Battery instead of lieutenant, and to-day I could do my duty up to the handle as a cannoneer; but when I can fill the place of captain, and get a chance to, I will do so; and if to-morrow I should receive the offer of any higher promotion, and thought that I could do the business of the place, I would not hesitate to accept it. "The tools to them that can use them;" given a certain amount of brains, industry, zeal, and right principle, to make it of the most use to the world and the right cause. . . . . I shall greatly envy you in your reading of "Œdipus Rex." I never read it, but went rapidly through the "Œdipus at Colonus," which I thought a story fully equal in pathos to King Lear, and in some parts not dissimilarly managed. . . . . For practical wrestling and pushing in the every-day world, both of thought and of action, Yale gives as good training as any college; but what inkling has a young Yale graduate of the beautiful world of literature, unless perchance he has neglected his studies. and lived in one of the libraries during his course. . . . . By the way, speaking of labor and study, there is a rather disagreeable article in the October "Atlantic," called "Life without Principle," some sentences in which I believe that I wrote myself, though I don't recollect ever publishing them. Especially the following: "I foresee that if my wants should be much increased, the labor required to supply them would become a drudgery. If I should sell both my forenoons and afternoons to society, as most appear to do, I am sure that, for me, there would be nothing left worth living for." I am already speculating what occupation will give me, when I return home, after supporting me simply on the food-and-shelter plan, the most time free to be employed as I wish, whether for self-improvement or that of others. But I am rather anticipating a subject which I might better discuss six months hence, when I shall have turned it over more.

You ask me for more minute experiences of my life as a soldier; these are hard to give, for very few of them are anything more than commonplace, and even the incidents of battle do not touch much more than the physical nature. The near approach of a battle can never be known with certainty; we are sometimes precipitated into an action which a few hours before we had not expected; and again, sometimes when we are all cocked and primed, and have screwed our courage to the fighting point, we are balked of our little muss; this last produces a sensation similar to that of going up one stair too many in the dark, and is altogether disgusting. We are marching quietly on, when suddenly we hear a cannonade a few miles off; this makes us all feel uneasy, as we would prefer to be either in the midst of the affair or else entirely absent. Then we get an order to pass the infantry in front and get to the field as quickly as possible; the rapid movement creates a certain physical excitement, which must be good for charging infantry, but is not the thing for artillery. At Gettysburg, when I trotted through the town with my Battery, to the front, saluted on all sides by ladies' smiles and good wishes, waving handkerchiefs and banners, I felt highly elated and excited, but this mostly passed away when we got to work. Every man, however brave, must feel unpleasantly when the shells begin to fall into the Battery before it is unlimbered, but as soon as the guns are "in battery," and the work has begun, this unpleasant sensation passes away, although more or less excitement is still felt, chiefly physical, I think, and which arises partly from the sense of bodily danger and of continual escape from it, and partly from the necessity of keeping all the senses on the *qui vive* to prevent the enemy from taking an advantage, by bringing out an enfilading battery, or by pushing forward suddenly a column of infantry to make a charge; I have felt greater *mental* excitement at the crisis of a game of chess played with an equal opponent. I speak this of an artillery fight on the level and in the open, subject to infantry and cavalry charges, as well as to the fire of hostile batteries; an artillery duel, from commanding and secure positions, is a different and much less exciting thing. An old soldier gets to be indifferent to danger so long as it does not affect him, but still he cannot help rejoicing continually that so many shots pass him by. As regards sleeping on the night before a battle, I don't think that the prospect of an Armageddon on the morrow, would keep me awake; it is not like a duel, you know, where a man centralizes and absorbs every feeling in himself, but here every man knows that it is his duty, and that he *must* do it, and the stronger his body is the better he can do that duty, and so he "puts in a big ration of sleep." On the night before July 2d, at Gettysburg, Major O., our Chief of Artillery, slept under my blankets with me, between two of my guns in battery on the crest of Cemetery Hill, and I don't think that either of us could accuse the other of either snoring or kicking.

So, you want me to violate the articles of war by pitching into my military superiors, do you? Well, I don't care if I do a little, seeing it's you. I rather like General Meade; he fought the battle of Gettysburg superbly, and I think that he did all that he could in the pursuit of Lee to Williamsport. Just think, in spite of all his losses, Lee was fully equal to us in numbers ; his excellent position at Gettysburg enabled him to get a day's start of us on his retreat, and thus to reach Williamsport first, where again his position was such as to prevent a successful reconnoissance, and it was impossible for Meade to know that the whole Rebel Army was not lying behind those rifle pits. It would have been the height of rashness for him to have attacked an army of equal strength in a strong position, and thereby to have lost all the advantages of the success at Gettysburg. I think that his course was just such a one as Washington would have pursued ; subsequent events have showed, and will show still more plainly, his capacity as a General. There was undoubtedly an immense amount of mismanagement about the battle of Chickamauga ; the men fought well, but were not well handled. I can't exactly find out how much Rosecrans was to blame, and don't like to think that he was to blame at all; McCook did certainly show great want of conduct, and had no control over his troops. General Thomas won a reputation at that battle by mere good luck, as his corps was heavily reinforced by forces from others, and no great generalship was required to drive Longstreet back, only some stubborn fighting; he is not considered of very heavy calibre. Granger is highly thought of and is a terror to the secesh. General Hooker is a splendid soldier, and is enthusiastically admired by his small force from the Army of the Potomac; there is a superabundant vitality about him which affects all who come near him, and makes one almost believe in some subtle magnetic or electric influence. On the march, he is continually among the troops, has always a friendly nod for the men and a kind word for the officers, and is to be seen at the toughest spots with advice and encouragement. He has such a fine physique, and seems to take such a pride and delight in soldiering, that it is a right pleasant event in a day's experience, to pass his head-quarters, and see him standing in front of his tent by the fire with his hands behind his back, his regular position. Grant I have seen two or three times, but not near enough to get any idea of his character from his phiz; he is said to be restless, full of energy and excitability, a steam-engine in pantaloons; he is in every respect boss of this Western shanty, *de jure* as well as *de facto*. Of General Howard, our Corps Commander, I don't care about speaking, except to say that he is a good and brave man, and a gentleman, but more adapted to the church than to the army.

Since writing most of the above, a day has passed, and it is now the evening of the 20th, and my Battery is under immediate marching orders "at a moment's notice;" General Sherman's troops have come in, and I think that we are going to have a row to-morrow. I am glad that I am to be at the front of it, and hope that we shall wallop them thoroughly. . . . . I have written you a long letter, my dear boy, but you won't mind if you are as fond of long letters as I am. Very much love to the Form; persuade him that this letter is to him also, and make him answer it.

BRIDGEPORT, ALABAMA, *January* 5, 1864.

. . . . From the effects of the battles at Chattanooga, and the ensuing forced march to Knoxville and back, I have hardly recovered yet, even bodily, although it is now nearly a fortnight since I rolled into my bed here, after a twenty-mile gallop, quite used up.

You must not lose track of me because I am so far off; in this army we experience lack of everything which we used to have so abundantly in the Army of the Potomac; but while we can stand being docked of our nice little supplies and winter comforts, we cannot stand being put on half rations of letters, and we shall get entirely uncivilized in this howling wilderness of Hoosiers, Buckeyes, Suckers, and Wolverines, unless you give us occasional glimpses of our dear Eastern home, and tell us that we are not entirely forgotten there.

. . . . My Battery has reënlisted under the Veteran Volunteer arrangement, and goes in for three years more, from the 1st of January, 1864; this movement was almost unanimous, almost every man reënlisting, and that when their feet were still bleeding and their bones still aching from the exposures and fatigues of the Knoxville march. We shall be mustered in, in a day or two, and then the Battery will probably go to New York on a thirty-day's furlough and to recruit. I shall not accompany them if I can possibly help it, as I could hardly bear the journey, and my health is greatly in need of a little rest; besides, I have a perfect horror of recruiting, and all its accompaniments. So now I am in for it until 1867, unless the world comes to an end in 1865, according to —— and Dr. Cummings, or some kindly shell or bullet gives me earlier relief. Don't think, from this, that I am low-spirited, or "down on my luck;" I am only half heart-broken about the state of the country now, and the state it must be in for a long time to come. The end and object of the war are most righteous and proper, and its final results will, after the lapse of years, be beneficial to all parties, and will aid the plan of Providence in teaching and elevating the nation, but all that does not shut my eyes to the terrible miseries which daily come to my notice. "Battle, murder, and sudden death," I can stand well enough; but the disruption of families, the destruction of homesteads, the closing of school-houses and churches, the starving of the people by subsisting large armies on the country, the emigration of hundreds of houseless wanderers, who, not long ago, were prosperous farmers, the disregard of all civil claims, and the treading down of the "Common Law" under the heel of the "Army Regulations, — " all this must be piteously painful to any one who calls himself a citizen of the United States; and equally so to me, although I have been often compelled to commit, in the line of duty, what I should once have called great outrages. . . . .

The country around Athens, Sweetwater, and Mouse Creek was a farmer's paradise; it looked lovely even in the middle of December, with its broad corn-lands and wheat fields, sugar-cane and cotton plant, and warm, delicious sun-light over all, undisturbed by winds or storms, — like the island valley of the Avilion, "deep-meadowed, happy, fair with orchard-lawns;" the very names, Sweetwater, Mouse Creek, speak of everything plentiful and quiet and cozy. Many pleasant Union demonstrations were made along the route; in some places really superb national flags, which the ladies had wrought with their own hands, and kept hidden from rebel eyes by many a cunning device, were given to the winds, and were accompanied by waving of handkerchiefs and by hearty greeting, to which the passing troops responded with roaring cheers. In some places the women jumped up and down with joy, and shouted "Hurrah for *our* side," which told a tale of the time when the *other* side had been uppermost, and those good people had suffered.

Sometimes this display of patriotism was prompted by mixed motives, as thus; the Battery was passing a house, at the door of which stood a woman, and on the opposite side of the road was walking a fat rooster; already a cannoneer had marked him for his own, and was *à la* David drawing a fatal *bead* on him with a "smooth pebble from the brook," when the old lady perceived the imminent danger of the bird, and determined to make a diversion in his favor; waving her hand, she exclaimed, as the swallow-tailed U. S. guidon was just passing, "Hurrah for that dear old flag! it does my eyes good to see it again." The diversion was successful, at least as far as we were concerned, and I am sure that the carcass of that rooster did *not* adorn the camp-kettles of the Thirteenth New York Battery.

BRIDGEPORT, ALA., *January* 17, 1864.

DEAR MOTHER, — .... I am particular anxious to get hold of those missing letters, which must suffice to me, this year, for Christmas and New Year's gifts, with their kind wishes and salutations. J.'s letter was a very delightful one, and made me feel quite homesick, and a longing desire that we might have met together at New Haven during that season.

What will you say to my coming home for a while? My Battery have reënlisted in superb style, only *two* remaining out who had a chance to go into the arrangement, and the

Thirteenth New York Battery has now been mustered into the service as a Veteran Volunteer Organization, "to serve for three years or during the war, unless sooner discharged, from January 1, 1864." Probably we shall start in a few days for New York, to give the men their thirty day's furlough in their State, and perhaps to recruit a little. I had not thought of continuing in the service longer than next fall, and consequently did not urge the men at all to reënlist. I simply stated the conditions, the bounty, the furlough, and read the order relating to such cases, and then said I would take the names of such as desired to enrol themselves for three years more of hardship and hard-tack. But they all asked me if I was going to remain with them, and made my promise to stay a sort of condition precedent to their reënlisting, so that I felt that if the gaining of these men for the service depended upon me, I had no right to selfishly consult my own feelings, and so gave the desired promise never to leave nor forsake them, and this promise I propose to keep, unless disabled in some way. It was not without a struggle that I gave up my dreams of home and friends, intellectual leisure and books, music and congenial society, all of which would be mine next October, when my time was out, and I could hang my sabre up as a relic, over my bookcase, feeling that the three years' hard work gave me a certain title to rest awhile ; but if this is not to be I may as well make up my mind to go without it, and for my personal wants and disappointments console myself with the increasing brightness of the national prospects, and the approaching probability of ultimate and entire success. We are going to give the rebs a queer stirring up down here, next spring. Knoxville and Chattanooga will both be thoroughly fortified and amply provisioned, so that we shall not have to depend upon the long line of railroad to Nashville for supplies, and will be able to make a formidable advance from either point, without endangering our communications. I think that in the next campaign the rebels will be obliged to abandon either Virginia or Georgia. If Lee concentrates his whole army against us, we are ready for him. We have been having terrible cold weather here; ten degrees below zero is not exactly comfortable in a tent. I am quite comfortable in my quarters, have a good fire-place, nice floor and good bed. I hope to be in New Haven by the middle of February, that is if you can tolerate the sight of soldiers away from their posts.

BRIDGEPORT, ALA., *March* 27, 1864.

In the midst of busy working and preparation, I take a few minutes to tell you of my safe arrival with my men in our Alabama home, after a pleasant journey from New York of a little more than six days. On Sunday I bade adieu to my New York friends, and Monday morning went to the Park Barracks, where I found most of my delinquents, and packed them on the Fort Schuyler steamer. I went, in the afternoon, to Fort Schuyler from Williams' Bridge in a wagon. We were doomed to wait for orders till Wednesday afternoon. A small tug took us to 31st Street, and we went to Albany by 7 P. M. train. On Thursday evening we were in Buffalo, Friday morning in Cleveland, and at 1 P. M. in Columbus. Here Lieutenant M. and I got out to take dinner, twenty minutes being advertised for that purpose, when we had the pleasure of seeing the train go off without us. So here were seven hours to be disposed of; when we had exhausted about every mode of slaughtering that most precious of earthly things, I had the good luck to stumble upon Henry Chittenden, who was most cordial, and took us both to his house, where we had supper and passed a very pleasant evening. We had a dreary night ride, and reached Cincinnati just before daybreak, where I found that trusty watch dog, the Orderly Sergeant, had got all his flock snugly gathered together in the barracks of the Sanitary Commission, and there the fourscore were snoring as if on a wager. I was right glad that my transportation to Louisville was by water. The men had only a deck passage, and had to stow themselves among the bales of merchandise, to keep warm. M. and I got a nice state-room, and I had a glorious nap, which was only interrupted by our arrival at Louisville on Sunday morning. An afternoon train took us on towards

Nashville, which we reached Monday morning. We found the place more horrible than ever; the dirt more abundant, and the dust flying in blinding clouds. The city was full of troops, waiting for transportation to the front, but was just beginning to be depleted, as an order had come for all infantry regiments to *march* out to Chattanooga. Owing to this we got shipped for Bridgeport on Tuesday afternoon; if we had had to wait for the whole of those 13,000 troops to be shipped, we might have stayed there a month. A ride of sixteen hours brought us safely to Bridgeport, with no other accident than being run into by the train behind us, and having our car pretty well smashed, though no one was hurt. We found nine inches of snow at Bridgeport, and through this we tramped from the depot to our camp; we passed over a little hill and came in sight of our old winter quarters, upon which the men broke out into loud and joyful cheers. But what especially pleased me was the sight of a row of beautiful, bright, brass, light twelve-pounders, or Napoleon guns, and as I ran my eyes along and counted, lo! there were six! I can assure you that I felt very ing in this respect. I was conducted to the stables, where much delighted at having the Battery restored to its old foot- nearly a hundred splendid horses were standing. It would do your eyes good to see how splendidly I have got them matched; hardly a single pair would disgrace a private carriage. It was the pleasantest thing of all, next to getting home, this getting back. The air is delicious, the snow is all gone, to-day has been a perfect Sunday, and I have been most happy in riding with M. across the river to call upon a Union family from the North, and having some first-rate church music together. On my return I have read in my new old Bible,[1] and thought of you all at home. I ought to have said that I found my box all right, and it warmed my heart to see all the nice things which home love had sent. I am very busy getting rid of my old guns, and fitting up the new ones. To-morrow morning I am to move across the river, into a work at the

---

[1] One given him by his grandfather to replace one lost with his luggage, given by him when six years old.

head of the bridge over the Tennessee, where I shall probably remain until the spring movement takes place. The corps which are to be put in most actively are the Eleventh, Twelfth, Fourteenth, and a Division of the Fourth Corps. The batteries will be fitted up in superb style, and will be expected to do the lion's share of the work. I am Chief of Artillery of the Third Division. My command is over twelve guns. I feel very happy at being at my work again, and am full of hope and courage, for the spring and summer campaign. I have enough to read for a good while, and hope to scare up some antagonists at chess. Have made good use of my little gun already, — have had some nice messes of quails and pigeons. I will write again as soon as we are settled in our new camp.

BRIDGEPORT, ALA., *April* 1, 1864.

. . . . I will not say that I felt as glad to see camp as I did to see New York; gladness does not express it at all; it was, rather, a quiet feeling of satisfaction and contentment, a happiness in being back at my work again, different in kind, but not inferior in degree, to the delight I felt in looking across the Jersey Flats, and seeing the spires of Trinity and St. John's. And it was very pleasant to feel this sense of contentment at coming back to the Army, and friends at home must not look upon it as evincing any want of affection for them, or any neglect of home; a man must do with his might what his hand findeth to do, and my job, at present, is to make my Battery efficient in the time of preparation, and active in the day of action; and to do this work well, all skill and thought and enthusiasm should be employed, and so I thank God that I am willing to leave New Haven, the opera, philharmonics, etc., for the "good time coming," whenever that may be. And yet it is right pleasant, when my officers have retired to their tents, to sit before the big fire-place in my rude quarters, and think over my thirty days at home, and recall so many dear faces, and the affection and kindness shown me by every one. It is the remembrance of such acts, and the words of approval and encouragement with which they are accompanied, that spirit a man up, and keep his heart warm and strong in his rough work. And I am sure that the harder and more sincerely a man does his duty, the more closely he loves and cherishes the remembrance of his friends. . . . . No man of taste cares for vulgar fame, but the thought of having the eyes he loves best smile approval, will nerve him up to anything. . . . ·

I found upon my arrival at Bridgeport, that I was already in possession of six fine brass guns, of the kind known as light twelve-pounders, or Napoleon guns ; they had been turned over by Battery F, of the Fourth United States Regulars, and are the *same guns* which young Frank Crosby commanded at Chancellorsville, and by which he fell. *May I never have a worse fate!* . . . .

Every day scores of the inhabitants, chiefly women, pass the camp on their way to procure supplies from the Commissaries, and I am sure that you never saw such creatures in your life,' so ragged, dirty, and woe-begone, — such spiritless faces, and drooping, slouching figures ; they are hardly worthy of being classed as Caucasians, but more nearly realize the idea of some intensely inferior race, the Papuans, or Australian Indians, or the Diggers. And I do not believe that the war has reduced them to this ; it is the normal condition of the " poor white trash." Nothing that I have ever heard or seen of the injustice and injury done by slavery to the blacks, ever made my blood boil so with indignation, as this spectacle of white men, the same flesh and blood as ourselves, offshoots, perhaps, of the same families that dispense such elegant hospitality in Virginia and South Carolina, to see these, I say, brought lower than the slave, and all by that same system of slavery that says, "we will not have the white man to work," and thus denying them the power of acquiring worldly prosperity, and at the same time, causing mind and body to rust in miserable inaction. The slave who works, thus becomes the physical and mental superior of the white who does not, and the slave-holders have little or nothing to fear from their degraded white brethren. There seems little chance of elevating these people for a generation to come ; we shall have to settle this country with Northern men, and then I am sure that Bridgeport, at the junction of two great railroads, on a most noble river, the centre of a region rich in coal, and iron, and saltpetre, and marble, and corn-lands, will one day be a splendid city ; under the hand of Southern enterprise it had grown to a place of *four* houses!

HEAD-QUARTERS OF 13TH N. Y. BATTERY,
BRIDGEPORT, ALA., *April* 21, 1864.

DEAREST MOTHER, — . . . . We have been in a regular fever of excitement here for a couple of weeks past, about the consolidation of these two Corps, — the Eleventh and Twelfth. Lookout Valley was the Mecca to which all curious officers made their pilgrimages, and every last arrival from that classic locality had to undergo a regular cross-examination as to the latest news, how Old Jose looked, what he said, and who were to have the new Divisions. The work is at last completed, and the new organization is announced ; the Generals of Division in the Twelfth Corps all retain their places, while those of the Eleventh Corps have to take a back seat. The German element is played out, and in everything except name, the Eleventh Corps is put with the Twelfth, our Divisions and even Brigades being broken up and distributed to the various Divisions, and even in name the Twelfth Corps will retain its identity ; the number of the new Corps is the Twentieth.

It is rather hard for an officer like myself, who has been with the Corps from the very first, and has shared its hardships and dangers, its good report of second Bull Run, Gettysburg, and Mission Ridge, and its evil report of Chancellorsville, to see the identity of the Corps merged into that of a rival Corps ; but orders are orders, and I consider nothing unbearable that comes from the proper authority.

The new Corps is going to be magnificently equipped, and commanded by a man who is more like old Stonewall Jackson, than any man in our army ; we shall have a force of over 30,000 men in one mass ; 25,000 of them for active service in the field, the remainder to guard the railroad, and if Fighting Joe does not make an impression on rebeldom, with this force, I shall be most grievously mistaken. It is a heart-stirring feeling, to belong to an army composed of such troops, so superbly equipped, and likely to have such a proud history. The Divisions of the new Corps are to be commanded as follows: First, General Williams; Second, General Geary; Third, General Rousseau: Fourth, General Butterfield; the artillery is assigned to Divisions, two batteries to each Division ; my Battery and Knapp's Pennsylvania Battery, a splendid volunteer battery, belong to General Geary's Division, and I am the Division Chief of Artillery. I have as fine a lot of horses as you would wish to see, and the other Battery has a supply equally fine, and when a few little deficiencies of equipment shall be supplied, and the spring movement takes place, I think that the Second Division will let itself be heard from. Major Reynolds, our chief of artillery, is an excellent officer, and very particular and critical. Lieutenant Mickle is his adjutant, and I am very glad that he remains connected with the artillery; he is a most cheerful and fine spirited fellow, and it does me good to meet him. I am afraid that I have bored you somewhat with my long account of the organizing of this army, but I want you to know just what I am about, and what my surroundings are. In every social point of view, the change is one for the better. I shall now be thrown among full-blooded Americans, and those mostly of the New York or New England type. I had a very pleasant introduction to some of my new comrades the other evening ; Colonel Ireland, who commands a brigade in General Geary's Division, gave a reception at his head-quarters at Stevenson, and F. S., who is an intimate friend of the Colonel's, asked me to go down there with him. Then we took the evening train at Bridgeport, and jolted down to Stevenson by 7.30 P. M. We were among the first arrivals, and I was very glad to have an opportunity of making the acquaintance of Mrs. Ireland. She is a very intimate friend of Captain S.'s wife, and his introduction was sufficient to insure me a cordial reception. The rooms were draped with flags of the regiments of the Brigade, and festooned with evergreen stars and loops, and ornaments of all kinds and shapes, formed from swords, bayonets, and sashes, lighted up the walls splendidly. In the hall hung the musket, knapsack, and accoutrements of a soldier, taken, the Colonel said, at hap-hazard from the ranks of a regiment. The musket shone like silver, not a speck of dust was on the equipments, and the knapsack, fully packed with overcoat and blanket, was a very neat and symmetrical object. Soon the guests began to arrive; a great many elegantly-dressed officers, and a very few ladies; it would make the eyes of a city belle snap to see the number of gentlemen that pounced upon each individual lady. The jolliest of the ladies was a Mrs. W., wife of Captain W. of the One Hundred and Forty-ninth New York, bearing certain proofs in his phiz of belonging to that noble race that bled at Concord. I took Mrs. W. in to supper, which, by the way, was a regular success for the field, as being substantial as well as elegant. The officers present danced with each other very gracefully, and treated me with great consideration, when they learned that I was assigned to their Division. The ladies from the country, who had been hunted up for this occasion, were a queer lot; one or two of them were said to be great heiresses, but of a different style from Northern girls whether heiresses or not. They did not know how to dance, to walk, to talk, or to appear at ease; and they seemed to look upon the fun and good hits made by the really smart officers, as very undignified; they actually behaved as if they had never seen a gentleman before in their lives. I never want to hear any one say anything in favor of Southern ladies, about their charming ways, and their graceful languor, — give me rather the poorest New England schoolmarm, — the force of language can no further go. S. and I came home at the respectable hours of $4\frac{1}{2}$ A. M., having had a very nice time. I like him better, the more I see of him. He is just as good as he can be; I like to hear him talk about his wife and children (he has four, three boys and a girl), in whom he is completely wrapped up; it really makes me feel quite a hankering after domesticity. I only hope that this new organization may not compel him to be assigned away from this Corps. Very many thanks to Mr. B. for his picture, and to Mr. D. for his, which I found in the box.

PEA VINE CHURCH, GA.,
May 6, 1864.

MY DEAREST MOTHER,— My doubt and anxiety about J. were brought to a painful certainty by your letter, which reached me just as we were marching from Bridgeport to the front, and filled me with very great sadness. I have always been very anxious about him, ever since he entered the service, and now perhaps almost the very worst of all is realized, a Richmond prison ; I cannot bear to think of him as having fallen. It will be with the greatest and most painful anxiety that I shall hear further news from him; whether he is wounded or not, and, if a prisoner, what his prospects of keeping up health and spirits until exchanged. . . . . But I cannot give way to feelings in this matter, as I have my own duties to attend to, and the perpetual consciousness of great sorrow such as this, would entirely incapacitate me from performing them in a proper manner ; so I cherish hope as much as I can, and rely upon the thought of J.'s energy and tact, which will enable him to alleviate some of the miseries of imprisonment, and to obtain for him release at the earliest possible day. I cannot help sympathizing with the mortification which his proud spirit must have felt, at being obliged to surrender after his almost first engagement,[1] but according to all accounts, the resistance made was most honorable and gallant, and General Wessells would have been to blame if he had not surrendered, when there was no more hope of receiving reënforcements. You must not allow yourself to grieve too much, my dearest mother, over this sad disaster ; we cannot do our duty in these stormy times, without many risks and sacrifices, and when J. and I came out into the field, we had no idea of avoiding our fair share of these dangers, and we are eternally grateful to

[1] His brother was taken prisoner at Plymouth.

you for your encouragement, and your sympathy in our plans and views of the right course to be pursued, so that we could go onward with everything in our favor, sense of duty, patriotism, and the cheering voice of those dearest to us. And so, no loss or sacrifice ought to be regretted, or unduly sorrowed over, when viewed in the light which Right and the splendid Future throw over the conflict. I shall not cease hoping that we shall once more meet under the family roof, and in the meantime I shall ask that strength may be given him to endure privation; and courage and cheerfulness to buoy his mind up in the dreariness of imprisonment. How can I communicate with him now? Shall I send my letter to you to be forwarded to him.

You will wish to know what brought me down into this region; on Monday night we received orders to move early the next morning, and so, on Tuesday, May 4, we broke up our camp at East Bridgeport, tore ourselves away from our comfortable quarters, and the delights of Tennessee River fish, and marched to Shellmound. The next day, after a most pitiless march up the valley, we crossed Lookout Mountain after nightfall, very completely done up, and joined the other Brigade of our Division, formerly the First Brigade, Second Division, Eleventh Corps. From this point, the southern base of Lookout, our Division marched, the next morning, through Russville, towards Ringgold, leaving that place to the left and marching towards a place called La Fayette. This morning we marched half a dozen miles further towards that place, but have now halted for a rest, and also to allow of the complete concentration of our Corps. It will form a most magnificent line, — almost as close as a line of battle, and containing nearly a hundred thousand men. If the rebs can make a stand against this force, they are smarter and stronger than I think them. I am quite delighted with my commanding officer, General Geary; he has great consideration for the Artillery, and tries to help it along as much as he can. He is very polite to me personally, and I feel quite at home in this strange Division already. The two batteries under my command, as

Division Chief of Artillery, are in fine order, and I shall be much disappointed if I do not do good service with them. It is impossible to say what the enemy propose to do. For my own part, I would rather have them stand and fight it out here, as I think that we are far enough from our supplies already. I do not allow myself to be over sanguine, in matters which are so vitally interesting to us all, and yet I should be greatly disappointed if we did not achieve some very decided success in the approaching battle. The country is hilly and undulating, and has been cultivated, but we see very few inhabitants; have not been able to forage much yet, and my fare is simple bacon, hard tack, and coffee; but the promised land can't be very far ahead, and there must be chickens there. I am very well indeed, and am getting my campaign tan on. If we have a fight here, look in the newspapers for accounts of Geary's Division, Twentieth Corps, and you will know where I have been at work. Let me know about J. as soon as you get any information, and how he is to be addressed.

NEAR RESACA, GA., *May* 14, 1864.

It seems a rather queer thing to be writing from a battlefield, and during a battle, but such is really the case. Not far from where I am sitting, the hostile batteries are fiercely playing on each other, and the infantry are beginning to tackle each other quite seriously; but as our Corps is in reserve, we don't trouble ourselves unduly about what Macpherson, or Logan, or Schofield, may be doing, and patiently await our turn to be called into the grand melée. The campaign has been a queer one, the object of it having been to amuse the enemy in front, and keep him at Dalton, while the bulk of the army should march along the range of hills within which Dalton liès, cross the ridge by one of the Gaps, cut the enemy from his communications, and take him in the rear. How far this plan has

---

[1] He never succeeded in communicating with his brother, who heard rumors of W.'s death when at Macon, from prisoners who were brought in, confirmed when he was at Savannah, in a letter received by a friend in S. from friends at the North.

succeeded I am as yet unable to inform you. It should have succeeded perfectly. The three principal Gaps in this range are, first, at Buzzard's Roost, next Mill Creek Gap; some ten miles further to the south, Snake Creek Gap. Buzzard's Roost, strongly fortified, was threatened by two Divisions of our Corps, while Geary marched against Mill Creek Gap. This is a very steep mountain pass, thickly wooded on all sides, and commanded on the crest by breastworks, in which a large force was posted. The Second Brigade of the Division was formed in the first line, and the First Brigade in the second, and an attempt was made to scale the mountain and take the pass, as was done at Lookout. But though the men did their best, scrambling from rock to rock, and pulling themselves up by trees and bushes, yet as fast as they showed their heads above the rocky parapets at the crest, an unseen foe picked them off, and even those who were but slightly wounded were in great danger of breaking their necks or limbs by falling from the rocky ledges. At times, small parties would succeed in reaching the summit, only to find themselves confronted by a strong breastwork, over which peeped the rifles of a foe. It was impossible to aid our men much with the artillery. However, I placed the rifled battery under my command in position, and threw some shells into the Gap, with what effect it was impossible to discover. The fight was kept up until night-fall, when our men retired down the mountain, protected by the artillery from being pursued, and camped just in front of the Gap; so that if the enemy would not let *us* over, we could be prepared to do the same by them. In this affair our Division lost about three hundred and fifty killed, wounded, and missing; but it was not labor in vain, as the attention of the enemy was thereby drawn to this Gap, and General Macpherson, with the Fifteenth and Sixteenth Corps, crossed the mountain at Snake Creek Gap almost without opposition; but I believe that he failed in thoroughly cutting the railroad communications at Resaca, and thus it is to be feared that the bulk of the enemy have slipped away to Atlanta, leaving only a rear guard before us. Since I have been writing this, the infantry firing has become much more heavy, and there is reason to hope that we are to have a chance at their main army. We lay for three days at Mill Creek Gap, and it rained frightfully and changed from extreme heat to severely chilly weather, which made us all a little ill. We marched on the 11th, passed through Snake Creek Gap, closely followed by the Eleventh and Twenty-third Corps, and yesterday began a lively skirmishing with the rebels, who are evidently on the retreat, — their object being to get safely off to Atlanta, and ours to cut them off, and make them fight. The result I cannot announce. I can only say that General Howard with the Fourth Corps took Dalton yesterday, and will be to-day on the enemy's rear, and that thus far everything looks well. Our hearts have been cheered by the glorious news from the Army of the Potomac; we all rejoice in their triumphs just as if we still belonged to that grand army. I only hope that we may be able to show some similar good service in the public cause. I continue in the same state of miserable uncertainty about my brother's fate. I am sure that you will let me know as soon as you hear anything. I wish that the present movements in Virginia might result in the release or escape of all our prisoners. Do not fail to write me soon, and let me know all you can learn about him and about all at home. Thus far this has not been a very severe campaign for either men or animals. I have kept my horses in pretty good condition, and my men have been well supplied with rations. For myself, in my capacity of Division Chief of Artillery, I held on to my ambulance for head-quarters, but fear greatly that it may be taken for general use in case of a big fight. It is very convenient as a dry and comfortable sleeping place, and I am now writing this letter from the driver's seat. Now I have written you a stupid letter, but one can't get up much on the edge of a battlefield, when in momentary expectation of being ordered in. Be sure that if we are I shall do my duty as I best know how.

CAMP NEAR CASSVILLE, GA.
May 20, 1864.

MY DEAR AUNT, — A day of rest at last, after so many spent in marching and fighting, enables me to answer your very kind letter, and to send assurances of my health and safety up to this date, to all the friends at home.

Your letter was a great relief, containing the information of J.'s comparative safety, even though he be a prisoner. Although I am not of a very sanguine temperament, yet I am very confident that his energy and tact will bring him safe through the horrors of even a Richmond prison, and that he will return again, alive and hearty. At any rate this is the view I must take; any more gloomy view of things would make me too wretched to perform my duty properly. When I wrote last to mother, we were lying in reserve, awaiting orders to move forward. In less than half an hour after that letter was mailed, our Corps began to move down toward the left, to form a junction with the Fourth Corps, under General Howard, against whom the rebels were massing heavily. I rode with General Geary in the advance of the Division, and reached the scene of conflict just in time to witness the most fortunate arrival of our men, who turned the enemy back, just as they were about to flank General Howard. A brigade of the First Division of our Corps took the Indiana Battery out of the very clutches of the rebs, as the covering infantry of the Fourth Corps had run away from it, and it was manfully holding its ground without support. This ended the fighting of the 14th May. The batteries of the Division marched to the left in the night, a most tedious and intricate march, requiring about eight hours to make five miles, and arriving in camp at 4.30 A. M. after a sleepless night. The next morning, Sunday, the 15th, the real fighting commenced. The enemy were intrenched on a line running almost north and south, parallel to, and covering the railroad; the country is very hilly and thickly wooded, admirably adapted to bushwhacking, but utterly unfit for extended movements in line, or for artillery operations. The rebel defenses consisted of rifle-pits and fence-rail breastworks at all points, and on the summits of the ridges were earthworks, and quite elaborate embrasured forts. The flanks were protected against any serious demonstration by the tangled character of the country. *My rôle* was of course not a very important one, but I placed the whole of the Thirteenth New York Battery in the best positions I could find, their brass guns being the only ones that could be used in such a country.

The assistance they gave did not amount to very much, but it would have been important in case our men had suffered any decided repulse.

The day was spent in assaults upon the enemy's position, points being gained and then lost again, but ground gradually gained until about four P. M. when General Hooker made an attack with his whole Corps, and took several of the fortified knobs; this decided the contest, and after making a midnight onslaught, to deceive us, and cover their retreat, the enemy decamped, and abandoned Resaca, moving directly south, both on the railroad and by roads running parallel to it. A similar mode of pursuit was adopted; Sherman did not give the enemy any head start, but pushed on at daybreak the next morning, moving the Fourth and Fourteenth Corps directly through Resaca, Macpherson's troops west, and our Corps east of the railroad, where we made a great circuit for the purpose of flanking Calhoun, and crossed the Conesauga River, but brought up against the Coosawatchee River, as we had neither pontoon bridge nor boats. In the night of the 16th we hunted up a couple of old ferry-boats, put them end for end, planked and secured them, and crossed the whole Corps the next morning, and marched to Calhoun, which the enemy had been obliged to leave. You see that General Sherman's plan of march is to move armies in parallel lines, but having them converge and concentrate at all important points. Thus, for example, we see the other Divisions of our Corps in the morning, lose them during the day, and meet again at night. This was also the style of marching we pursued in going to Knoxville. On the 19th General

Howard had quite a sharp fight with the rebs, but outfought them and pushed on. The other Corps continued the flank march, and the advance of our army is at Kingston, the junction of the branch railroad to Rome, thus cutting off that important place and compelling its abandonment. We are at Cassville, east of Kingston, in the beautiful valley of the Etowah, enjoying supremely a few hours' rest after our hard marches. The country is very lovely and well cultivated, as far as it is cleared; but immense tracts in this section are still covered with heavy timber, chiefly oak and nut-wood. The inhabitants have generally vamosed, the male ones almost without exception, and have taken with them their two legged property, evidently looking upon that as too portable to be left to the Yanks. Thus far the campaign has been a severe one on both men and horses, as far as fatigue and work are concerned, but supplies have come up with great regularity, and we have not been compelled to forage on the country, though I think that we shall come to that soon. Our Corps lost heavily in the battle of the 15th, the entire loss being about two thousand. What the loss of the whole army is I do not know, but should think that five thousand ought to cover it. We have taken a number of prisoners, and about twenty guns. Several of my friends were killed or wounded. Lieutenant-colonel Lloyd of the One Hundred and Nineteenth New York, was killed, and the Adjutant of the One Hundred and Thirty-fourth New York wounded in the head. While passing from one of my batteries to the other, I got by mistake into a cross-fire, and found it very hot for a few minutes, and got a smart slap on the arm from a spent ball. Still all our fighting here has been mere child's play compared with that in Virginia. If we could only get a fair chance, on a fair field, we would give you a victory to record not much inferior to those of the Army of the Potomac. I do not like to see all the work being done by others when we are ready and willing to do our share. If the work goes on through the summer as it has begun, I shall be able to leave the service at the expiration of my term with a clear conscience.

We are in pretty light marching order, as all wagons containing officers' baggage have been sent to Ringgold, unloaded, and sent again to the front with forage. I have seen my old friend Captain S. once or twice on this march. He is now Division Quartermaster in the Fourteenth Corps. I take great interest in everything, even the smallest detail, from New Haven, and your letters are sure to entertain me.

To L. R. P.

CASSVILLE, GA., *May* 22, 1864.

MY DEAR BOY, — As to-day is a real "day of rest," unlike the last two Sundays, which were spent in fighting, and as letter-writing is not only permitted but also encouraged by General Sherman, in a very spicy circular issued yesterday, in which he gave the press correspondents a gorgeous rap over the knuckles, and as to-morrow we resume our line of march for Atlanta, with the prospect of a very sound bellyful of hard work and hard fighting before we reach that interesting spot, I think that I will try to start with as clean a record as possible with my correspondents, and your letter dated April 27 is very noisy and clamorous in its demands to be attended to, so that after reflecting for some time whether I had better take the bantling up and spank it thoroughly or administer a soothing dose of paregoric, I have decided upon the latter course. I desire, in the first place, to object to a statement of yours to the effect that you were not in my debt; if you were not, you certainly ought to be, for I spread myself on an epistle to you shortly before I left Bridgeport, and really I cannot be held responsible for the bulls of Uncle Sam's Briefträgers ; you must write me whenever you feel like it and the gadfly of Sanskrit remits his exertions for a season, without revolving the question of who wrote last, or casting up our epistolary accounts to see where the balance lies, and I am sure that you will be good and kind enough to do so. I love to read your letters ; you can't talk too much "shop" for me ; some other people talk about marriages, and removals, and fairs, and concerts, and similar pomps and vanities of this wicked world, and seem to think I have not retained civilization enough to care for culture or scholarship; while you pay me the compliment of taking it for granted that I have not, in a couple of hard, rough years, thrown off my love for those beautiful studies. I don't care how deep you go into questions, or how dark and abstruse they may seem to me; it is like looking into the dusky alcove of a superb library; you *know* that there are treasures there, and that when your eyes become accustomed to that solemn light, you can find them. As for your proposition to get up a translation in the way you spoke of, it was most kind of you to be willing to ask me with my dim ideas of grammar and roots, to go with you in such an undertaking; but perhaps some of these days, when I shall have emerged from the nomadic state, I may take you at your word; though even in literature and æsthetics I should require a considerable amount of refreshing and posting.

Did it ever occur to you to place Shakespeare beside any one of the three great Greek dramatists? I was thinking about it only to-day, and carried out the thought to some length, although it was an unsatisfactory business without the text of any of them at hand. Has it been done already; and if so, how and by whom? I should really like at some time to put down some of my ideas on this point. I do not think that the study of Tennyson would help a man much in working up Sophocles; he is, I think, eminently unclassic, except, perhaps, in his beautiful rhythm: he might have written fine Greek lines at the University, but his ideas are not Greek. There is no modern production to be compared with the "Hermann and Dorothea" of Goethe in its classic beauty; I read it once more when I was at home, and was more charmed than ever. Tennyson is essentially a writer of the Romance school, strongly tinged and influenced by the liberal Christianity of the Broad Church; a man who has deeply studied the best models, and has profited vastly by the study; he has caught the rhythm and melody of the Greeks, but not their power. "Ulysses" is a modern picture on an ancient subject, and the superb lines in it, as well as the whole casting, are from Dante. "Morte d'Arthur" is only a translation of the old legend into sonorous verse, containing a few lines almost literal from Homer, and a passage on prayer which reminds me always of that about the Λιται.[1] For *my* part, I should as soon look to a star to explain the source of light in the sun, as study Tennyson preparatory to pitching into Sophocles.

I propose, one of these days, when we commence that translation together, to begin also another job with you, namely, a literary course based on the classics and beginning with Dante (your nose having been previously kept on the Italian grindstone long enough to post you on the original), then Shakespeare, a little of Milton, Rabelais, Cervantes, and Sir Thomas Browne. I am also desirous of knowing something for myself of those bugbears of our youth, Voltaire, Rousseau, Diderot, and Helvetius; if I read these with you, it would do me no harm, you know.

But enough of books; you will want to know where I am at this present writing. We are about half a mile from the pretty village of Cassville, county seat of Cass County, Georgia, which is really quite charming for a Southern town, and contains several churches, a college (which has for some time been used as a hospital), and a Ladies' Seminary: this last affair was occupied up to the last moment by the fair schoolgirls, who at last fled with great precipitation, leaving many of their clothes and toilet articles a prey to the Yankee invader; even sweet little notes were picked up, wherein gallant young reb officers expressed their thanks for bouquets of flowers, and "sich like." The valley of the Etowah is very beautiful, and in Northern hands would be a paradise; it seems too bad for this lovely country to be ravaged by war,

[1] The passage from Tennyson is, —

"For what are men better than sheep or goat
That nourish a blind life within the brain,
If, knowing God, they lift not hands of prayer
Both for themselves, and those who call them friend?
For so the whole round earth is every way
Bound by gold chains about the feet of God."

but the people would not be warned, and now they are reaping the fruits of their folly. Every house is either entirely deserted, or else occupied only by a few women and children; a man at home is a curiosity. Our Division Head-quarters is in a fine house out of town, where I love to go and loaf, and look at the roses, and scent the honeysuckles and jessamines that run all over the porch and up the trees, and make me think of that arbor at the hotel in Athens, six years ago this month. I won't bother you with any account of our fight at Resaca; we whipped the rebs well, and most of the fighting was done by our Corps, though the Batteries did not have a great deal to do. We have all been indignant at General McPherson for not cutting the enemy off as early as May 10th; he had the chance, and might have done it. If Hooker had been in his place, we might have captured the whole of Johnston's army; as it was, we only forced him to make a clean and orderly retreat, and to-morrow we start to break our heads against Atlanta or any intervening obstacles. I hope that the blows struck may be heavy and incessant; then, perhaps, we may settle all the heads of this Hydra.

INTRENCHMENTS ON THE BATTLEFIELD,
NEAR DALLAS, GA., *May* 30, 1864.

I can't say exactly how the epistolary account stands between us, but am inclined to think that I am quite decidedly your debtor, and so here goes for a few words, although the first line of works, not more than two hundred yards from the enemy's position, where bullets are constantly flying within a few yards of my paper, is not exactly the best place for a quiet and thoughtful chat. But we have been lying here for four days now, and are getting accustomed to the steady whiz of the bullets, to say nothing of the occasional boom of a rebel shell, and the idea of writing you a letter under fire is rather amusing than otherwise, so I snatch a scrap of my rapidly diminishing stock of paper, borrow the finest pen in the crowd, and try to see how much I can work in on a little space. I do not need to tell you that I have been preserved safe and sound through the fight at Rocky-faced Ridge, the battle at Resaca, and the action of the 25th at this place. Suffice it to say, that they were bloody affairs for our Corps and Division; the losses of the Twentieth Corps since we left Bridgeport amounting to nearly five thousand. The action of Wednesday last was a curious one. We had left the fertile valley of the Etowah, and had entered the woody and mountainous country on the western part of the Altoona ridge, hoping to be able to anticipate the enemy in reaching one of the gaps, and to compel him to give battle in the comparatively level country before Altoona. On Wednesday morning we pushed forward from Burnt Hickory to Pumpkin Vine Creek, repaired the bridge which the pickets had half burned, and crossed our Division over, the other Divisions being on other roads. After marching a couple of miles, we met the enemy in force and attacked him fiercely, driving his force back. It was very lucky for us that we did so, as we learned from prisoners that Johnston's whole army was before us, and nothing but our anxiety had prevented the whole Division from being taken or cut to pieces. The other Divisions were sent for and came up at double-quick, when Hooker hurled them upon the enemy with his customary impetuosity, and drove them back about a mile and a half, storming one of their best positions, — that which we are now holding; and I sincerely believe that nothing but the coming on of a most thick darkness prevented him from driving them headlong from their stronghold. Our loss was heavy; about two thousand. General Howard, General Palmer, and General Schofield arrived with their Corps the next day, and we took up a line opposite to that of the enemy, and since then the Vicksburg tactics of fighting from trenches have been adopted, — a most tedious and vexatious way of fighting, I think, and one calculated to demoralize an army of spirit. Here we have been for four days in dirty trenches, without taking off our clothes, and started up every few hours by an attack either real or sham. Last night the rebs made a serious attempt to drive us out, and we awaked from our first sleep at about 11 P. M. to hear a most ferocious fire from their line which had advanced to within one hundred yards of our works. My men sprang to their guns and treated them to a few doses of canister that soon drove them back, and their officers could not get them out again. Our works alone saved us from destruction. I anticipate a still rougher assault to-night, but they won't get the Thirteenth New York Battery without pretty hard work. This whole campaign is going to be a severe and deadly one, and I don't much expect to come out of it all right; and it is for this very reason that I write you under these very peculiar circumstances to assure you once more of my unaltered esteem and love for you, which have now continued the same from childhood up. My dearest brother is a prisoner, and you must join with me in prayers and hopes that he may have strength to bear, with patience and cheerfulness, the severe trial of personal confinement and mental inactivity. May he be restored to his home, without suffering any shock either to his health or spirits. I feel at times almost desperate when I think of the still distant termination of the war, and of the blood and treasure that must yet be expended before truth and justice shall prevail; but I think that a man is less miserable when actively engaged in the war, than when an anxious watcher and spectator at home. Perhaps the poor fellows who fell the other evening, and whose graves are at my feet as I write, are the happiest and most enviable of all. You must not think that I am downhearted; but the constant strain of lying here under fire, and witnessing the constant slaughter going on, on the skirmish line, while the air is heavy and polluted with the smell of dead men and horses yet unburied, does not tend to make a man's fancy bright or his spirits high. I almost envy the lot of the men of the Army of the Potomac. They have the heavy fighting and also the greater and fairer wreaths of laurel. I am afraid that the country will ask Sherman what he has been doing all this time, while his brother in arms has been doing so much. Rumors are prevalent that our Corps is to be relieved from this trench-work, and is to be employed on a flank movement.

I earnestly hope that it may be the case, as I am about used up. I hope that my next letter home may be from Atlanta, though perhaps that is a little too sanguine; only, if with our force we don't put the rebs through here, we ought to be ashamed of ourselves.

But I must close, as it is growing dark, and there is every prospect of a lively affair to-night. If this letter is duly sent, you may take it for granted that I got through all right. Now, my dearest cousin, write me soon, and at length, and give me good words which shall make my heart feel warm and strong in this distant land and rough life.

THE LAST LETTER RECEIVED BY ME. T. D. W.

CAMP NEAR ACWORTH, GA.,
June 8, 1864.

MY DEAREST MOTHER,— .... I think that I have not written home directly since we were at Cassville, though I sent off a short epistle to Annie from our trenches, written under a heavy fire; but this was more for the oddity of the thing, and I know that it was a very absurd letter. We have had a very hard and fatiguing fortnight of it since leaving Cassville; we started on May 23, marched through the rich and beautiful valley of the Etowah, which is worthy of being possessed and worked by free people, crossed the Etowah on pontoons, and massed our forces on its south bank. The next day we pushed cautiously ahead, through a town called Stilesborough, where large quantities of cotton had been destroyed the day before, then began to leave the rich and fertile valley, and to enter the oak forests and barren districts of the eastern Altoona ridge, until we camped in a place bearing the euphonious name of Burnt Hickory. On Wednesday we marched through the mountains by parallel roads, toward a creek called Pumpkin Vine Creek; our Division being considerably in the advance, the other Divisions making flank demonstrations towards Dallas. At Pumpkin Vine Creek we found the bridge half burned by the rebel cavalry; but it was soon repaired, and our Division began to cross, and to pass into a ridgy wooded country, where, about two miles from the creek, we found the enemy in force, and attacked him with our first Brigade, driving his forces back quite a distance. Here very large forces of the rebels could be seen coming up, and their artillery was being planted. To our dismay, we learned from prisoners, that nearly the whole of the rebel army was in our front, both Hood and Hardee being present with their Corps. Nothing but our first brisk attack had saved us; the enemy supposed that our whole army must also be there; a determined advance on their part would have cut Geary's whole Division in pieces before it could have retreated. We made our preparations for a vigorous defense; I took my batteries back across the creek, and placed them in strong positions, to cover the crossing, and the Divisions of Williams and Butterfield, and General Howard's Corps, were ordered up on double quick. You can imagine our anxiety until they arrived; but the critical moment went by, the rebels did not improve their golden time, and as soon as General Hooker had got his three lines of battle, — General Williams' Division forming the first two lines, General Butterfield's the third, while our Division, which had been all day long skirmishing and holding the enemy in check, formed the reserve, — I followed the first line of battle with a section of my Battery, ready to place it in position as soon as a position could be found, which was too rare in that heavily wooded country. I had a fine opportunity of observing General Hooker, who rode close behind the first line, and encouraged the men immensely by his cool and easy bearing and his cheering words. Perhaps he exposes himself too much, but he gets more fight out of his men than any officer I ever saw. The men went into the fight superbly; the rebels were driven steadily back, and back, until they reached a strongly fortified position that they had prepared; here they made a stand and checked our advance, and the fighting became very severe. The second line relieved the first, and the third the second; rebel batteries poured shell and canister into our ranks, and yet they pushed on. Just before dark our Division was sent in, and with two good hours for work would have carried the rebel position; but a pitchy darkness came on, and the fighting on both sides ceased almost instantaneously, and both sides began to intrench the positions in which they were resting. We had not won everything, but we had gained the crossing of Pumpkin Vine Creek, a serious obstacle, and had pushed the enemy back two miles by determined fighting, and had even gained a footing on the crest of his position. The next day was spent in strengthening the works thrown up on the night of the 25th. At daybreak on Wednesday, the 27th, the three brass batteries of the Corps were placed in position in these works.

Here we remained six days without relief, under a burning sun, constantly under fire, with the rebel works less than two hundred yards distant from us, and their sharp-shooters often stealing up to within one hundred and fifty yards, and sending their bullets into our embrasures with disagreeable sharpness and precision. Fortunately their advanced works were in a hollow, and so they overshot our breastworks as a general rule; but sometimes an enterprising reb would climb a tree and get a very fair view of us, as we took our ease on the sharp stones behind our works, and then we would find it convenient to huddle up pretty close into the trenches. Night was the worst time of all; the short distance between the lines made a rush possible, at any time, from the enemy's works to ours; and then the Fourth Corps, which occupied the works to our left, had a nervous way of getting up a false alarm about three times in the course of the night, and making us tumble up to our posts, thus completely breaking our rest and depriving us of sleep. On Sunday night the rebs undertook to see if they could oust us, and came up to within fifty yards of our works in a very threatening manner; but we were wide awake, and after a hot little fight of about half an hour, they got back to their works very rapidly, and their officers could not get them out to make another assault. We must have mowed them pretty badly, as we fired twenty-four rounds of canister into them at short range. Pretty business for Sunday night, was it not? We were at last relieved in the trenches by some of the Fifteenth Corps, General Logan's, and moved off to the left of the army. The exposure and wearing excitement had made us all more or less unwell. I came off better than most of the others, and a dose of opium broke up a severe attack of dysentery that had begun to come on. Since then there has been more or less fighting, mostly to our advantage. We now hold the railroad to Altoona; our next point is Marietta, then the passage of the Chattahooche River, and then onward to Atlanta. We march probably to the river to-morrow morning, and it is impossible to say when a general engagement may come on. When it does, we are confident of success, and especially that the Twentieth Corps will have plenty to do and will do it well. Our Corps has done almost all the fighting in this campaign, and has sustained a very large proportion of the losses. I think that the entire loss of our Corps since we left Bridgeport must be rather over than under five thousand. Our battles have seemed small and pigmy-like beside those in Virginia, still we are not idle and are making progress. . . . . The climate suits me as well as, or better than Virginia. In the morning and evening the air is full of the delicious perfume from the blossoms of the wild grape and the hawthorn, from thyme and other sweet grasses. The smell of these last make me think of Athens and Mount Hymettus. Think of me as well and strong, and doing the best I can, and always longing to hear from my dearest mother.

Your ever loving son,
WILLIAM WHEELER.

The following letter to Professor Henry H. Hadley will serve to introduce, and add to the interest of, the next and final letter of this collection, as coming from the soldier to whom reference is herein made.

ARMY LIFE AND SERVICE. 467

HEAD-QUARTERS THIRTEENTH NEW YORK BATTERY,
BRIDGEPORT, ALA., *April* 14, 1864.

MY DEAR MR. HADLEY, — Your kind note, in reference to Mr. Lee, whom you caused to enlist for my Battery, has been duly received, and permit me to thank you most sincerely for the interest you have taken in my command. The acquisition of a single good man is right acceptable, and the Spring is just the time when we need all our available force at the front. I think that I shall be able to make it comfortable for this new recruit, physically at least; the moral and religious advantages of a Battery are not very great, but I think that the general tone, and the sense of self-respect, are much higher than in the Infantry. He will, at least, have an opportunity of doing and enduring in the cause. My Battery has never been in the reserve, and this spring it will probably have a prominent part to play, as it belongs to General Hooker's new Corps, the Twentieth, which will doubtless be pushed into the thickest of all the fights. If I survive the campaign, I shall hope to thank you in person for your kindness and thoughtfulness in my behalf.

IN FIELD, *June* 23, 1864.
CAMP NEAR MARIETTA.

PROFESSOR HADLEY : —

My dear Sir, — The painful intelligence I have to communicate, of Captain Wheeler's death, you will receive through other sources before this reaches you. The envelope which I send, you will observe, has his frank, which I obtained yesterday morning, there being no stamps to be procured in the Battery. When I went to him he was sitting in the ambulance writing, unconscious as I was, no doubt, of the fate that so soon awaited him. I will give the circumstances of his death as near as I am informed. At noon, yesterday, the 22d, we had orders to advance to a new position in front, the enemy having fallen back about a mile for fear of a flank movement. Captain Wheeler, being acting Chief of Artillery for the Division, took Knapp's Pennsylvania Battery forward, while we remained where we were. Shortly after, or while they were getting the Battery in position, the enemy made two or three charges, evidently with a view of capturing it, as we had no breastworks. They were repulsed and driven back, however, every time, by the fire of the infantry and the artillery. It was while they were making one of these charges, as Captain Wheeler stood partly behind a tree, making observations and giving orders, that a ball from a sharp-shooter struck him in the left breast, piercing him through the heart, from the effects of which he died almost instantly. . . . . His death created a deep and solemn impression in the Battery, and a general expression of regret was manifested by all. . . . .

Most sincerely yours,
FRANK M. LEE.

www.ingramcontent.com/pod-product-compliance
Lightning Source LLC
Chambersburg PA
CBHW051858300426
44117CB00006B/441